Greek Style Beans with Mushrooms

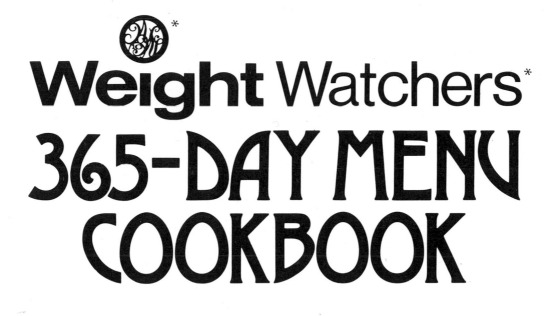

Weight Watchers*
365-DAY MENU COOKBOOK

NEW ENGLISH LIBRARY

The preparation of this book has involved so many different people. Recipes have been created, tested and tasted; photographs planned and taken; the results all checked and edited. Many members of Weight Watchers U.K. staff have given their enthusiasm and skills to produce a whole year's outline of good food. To all these people we say a sincere 'Thank you'.

We wish, also, to acknowledge the contribution of Felice Lippert, Advisor and Consultant to the Food Research and Development Department. The original conception of this book was hers.

Dr Lelio G. Parducci
Vice President
Food Research & Development
Department.

For more information about the Weight Watchers Classroom Programme, contact:
Weight Watchers U.K. Limited
11-12 Fairacres
Dedworth Road
Windsor
Berkshire SL4 4UY
Telephone: Windsor (95) 56751

Weight Watchers 365-day menu cookbook
1. Reducing diets – Recipes
I. Weight Watchers
641.5'635   RM222.2

ISBN 0-450-06034-9

Reprinted by arrangement with New English Library.

Weight Watchers* and ⬤* are registered trademarks of Weight Watchers International, Inc. and are used under its control by the Publisher.

Design: Ian Hughes
Photography: David Rudkin
Illustrations: kitchen equipment by courtesy of Covent Garden Kitchen Supplies

Photoset by South Bucks Photosetters Ltd.

Printed and Bound by Hazell, Watson and Viney Ltd., Aylesbury.

CONTENTS

A Note from Jean Nidetch	**3**
General Information	**4**
Menu Plans	**6**
Starters	**110**
Eggs and Cheese	**116**
Poultry, Veal and Rabbit	**127**
Meats	**136**
Fish	**152**
Dried Peas/Beans and Peanut Butter	**164**
Vegetables	**168**
Grains, Pasta and Potatoes	**174**
Salads	**178**
Sauces, Salad Dressings and Dips	**182**
Desserts, Snacks and Drinks	**186**
Index	**198**

A NOTE FROM JEAN NIDETCH

Are you the type of shopper who casts a careful eye on labels?

There's a 'label' on this book that you can be assured stands for Grade-A quality. I refer to the two simple words: Weight and Watchers. Together they stand for the largest weight-control company in the world, and the most respected.

If I may take a nostalgic journey, come with me to the apartment house I lived in, in Little Neck, New York. That's where our first meetings were held, back in 1962. We began with just six women . . . . I went to the New York City Board of Health Obesity Clinic for help. The diet they gave me, which was to become the basis of the original Weight Watchers Food Plan, was well balanced. However, I sensed that something more than calorie counting was needed: the missing ingredient was the 'I-know-just-what-you-mean' that only comes from fellow sufferers.

Our recipe for success was something called group support. It was to become the hallmark of the Weight Watchers Organisation, for the hands joined together now encircle the globe. The six have multiplied astoundingly into more than twelve million. So universal was and is the need that today the sun seldom sets on Weight Watchers classes. They can be found in nearly every corner of the world. Our members span the decades (from teens to nineties) and encompass all races, religions, careers and social levels, for overweight is no respecter of these boundaries.

The help we offer extends far beyond the classes. Our 'label' appears on best-selling cookbooks and magazines. And wherever the name 'Weight Watchers' is seen or heard, you have the satisfaction of knowing it is backed up by the expertise of highly skilled professionals. Many of them have lent their nutritional knowledge and culinary abilities to the making of this cookbook.

But you don't have to be on a diet to find this book an invaluable 'partner'. What it does is take the burden of meal-planning off your shoulders by supplying well-balanced, carefully thought out menu plans. For the first time, we have divided a cookbook into daily menus – appropriately so, since eating successfully is a day-to-day challenge!

Now you have a chance to sample our exciting world for yourself and discover that it is possible to eat healthfully and control your weight without starvation, without boredom, without even having to forfeit many favourites. In a word: enjoyably!

Isn't it delicious to know that with this book that 'choice' is yours?

Jean Nidetch
Founder, Weight Watchers
International, Inc.

GENERAL INFORMATION

1. **These weekly menu plans are designed to start in January – Week 1. The ingredients and recipes are linked to seasonal availability of foods and to dishes traditionally associated with annual festivals and events. You can, if you wish, take any one week's menu plan out of sequence, as the calorie count and nutrition values hold good whenever the week's plan is used, but you may prefer to slot into the year's plans at the appropriate week in the calendar when you first use this book.**

2. Each menu plan has been developed to fulfill the requirements of a complete week in accordance with the Weight Watchers Full Choice Food Plan for Women. The amounts indicated are for one serving. When a serving-size range is given, Men should choose the upper end of the range; the entire range is available to Teenagers (males 11 to 17 and females 11 to 14). Additions for Men and Teenagers are indicated on each menu plan.

3. The menu plans were developed with an eye to seasonal availability of fresh fruits and vegetables. However, if fresh is not available, frozen or canned may be substituted.

4. The weights indicated on the menu plans for poultry, meat and fish do not include skin or bones. Before eating poultry, remove and discard the skin.

5. Not every menu includes a drink. Water, soda water, mineral water, coffee or tea may be added to any meal.

6. 'Snacks, at Planned Times' may be consumed with any of the day's meals instead of being taken as snacks.

7. Check the menu plan and make a weekly shopping list. Before beginning to prepare a recipe, make certain every item is on hand.

Oven Temperatures

250° to 275°F	Very slow oven	Regulo 1
300° to 325°F	Slow oven	2–3
350° to 375°F	Moderate oven	4–5
400° to 425°F	Hot oven	6–7
450° to 475°F	Very hot oven	8–9
500° to 525°F	Extremely hot oven	10+

Microwave Ovens

Many of our recipes can be cooked in a microwave oven. Since there is no one standard that applies to all ovens, you will have to experiment with your unit and follow the manufacturer's advice for timing. Generally, you should allow about ¼ of the cooking time. This means that if our recipe suggests 20 minutes, allow 5 minutes in your microwave oven (or slightly less, since it's wiser to undercook than overcook). Plastic racks are available for use in microwave ovens.

8. Non-stick cookware makes it possible to cook without fat.

9. For best recipe results, always take time to measure and weigh – don't try to judge portions by eye. We recommend the use of the following items to help you with portion control: a scale for weighing food, measuring jugs for both liquid and dry measures and measuring spoons. (Teaspoon 5ml size. Tablespoon 15ml size). All dry measurements should be level. Recipe directions may sometimes look as if they're taking the long way around, but remember, they're all shortcuts to weight control.

10. The herbs used in these recipes are dried unless otherwise indicated. If you are using fresh herbs, use approximately four times the amount of dried.

11. All fruit and juice should be fresh or frozen or canned with no sugar added. Canned fruit may be packed in its own or another juice, in a juice blend, in water and with artificial sweetener.

12. The vegetables are fresh unless otherwise indicated. If you use frozen or canned vegetables, it may be necessary to adjust cooking times accordingly.

13. Meat should be trimmed of all visible fat, and note that beef, ham, lamb or pork require the use of a rack when roasting so that fat drains off into the pan.

14. Canned fish in oil, brine or tomato sauce should be well drained before weighing.

15. When vegetable oil is called for, oils such as safflower, sunflower, soybean, corn, cottonseed, olive or sesame, or any of these combined may be used. Margarine – be sure to use margarine high in polyunsaturates.

16. We have included recipes for Chicken and Beef Stock, should you want to make your own. Quantities stay the same.

17. In any recipe for more than one serving it is important to mix ingredients well and to divide evenly, so that each portion will be the same size.

18. The only breakfast cereals *not* allowed are the sugar-coated variety.

19. All yogurt used must be 'natural' and unsweetened.

Slow Cookers
If you enjoy cooking with this appliance, there's no reason why you can't adapt many of our recipes to its use.

Artificial Sweeteners
The use of artificial sweeteners on the Weight Watchers Food Plan has always been optional. Natural sweetness is available in the form of fruits and honey. You may also use white and brown sugar, fructose and golden syrup.

Nutrition Notes
This cookbook contains menu plans and recipes and all the recipes are calorie-counted. The menus provide approximately 1,200 calories per day for women, 1,600 calories for men and 1,700 calories for teenagers. These daily averages are based on one week's intake. The menus will allow you to plan nutritious meals, expand your choice of selections, help with portion control and maintain a well-balanced diet.

WEEK 1

Now is the time to make your New Year Resolutions. As you are reading this book, one of yours will probably be concerned with losing weight. In which case, you have made an excellent start, for within these covers you will find menus for every day of the year. They are planned to fulfil the principles of a good weight-reducing regime.

Your nutritional needs will be well cared for and your health maintained. Your weight loss will be gradual, consistent and safe.

You will be enjoying food and drink in delicious variety.

This combination of a pleasing, varied diet, the joy of good health and a satisfactory weight loss will help you to 'stay with it' until you reach your chosen goal weight.

DAY 1

MORNING MEAL
4 oz (120 g) canned fruit cocktail
¾ oz (20 g) cornflakes
5 fl oz (150 ml) skim milk
tea or coffee

MIDDAY MEAL
3-4 oz (90-120 g) cooked chicken, sliced, served on 1 slice (1 oz/30 g) bread, with lettuce and radish salad, with **Tarragon Vinaigrette** (page 183)
½ medium grapefruit
tea or coffee

EVENING MEAL
Cauliflower and Courgette Soup (page 110)
Prawns with Crispy Topping (page 163)
3 oz (90 g) steamed broccoli
green salad with 2 teaspoons (10 ml) low-calorie mayonnaise
Frozen Apple-Banana Dessert (page 191)
tea or coffee

SNACKS OR DRINKS AT PLANNED TIMES
1 digestive biscuit, 5 fl oz (150 ml) skim milk

Serving Information
Men and Teenagers: Add 2 slices (1 oz/30 g each) rye bread and 1 medium orange
Teenagers: Add ½ pint (300 ml) skim milk

DAY 4

MORNING MEAL
4 fl oz (120 ml) grapefruit juice
¾ oz (20 g) wheat flakes
5 fl oz (150 ml) skim milk
1 slice (1 oz/30 g) wholemeal bread, toasted
1 teaspoon (5 ml) margarine
1 teaspoon (5 ml) marmalade
tea or coffee

MIDDAY MEAL
4 breadcrumbed fish fingers, grilled
3 oz (90 g) cooked carrots
1 teaspoon (5 ml) margarine
iceberg lettuce with lemon juice
1 medium apple
tea or coffee

EVENING MEAL
Beef and Corn Casserole (page 148)
green salad with **Basic Vinaigrette** (page 183)
4 oz (120 g) canned peach slices
tea or coffee

SNACKS OR DRINKS AT PLANNED TIMES
1 slice (1 oz/30 g) currant bread,
    15 fl oz (450 ml) skim milk

Serving Information
Men and Teenagers: Add 1 slice (1 oz/30 g) currant bread and 4 dried dates
Teenagers: Add 5 fl oz (150 ml) natural yogurt

DAY 5

MORNING MEAL
1 medium orange
3 oz (90 g) baked beans
1 slice (1 oz/30 g) bread, toasted
tea or coffee

MIDDAY MEAL
Mushroom Omelette (page 120)
3 oz (90 g) cooked peas
1-oz (30-g) wholemeal roll
2 teaspoons (10 ml) low-fat spread
4 oz (120 g) fresh fruit salad
tea or coffee

EVENING MEAL
3-4 oz (90-120 g) poached cod fillet
2 teaspoons (10 ml) tomato relish
Slow-Cooked Vegetable Medley (page 172)
1 medium apple
tea or coffee

SNACKS OR DRINKS AT PLANNED TIMES
½ pint (300 ml) skim milk, 5 fl oz (150 ml) natural yogurt

Serving Information
Men and Teenagers: Add 1-oz (30-g) wholemeal roll, 1 medium banana, 1 digestive biscuit
Teenagers: Add ½ pint (300 ml) skim milk

DAY 2

MORNING MEAL
2-inch (5-cm) wedge honeydew melon
2½ oz (75 g) cottage cheese
1 slice (1 oz/30 g) currant bread
tea or coffee

MIDDAY MEAL
3-4 oz (90-120 g) grilled lamb's liver
3 oz (90 g) sliced onion, sauteed in 1½ teaspoons (7.5 ml)
    vegetable oil
3 oz (90 g) cooked green beans with diced red pepper
sparkling mineral water
tea or coffee

EVENING MEAL
3-4 oz (90-120 g) grilled chicken
Cucumber and Tomato Salad (page 179)
2 oz (60 g) cooked noodles
4 oz (120 g) stewed apples with 2 tablespoons (30 ml) raisins
tea or coffee

SNACKS OR DRINKS AT PLANNED TIMES
5 fl oz (150 ml) natural yogurt with 1 teaspoon (5 ml) low-calorie
    jam, **Hot Mocha Milk** (page 192)

Serving Information
Men and Teenagers: Add 2 oz (60 g) cooked noodles at Evening
    Meal; 1 slice (1 oz/30 g) currant bread, 1 large tangerine, 2
    tablespoons (30 ml) raisins
Teenagers: Add ½ pint (300ml) skim milk

DAY 3

MORNING MEAL
4 fl oz (120 ml) grapefruit juice
1 poached egg
1 slice (1 oz/30 g) wholemeal bread
tea or coffee

MIDDAY MEAL
5 oz (150 g) cottage cheese
¾ oz (20 g) melba toast
1½ teaspoons (7.5 ml) margarine
green salad with lemon juice
4 oz (120 g) canned peach slices
tea or coffee

EVENING MEAL
Baked Fish Casserole (page 162)
1 medium tomato, sliced on lettuce with cider vinegar
1 medium pear
tea or coffee

SNACKS OR DRINKS AT PLANNED TIMES
¾-oz (20-g) scone, 7½ fl oz (225 ml) skim milk, 5 fl oz (150 ml)
    natural yogurt

Serving Information
Men and Teenagers: Add 4 fl oz (120 ml) grapefruit juice, 1 slice
    (1 oz/30 g) wholemeal bread, 1 medium apple
Teenagers: Add ½ pint (300 ml) skim milk

DAY 6

MORNING MEAL
2½ fl oz (75 ml) prune juice
2½ oz (75 g) cottage cheese
1 slice (1 oz/30 g) bread with 1 teaspoon (5 ml) low-fat spread
tea or coffee

MIDDAY MEAL
2 oz (60 g) canned tuna
1 hard-boiled egg
sliced tomato and onion salad with wine vinegar and pinch
    oregano
1½ teaspoons (7.5 ml) mayonnaise
1 slice (1 oz/30 g) bread
mineral water with lemon slice
tea or coffee

EVENING MEAL
Sesame Chicken with Green Beans (page 131)
2 oz (60 g) cooked brown rice
green salad with lemon juice
1 medium orange
tea or coffee

SNACKS OR DRINKS AT PLANNED TIMES
½ pint (300 ml) skim milk, 5 fl oz (150 ml) natural yogurt, ¼ small
    pineapple

Serving Information
Men and Teenagers: Add extra 2 oz (60 g) cooked brown rice at
    Evening Meal; 1 medium pear
Teenagers: Add ½ pint (300 ml) skim milk

DAY 7

MORNING MEAL
½ medium banana
¾ oz (20 g) muesli
5 fl oz (150 ml) skim milk □ tea or coffee

MIDDAY MEAL
3-4 oz (90-120 g) roast pork
3 oz (90 g) cooked Brussels sprouts
3-oz (90-g) baked jacket potato
2 teaspoons (10 ml) low-fat spread
2 oz (60 g) stewed apple
3-oz (90-g) baked onion, sprinkled with sage
4 fl oz (120 ml) white wine
2-inch (5-cm) wedge honeydew melon
tea or coffee

EVENING MEAL
3-4 oz (90-120 g) sardines
2 teaspoons (10 ml) mayonnaise
sliced tomato and onion on green salad
1 slice (1 oz/30 g) wholemeal bread
mineral water with lemon slice □ tea or coffee

SNACKS OR DRINKS AT PLANNED TIMES
5 fl oz (150 ml) skim milk, 5 fl oz (150 ml) natural yogurt, 1
    tablespoon (15 ml) raisins

Serving Information
Men and Teenagers: Add extra 3-oz (90-g) baked jacket potato
    at Midday Meal; 1 digestive biscuit, 2-inch (5-cm) wedge
    honeydew melon
Teenagers: Add ½ pint (300 ml) skim milk

WEEK 2

The avoidance of boredom is an essential part of any weight-loss scheme. Food means more than nourishment to us all. We associate it, probably unconsciously, with warmth, affection, hospitality, relaxation. If our diet is restricted to a monotonous regime, and if most of the regime consists of items which we don't especially enjoy anyway, then we are very easily diverted from it. The strongest will, the best of intentions bend under such pressure and the good effect of several days' sensible eating is undone in one foolish moment.

The variety of foods and the range of cooking methods within this week's menu plan ensure that boredom is kept at bay, while healthy weight loss is ensured.

DAY 1

MORNING MEAL
½ medium grapefruit
¾ oz (20 g) porridge oats cooked with water
5 fl oz (150 ml) skim milk
tea or coffee

MIDDAY MEAL
3-4 oz (90-120 g) canned tuna served on lettuce leaves
2 teaspoons (10 ml) mayonnaise
3 oz (90 g) canned asparagus tips
1 oz (30 g) pitta bread
1 teaspoon (5 ml) margarine
tea or coffee

EVENING MEAL
Lamb's Liver Creole (page 143)
2 oz (60 g) cooked rice
4 oz (120 g) fresh fruit salad
tea or coffee

SNACKS OR DRINKS AT PLANNED TIMES
1 medium orange, **Hot Cocoa** (page 191)
5 fl oz (150 ml) skim milk

Serving Information
Men and Teenagers: Add 1 oz (30 g) pitta bread, 2 medium apples, 1 digestive biscuit
Teenagers: Add ½ pint (300 ml) skim milk

DAY 4

MORNING MEAL
2½ fl oz (75 ml) apple juice
1 scrambled egg
2 teaspoons (10 ml) tomato ketchup
1 slice (1 oz/30 g) wholemeal bread
tea or coffee

MIDDAY MEAL
Cold Chicken Platter (page 134)
1 slice (1 oz/30 g) wholemeal bread
2-inch (5-cm) wedge honeydew melon
tea or coffee

EVENING MEAL
Grilled Ham Steak with Pineapple (page 139)
3 oz (90 g) cooked peas
3 oz (90 g) steamed cauliflower
green salad with **Herb Dressing** (page 184)
3 oz (90 g) grapes
tea or coffee

SNACKS OR DRINKS AT PLANNED TIMES
2½ fl oz (75 ml) natural yogurt with 1 digestive biscuit, ½ pint (300 ml) skim milk

Serving Information
Men and Teenagers: Add 2½ fl oz (75 ml) apple juice, 1 slice (1 oz/30 g) wholemeal bread and 1 digestive biscuit
Men: Add 1 oz (30 g) extra cooked ham at Evening Meal
Teenagers: Add ½ pint (300 ml) skim milk

DAY 5

MORNING MEAL
1 medium orange
1 oz (30 g) Cheddar cheese
1 slice (1 oz/30 g) wholemeal bread
1 teaspoon (5 ml) low-fat spread
tea or coffee

MIDDAY MEAL
3 tablespoons (45 ml) peanut butter
2 slices (1 oz/30 g each) white bread
3 oz (90 g) grapes
tea or coffee

EVENING MEAL
3-4 oz (90-120 g) grilled veal chop
3 oz (90 g) steamed Brussels sprouts with **Lemon 'Butter' Sauce** (page 184)
Mixed Vegetable Salad (page 179)
1 medium pear
tea or coffee

SNACKS OR DRINKS AT PLANNED TIMES
1 pint (600 ml) skim milk

Serving Information
Men and Teenagers: Add 1 medium pear, 2 tablespoons (30 ml) raisins and 2 cream crackers
Teenagers: Add ½ pint (300 ml) skim milk

DAY 2

MORNING MEAL
4 fl oz (120 ml) orange juice
2½ oz (75 g) cottage cheese
1 slice (1 oz/30 g) brown bread
tea or coffee

MIDDAY MEAL
French Omelette (page 120)
1 slice (1 oz/30 g) brown bread
1 teaspoon (5 ml) margarine
3 oz (90 g) steamed broccoli
tea or coffee

EVENING MEAL
3-4 oz (90-120 g) grilled chicken
3 oz (90 g) steamed courgettes with oregano
3 oz (90 g) steamed carrots
green salad with **Thousand Island Dressing** (page 182)
½ medium banana
tea or coffee

SNACKS OR DRINKS AT PLANNED TIMES
1 medium apple, ½ pint (300 ml) skim milk, **Coconut-Coffee Mounds** (page 192)

Serving Information
Men and Teenagers: Add 2 slices (1 oz/30 g each) brown bread, ¼ small pineapple, and ½ medium banana
Teenagers: Add ½ pint (300 ml) skim milk

DAY 3

MORNING MEAL
4 oz (120 g) canned grapefruit sections
¾ oz (20 g) ready-to-eat cereal
5 fl oz (150 ml) skim milk
tea or coffee

MIDDAY MEAL
Tomato Stuffed with Herb Cheese (page 126)
green salad with 1 teaspoon (5 ml) mayonnaise
1 (1-oz/30-g) bread roll
2 teaspoons (10 ml) low-fat spread
3 oz (90 g) grapes
tea or coffee

EVENING MEAL
3-4 oz (90-120 g) grilled plaice
3-oz (90-g) baked jacket potato with 2½ fl oz (75 ml) natural yogurt with chives
3 oz (90 g) cooked spinach
chicory salad with **Garlic Vinaigrette** (page 183)
1 medium pear
tea or coffee

SNACKS OR DRINKS AT PLANNED TIMES
½ pint (300 ml) skim milk

Serving Information
Men and Teenagers: Add 3-oz (90-g) baked jacket potato at Evening Meal; and 1 (1-oz/30-g) bread roll and 1 tangerine
Teenagers: Add 5 fl oz (150 ml) natural yogurt

DAY 6

MORNING MEAL
Honey Stewed Prunes (page 192)
¾ oz (20 g) porridge oats cooked with water
5 fl oz (150 ml) skim milk
tea or coffee

MIDDAY MEAL
Sardine Salad (page 156)
3-oz (90-g) tomato, sliced
1-oz (30-g) onion, sliced
1-oz (30-g) bread roll
3 teaspoons (15 ml) low-fat spread
5 fl oz (150 ml) natural yogurt
tea or coffee

EVENING MEAL
3-4 oz (90-120 g) grilled beefburger
1 x 2-oz (60-g) hamburger bap
2 teaspoons (10 ml) tomato ketchup
1 pickled cucumber
Curried Cole Slaw (page 178)
1 medium orange
tea or coffee

SNACKS OR DRINKS AT PLANNED TIMES
1 medium pear, 5 fl oz (150 ml) skim milk

Serving Information
Men and Teenagers: Add 1 orange, 2 digestive biscuits
Teenagers: Add ½ pint (300 ml) skim milk

DAY 7

MORNING MEAL
½ medium grapefruit
1 poached egg
1 slice (1 oz/30 g) bread, toasted
2 teaspoons (10 ml) low-fat spread
tea or coffee

MIDDAY MEAL
3-4 oz (90-120 g) grilled lemon sole with lemon juice
2 oz (60 g) cooked noodles
1 teaspoon (5 ml) low-fat spread
3 oz (90 g) steamed broccoli
green salad with **Lemon Salad Dressing** (page 182)
4 fl oz (120 ml) white wine
2 canned peach halves
tea or coffee

EVENING MEAL
7-8 oz (210-240 g) baked beans
1 slice (1 oz/30 g) bread, toasted
1 teaspoon (5 ml) margarine
4 oz (120 g) fruit salad
tea or coffee

SNACKS OR DRINKS AT PLANNED TIMES
½ pint (300 ml) skim milk and 5 fl oz (150 ml) natural yogurt

Serving Information
Men and Teenagers: Add 3-oz (90-g) potato, 2 canned peach halves
Teenagers: Add ½ pint (300 ml) skim milk

WEEK 3

Our ancestors believed that if they wore a clove of garlic on a string around the neck, they would never be troubled by unwelcome attentions from vampires and witches. They also believed that the evil eye could be kept averted from any home in which a garlic clove was hung.

Today we rely less on the supernatural properties of this pungent little plant and use it, rather, to enhance the flavour of savoury dishes. A little goes a long way, so handle it with caution. And if you don't want your breath to betray that you have just enjoyed a garlic-laden feast after Day 5's Garlic Bread, then chew a little fresh parsley to disguise the fact.

DAY 1

MORNING MEAL
4 fl oz (120 ml) orange juice
¾ oz (20 g) wheat flakes served with 5 fl oz (150 ml) skim milk
tea or coffee

MIDDAY MEAL
Open Grilled Cheese Sandwich (page 122)
green salad with **Basic Vinaigrette** (page 183)
4 oz (120 g) canned mandarin orange sections sprinkled with 1 teaspoon (5 ml) shredded coconut
tea or coffee

EVENING MEAL
3-4 oz (90-120 g) grilled veal chop
3 oz (90 g) cooked Brussels sprouts
3-oz (90-g) grilled tomato
sliced chicory on lettuce with 1 teaspoon (5 ml) mayonnaise
Baked Apple (page 188)
tea or coffee

SNACKS OR DRINKS AT PLANNED TIMES
5 fl oz (150 ml) skim milk, 2 cream crackers with 1 teaspoon (5 ml) margarine and 2 teaspoons (10 ml) grated Cheddar cheese, 5 fl oz (150 ml) natural yogurt

Serving Information
Men and Teenagers: Add 2 (1 oz/30 g) slices bread and 1 medium apple
Teenagers: Add ½ pint (300 ml) skim milk

DAY 4

MORNING MEAL
4 fl oz (120 ml) orange juice
2½ oz (75 g) cottage cheese
¾ oz (20 g) crispbread
tea or coffee

MIDDAY MEAL
Salmon Mousse (page 152)
chicory and watercress salad with lemon juice
2 cream crackers
1 medium apple
tea or coffee

EVENING MEAL
Mediterranean Stew (page 136)
3 oz (90 g) steamed broccoli
3 oz (90 g) steamed French beans
2 oz (60 g) cooked pasta shells
3 fl oz (90 ml) orange juice
tea or coffee

SNACKS OR DRINKS AT PLANNED TIMES
15 fl oz (450 ml) skim milk

Serving Information
Men and Teenagers: Add 1 medium apple, 2 oz (60 g) cooked pasta shells and 2 tablespoons (30 ml) raisins
Teenagers: Add ½ pint (300 ml) skim milk

DAY 5

MORNING MEAL
4 oz (120 g) canned grapefruit sections
¾ oz (20 g) porridge oats cooked with water and served with 5 fl oz (150 ml) skim milk
tea or coffee

MIDDAY MEAL
5 oz (150 g) cottage cheese
sliced tomatoes on bed of lettuce
1 teaspoon (5 ml) vegetable oil
Garlic Bread (page 175)
Pear Frozen Yogurt (page 195)
tea or coffee

EVENING MEAL
3-4 oz (90-120 g) grilled chicken livers sprinkled with lemon juice
3 oz (90 g) cooked peas with 1 teaspoon (5 ml) margarine
3 oz (90 g) steamed cauliflower
2 oz (60 g) cooked rice
4 fl oz (120 ml) red or white wine
tea or coffee

SNACKS OR DRINKS AT PLANNED TIMES
1 medium orange, 1 digestive biscuit, 5 fl oz (150 ml) skim milk

Serving Information
Men and Teenagers: Add 1 medium orange, 2 digestive biscuits
Teenagers: Add ½ pint (300 ml) skim milk

DAY 2

MORNING MEAL
1 medium orange
2½ oz (75 g) curd cheese with 2 teaspoons (10 ml) low-calorie jam
1 slice (1 oz/30 g) bread, toasted
tea or coffee

MIDDAY MEAL
3-4 oz (90-120 g) corned beef on 1 slice (1 oz/30 g) bread with 2 teaspoons (10 ml) horseradish sauce
tomato and cucumber salad with 1 teaspoon (5 ml) vegetable oil
1 medium apple
tea or coffee

EVENING MEAL
Egg Salad (page 123)
3 oz (90 g) cooked peas
3 oz (90 g) cooked carrots
2 canned pear halves
tea or coffee

SNACKS OR DRINKS AT PLANNED TIMES
2 oz (60 g) vanilla ice cream, 2 cream crackers, 1 pint (600 ml) skim milk

Serving Information
Men and Teenagers: Add 1 medium apple 6-oz (180-g) jacket potato
Teenagers: Add ½ pint (300 ml) skim milk

DAY 3

MORNING MEAL
1 large tangerine
¾ oz (20 g) ready-to-eat cereal with 5 fl oz (150 ml) skim milk
tea or coffee

MIDDAY MEAL
1 hard-boiled egg
1 oz (30 g) Cheddar cheese
green salad with **Russian Dressing** (page 184)
1 slice (1 oz/30 g) wholemeal bread
1 teaspoon (5 ml) margarine
1 medium orange
tea or coffee

EVENING MEAL
3-4 oz (90-120 g) grilled cod
3 oz (90 g) steamed broccoli
3 oz (90 g) steamed carrots
1 slice (1 oz/30 g) wholemeal bread
3-oz (90-g) baked jacket potato
1 teaspoon (5 ml) margarine
tea or coffee

SNACKS OR DRINKS AT PLANNED TIMES
5 fl oz (150 ml) skim milk, 5 fl oz (150 ml) natural yogurt with ½ medium banana, sliced

Serving Information
Men and Teenagers: Add ¾ oz (20 g) ready-to-eat cereal at Morning Meal; and 3-oz (90-g) baked jacket potato at Evening Meal, 1 medium apple
Teenagers: Add ½ pint (300 ml) skim milk

DAY 6

MORNING MEAL
4 fl oz (120 ml) orange juice
1 poached egg on 1 slice (1 oz/30 g) wholemeal bread, toasted
1½ teaspoons (7.5 ml) margarine
tea or coffee

MIDDAY MEAL
Curried Chicken Salad (page 135)
chicory and sliced red pepper salad with 1 teaspoon (5 ml) low-calorie mayonnaise
1-oz (30-g) wholemeal roll
tea or coffee

EVENING MEAL
3-4 oz (90-120 g) grilled plaice
3 oz (90 g) cooked peas
3 oz (90 g) boiled potato, mashed
1 medium pear
tea or coffee

SNACKS OR DRINKS AT PLANNED TIMES
½ pint (300 ml) skim milk, 5 fl oz (150 ml) natural yogurt, 1 tablespoon (15 ml) raisins

Serving Information
Men and Teenagers: Add 3-oz (90-g) boiled potato at Evening Meal; 1 medium pear
Teenagers: Add ½ pint (300 ml) skim milk

DAY 7

MORNING MEAL
4 oz (120 g) canned grapefruit sections
2½ oz (75 g) curd cheese with chopped chives
1 slice (1 oz/30 g) wholemeal bread
tea or coffee

MIDDAY MEAL
3-4 oz (90-120 g) roast chicken
Orange Broccoli (page 170)
tomato salad with lettuce, with **Gingered Vinaigrette** (page 183)
Coconut Honey Shake (page 192)
tea or coffee

EVENING MEAL
3-4 oz (90-120 g) cooked tongue
3 oz (90 g) sliced beetroot and watercress
cucumber salad with 1 teaspoon (5 ml) mayonnaise
1-oz (30-g) wholemeal roll
2 canned pineapple slices
tea or coffee

SNACKS OR DRINKS AT PLANNED TIMES
15 fl oz (450 ml) skim milk, 1 small mandarin orange, 1 digestive biscuit

Serving Information
Men and Teenagers: Add 2 medium apples, 1-oz (30-g) wholemeal roll
Teenagers: Add ½ pint (300 ml) skim milk

WEEK 4

Burns Night falls on January 25th and good Scots all over the world spare a nostalgic thought for the poetry and songs of their celebrated kinsman. Perhaps they enjoy the traditional Scottish meal too – 'Haggis wi' bashed neeps and tatties'. 'Neeps' are swede and 'bashed' a vivid description of the mashing process! Burns actually wrote 'An Address to a Haggis' and called it 'Great chieftain o' the pudding-race'. But perhaps it takes a true Scot to appreciate the dish.

Sassenachs can enjoy this week's dishes quite as much – from Crab Meat Mould to Chicken Greek Style, there's something to please every taste.

DAY 1

MORNING MEAL
4 oz (120 g) canned mandarin oranges
1 scrambled egg
1 slice (1 oz/30 g) wholemeal bread
tea or coffee

MIDDAY MEAL
2 oz (60 g) Cheshire cheese on ¾ oz (20 g) melba toast
1 medium tomato, sliced on shredded lettuce with **Cole Slaw Vinaigrette** (page 178)
5 oz (150 g) melon balls
tea or coffee

EVENING MEAL
3-4 oz (90-120 g) grilled salmon steak
Courgettes Italian Style (page 170)
chicory salad with **Basic Vinaigrette** (page 183)
2 canned pear halves
tea or coffee

SNACKS OR DRINKS AT PLANNED TIMES
½ pint (300 ml) skim milk, clear soup made with ½ stock cube, 2 cream crackers, 5 fl oz (150 ml) natural yogurt

Serving Information
Men and Teenagers: Add 1 slice (1 oz/30 g) bread, 2 medium plums and 1 medium orange
Teenagers: Add ½ pint (300 ml) skim milk

DAY 4

MORNING MEAL
4 oz (120 g) fruit salad
1 poached egg
1 slice (1 oz/30 g) brown bread, toasted
1 teaspoon (5 ml) low-fat spread
tea or coffee

MIDDAY MEAL
Liver Venetian (page 143)
3 oz (90 g) cooked cauliflower florets
green salad with **Vinaigrette Parmesan** (page 184)
6 canned apricot halves
tea or coffee

EVENING MEAL
3-4 oz (90-120 g) sliced roast chicken, on 1 slice (1 oz/30 g) wholemeal bread with lettuce, tomato slices and 1 teaspoon (5 ml) mayonnaise
3 oz (90 g) canned cream-style corn
3 oz (90 g) cooked carrots
1 medium orange
tea or coffee

SNACKS OR DRINKS AT PLANNED TIMES
½ pint (300 ml) skim milk, 5 fl oz (150 ml) natural yogurt

Serving Information
Men and Teenagers: Add 1½-oz (45-g) muffin, toasted, with 2 teaspoons (10 ml) low-calorie raspberry jam, 6 canned apricot halves
Teenagers: Add ½ pint (300 ml) skim milk

DAY 5

MORNING MEAL
4 fl oz (120 ml) orange juice
1 oz (30 g) Cheddar cheese
1 slice (1 oz/30 g) wholemeal bread
tea or coffee

MIDDAY MEAL
Tuna Boats (page 159)
Bean Salad (page 179)
1 slice (1 oz/30 g) white bread
1 medium orange
5 fl oz (150 ml) natural yogurt
tea or coffee

EVENING MEAL
3-4 oz (90-120 g) grilled beef sausages
4 oz (120 g) steamed mushrooms
3 oz (90 g) grated beetroot on lettuce with cider vinegar
½ pint (300 ml) beer
tea or coffee

SNACKS OR DRINKS AT PLANNED TIMES
4 oz (120 g) canned fruit cocktail, ½ pint (300 ml) skim milk

Serving Information
Men and Teenagers: Add 4 fl oz (120 g) orange juice and 2-oz (60-g) bread roll
Teenagers: Add ½ pint (300 ml) skim milk

MORNING MEAL
½ medium grapefruit
¾ oz (20 g) muesli
5 fl oz (150 ml) skim milk
tea or coffee

MIDDAY MEAL
Crab Meat Mould (page 160)
2 cream crackers
¼ small pineapple
tea or coffee

EVENING MEAL
3-4 oz (90-120 g) grilled chicken with herbs and lemon juice
3 oz (90 g) steamed cauliflower
3 oz (90 g) steamed carrots
lettuce with **Dijon-Herb Dressing** (page 182)
½ medium banana with 2½ fl oz (75 ml) natural yogurt
tea or coffee

SNACKS OR DRINKS AT PLANNED TIMES
1 slice (1 oz/30 g) currant bread, toasted, with 1 teaspoon (5 ml)
   low-fat spread, 5 fl oz (150 ml) skim milk

Serving Information
Men and Teenagers: Add 1 digestive biscuit, 2 tablespoons
   (30 ml) raisins, 1 medium apple, 1-oz (30-g) wholemeal roll
Teenagers: Add ½ pint (300 ml) skim milk

MORNING MEAL
½ medium grapefruit
¾ oz (20 g) porridge oats cooked with water and served with
   5 fl oz (150 ml) skim milk
tea or coffee

MIDDAY MEAL
3-4 oz (90-120 g) grilled beefburger
3 oz (90 g) steamed spinach
3 oz (90 g) steamed carrots
green salad with **Russian Dressing** (page 184)
tea or coffee

EVENING MEAL
Burns Supper
Cock-A-Leekie (page 111)
3-4 oz (90-120 g) cooked haggis
3 oz (90 g) cooked swede mashed with 1 teaspoon (5 ml) low-fat
   spread and pinch nutmeg, salt and pepper
6 oz (180 g) cooked potatoes, mashed with 3 teaspoons
   (15 ml) low-fat spread and pinch each salt and pepper
5 oz (150 g) raspberries
1½ fl oz (45 ml) whisky □ tea or coffee

SNACKS OR DRINKS AT PLANNED TIMES
1 medium orange, 5 fl oz (150 ml) skim milk, 5 fl oz (150 ml)
   natural yogurt

Serving Information
Men and Teenagers: Add 5 oz (150 g) raspberries, 3 oz (90 g)
   mashed potato and 1 digestive biscuit
Teenagers: Add ½ pint (300 ml) skim milk

MORNING MEAL
5 oz (150 g) honeydew or cantaloupe melon balls
¾ oz (20 g) cornflakes
5 fl oz (150 ml) skim milk
tea or coffee

MIDDAY MEAL
Chicken Greek Style (page 132)
green salad with sliced red onion and **Basic Vinaigrette** (page
   183)
1-oz (30-g) bread roll
5 oz (150 g) stewed blackcurrants

EVENING MEAL
5 oz (150 g) curd cheese mixed with cinnamon and artificial
   sweetener
1 slice (1 oz/30 g) brown bread, toasted
1 medium tomato
hearts of lettuce with **Russian Dressing** (page 184)
Baked Apple (page 188)
tea or coffee

SNACKS OR DRINKS AT PLANNED TIMES
5 fl oz (150 ml) skim milk, 5 fl oz (150 ml) natural yogurt

Serving Information
Men and Teenagers: Add 1 digestive biscuit with 2 teaspoons
   (10 ml) low-calorie strawberry jam, 1 medium banana
Teenagers: Add ½ pint (300 ml) skim milk

MORNING MEAL
1 medium orange, cut into wedges
1 oz (30 g) ham
1 slice (1 oz/30 g) rye bread
tea or coffee

MIDDAY MEAL
Mushroom Omelette (page 120)
mixed salad with lemon juice
¾ oz (20 g) crispbread
2 canned peach halves with 5 fl oz (150 ml) natural yogurt
tea or coffee

EVENING MEAL
Fillet of Sole Florentine (page 159)
3 oz (90 g) cooked mashed swede
3 oz (90 g) steamed carrot slices
sliced radishes and celery on shredded lettuce with 1 teaspoon
   (5 ml) mayonnaise, sprinkled with chopped chives

SNACKS OR DRINKS AT PLANNED TIMES
½ pint (300 ml) skim milk, 1 medium apple

Serving Information
Men and Teenagers: Add 1½-oz (75-g) muffin, split and toasted,
   with 1 teaspoon (5 ml) golden syrup, 2 tablespoons (30 ml)
   raisins and 4 oz (120 g) canned mandarin orange sections
Teenagers: Add ½ pint (300 ml) skim milk

WEEK 5

The taste of a dish is what we enjoy. The 'look' of it is important, of course, but the most pleasing presentation won't make up for a taste of warm flannel. Herbs and spices can make all the difference, and as they have negligible calorie content plus maximum taste-bud impact, they are a real boon to the serious dieter.

This week's menus include a simple, tasty item – Cinnamon-Cheese Toast.

Cinnamon comes from the bark of the evergreen cinnamon tree – a member of the laurel family and a native of the Far East. The bark is dried and becomes the cinnamon sticks or powder which we buy here. It is one of the first spices to have been enjoyed by man and was valued as a medicine and a perfume as well as a flavouring. We enjoy it now as a pungent, sweet addition to dishes both savoury and sweet.

DAY 1

MORNING MEAL
4 oz (120 g) canned crushed pineapple
2½ oz (75 g) curd cheese
1 slice (1 oz/30 g) currant bread
tea or coffee

MIDDAY MEAL
Salmon Salad (page 162)
celery sticks, cucumber sticks, and 2 green olives
1 slice (1 oz/30 g) rye bread
1½ teaspoons (7.5 ml) margarine
tea or coffee

EVENING MEAL
3-4 oz (90-120 g) grilled calf liver
3 oz (90 g) steamed courgettes
3 oz (90 g) steamed green beans
Radish Salad (page 180)
4 oz (120 g) orange and grapefruit sections
tea or coffee

SNACKS OR DRINKS AT PLANNED TIMES
1 pint (600 ml) skim milk, 1 digestive biscuit, 2 canned pear halves

Serving Information
Men and Teenagers: Add 1 medium apple and 2 slices (1 oz/30 g each) bread
Teenagers: Add ½ pint (300 ml) skim milk

DAY 4

MORNING MEAL
4 oz (120 g) grapefruit sections
¾ oz (20 g) ready-to-eat cereal
5 fl oz (150 ml) skim milk
tea or coffee

MIDDAY MEAL
3-4 oz (90-120 g) canned drained tuna
mixed salad with pepper rings
1 teaspoon (5 ml) margarine
1 slice (1 oz/30 g) rye bread
2 medium plums
tea or coffee

EVENING MEAL
3-4 oz (90-120 g) grilled steak
3-oz (90-g) baked jacket potato
3 oz (90 g) cooked broccoli spears
iceberg lettuce with **Russian Dressing** (page 184)
1 large mandarin orange
tea or coffee

SNACKS OR DRINKS AT PLANNED TIMES
watercress and mushroom salad with **Basic Vinaigrette** (page 183), 15 fl oz (450 ml) skim milk

Serving Information
Men and Teenagers: Add 4 fl oz (120 ml) orange juice, 2 medium plums, 4 cream crackers
Teenagers: Add ½ pint (300 ml) skim milk

DAY 5

MORNING MEAL
4 oz (120 g) grapefruit sections
1 poached egg
1 slice (1 oz/30 g) wholemeal bread
1 teaspoon (5 ml) margarine
tea or coffee

MIDDAY MEAL
Cream of Cauliflower Soup (page 115)
3-4 oz (90-120 g) sliced roast turkey
chicory salad with **Garlic Vinaigrette** (page 183)
1 medium pickled cucumber
1-oz (30-g) roll □ tea or coffee

EVENING MEAL
3-4 oz (90-120 g) grilled halibut
Green Beans and Tomatoes Hungarian Style (page 168)
crisp lettuce with cucumber slices and 2½ fl oz (75 ml) natural yogurt
4 oz (120 g) canned mandarin sections
tea or coffee

SNACKS OR DRINKS AT PLANNED TIMES
12 fl oz (375 ml) skim milk, 1 medium kiwi fruit or 4 oz (120 g) canned pineapple chunks

Serving Information
Men and Teenagers: Add 4 oz (120 g) grapefruit sections, ¾-oz (20-g) muffin, toasted, 4 oz (120 g) canned pineapple chunks and 1 slice (1 oz/30 g) rye bread
Teenagers: Add ½ pint (300 ml) skim milk or 5 fl oz (150 ml) natural yogurt

DAY 2

MORNING MEAL
2½ fl oz (75 ml) apple juice
¾ oz (20 g) ready-to-eat cereal
5 fl oz (150 ml) skim milk
tea or coffee

MIDDAY MEAL
Chili-Cheese Rarebit (page 119)
green salad with **Tarragon Vinaigrette** (page 183)
tea or coffee

EVENING MEAL
3-4 oz (90-120 g) grilled haddock with lemon wedge
3 oz (90 g) whole kernel canned corn with 1 teaspoon (5 ml)
   margarine
Savoury Grilled Tomatoes (page 172)
3 oz (90 g) cooked chopped spinach
2-inch (5-cm) wedge melon
tea or coffee

SNACKS OR DRINKS AT PLANNED TIMES
2 chopped dried dates with 5 fl oz (150 ml) natural yogurt
5 fl oz (150 ml) skim milk

Serving Information
Men and Teenagers: Add 2½ fl oz (75 ml) apple juice, 1 digestive
   biscuit and ½ medium grapefruit; Add 3 oz (90 g) mashed
   potato at Evening Meal
Teenagers: Add ½ pint (300 ml) skim milk

DAY 3

MORNING MEAL
4 oz (120 g) orange sections
Cinnamon-Cheese Toast (page 123)
tea or coffee

MIDDAY MEAL
Mushroom-Stuffed Eggs (page 123)
sliced red and green pepper rings on lettuce
1 slice (1 oz/30 g) rye bread
tea or coffee

EVENING MEAL
3-4 oz (90-120 g) grilled chicken
3 oz (90 g) cooked carrot slices with 3 oz (90 g) cooked peas
green salad with 1 teaspoon (5 ml) mayonnaise
4 oz (120 g) fruit salad
tea or coffee

SNACKS OR DRINKS AT PLANNED TIMES
2 canned peach halves, ½ pint (300 ml) skim milk, 5 fl oz (150 ml)
   natural yogurt

Serving Information
Men and Teenagers: Add 4 oz (120 g) fruit salad, 2 digestive
   biscuits
Teenagers: Add ½ pint (300 ml) skim milk

DAY 6

MORNING MEAL
½ medium grapefruit
1 oz (30 g) smoked salmon with lemon wedge
1 slice (1 oz/30 g) brown bread
1 teaspoon (5 ml) low-fat spread
tea or coffee

MIDDAY MEAL
1 oz (30 g) Emmenthal cheese, sliced
1 oz (30 g) Edam cheese, sliced
¾ oz (20 g) melba toast
green salad with lemon juice
4 fl oz (120 ml) white wine
tea or coffee

EVENING MEAL
3-4 oz (90-120 g) roast veal
3 oz (90 g) braised celery
2 oz (60 g) cooked rice with chopped spring onion and green
   pepper
iceberg lettuce with **Herb Dressing** (page 184)
tea or coffee

SNACKS OR DRINKS AT PLANNED TIMES
Curried Bananas (page 194)
½ pint (300 ml) skim milk

Serving Information
Men and Teenagers: Add ¾ oz (20 g) melba toast, 1 slice
   (1 oz/30 g) brown bread and 2½ fl oz (75 ml) pineapple juice
Teenagers: Add ½ pint (300 ml) skim milk

DAY 7

MORNING MEAL
1 medium banana
¾ oz (20 g) porridge oats cooked with water
5 fl oz (150 ml) skim milk
tea or coffee

MIDDAY MEAL
1 scrambled egg
3 oz (90 g) bean sprouts with sliced radishes on lettuce with
   1 teaspoon (5 ml) mayonnaise
1½ tablespoons (22.5 ml) peanut butter on 1 slice (1 oz/30 g)
   wholemeal bread, with 1 teaspoon (5 ml) low-calorie jam
tea or coffee

EVENING MEAL
Pork Goulash (page 136)
leek and mushroom salad with **Tarragon Vinaigrette** (page
   183)
½ medium grapefruit
½ pint cider or beer □ tea or coffee

SNACKS OR DRINKS AT PLANNED TIMES
1 digestive biscuit, 5 fl oz (150 ml) natural yogurt with
   ½ teaspoon (2.5 ml) honey, 2½ fl oz (75 ml) skim milk

Serving Information
Men and Teenagers: Add 1 slice (1 oz/30 g) wholemeal bread,
   4 oz (120 g) canned mandarin orange sections, and 1 digestive
   biscuit
Teenagers: Add ½ pint (300 ml) skim milk

WEEK 6

The aubergine features in this week's plan. Sometimes known as 'eggplant', this vegetable is a native of southern Asia but is now common in Europe. They grow well here in a greenhouse, for they need plenty of heat. They are most attractive, too, having a glossy dark purple skin and a pleasing long egg-shaped contour. Much of the aubergine's flavour lies in the skin, so avoid peeling unless this is absolutely necessary, but it is advisable to sprinkle the cut slices with salt, then drain and dry, to eliminate the excess fluid and slightly bitter taste.

The aubergine combines well with cheese – as in this week's recipe, Layered Aubergine Cheese Bake.

DAY 1

MORNING MEAL
2½ fl oz (75 ml) pineapple juice
1 poached egg
1 slice (1 oz/30 g) white bread, toasted
1 teaspoon (5 ml) margarine
tea or coffee

MIDDAY MEAL
Layered Aubergine Cheese Bake (page 119)
3 oz (90 g) sliced beetroot
crisp lettuce with **Thousand Island Dressing** (page 182)
1-oz (30-g) wholemeal roll
1 teaspoon (5 ml) margarine
1 medium apple
tea or coffee

EVENING MEAL
3-4 oz (90-120 g) steamed plaice
3 oz (90 g) steamed carrots
3 oz (90 g) cooked cabbage
4 fl oz (120 ml) white wine
tea or coffee

SNACKS OR DRINKS AT PLANNED TIMES
4 oz (120 g) grapefruit sections, 15 fl oz (450 ml) skim milk, ¾ oz (20 g) crispbread

Serving Information
Men and Teenagers: Add 2½ fl oz (75 ml) pineapple juice, 1 slice (1 oz/30 g) wholemeal bread and 4 oz (120 g) canned peach slices
Teenagers: Add ½ pint (300 ml) skim milk

DAY 4

MORNING MEAL
½ medium banana
¾ oz (20 g) bran flakes
5 fl oz (150 ml) skim milk
tea or coffee

MIDDAY MEAL
Open Grilled Cheese Sandwich (page 122)
1 medium tomato, grilled
6 medium cooked asparagus spears
tea or coffee

EVENING MEAL
3-4 oz (90-120 g) grilled trout
3 oz (90 g) cooked peas
3 oz (90 g) poached mushrooms
3-oz (90-g) boiled potato
3 teaspoons (15 ml) margarine
2 canned pear halves
tea or coffee

SNACKS OR DRINKS AT PLANNED TIMES
1 medium orange, 15 fl oz (450 ml) skim milk

Serving Information
Men and Teenagers: Add 1 slice (1 oz/30 g) wholemeal bread, 4 oz (120 g) canned pineapple chunks, and 1-oz (30-g) wholemeal roll
Teenagers: Add ½ pint (300 ml) skim milk

DAY 5

MORNING MEAL
Honey-Stewed Prunes (page 192)
2½ oz (75 g) cottage cheese
1 slice (1 oz/30 g) pumpernickel bread
1 teaspoon (5 ml) margarine
tea or coffee

MIDDAY MEAL
2½ fl oz (75 ml) apple juice
3-4 oz (90-120 g) canned tuna
green pepper and cucumber slices with 1½ teaspoons (7.5 ml) mayonnaise
¾ oz (20 g) melba toast
tea or coffee

EVENING MEAL
3-4 oz (90-120 g) corned beef
3 oz (90 g) cooked peas
3 oz (90 g) cooked diced carrot
spinach and mushroom salad with **Dill Vinaigrette** (page 183)
5 oz (150 g) honeydew melon balls with lemon wedge
tea or coffee

SNACKS OR DRINKS AT PLANNED TIMES
5 fl oz (150 ml) natural yogurt with 1 teaspoon (5 ml) low-calorie jam, ½ pint (300 ml) skim milk

Serving Information
Men and Teenagers: Add 2 slices (2 oz/60 g) pumpernickel bread, 4 oz (120 g) fruit salad, 2 dried dates
Teenagers: Add 5 fl oz (150 ml) natural yogurt

DAY 2

MORNING MEAL
1 oz (30 g) dried apricot halves
¾ oz (20 g) porridge oats cooked with water
5 fl oz (150 ml) skim milk □ tea or coffee

MIDDAY MEAL
3-4 oz (90-120 g) sliced roast turkey with **Russian Dressing**
(page 184)
4 oz (120 g) chilled cooked artichoke hearts
mixed salad with lemon juice
1 slice (1 oz/30 g) rye bread
1 teaspoon (5 ml) margarine
1 medium orange
tea or coffee

EVENING MEAL
3-4 oz (90-120 g) grilled lamb's liver
3 oz (90 g) steamed cauliflower
3 oz (90 g) cooked spinach
shredded lettuce and sliced radishes with ¼ recipe **Yogurt
Dressing** (page 182)
Frozen Apple-Banana Dessert (page 191)
tea or coffee

SNACKS OR DRINKS AT PLANNED TIMES
¾ oz (20 g) melba toast and 1 teaspoon (5 ml) margarine,
2½ fl oz (75 ml) skim milk

Serving Information
Men and Teenagers: Add 1 slice (1 oz/30 g) rye bread, 1½-oz
(45 g) muffin, split and toasted and 1 medium pear
Teenagers: Add ½ pint (300 ml) skim milk

DAY 3

MORNING MEAL
4 fl oz (120 ml) orange juice
2½ oz (75 g) cottage cheese
1 slice (1 oz/30 g) bread
1 teaspoon (5 ml) margarine
tea or coffee

MIDDAY MEAL
Cod-Vegetable Bake (page 154)
chicory and lettuce salad with 2 green olives, capers, and **Basic
Vinaigrette** (page 183)
tea or coffee

EVENING MEAL
3-4 oz (90-120 g) grilled beefburger with 2 teaspoons (10 ml)
ketchup mixed with 1 teaspoon (5 ml) mayonnaise
2-oz (60-g) bap
½ medium pickled cucumber, sliced
1 medium tomato, sliced
4 oz (120 g) canned fruit cocktail
tea or coffee

SNACKS OR DRINKS AT PLANNED TIMES
5 fl oz (150 ml) natural yogurt, ½ medium banana, ½ pint (300
ml) skim milk

Serving Information
Men and Teenagers: Add 1 slice (1 oz/30 g) bread, 2 medium
plums, 1 digestive biscuit and 4 oz (120 g) canned fruit cocktail
Teenagers: Add ½ pint (300 ml) skim milk

DAY 6

MORNING MEAL
Apple and Oatmeal Breakfast (page 176) with 1 tablespoon
(15 ml) raisins
tea or coffee

MIDDAY MEAL
5 oz (150 g) cottage cheese mixed with 4 oz (120 g) canned
crushed pineapple arranged on lettuce
1 medium tomato, sliced
¾ oz (20 g) crispbread
2 teaspoons (10 ml) low-fat spread
tea or coffee

EVENING MEAL
2-egg omelette filled with 3 oz (90 g) sliced poached mushrooms
green salad with 1 teaspoon (5 ml) mayonnaise
tea or coffee

SNACKS OR DRINKS AT PLANNED TIMES
¾-oz (20 g) melba toast, **Mushroom Dip** (page 195)
½ pint (300 ml) beer or cider, 1 medium orange, 5 fl oz (150 ml)
skim milk

Serving Information
Men and Teenagers: Add 4 fl oz (120 ml) orange juice, 2 canned
peach halves, 2 digestive biscuits
Teenagers: Add ½ pint (300 ml) skim milk

DAY 7

MORNING MEAL
½ medium grapefruit
1 poached egg
1 slice (1 oz/30 g) bread, toasted
1 teaspoon (5 ml) margarine
tea or coffee

MIDDAY MEAL
Chicken Kebabs (page 128)
celery and beansprout salad with **Dijon-Herb Dressing** (page
182)
1 large mandarin orange
tea or coffee

EVENING MEAL
7-8 oz (210-240 g) baked beans
1 slice (1 oz/30 g) bread, toasted
1 teaspoon (5 ml) low-fat spread
1 medium tomato, sliced on a green salad with 1 teaspoon (5 ml)
vegetable oil with wine vinegar
tea or coffee

SNACKS OR DRINKS AT PLANNED TIMES
1 medium apple, 1 digestive biscuit, 1 pint (600 ml) skim milk

Serving Information
Men and Teenagers: Add 1½-oz (45-g) scone, 1 medium apple,
1 large mandarin orange
Teenagers: Add ½ pint (300 ml) skim milk

WEEK 7

February 14th – St Valentine's day, when (so legend says) the birds choose their mates and lovers everywhere exchange cards and greetings. On Tuesday of this week we suggest a special dinner of roast chicken with vegetables and salad followed by Pineapple Sorbet and with a glass of champagne – a feast to flatter any loving heart.

The tomato was known as the 'love apple' when it first found its way from South America to Europe. Sir Walter Raleigh is said to have given them to Queen Elizabeth I as a token of his admiration. So it's quite appropriate to include them on the 14th too – in the salad which accompanies the midday meal.

DAY 1

MORNING MEAL
½ medium grapefruit
1 poached egg
1 slice (1 oz/30 g) bread, toasted
1 teaspoon (5 ml) low-fat spread
tea or coffee

MIDDAY MEAL
3-4 oz (90-120 g) grilled sole
3 oz (90 g) cooked peas
green salad with **Basic Vinaigrette** (page 183)
1 large mandarin orange
tea or coffee

EVENING MEAL
Pork with Fennel Seeds (page 142)
3 oz (90 g) boiled potatoes
3 oz (90 g) cooked green beans
chicory and pimiento salad with ½ teaspoon (2.5 ml) vegetable oil plus cider vinegar
tea or coffee

SNACKS OR DRINKS AT PLANNED TIMES
5 fl oz (150 ml) natural yogurt with 2 teaspoons (10 ml) low-calorie jam, ½ pint (300 ml) skim milk, 4 oz (120 g) canned crushed pineapple

Serving Information
Men and Teenagers: Add 1½-oz (45-g) scone, 4 oz (120 g) canned crushed pineapple, 1 medium apple
Teenagers: Add ½ pint (300 ml) skim milk

DAY 4

MORNING MEAL
4 oz (120 g) canned apple slices
¾ oz (20 g) porridge oats cooked with water
5 fl oz (150 ml) skim milk
tea or coffee

MIDDAY MEAL
3-4 oz (90-120 g) canned tuna
radishes, 2 small tomatoes and 2 black olives on lettuce with 1 teaspoon (5 ml) mayonnaise
¾ oz (20 g) melba toast
4 oz (120 g) canned fruit cocktail with 5 fl oz (150 ml) natural yogurt
tea or coffee

EVENING MEAL
Chicken Salad Oriental (page 135)
spinach and mushroom salad with 1 teaspoon (5 ml) imitation bacon bits, 1 teaspoon (5 ml) sesame oil and wine vinegar
tea or coffee

SNACKS OR DRINKS AT PLANNED TIMES
4 oz (120 g) grapefruit sections, 5 fl oz (150 ml) skim milk, 1 digestive biscuit

Serving Information
Men and Teenagers: Add ¾ oz (20 g) crispbread, 1-oz (30-g) wholemeal roll and 4 oz (120 g) canned grapefruit sections
Teenagers: Add ½ pint (300 ml) skim milk

DAY 5

MORNING MEAL
4 fl oz (120 ml) orange juice
¾ oz (20 g) cornflakes
5 fl oz (150 ml) skim milk
tea or coffee

MIDDAY MEAL
1 oz (30 g) Cheddar cheese, grilled on 1 slice (1 oz/30 g) bread, toasted and topped with 1 poached egg
Broccoli Salad (page 179)
tea or coffee

EVENING MEAL
3-4 oz (90-120 g) steamed plaice
3 oz (90 g) cooked peas
green pepper rings on lettuce with 1 teaspoon (5 ml) mayonnaise
4 oz (120 g) canned mandarin orange sections with 5 fl oz (150 ml) natural yogurt
tea or coffee

SNACKS OR DRINKS AT PLANNED TIMES
5 fl oz (150 ml) skim milk, 8 fl oz (240 ml) tomato juice with 2 water biscuits

Serving Information
Men and Teenagers: Add ¾ oz (20 g) cornflakes at Morning Meal; 2 dried dates, 1 slice (1 oz/30 g) white bread
Teenagers: Add ½ pint (300 ml) skim milk

DAY 2

MORNING MEAL
4 oz (120 g) stewed apple with 1 teaspoon (5 ml) honey
1 tablespoon (15 ml) peanut butter spread on ¾ oz (20 g)
  crispbread
tea or coffee

MIDDAY MEAL
3-4 oz (90-120 g) grilled halibut
3 oz (90 g) cooked peas
1 slice (1 oz/30 g) white bread
1 teaspoon (5 ml) margarine
shredded lettuce with 2 small tomatoes, 2 green olives
tea or coffee

EVENING MEAL
3-4 oz (90-120 g) sliced roast chicken
3 oz (90 g) cooked green beans
beansprouts and carrot salad with **Basic Vinaigrette** (page 183)
4 fl oz (120 ml) champagne
Pineapple Sorbet (page 190)
tea or coffee

SNACKS OR DRINKS AT PLANNED TIMES
½ pint (300 ml) skim milk, 1 medium orange and 2 cream
  crackers

Serving Information
Men and Teenagers: Add 4 oz (120 g) canned sliced peaches
  and 2 digestive biscuits
Teenagers: Add 5 fl oz (150 ml) natural yogurt

DAY 3

MORNING MEAL
¾ oz (20 g) bran flakes with ½ medium banana, sliced
5 fl oz (150 ml) skim milk
tea or coffee

MIDDAY MEAL
Cheese-Salad Sandwich (page 119)
carrot and celery sticks
1 medium orange
tea or coffee

EVENING MEAL
Sole Veronique (page 158)
1-oz (30-g) bread roll
2 oz (60 g) vanilla ice cream
tea or coffee

SNACKS OR DRINKS AT PLANNED TIMES
12½ fl oz (375 ml) skim milk

Serving Information
Men and Teenagers: Add 1 tablespoon (15 ml) raisins, 2
  digestive biscuits, 5 oz (150 g) raspberries
Teenagers: Add ½ pint (300 ml) skim milk

DAY 6

MORNING MEAL
Honey-Stewed Prunes (page 192)
2½ oz (75 g) cottage cheese
1 slice (1 oz/30 g) bread
1 teaspoon (5 ml) low-fat spread
tea or coffee

MIDDAY MEAL
3-4 oz (90-120 g) grilled beefburger
1 tablespoon (15 ml) relish, any type
1 slice (1 oz/30 g) rye bread
Curried Cole Slaw (page 178)
1 medium orange
tea or coffee

EVENING MEAL
Chicken Liver Pilaf (page 146)
2 small grilled tomatoes
green salad with capers and **Garlic Vinaigrette** (page 183)
5 fl oz (150 ml) natural yogurt mixed with 1 oz (30 g) dried apricot
  halves, chopped
tea or coffee

SNACKS OR DRINKS AT PLANNED TIMES
½ pint (300 ml) skim milk, 5 oz (150 g) honeydew or cantaloupe
  melon balls

Serving Information
Men and Teenagers: Add 1 slice (1 oz/30 g) rye bread, 1 medium
  pear, 1 digestive biscuit and 2 dried dates
Teenagers: Add ½ pint (300 ml) skim milk

DAY 7

MORNING MEAL
2½ fl oz (75 ml) pineapple juice
1 scrambled egg cooked with 1 teaspoon (5 ml) margarine
1 slice (1 oz/30 g) brown bread, toasted
tea or coffee

MIDDAY MEAL
Vegetable Medley Soup (page 111)
3 4 oz (90 120 g) grilled lamb chop
3 oz (90 g) cooked chopped broccoli
2 oz (60 g) coffee ice cream
tea or coffee

EVENING MEAL
Baked Cheese Souffle (page 116)
mixed salad with **Tarragon Vinaigrette** (page 183)
1 medium orange
tea or coffee

SNACKS OR DRINKS AT PLANNED TIMES
1 medium apple with 5 fl oz (150 ml) natural yogurt, ¾ pint (225
  ml) skim milk

Serving Information
Men and Teenagers: Add 2½ fl oz (75 ml) pineapple juice, 1 slice
  (1 oz/30 g) rye bread
Teenagers: Add ½ pint (300 ml) skim milk

WEEK 8

Fennel was said by the Normans to have slimming properties, so it's a very suitable vegetable for users of this book! It's grown for its bulbous base rather than its leaves and it has a delicious taste of mild aniseed. It can be used raw in salads and cold dishes, or – as we use it here on Day 1 – cooked with cheese and garlic. If you like to grow your own vegetables, you will find fennel very easy to cultivate and it can be lifted from September onwards. Enjoy it with fish and with chicken as well as with cheese. Vegetarians too will love its versatility in their dishes.

DAY 1

MORNING MEAL
4 oz (120 g) grapefruit sections
2½ oz (75 g) cottage cheese
1 medium tomato, sliced
¾ oz (20 g) melba toast
tea or coffee

MIDDAY MEAL
3-4 oz (90-120 g) sliced cooked chicken
Fennel with Parmesan Cheese (page 172)
green salad with 1½ teaspoons (7.5 ml) vegetable oil with wine vinegar
1-oz (30-g) bread roll
4 fl oz (120 ml) white wine
tea or coffee

EVENING MEAL
5-6 oz (150-180 g) uncooked liver sauteed with 3 oz (90 g) sliced onion in 1½ teaspoons (7.5 ml) vegetable oil
3 oz (90 g) cooked green beans
1 medium pear
tea or coffee

SNACKS OR DRINKS AT PLANNED TIMES
½ pint (300 ml) skim milk, 5 fl oz (150 ml) natural yogurt, 4 oz (120 g) fruit salad, 1 digestive biscuit

Serving Information
Men and Teenagers: Add 4 oz (120 g) fruit salad, 1 medium pear, 1 digestive biscuit
Teenagers: Add ½ pint (300 ml) skim milk

DAY 4

MORNING MEAL
1 medium orange
1 poached egg
1 slice (1 oz/30 g) bread, toasted
1 teaspoon (5 ml) low-fat spread
tea or coffee

MIDDAY MEAL
3-4 oz (90-120 g) canned salmon with green salad, sliced tomato and cucumber
2 small satsumas
tea or coffee

EVENING MEAL
Chicken Provencale (page 132)
3-oz (90-g) baked jacket potato
lettuce and grated carrot salad with 1 teaspoon (5 ml) salad cream
4 fl oz (120 ml) white wine
Cherry Tarts (page 187)
tea or coffee

SNACKS OR DRINKS AT PLANNED TIMES
½ pint (300 ml) skim milk, 5 fl oz (150 ml) natural yogurt

Serving Information
Men and Teenagers: Add 1 slice (1 oz/30 g) bread, 3-oz (90-g) baked jacket potato, 2 medium apples
Teenagers: Add ½ pint (300 ml) skim milk

DAY 5

MORNING MEAL
4 oz (120 g) canned grapefruit sections
¾ oz (20 g) ready-to-eat cereal with 5 fl oz (150 ml) skim milk
tea or coffee

MIDDAY MEAL
Gypsy Cheese Salad (page 122)
1 tablespoon (15ml) low-calorie salad dressing
2 (1 oz/30 g each) wholemeal rolls
2 teaspoons (10 ml) low-fat spread
tea or coffee

EVENING MEAL
Savoury Tripe (page 150)
3 oz (90 g) steamed cauliflower
3 oz (90 g) steamed carrots
6 oz (180 g) canned peaches
tea or coffee

SNACKS OR DRINKS AT PLANNED TIMES
¾ oz (20 g) crispbread with 2 teaspoons (10 ml) low-fat spread, 5 fl oz (150 ml) skim milk; 5 fl oz (150 ml) natural yogurt with one medium portion stewed rhubarb

Serving Information
Men and Teenagers: Add ¾ oz (20 g) crispbread, 3 oz (90 g) grapes, 1 medium orange
Teenagers: Add ½ pint (300 ml) skim milk

DAY 2

MORNING MEAL
4 fl oz (120 ml) orange juice
1 egg, scrambled with 1 teaspoon (5 ml) margarine on 1 slice (1 oz/30 g) bread, toasted
tea or coffee

MIDDAY MEAL
4 breadcrumbed fish fingers, grilled
3 oz (90 g) cooked peas
3 oz (90 g) steamed cauliflower
1 medium apple
tea or coffee

EVENING MEAL
Stuffed Mushroom Starter (page 112)
3-4 oz (90-120 g) roast chicken
3 oz (90 g) canned sweet corn
green salad with 1 teaspoon (5 ml) low-calorie mayonnaise
½ medium banana, sliced into 5 fl oz (150 ml) natural yogurt, sprinkled with pinch of cinnamon
tea or coffee

SNACKS OR DRINKS AT PLANNED TIMES
½ pint (300 ml) skim milk, ¾-oz (20-g) plain scone with 1 teaspoon (5 ml) margarine, 1 teaspoon (5 ml) low-calorie jam

Serving Information
Men and Teenagers: Add 2 medium apples, 1 digestive biscuit and ¾-oz (20-g) plain scone
Teenagers: Add 5 fl oz (150 ml) natural yogurt

DAY 3

MORNING MEAL
½ medium banana
¾ oz (20 g) ready-to-eat cereal with 2 tablespoons (30 ml) sultanas
5 fl oz (150 ml) skim milk
tea or coffee

MIDDAY MEAL
5 oz (150 g) curd cheese on green salad
1 medium tomato, sliced with 2 teaspoons (10 ml) vegetable oil, mixed with cider vinegar
2-oz (60-g) bread roll
tea or coffee

EVENING MEAL
3-4 oz (90-120 g) grilled veal chop
3 oz (90 g) cooked spinach with lemon juice
3 oz (90 g) cooked courgettes
5 oz (150 g) melon balls
tea or coffee

SNACKS OR DRINKS AT PLANNED TIMES
15 fl oz (450 ml) skim milk, 1-oz (30-g) bread roll with 1 teaspoon (5 ml) margarine and 1 teaspoon (5 ml) honey

Serving Information
Men and Teenagers: Add ½ medium banana, 4 oz (120 g) fruit salad; 6 oz (180 g) boiled potato at Evening Meal
Teenagers: Add ½ pint (300 ml) skim milk

DAY 6

MORNING MEAL
4 fl oz (120 ml) orange juice
2½ oz (75 g) cottage cheese lightly grilled on 1 slice (1 oz/30 g) wholemeal bread, toasted
tea or coffee

MIDDAY MEAL
2-egg omelette, cooked with 1 teaspoon (5 ml) vegetable oil, filled with 3 oz (90 g) cooked mushrooms
3 oz (90 g) cooked courgettes
2 cream crackers
2 teaspoons (10 ml) low-fat spread
tea or coffee

EVENING MEAL
3-4 oz (90-120 g) baked trout with lemon wedges
3 oz (90 g) cooked peas
3 oz (90 g) whole kernel sweet corn
sliced chicory with **Oregano Vinaigrette** (page 183)
4 fl oz (120 ml) white wine
Coconut Coffee Mounds (page 192)
tea or coffee

SNACKS OR DRINKS AT PLANNED TIMES
Baked Apple (page 188), 5 fl oz (150 ml) natural yogurt with 2 tablespoons (30 ml) raisins, 5 fl oz (150 ml) skim milk

Serving Information
Men and Teenagers: Add 1 medium pear; add extra 3 oz (90 g) whole kernel sweet corn at Evening Meal
Teenagers: Add ½ pint (300 ml) skim milk

DAY 7

MORNING MEAL
4 oz (120 g) canned grapefruit sections
¾ oz (20 g) uncooked porridge oats cooked with water
5 fl oz (150 ml) skim milk ☐ tea or coffee

MIDDAY MEAL
3-4 oz (90-120 g) grilled steak
3 oz (90 g) boiled and mashed potatoes with 1 teaspoon (5 ml) margarine
3 oz (90 g) steamed red cabbage
3 oz (90 g) cooked peas
1 grilled tomato
1 medium orange ☐ tea or coffee

EVENING MEAL
3-4 oz (90-120 g) grilled lemon sole
3 oz (90 g) cooked green beans
3 oz (90 g) cooked carrot slices
1 slice (1 oz/30 g) wholemeal bread
1 teaspoon (5 ml) margarine
tea or coffee

SNACKS OR DRINKS AT PLANNED TIMES
½ medium banana, 5 fl oz (150 ml) natural yogurt, 1 slice (1 oz/30 g) currant bread, 2 teaspoons (10 ml) low-fat spread, 5 fl oz (150 ml) skim milk

Serving Information
Men and Teenagers: Add ½ medium banana, 2 slices (2 oz/60 g) currant bread
Teenagers: Add ½ pint (300 ml) skim milk

WEEK 9

St David's Day falls on March 1st and we remember that the leek (with the daffodil) is a Welsh emblem. It is said to be good for the voice – and all those splendid choirs prove that there surely must be something in the belief.

The leek is a most versatile vegetable with a far-back history record too. The Egyptians enjoyed it and the Romans introduced it into Britain. It has a subtle taste of onion, gives a marvellous flavour to other dishes and stands well in its own right when served alone or as an accompaniment to meat. We suggest Cream of Asparagus and Leek Soup for March 1st, and what could be more suitable to start this day with than Welsh Rarebit for breakfast?

DAY 1

MORNING MEAL
Honey-Stewed Prunes (page 192)
1 boiled egg
1 slice (1 oz/30 g) wholemeal bread, toasted
1 teaspoon (5 ml) margarine
tea or coffee

MIDDAY MEAL
Chick Pea Croquettes (page 165)
salad of sliced tomato on shredded lettuce with 1 teaspoon (5 ml) low-calorie mayonnaise
2 water biscuits
2 canned pear halves
tea or coffee

EVENING MEAL
Fish Greek Style (page 159)
3 oz (90 g) cooked broccoli spears with lemon wedge
green salad with **Dijon-Herb Dressing** (page 182)
4 fl oz (120 ml) white wine
tea or coffee

SNACKS OR DRINKS AT PLANNED TIMES
½ medium grapefruit, ½ pint (300 ml) skim milk

Serving Information
Men and Teenagers: Add 1 medium grapefruit, 2-oz (60-g) bread roll, 4 oz (120 g) canned fruit cocktail
Men: Add ½ oz (15 g) Cheddar cheese to salad
Teenagers: Add ½ pint (300 ml) skim milk

DAY 4

MORNING MEAL
½ medium grapefruit
Welsh Rarebit (page 118)
tea or coffee

MIDDAY MEAL
5 oz (150 g) cottage cheese on lettuce leaves with 1 medium tomato, sliced
1 slice (1 oz/30 g) bread
1 medium orange, sliced with 5 fl oz (150 ml) natural yogurt
tea or coffee

EVENING MEAL
Cream of Asparagus and Leek Soup (page 112)
3-4 oz (90-120 g) grilled plaice
3 oz (90 g) carrot sticks, sauteed in 1 teaspoon (5 ml) margarine
3 oz (90 g) steamed broccoli
4 oz (120 g) canned apple slices
tea or coffee

SNACKS OR DRINKS AT PLANNED TIMES
9 fl oz (270 ml) skim milk, ¾-oz (20-g) scone with 1 teaspoon (5 ml) low-calorie strawberry jam

Serving Information
Men and Teenagers: Add 1½-oz (45-g) scone with 2 teaspoons (10 ml) low-calorie strawberry jam, 4 oz (120 g) canned apple slices and 1 medium pear
Teenagers: Add ½ pint (300 ml) skim milk

DAY 5

MORNING MEAL
2-inch (5-cm) wedge honeydew melon
1 egg, scrambled with 1 teaspoon (5 ml) margarine
1 slice (1 oz/30 g) bread, toasted
tea or coffee

MIDDAY MEAL
3-4 oz (90-120 g) canned sardines
3-4 green pepper and onion rings on lettuce with 1 teaspoon (5 ml) mayonnaise
¾ oz (20 g) crispbread
5 fl oz (150 ml) natural yogurt with coffee flavouring and sweetener to taste
tea or coffee

EVENING MEAL
3-4 oz (90-120 g) grilled steak
3 oz (90 g) hot baked beans
3 oz (90 g) cooked Brussels sprouts
lettuce with **Savory Vinaigrette** (page 183)
4 oz (120 g) fruit salad
tea or coffee

SNACKS OR DRINKS AT PLANNED TIMES
2 medium plums, ½ pint (300 ml) skim milk

Serving Information
Men and Teenagers: Add 1 slice (1 oz/30 g) bread, 1 medium orange; add extra 3 oz (90 g) baked beans at Evening Meal
Teenagers: Add ½ pint (300 ml) skim milk

DAY 2

MORNING MEAL
1 oz (30 g) dried apricots, chopped, with ¾ oz (20 g) muesli
5 fl oz (150 ml) natural yogurt
tea or coffee

MIDDAY MEAL
3-4 oz (90-120 g) canned tuna
mixed green salad with 1 teaspoon (5 ml) mayonnaise
1 medium tomato
1 slice (1 oz/30 g) bread
1 teaspoon (5 ml) margarine
Spiced Orange Ambrosia (page 187)
tea or coffee

EVENING MEAL
3-4 oz (90-120 g) roast beef
2 oz (60 g) cooked brown rice
3 oz (90 g) cooked green beans
lettuce and cucumber salad with **Basic Vinaigrette** (page 183)
5 oz (150 g) melon chunks
tea or coffee

SNACKS OR DRINKS AT PLANNED TIMES
½ pint (300 ml) skim milk

Serving Information
Men and Teenagers: Add 2 oz (60 g) cooked brown rice,
    1 digestive biscuit, 5 oz (150 g) melon chunks, 1 medium
    orange
Teenagers: Add ½ pint (300 ml) skim milk

DAY 3

MORNING MEAL
Oatmeal with Spiced Fruit Ambrosia (page 176)
tea or coffee

MIDDAY MEAL
3-4 oz (90-120 g) grilled, thinly-sliced pig's liver
1 medium onion, sauteed for 2-3 minutes in 1 teaspoon (5 ml)
    vegetable oil
3 oz (90 g) cauliflower
3 oz (90 g) grilled tomatoes
1 slice (1 oz/30 g) bread with 1 teaspoon (5 ml) margarine
tea or coffee

EVENING MEAL
3-4 oz (90-120 g) grilled veal steak
3 oz (90 g) boiled potato
3 oz (90 g) cooked green beans
Chicory and Beetroot Salad (page 178)
4 oz (120 g) orange sections
tea or coffee

SNACKS OR DRINKS AT PLANNED TIMES
5 fl oz (150 ml) skim milk, 5 fl oz (150 ml) natural yogurt, 4 oz
    (120 g) canned pineapple chunks

Serving Information
Men and Teenagers: Add 3-oz (90-g) potato at Evening Meal;
    1 medium apple, 4 oz (120 g) canned pineapple chunks, and
    ¾-oz (20-g) scone
Teenagers: Add ½ pint (300 ml) skim milk

DAY 6

MORNING MEAL
4 fl oz (120 ml) grapefruit juice
¾ oz (20 g) cornflakes
5 fl oz (150 ml) skim milk
tea or coffee

MIDDAY MEAL
Chicken Donna (page 130)
Chinese Cabbage and Tomato Medley (page 171)
¾ oz (20 g) melba toast
1 medium pear
tea or coffee

EVENING MEAL
1-egg omelette cooked in 1 teaspoon (5 ml) vegetable oil, filled
    with 1 oz (30 g) Cheddar cheese, grated
Webb lettuce, sliced radishes and ½ teaspoon (2.5 ml) imitation
    bacon bits with ½ recipe **Yogurt Dressing** (page 182)
1 slice (1 oz/30 g) wholemeal bread
1 medium apple
tea or coffee

SNACKS OR DRINKS AT PLANNED TIMES
12½ fl oz (375 ml) skim milk, 4 fl oz (120 ml) red wine

Serving Information
Men and Teenagers: Add 1½-oz (45-g) scone, 1 medium
    banana
Teenagers: Add ½ pint (300 ml) skim milk

DAY 7

MORNING MEAL
4 oz (120 g) orange and grapefruit sections
1 poached egg
1 slice (1 oz/30 g) bread
1 teaspoon (5 ml) margarine
tea or coffee

MIDDAY MEAL
3-4 oz (90-120 g) grilled haddock
3 oz (90 g) steamed mushrooms
watercress and sliced cucumber with **Lemon Salad Dressing**
    (page 182)
Pineapple-Orange 'Cream' (page 188)
tea or coffee

EVENING MEAL
Beef Pie (page 147)
3 oz (90 g) steamed cauliflower dotted with 1½ teaspoons
    (7.5 ml) margarine
½ pint (300 ml) lager
tea or coffee

SNACKS OR DRINKS AT PLANNED TIMES
5 oz (150 g) canned strawberries with 5 fl oz (150 ml) natural
    yogurt, 1 digestive biscuit, 5 fl oz (150 ml) skim milk

Serving Information
Men and Teenagers: Add 1 medium apple, 2 digestive biscuits
Teenagers: Add ½ pint (300 ml) skim milk

WEEK 10

Shrove Tuesday is the last day before Lent begins on Ash Wednesday. The Church imposed strict rules of self-denial on all the congregation during Lent. Meat and dairy products were forbidden and so the house had to be cleared of these goods. On Shrove Tuesday all milk and eggs in the larder were used up in pancakes – the last indulgence until Easter Day.

We suggest pancakes served with lemon juice on Day 2 of this week. Remember that although they taste best served as soon as cooked, it is possible to keep them for a short time if they are layered on a plate which rests over a pan of gently simmering water.

DAY 1

MORNING MEAL
4 oz (120 g) canned fruit cocktail
¾ oz (20 g) puffed wheat
5 fl oz (150 ml) skim milk
tea or coffee

MIDDAY MEAL
2½ oz (75 g) cottage cheese
3 oz (90 g) cooked beetroot
green salad with 2 teaspoons (10 ml) low-calorie mayonnaise
1 slice (1 oz/30 g) wholemeal bread
1 medium orange
tea or coffee

EVENING MEAL
3-4 oz (90-120 g) grilled beefburger
3 oz (90 g) cooked green beans
sliced tomato, cucumber and mushrooms on lettuce with 2 teaspoons (10 ml) mayonnaise
Lady Fingers (page 196)
tea or coffee

SNACKS OR DRINKS AT PLANNED TIMES
5 fl oz (150 ml) skim milk, 5 fl oz (150 ml) natural yogurt with one medium portion of stewed rhubarb

Serving Information
Men and Teenagers: Add 2-oz (60-g) hamburger roll at Evening Meal; 4 oz (120 g) canned fruit cocktail and 1 medium pear
Teenagers: Add ½ pint (300 ml) skim milk

DAY 4

MORNING MEAL
4 fl oz (120 ml) orange juice
2½ oz (75 g) quark cheese with 1 tablespoon (15 ml) raisins and grated rind of ½ lemon
¾ oz (20 g) crispbread □ tea or coffee

MIDDAY MEAL
3-4 oz (90-120 g) sliced liver sausage
1 oz (30 g) sliced onion
lettuce and tomato salad with 1 teaspoon (5 ml) olive oil and 1 tablespoon (15 ml) vinegar
1 slice (1 oz/30 g) rye bread
1 teaspoon (5 ml) margarine
½ oz (15 g) dried apricots chopped and added to 5 fl oz (150 ml) natural yogurt □ tea or coffee

EVENING MEAL
3-4 oz (90-120 g) roast chicken
Herbed Vegetables (page 168)
green salad with lemon juice
5 oz (150 g) stewed blackcurrants
2 oz (60 g) vanilla ice cream □ tea or coffee

SNACKS OR DRINKS AT PLANNED TIMES
½ pint (300 ml) skim milk

Serving Information
Men and Teenagers: Add extra 4 fl oz (120 ml) orange juice at Morning Meal; extra 1 slice (1 oz/30 g) rye bread and 3 oz (90 g) canned whole kernel sweet corn at Midday Meal, and 3 oz (90 g) grapes
Teenagers: Add ½ pint (300 ml) skim milk

DAY 5

MORNING MEAL
½ medium grapefruit
¾ oz (20 g) bran flakes
5 fl oz (150 ml) skim milk □ tea or coffee

MIDDAY MEAL
Sweet and Sour Liver (page 147)
3 oz (90 g) steamed cauliflower
3 oz (90 g) steamed courgettes
1 teaspoon (5 ml) low-fat spread
5 fl oz (150 ml) natural yogurt
tea or coffee

EVENING MEAL
3-4 oz (90-120 g) grilled cod with lemon wedge
3 oz (90 g) steamed kale
3 oz (90 g) steamed carrots
1 teaspoon (5 ml) low-fat spread
green salad with chopped onion
2 teaspoons (10 ml) salad cream
4 oz (120 g) stewed apples with 1 tablespoon (15 ml) raisins
tea or coffee

SNACKS OR DRINKS AT PLANNED TIMES
1½-oz (45-g) muffin, split and toasted with 1 teaspoon (5 ml) low-fat spread and 1 teaspoon (5 ml) low-calorie jam, 5 fl oz (150 ml) skim milk

Serving Information
Men and Teenagers: Add 4 oz (120 g) cooked noodles at Midday Meal, 1 medium banana
Teenagers: Add ½ pint (300 ml) skim milk

DAY 2

MORNING MEAL
¾ oz (20 g) muesli
½ medium banana
5 fl oz (150 ml) skim milk
tea or coffee

MIDDAY MEAL
3½-4 oz (105-120 g) baked beans
1 poached egg
2 slices (1 oz/30 g each) wholemeal bread, toasted
2 teaspoons (10 ml) margarine
3 oz (90 g) poached mushrooms
1 medium grilled tomato
3 oz (90 g) grapes
tea or coffee

EVENING MEAL
5 oz (150 g) melon balls
3-4 oz (90-120 g) sliced roast turkey
3 oz (90 g) sliced cooked beetroot
tomato and onion salad with ½ teaspoon (2½ ml) vegetable oil,
    wine vinegar and oregano
Pancake with Lemon Juice (page 119)
tea or coffee

SNACKS OR DRINKS AT PLANNED TIMES
12½ fl oz (375 ml) skim milk

Serving Information
Men and Teenagers: Add extra 3 oz (90 g) baked beans at
    Midday Meal; 1 digestive biscuit, 3 oz (90 g) grapes and ½
    banana
Teenagers: Add ½ pint (300 ml) skim milk

DAY 3

MORNING MEAL
4 fl oz (120 ml) orange juice
1 egg cooked in 1 teaspoon (5 ml) low-fat spread
1 slice (1 oz/30 g) wholemeal bread
tea or coffee

MIDDAY MEAL
2 oz (60 g) Cheddar cheese toasted on 1 slice (1 oz/30 g)
    wholemeal bread
iceberg lettuce with 1 teaspoon (5 ml) imitation bacon bits and 2
    teaspoons (10 ml) low-calorie mayonnaise
1 medium apple □ tea or coffee

EVENING MEAL
3-4 oz (90-120 g) grilled plaice
3 oz (90 g) steamed artichoke hearts with 1 teaspoon (5 ml)
    low-fat spread
3 oz (90 g) steamed spinach
green salad with 1 teaspoon (5 ml) olive oil and 1 tablespoon
    (15 ml) wine vinegar
2 canned peach halves
5 fl oz (150 ml) natural yogurt
tea or coffee

SNACKS OR DRINKS AT PLANNED TIMES
½ pint (300 ml) skim milk

Serving Information
Men and Teenagers: Add 8 fl oz (240 ml) tomato juice at Midday
    Meal; 6 oz (180 g) steamed potatoes at Evening Meal and 2
    canned peach halves
Teenagers: Add ½ pint (300 ml) skim milk

DAY 6

MORNING MEAL
1 medium orange
2½ oz (75 g) cottage cheese
1 slice (1 oz/30 g) currant bread □ tea or coffee

MIDDAY MEAL
3-4 oz (90-120 g) grilled chicken with lemon juice and mixed
    herbs
green salad with 1 teaspoon (5 ml) vegetable oil and wine
    vinegar
3 oz (90 g) cooked green beans
3-oz (90-g) baked jacket potato
2 teaspoons (10 ml) low-fat spread
1 medium pear □ tea or coffee

EVENING MEAL
1 hard-boiled egg
1 oz (30 g) cheddar cheese
2 sticks celery
1 medium tomato
¾ oz (20 g) crispbread
2 teaspoons (10 ml) low-fat spread
4 oz (120 g) fresh fruit salad
tea or coffee

SNACKS OR DRINKS AT PLANNED TIMES
½ pint (300 ml) skim milk, 5 fl oz (150 ml) natural yogurt

Serving Information
Men and Teenagers: Add extra 3-oz (90-g) baked jacket potato
    at Midday Meal and 4 dried dates
Teenagers: Add ½ pint (300 ml) skim milk

DAY 7

MORNING MEAL
½ medium banana
¾ oz (20 g) porridge oats cooked with water
5 fl oz (150 ml) skim milk □ tea or coffee

MIDDAY MEAL
3-4 oz (90-120 g) roast pork
3 oz (90 g) steamed spring cabbage
3 oz (90 g) steamed carrots
3 oz (90 g) steamed potatoes
2 teaspoons (10 ml) low-fat spread
1 medium baked apple
4 fl oz (120 ml) white wine □ tea or coffee

EVENING MEAL
3-4 oz (90-120 g) peeled prawns with 2 teaspoons (10 ml)
    low-calorie mayonnaise
3 oz (90 g) canned asparagus spears
tomato, cucumber and lettuce salad with lemon juice
¾ oz (20 g) crispbread
2 teaspoons (10 ml) low-fat spread
4 oz (120 g) orange sections □ tea or coffee

SNACKS OR DRINKS AT PLANNED TIMES
5 fl oz (150 ml) skim milk, 5 fl oz (150 ml) natural yogurt

Serving Information
Men and Teenagers: Add extra 3-oz (90-g) steamed potato at
    Midday Meal; ¾-oz (20-g) plain scone with 1 teaspoon (5 ml)
    low-calorie jam at Evening Meal; ½ medium banana and 2
    tablespoons (30 ml) raisins
Teenagers: Add ½ pint (300 ml) skim milk

WEEK 11

What else could we suggest for St Patrick's day on March 17th but Irish Stew? Traditionally it is based on neck of lamb cooked with onions and potatoes.

We regard the potato as a nourishing and inexpensive addition to most of our main meals, but it was not until the 18th Century that they were under widespread cultivation in Great Britain. Sir John Hawkins brought them here from America in 1563 and in 1586 Sir Francis Drake carried them here too. They were rare and therefore expensive, and grown only in the gardens of the Royal household and the nobility. It's odd to realise that one of our staple foods was once an exotic delicacy!

MORNING MEAL
4 fl oz (120 ml) orange juice
2½ oz (75 g) cottage cheese
1 slice (1 oz/30 g) raisin bread
1 teaspoon (5 ml) low-fat spread ☐ tea or coffee

MIDDAY MEAL
3-4 oz (90-120 g) crab meat
green salad
1 medium tomato
2 teaspoons (10 ml) low-calorie mayonnaise
1 oz (30 g) pitta bread
1 medium pear ☐ tea or coffee

EVENING MEAL
3-4 oz (90-120 g) grilled lamb's liver
3 oz (90 g) steamed cauliflower
3 oz (90 g) steamed courgettes
green salad with lemon juice
2 teaspoons (10 ml) low-fat spread
¼ small pineapple ☐ tea or coffee

SNACKS OR DRINKS AT PLANNED TIMES
1 slice (1 oz/30 g) wholemeal bread with 1 teaspoon (5 ml)
low-fat spread and 1 teaspoon (5 ml) low-calorie raspberry
jam, 5 fl oz (150 ml) natural yogurt, ½ pint (300 ml) skim milk

Serving Information
Men and Teenagers: Add 1 oz (30 g) pitta bread at Midday Meal;
¼ small pineapple at Evening Meal; 4 fl oz (120 ml) orange
juice
Teenagers: Add ½ pint (300 ml) skim milk

MORNING MEAL
2½ fl oz (75 ml) apple juice
¾ oz (20 g) porridge oats cooked in water with 5 fl oz (150 ml)
skim milk and ½ teaspoon (2.5 ml) golden syrup
tea or coffee

MIDDAY MEAL
2 eggs, scrambled in 1 teaspoon (5 ml) margarine
1½ oz (45 g) sliced red peppers
1 slice (1 oz/30 g) wholemeal bread, toasted
1 teaspoon (5 ml) low-fat spread
1 medium orange ☐ tea or coffee

EVENING MEAL
3-4 oz (90-120 g) roast beef
3-oz (90-g) baked jacket potato with 1 teaspoon (5 ml) low-fat
spread
3 oz (90 g) cooked green beans
green salad with 1 medium tomato, 1 teaspoon (5 ml) olive oil
and wine vinegar
¼ small pineapple ☐ tea or coffee

SNACKS OR DRINKS AT PLANNED TIMES
5 fl oz (150 ml) skim milk, 5 fl oz (150 ml) natural yogurt,
1 digestive biscuit with 1 teaspoon (5 ml) low-calorie
raspberry jam

Serving Information
Men and Teenagers: Add 3-oz (90-g) baked jacket potato at
Evening Meal; 2½ fl oz (75 ml) apple juice and ¼ small
pineapple
Teenagers: Add ½ pint (300 ml) skim milk

MORNING MEAL
½ medium cantaloupe melon
1 oz (30 g) Cheddar cheese on 1 slice (1 oz/30 g) bread, toasted,
with dash Worcestershire sauce
tea or coffee

MIDDAY MEAL
3-4 oz (90-120 g) tuna mixed with 1 teaspoon (5 ml) mayonnaise
green pepper, tomato and onion salad with iceberg lettuce and
lemon juice
1 slice (1 oz/30 g) wholemeal bread
1 teaspoon (5 ml) low-fat spread ☐ tea or coffee

EVENING MEAL
Chicken and Bean Casserole (page 131)
3 oz (90 g) cooked spinach
mixed green salad with 1 teaspoon (5 ml) olive oil, wine vinegar
and seasoning salt
1 oz (30 g) French bread
1 teaspoon (5 ml) low-fat spread
4 oz (120 g) canned pineapple chunks ☐ tea or coffee

SNACKS OR DRINKS AT PLANNED TIMES
½ pint (300 ml) skim milk, 5 fl oz (150 ml) natural yogurt,
2 tablespoons (30 ml) sultanas, 1 medium portion stewed
rhubarb

Serving Information
Men and Teenagers: Add 2 oz (60 g) French bread at Evening
Meal; 8 fl oz (240 ml) tomato juice
Men: Add ½ oz (15 g) tuna at Midday Meal
Teenagers: Add ½ pint (300 ml) skim milk

DAY 2

MORNING MEAL
½ medium banana
¾ oz (20 g) muesli
5 fl oz (150 ml) skim milk
tea or coffee

MIDDAY MEAL
3-4 oz (90-120 g) sliced roast chicken
3 oz (90 g) sliced cucumber and green pepper
2 slices (1 oz/30 g each) rye bread
2 teaspoons (10 ml) mayonnaise mixed with 1 teaspoon (5 ml)
    tomato ketchup
5 fl oz (150 ml) natural yogurt with 1 teaspoon (5 ml) honey and 2
    tablespoons (30 ml) sultanas
tea or coffee

EVENING MEAL
Cod with Lemon (page 154)
2 oz (60 g) cooked rice
3 oz (90 g) cooked green beans
iceberg lettuce with garlic salt, lemon juice and wine vinegar
4 oz (120 g) orange sections
tea or coffee

SNACKS OR DRINKS AT PLANNED TIMES
5 fl oz (150 ml) skim milk

Serving Information
Men and Teenagers: Add ¾ oz (20 g) muesli at Morning Meal;
    with ½ medium banana and 2 oz (60 g) rice at Evening Meal; 1
    medium apple
Teenagers: Add ½ pint (300 ml) skim milk

DAY 3

MORNING MEAL
4 oz (120 g) orange sections
1 oz (30 g) Cheddar cheese
1 slice (1 oz /30 g) bread
tea or coffee

MIDDAY MEAL
3-4 oz (90-120 g) grilled beefburgers
1-oz (30-g) hamburger roll
1 teaspoon (5 ml) mustard
tomato and onion salad with 1 teaspoon (5 ml) olive oil, wine
    vinegar and pinch oregano
4 oz (120 g) canned sliced peaches
tea or coffee

EVENING MEAL
3-4 oz (90-120 g) poached chicken
3 oz (90 g) cooked peas with 2 tablespoons (30 ml) cooked pearl
    onions and 1 teaspoon (5 ml) margarine
green salad with 1 teaspoon (5 ml) mayonnaise
5 oz (150 g) strawberry jelly and 5 oz (150 g) raspberries
tea or coffee

SNACKS OR DRINKS AT PLANNED TIMES
½ pint (300 ml) skim milk, 5 fl oz (150 ml) natural yogurt

Serving Information
Men and Teenagers: Add 1-oz (30-g) hamburger roll at Midday
    Meal; and 2 oz (60 g) cooked noodles at Evening Meal; 2
    tablespoons (30 ml) raisins, and 2 dried dates
Teenagers: Add ½ pint (300 ml) skim milk

DAY 6

MORNING MEAL
½ medium grapefruit
¾ oz (20 g) cornflakes
5 fl oz (150 ml) skim milk □ tea or coffee

MIDDAY MEAL
1 hardboiled egg
1 oz (30 g) Cheddar cheese
3 oz (90 g) mushrooms on lettuce with 1 tablespoon (15 ml)
    mayonnaise
4 oz (120 g) fresh fruit salad
1-oz (30-g) bread roll
tea or coffee

EVENING MEAL
Irish Stew (page 144)
2 canned peach halves
2 oz (60 g) vanilla ice cream
tea or coffee

SNACKS OR DRINKS AT PLANNED TIMES
5 fl oz (150 ml) skim milk, 5 fl oz (150 ml) natural yogurt

Serving Information
Men and Teenagers: Add 1½-oz (45-g) potato scone with
    2 teaspoons (10 ml) low-calorie marmalade at Morning Meal;
    1 medium banana
Teenagers: Add ½ pint (300 ml) skim milk

DAY 7

MORNING MEAL
½ medium grapefruit
1 poached egg
¾-oz (20-g) muffin, toasted
1 teaspoon (5 ml) margarine □ tea or coffee

MIDDAY MEAL
Ginger-Grilled Chicken (page 130)
3 oz (90 g) cooked mange tout peas, sliced
celery, cucumber and mushroom salad with **Garlic Vinaigrette**
    (page 183)
3 oz (90 g) canned whole kernel sweet corn
1 medium apple □ tea or coffee

EVENING MEAL
3-4 oz (90-120 g) cooked peeled prawns
2 oz (60 g) cooked pasta shells mixed with 1 tablespoon (15 ml)
    chopped red pepper and 2 teaspoons (10 ml) low-calorie
    mayonnaise
tomato and lettuce salad
5 fl oz (150 ml) natural yogurt with 1 oz (30 g) chopped dried
    apricots
tea or coffee

SNACKS OR DRINKS AT PLANNED TIMES
½ pint (300 ml) skim milk

Serving Information
Men and Teenagers: Add extra ¾-oz (20-g) muffin at Morning
    Meal; add extra 2 oz (60 g) cooked pasta shells at Evening
    Meal; 2 tablespoons (30 ml) sultanas
Teenagers: Add ½ pint (300 ml) skim milk

WEEK 12

There's an oriental flavour to Chicken Teriyaki (Day 6) with its marinade sauce and sauted vegetable accompaniment. The term 'saute' means 'to cook quickly in a small amount of oil until brown and tender'. The word comes from the French 'sauter – to jump' and it's an apt description because the food being sauteed must be constantly in motion as it is cooked. It's best to use a pan with sloping sides and you need a good heat.

DAY 1

MORNING MEAL
½ medium grapefruit
¾ oz (20 g) cornflakes
5 fl oz (150 ml) skim milk
tea or coffee

MIDDAY MEAL
Stuffed French Toast (page 122)
carrot and celery sticks
tea or coffee

EVENING MEAL
3-4 oz (90-120 g) roast chicken
3 oz (90 g) cooked peas
3 oz (90 g) steamed red cabbage
mixed green salad with **Dill Vinaigrette** (page 183)
1-oz (30-g) bread roll
1 teaspoon (5 ml) margarine
Stuffed Baked Apple (page 190)
tea or coffee

SNACKS OR DRINKS AT PLANNED TIMES
5 fl oz (150 ml) skim milk, 5 fl oz (150 ml) natural yogurt

Serving Information
Men and Teenagers: Add extra ¾ oz (20 g) cornflakes at
    Morning Meal and extra 1-oz (30-g) bread roll at Evening Meal;
    1 medium banana
Teenagers: Add ½ pint (300 ml) skim milk

DAY 4

MORNING MEAL
½ medium banana
¾ oz (20 g) muesli
5 fl oz (150 ml) skim milk
tea or coffee

MIDDAY MEAL
Chicken Livers Sauteed in Wine (page 00)
sliced cucumber and tomato salad
1-oz (30-g) wholemeal roll
1 teaspoon (5 ml) margarine
4 oz (120 g) canned pears
tea or coffee

EVENING MEAL
3-4 oz (90-120 g) veal escalope
1 teaspoon (5 ml) vegetable oil
3 oz (90 g) cooked peas
3 oz (90 g) steamed broccoli
3 oz (90 g) steamed potatoes
4 oz (120 g) grapefruit and orange sections
tea or coffee

SNACKS OR DRINKS AT PLANNED TIMES
5 fl oz (150 ml) skim milk, 5 fl oz (150 ml) natural yogurt,
    1 medium portion stewed rhubarb

Serving Information
Men and Teenagers: Add ¾ oz (20 g) muesli at Morning Meal;
    3 oz (90 g) steamed potatoes at Evening Meal; ½ medium
    banana
Teenagers: Add ½ pint (300 ml) skim milk

DAY 5

MORNING MEAL
4 fl oz (120 ml) orange juice
1 boiled egg
1 slice (1 oz/30 g) bread, toasted
1 teaspoon (5 ml) margarine □ tea or coffee

MIDDAY MEAL
3-4 oz (90-120 g) grilled cod
3 oz (90 g) cooked green beans
3 oz (90 g) steamed carrots
watercress and lettuce salad and 1 teaspoon (5 ml) mayonnaise
1 slice (1 oz/30 g) wholemeal bread
1 teaspoon (5 ml) margarine
5 oz (150 g) canned blackcurrants with **Custard** (page 191)
tea or coffee

EVENING MEAL
3 oz (90 g) cooked ham
3 oz (90 g) steamed mange tout peas
3 oz (90 g) poached mushrooms
1 medium grilled tomato
1 medium apple □ tea or coffee

SNACKS OR DRINKS AT PLANNED TIMES
5 fl oz (150 ml) skim milk, 5 fl oz (150 ml) natural yogurt

Serving Information
Men and Teenagers: Add 3 oz (90 g) steamed potatoes at
    Midday Meal; 2 oz (60 g) cooked noodles at Evening Meal;
    2 tablespoons (30 ml) raisins
Men: Add 1 oz (30 g) cooked ham at Evening Meal
Teenagers: Add ½ pint (300 ml) skim milk

DAY 2

MORNING MEAL
4 fl oz (120 ml) orange juice
1 poached egg
1 slice (1 oz/30 g) wholemeal bread
tea or coffee

MIDDAY MEAL
3-4 oz (90-120 g) tuna
2 teaspoons (10 ml) mayonnaise
iceberg lettuce with sliced tomatoes
3 oz (90 g) cooked beetroot
¾ oz (20 g) crispbread with 2 teaspoons (10 ml) low-fat spread
tea or coffee

EVENING MEAL
3-4 oz (90-120 g) grilled lamb chop
3 oz (90 g) baked jacket potato
sliced red pepper rings and cucumber slices on lettuce with
   lemon juice
4 fl oz (120 ml) red wine
4 oz (120 ml) fresh fruit salad
tea or coffee

SNACKS OR DRINKS AT PLANNED TIMES
4 oz (120 g) canned pears, ½ pint (300 ml) skim milk, 5 fl oz
   (150 ml) natural yogurt

Serving Information
Men and Teenagers: Add extra 3-oz (90-g) baked jacket potato
   and extra 4 oz (120 g) fruit salad at Evening Meal; 1 digestive
   biscuit
Teenagers: Add ½ pint (300 ml) skim milk

DAY 3

MORNING MEAL
2-inch (5-cm) wedge honeydew melon
1 oz (30 g) Cheddar cheese, grilled on 1 slice (1 oz/30 g)
   wholemeal bread, toasted
tea or coffee

MIDDAY MEAL
1½-2 oz (45-60 g) sliced cooked chicken and 1 sliced hard-boiled
   egg on lettuce
tomato and spring onion salad
Fruit Slaw (page 180)
tea or coffee

EVENING MEAL
3-4 oz (90-120 g) grilled haddock with lemon wedges
3 oz (90 g) cooked sliced beetroot
3 oz (90 g) steamed spinach
green salad with 1½ teaspoons (7.5 ml) salad cream
¾-oz (20-g) muffin, toasted
1 teaspoon (5 ml) low-fat spread
1 medium apple
tea or coffee

SNACKS OR DRINKS AT PLANNED TIMES
7½ fl oz (225 ml) skim milk, 5 fl oz (150 ml) natural yogurt, 1
   tablespoon (15 ml) raisins

Serving Information
Men and teenagers: Add 6 oz (180 g) steamed potatoes at
   Evening Meal; 2-inch (5-cm) wedge honeydew melon
Teenagers: Add ½ pint (300 ml) skim milk

DAY 6

MORNING MEAL
1 medium orange
2½ oz (75 g) cottage cheese
1 slice (1 oz/30 g) raisin bread, toasted
1 teaspoon (5 ml) low-fat spread
tea or coffee

MIDDAY MEAL
Chicken Teriyaki (page 132)
2 oz (60 g) cooked rice
beansprouts, sliced onions and green peppers, sauteed in
   1 teaspoon (5 ml) vegetable oil
2-inch (5-cm) wedge honeydew melon
tea or coffee

EVENING MEAL
3-4 oz (90-120 g) grilled plaice
1 medium grilled tomato
3 oz (90 g) steamed broccoli
cucumber, radish and green pepper slices on lettuce with
   2 teaspoons (10 ml) salad cream
tea or coffee

SNACKS OR DRINKS AT PLANNED TIMES
½ pint (300 ml) skim milk, 5 fl oz (150 ml) natural yogurt with
   1 tablespoon (15 ml) raisins

Serving Information
Men and Teenagers: Add extra 4 oz (120 g) cooked rice at
   Midday Meal; 1 medium banana
Teenagers: Add ½ pint (300 ml) skim milk

DAY 7

MORNING MEAL
½ medium grapefruit
¾ oz (20 g) porridge oats cooked with water, served with 5 fl oz
   (150 ml) skim milk □ tea or coffee

MIDDAY MEAL
4½-6 oz (135-180 g) grilled rump steak
3 oz (90 g) steamed kale
3-oz (90-g) baked jacket potato
2 teaspoons (10 ml) low-fat spread
green salad with 1 teaspoon (5 ml) mayonnaise
4 fl oz (120 ml) red wine
2 canned pear halves
tea or coffee

EVENING MEAL
1 oz (30 g) Cheddar cheese toasted on 1 slice (1 oz/30 g) bread
green pepper, tomato and onion slices with 1 teaspoon (5 ml)
   olive oil, wine vinegar and pinch oregano
5 fl oz (150 ml) natural yogurt with 1 teaspoon (5 ml) honey and
   2 dried dates, chopped

SNACKS OR DRINKS AT PLANNED TIMES
5 fl oz (150 ml) skim milk

Serving Information
Men and Teenagers: Add 1 slice (1 oz/30 g) currant bread,
   ½ teaspoon (2.5 ml) marmalade at Morning Meal; 3-oz (90-g)
   baked jacket potato at Midday Meal; 1 oz (30 g) chopped dried
   apricots to yogurt at Evening meal
Teenagers: Add ½ pint (300 ml) skim milk

WEEK 13

The mid-Lent Sunday was traditionally the day when people went to their 'Mother-Church' and it was thus called 'Mothering Sunday'. For young people working away in service, this church visit meant a journey back to the home and family too, and it was the custom to take a cake to Mother and to gather bunches of violets and primroses from those which grew wild at the roadside.

Today's version of making a fuss of Mother could well be to take her breakfast in bed or to prepare a special evening meal, so that she can have a rest and a day free from domestic chores. With this in mind we suggest, for Mother's Day breakfast, a simple menu of cheese grilled on toast plus fruit juice and tea or coffee – any child could manage that. And for a dinnertime treat, we plan Red Pepper Steak with a glass of red wine. Mother should like it!

DAY 1

MORNING MEAL
6 canned apricot halves
2½ oz (75 g) cottage cheese
1 slice (1 oz/30 g) wholemeal bread □ tea or coffee

MIDDAY MEAL
2-egg omelette with pinch mixed herbs cooked in 1 teaspoon (5 ml) vegetable oil
3 oz (90 g) grilled mushrooms
2 medium grilled tomatoes
¾ oz (20 g) crispbread
1 teaspoon (5 ml) low-fat spread
2-inch (5-cm) wedge honeydew melon
tea or coffee

EVENING MEAL
3-4 oz (90-120 g) grilled halibut
3 oz (90 g) cooked carrots
iceberg lettuce with 1 teaspoon (5 ml) mayonnaise
1-oz (30-g) bread roll
1 teaspoon (5 ml) low-fat spread
4 oz (120 g) stewed apple with **Custard** (page 191)
tea or coffee

SNACKS OR DRINKS AT PLANNED TIMES
5 fl oz (150 ml) skim milk, 5 fl oz (150 ml) natural yogurt

Serving Information
Men and Teenagers: Add 6 oz (180 g) cooked potatoes at Evening Meal; 2-inch (5-cm) wedge honeydew melon, and 6 canned apricot halves
Teenagers: Add ½ pint (300 ml) skim milk

DAY 4

MORNING MEAL
½ medium banana
¾ oz (20 g) bran flakes
5 fl oz (150 ml) skim milk
1 slice (1 oz/30 g) wholemeal bread
1 teaspoon (5 ml) margarine □ tea or coffee

MIDDAY MEAL
shredded iceberg lettuce with sliced mushrooms
1 hard-boiled egg, sliced
1 oz (30 g) grated Cheddar cheese and tomato wedges with **Oregano Vinaigrette** (page 183)
¾ oz (20 g) crispbread
5 oz (150 g) orange jelly with 4 oz (120 g) orange slices
tea or coffee

EVENING MEAL
3-4 oz (90-120 g) grilled haddock with lemon wedges
3 oz (90 g) steamed broad beans
3 oz (90 g) steamed carrots
3 oz (90 g) steamed potatoes
2 teaspoons (10 ml) low-fat spread
5 oz (150 g) frozen raspberries with 5 fl oz (150 ml) natural yogurt
1½ teaspoons (7.5 ml) sugar □ tea or coffee

SNACKS OR DRINKS AT PLANNED TIMES
5 fl oz (150 ml) skim milk

Serving Information
Men and Teenagers: Add 3 oz (90 g) steamed potatoes at Evening Meal; 1 digestive biscuit and 1 medium pear
Teenagers: Add ½ pint (300 ml) skim milk

DAY 5

MORNING MEAL
½ medium grapefruit
2½ oz (75 g) cottage cheese with 1 teaspoon (5 ml) chopped chives
1 oz (30 g) French bread □ tea or coffee

MIDDAY MEAL
3-4 oz (90-120 g) cold roast chicken
tomato and watercress salad with 1 teaspoon (5 ml) vegetable oil and wine vinegar
1 slice (1 oz/30 g) wholemeal bread
1 teaspoon (5 ml) low-fat spread
4 oz (120 g) fresh fruit salad with 3 tablespoons (45 ml) single cream □ tea or coffee

EVENING MEAL
3-4 oz (90-120 g) grilled lamb's liver
3 oz (90 g) sliced onion, sauteed in 1 teaspoon (5 ml) margarine
3 oz (90 g) steamed carrots
3 oz (90 g) steamed broccoli
1 teaspoon (5 ml) low-fat spead
5 fl oz (150 ml) natural yogurt with ½ medium banana
tea or coffee

SNACKS OR DRINKS AT PLANNED TIMES
½ pint (300 ml) skim milk, 1 digestive biscuit

Serving Information
Men and Teenagers: Add 3 oz (90 g) steamed potatoes at Evening Meal; ½ medium banana and 4 oz (120 g) fresh fruit salad
Teenagers: Add ½ pint (300 ml) skim milk

DAY 2

MORNING MEAL
4 fl oz (120 ml) orange juice
¾ oz (20 g) cornflakes
5 fl oz (150 ml) skim milk
tea or coffee

MIDDAY MEAL
Baked 'Cheesy' Pitta Bread (page 122)
green salad with sliced tomatoes and onions with 2 teaspoons
  (10 ml) salad cream and 1 tablespoon (15 ml) wine vinegar
4 oz (120 g) canned fruit cocktail
tea or coffee

EVENING MEAL
6 oz (180 g) boil-in-the-bag fish in sauce (any type)
3 oz (90 g) cooked carrots
3 oz (90 g) cooked green beans
3-oz (90-g) boiled potato
2 teaspoons (10 ml) low-fat spread
sparkling mineral water with lemon twist
tea or coffee

SNACKS OR DRINKS AT PLANNED TIMES
5 fl oz (150 ml) skim milk, 5 fl oz (150 ml) natural yogurt, 5 oz
(150 g) canned blackcurrants

Serving Information
Men and Teenagers: Add 1 oz (30 g) pitta bread at Midday Meal;
  4 oz (120 g) fruit cocktail and 1 digestive biscuit
Teenagers: Add ½ pint (300 ml) skim milk

DAY 3

MORNING MEAL
½ medium grapefruit
1 egg, scrambled in 1 teaspoon (5 ml) margarine
1 slice (1 oz/30 g) wholemeal bread, toasted
1 teaspoon (5 ml) margarine □ tea or coffee

MIDDAY MEAL
3-4 oz (90-120 g) grilled chicken with lemon juice and pinch each
  garlic salt and paprika
2 small grilled tomatoes
3 oz (90 g) cooked peas
2 oz (60 g) cooked noodles □ tea or coffee

EVENING MEAL
3-4 oz (90-120 g) roast beef
3-oz (90-g) baked jacket potato with 2½ fl oz (75 ml) natural
  yogurt and chopped chives
tomato, lettuce and onion salad with 1 teaspoon (5 ml) vegetable
  oil and 1 tablespoon (15 ml) wine vinegar
4 oz (120 g) canned pineapple cubes with 2½ fl oz (75 ml) natural
  yogurt
tea or coffee

SNACKS OR DRINKS AT PLANNED TIMES
½ pint (300 ml) skim milk, 1 medium apple

Serving Information
Men and Teenagers: Add extra 2 oz (60 g) noodles at Midday
  Meal; 3-oz (90-g) baked jacket potato at Evening Meal;
  1 medium orange
Teenagers: Add ½ pint (300 ml) skim milk

DAY 6

MORNING MEAL
1 medium orange
¾ oz (20 g) muesli
5 fl oz (150 ml) skim milk □ tea or coffee

MIDDAY MEAL
Curried Kidney Beans (page 167)
lettuce and onion salad with **Basic Vinaigrette** (page 183)
1 oz (30 g) pitta bread
5 fl oz (150 ml) natural yogurt with 1 tablespoon (15 ml) raisins
  and ½ teaspoon (2.5 ml) rum flavouring
tea or coffee

EVENING MEAL
3-4 oz (90-120 g) grilled veal chop
6 medium cooked asparagus spears
3 oz (90 g) cooked celery hearts
1 oz (30 g) French bread
1 teaspoon (5 ml) low-fat spread
½ medium cantaloupe melon
tea or coffee

SNACKS OR DRINKS AT PLANNED TIMES
5 fl oz (150 ml) skim milk

Serving Information
Men and Teenagers: Add 1 oz (30 g) pitta bread at Midday Meal;
  2 tablespoons (30 ml) raisins and 1 oz (30 g) French bread at
  Evening Meal; 4 fl oz (120 ml) orange juice
Men: Add ½ oz (15 g) grated Cheddar cheese to salad at Midday
  Meal
Teenagers: Add ½ pint (300 ml) skim milk

DAY 7

MORNING MEAL
4 fl oz (120 ml) orange juice
1 oz (30 g) Cheddar cheese and 1 medium sliced tomato grilled
  on 1 slice (1 oz/30 g) wholemeal bread, toasted
tea or coffee

MIDDAY MEAL
3-4 oz (90-120 g) sardines
green salad with sliced tomatoes and sliced onions
1 teaspoon (5 ml) low-calorie mayonnaise
2 slices canned pineapple
tea or coffee

EVENING MEAL
Red Pepper Steak (page 138)
4 oz (120 g) cooked rice
3 oz (90 g) steamed courgettes
iceberg lettuce with 1 teaspoon (5 ml) olive oil and wine vinegar
4 oz (120 g) canned sliced peaches
4 fl oz (120 ml) glass red wine
tea or coffee

SNACKS OR DRINKS AT PLANNED TIMES
5 fl oz (150 ml) natural yogurt with 2 teaspoons (10 ml) low-
  calorie jam
½ pint (300 ml) skim milk

Serving Information
Men and Teenagers: Add 2 cream crackers at Midday Meal,
  1 digestive biscuit and 1 medium banana
Teenagers: Add ½ pint (300 ml) skim milk

WEEK 14

If you think that 'salad' means 'lettuce', then you're in for a shock. We believe that a collection of crisp and colourful salad greens and vegetables gives a boost to the food plan of anyone who wants to lose weight. They look so attractive, they taste good if they are properly 'dressed', they are filling and nutritious and they help to provide the dietary fibre which we all need.

We suggest several salads for you this week. You will find combinations of lettuce and celery, peppers, potatoes in special dressing, watercress and radish, tomato and onion as well as the more conventional tomato and cucumber.

Don't imagine that there's only one lettuce either – the family contains many branches – round, cos, iceberg to mention only the obvious ones. Try its other relations too – endive, cress, escarole, spinach for instance. There's a whole new experience there if you are prepared to be adventurous.

DAY 1

MORNING MEAL
4 fl oz (120 ml) orange juice
1 poached egg
1 slice (1 oz/30 g) wholemeal bread
1 teaspoon (5 ml) margarine
tea or coffee

MIDDAY MEAL
3-4 oz (90-120 g) grilled haddock
3 oz (90 g) steamed spinach
3 oz (90 g) steamed carrots
3 oz (90 g) steamed potatoes
1 teaspoon (5 ml) margarine
½ medium cantaloupe melon
tea or coffee

EVENING MEAL
3-4 oz (90-120 g) roast chicken
3 oz (90 g) steamed cauliflower
3 oz (90 g) steamed Brussels sprouts
grated red cabbage and beansprouts with **Cider Vinaigrette**
  (page 183)
1 medium apple □ tea or coffee

SNACKS OR DRINKS AT PLANNED TIMES
5 fl oz (150 ml) natural yogurt, ½ pint (300 ml) skim milk

Serving Information
Men and Teenagers: Add 3 oz (90 g) steamed potato at Midday
  Meal; 3 oz (90 g) canned sweet corn at Evening Meal;
  2 tablespoons (30 ml) raisins and 4 fl oz (120 ml) orange juice
Teenagers: Add ½ pint (300 ml) skim milk

DAY 4

MORNING MEAL
2½ fl oz (75 ml) apple juice
2½ oz (75 g) cottage cheese
1-oz (30-g) bread roll
1 teaspoon (5 ml) yeast extract
tea or coffee

MIDDAY MEAL
2-egg omelette cooked in 1 teaspoon (5 ml) vegetable oil
watercress and radish salad with lemon juice
1 slice (1 oz/30 g) wholemeal bread
2 teaspoons (10 ml) low-fat spread
tea or coffee

EVENING MEAL
Savoury Butter Bean Salad (page 166)
3 oz (90 g) steamed spinach
green salad with wine vinegar
1 medium orange
tea or coffee

SNACKS OR DRINKS AT PLANNED TIMES
Strawberry-Apple Frost (page 187)
½ pint (300 ml) skim milk

Serving Information
Men and Teenagers: Add 2 oz (60 g) bread roll, 1 medium
  banana
Men: Add 2 oz (60 g) cooked butter beans at Evening Meal
Teenagers: Add 5 fl oz (150 ml) natural yogurt

DAY 5

MORNING MEAL
4 oz (120 g) canned grapefruit sections
¾ oz (20 g) cornflakes
5 fl oz (150 ml) skim milk □ tea or coffee

MIDDAY MEAL
3-4 oz (90-120 g) peeled prawns
2 teaspoons (10 ml) low-calorie seafood sauce
3 oz (90 g) steamed green beans
tomato, pepper and cucumber salad with 1 teaspoon (5 ml) olive
  oil and vinegar
1 slice (1 oz/30 g) wholemeal bread
1 teaspoon (5 ml) margarine
2 oz (60 g) stewed apple with **Custard** (page 191)
tea or coffee

EVENING MEAL
3-4 oz (90-120 g) grilled pork chop
2 oz (60 g) cooked apple, pureed
3 oz (90 g) cooked cauliflower
3 oz (90 g) cooked beetroot
2 teaspoons (10 ml) low-fat spread
green salad with lemon juice
4 fl oz (120 ml) red wine □ tea or coffee

SNACKS OR DRINKS AT PLANNED TIMES
1 medium pear, 1 digestive biscuit, ½ pint (300 ml) skim milk

Serving Information
Men and Teenagers: Add 4 oz (120 g) cooked noodles at
  Evening Meal; 6 oz (180 g) grapes
Teenagers: Add 5 fl oz (150 ml) natural yogurt

DAY 2

MORNING MEAL
8 fl oz (240 ml) tomato juice
1 oz (30 g) Cheddar cheese
1 slice (1 oz/30 g) bread
1 teaspoon (5 ml) margarine
tea or coffee

MIDDAY MEAL
3-4 oz (90-120 g) cold chicken
tomato and cucumber slices on lettuce with 1 teaspoon (5 ml)
    low-calorie mayonnaise
1 slice (1 oz/30 g) wholemeal bread
2 canned peach halves
tea or coffee

EVENING MEAL
Pork and Vegetable Medley (page 148)
3 oz (90 g) cooked broccoli
shredded lettuce and sliced celery with 1 teaspoon (5 ml)
    imitation bacon bits and 2 teaspoons (10 ml) low-calorie
    French dressing
½ medium grapefruit □ tea or coffee

SNACKS OR DRINKS AT PLANNED TIMES
5 fl oz (150 ml) **Hot Mocha Milk** (page 192) ½ pint (300 ml) skim
    milk, 5 fl oz (150 ml) natural yogurt

Serving Information
Men and Teenagers: Add 1 slice (1 oz/30 g) wholemeal bread at
    Midday Meal; 1 digestive biscuit, 2 canned peach halves
Teenagers: Add ½ pint (300 ml) skim milk

DAY 3

MORNING MEAL
½ medium banana
¾ oz (20 g) bran flakes
5 fl oz (150 ml) skim milk □ tea of coffee

MIDDAY MEAL
5-6 oz (150-180 g) uncooked chicken livers, sauteed in
    1 teaspoon (5 ml) vegetable oil
Bacon-Flavoured Potato Salad (page 175)
1 slice (1 oz/30 g) wholemeal bread
1 teaspoon (5 ml) margarine
4 oz (120 g) canned fruit cocktail
tea or coffee

EVENING MEAL
3-4 oz (90-120 g) grilled haddock
3 oz (90 g) cooked peas
2 oz (60 g) cooked sliced mushrooms
red and green peppers sliced on lettuce with wine vinegar
4 fl oz (120 ml) white wine
tea or coffee

SNACKS OR DRINKS AT PLANNED TIMES
5 fl oz (150 ml) natural yogurt with ½ teaspoon (2.5 ml) vanilla
    flavouring and artificial sweetener, 1 medium orange, 5 fl oz
    (150 ml) skim milk

Serving Information
Men and Teenagers: Add 2 tablespoons (30 ml) raisins, 4 oz
    (120 g) stewed apple; add 2-oz (60-g) bread roll at Evening
    Meal
Teenagers: Add ½ pint (300 ml) skim milk

DAY 6

MORNING MEAL
1 medium orange
1 boiled egg
¾ oz (20 g) crispbread with 1 teaspoon (5 ml) marmalade
tea or coffee

MIDDAY MEAL
3 tablespoons (45 ml) peanut butter
1 slice (1 oz/30 g) wholemeal bread
tomato, lettuce and cucumber salad with lemon juice
1 medium pear □ tea or coffee

EVENING MEAL
Braised Chicken with Vegetables (page 127)
3 oz (90 g) steamed spinach
3 oz (90 g) steamed carrots
2 slices canned pineapple □ tea or coffee

SNACKS OR DRINKS AT PLANNED TIMES
5 fl oz (150 ml) natural yogurt with 2 teaspoons (10 ml) low-
    calorie apricot jam, ½ pint (300 ml) skim milk

Serving Information
Men and Teenagers: Add 4 oz (120 g) steamed rice at Evening
    Meal; 6 oz (180 g) grapes
Teenagers: Add ½ pint (300 ml) skim milk

DAY 7

MORNING MEAL
½ medium banana
¾ oz (20 g) muesli
5 fl oz (150 ml) skim milk
tea or coffee

MIDDAY MEAL
Marinated Rump Steak (page 150)
3 oz (90 g) steamed courgettes
3 oz (90 g) steamed broccoli
2 teaspoons (10 ml) low-fat spread
tomato and onion salad with vinegar and garlic salt
4 oz (120 g) fresh fruit salad
2 oz (60 g) vanilla ice cream □ tea or coffee

EVENING MEAL
3 breadcrumbed fish cakes, grilled
3 oz (90 g) baked beans
green salad with 2 teaspoons (10 ml) low-calorie mayonnaise
1-oz (30-g) bread roll
2 teaspoons (10 ml) low-fat spread
8 fl oz (240 ml) tomato juice □ tea or coffee

SNACKS OR DRINKS AT PLANNED TIMES
5 fl oz (150 ml) natural yogurt with coffee flavouring and artificial
    sweetener, 5 fl oz (150 ml) skim milk

Serving Information
Men and Teenagers: Add ¾ oz (20 g) muesli at Morning Meal
    with extra ½ medium banana; add 1-oz (30-g) bread roll at
    Evening Meal
Teenagers: Add ½ pint (300 ml) skim milk

WEEK 15

Spring should be showing her colours now and the joys of early vegetables and fruits, together with better weather and lighter evenings, bring on a happy state of Spring Fever. Sunday dinner gives a good opportunity to enjoy young lamb and we've suggested a splendid way to cook it, with orange and rosemary to enhance the flavour.

Rosemary is a wonderfully aromatic herb. It's a symbol of fidelity and was supposed to grow only in the gardens of righteous people! Its pungent scent was said to have the power of fighting infection and it is sometimes used, even now, as an infusion to benefit hair and skin.

There is no end to its culinary uses, both sweet and savoury. It goes especially well with lamb and fish, but try it, too, with sauteed potatoes or raw vegetables.

DAY 1

MORNING MEAL
4 fl oz (120 ml) grapefruit juice
1 boiled egg
1 slice (1 oz/30 g) bread
1 teaspoon (5 ml) margarine
tea or coffee

MIDDAY MEAL
tuna fish salad made with 3-4 oz (90-120 g) canned tuna on
    shredded lettuce with 1 medium tomato, sliced, and 2-inch
    (5-cm) chunk cucumber, sliced
1 slice (1 oz/30 g) bread
1 teaspoon (5 ml) margarine
1 medium apple
tea or coffee

EVENING MEAL
Chicken Breasts with Tarragon (page 135)
3 oz (90 g) steamed cauliflower
3 oz (90 g) cooked peas
2 oz (60 g) boiled rice
1 medium orange
tea or coffee

SNACKS OR DRINKS AT PLANNED TIMES
½ pint (300 ml) skim milk, 5 fl oz (150 ml) natural yogurt

Serving Information
Men and Teenagers: Add 1 slice (1 oz/30 g) brown bread and
    2 oz (60 g) boiled rice at Evening Meal; 1 medium banana
Teenagers: Add ½ pint (300 ml) skim milk

DAY 4

MORNING MEAL
½ medium grapefruit
1 scrambled egg with 1 medium tomato, halved and grilled
1 slice (1 oz/30 g) bread, toasted
1 teaspoon (5 ml) margarine
tea or coffee

MIDDAY MEAL
sardine salad made with 3-4 oz (90-120 g) canned sardines,
    served on shredded lettuce, with sliced tomato and
    cucumber, with mustard and cress as a garnish topped with 1
    teaspoon (5 ml) vegetable oil
2 water biscuits
2 teaspoons (10 ml) low-fat spread
3 oz (90 g) grapes
tea or coffee

EVENING MEAL
3 oz (90 g) thick slice ham, grilled with 2 canned pineapple slices
3 oz (90 g) cooked peas
3 oz (90 g) steamed broccoli

SNACKS OR DRINKS AT PLANNED TIMES
½ pint (300 ml) skim milk, 5 fl oz (150 ml) natural yogurt

Serving Information
Men and Teenagers: Add extra 2 water biscuits and 1 slice
    (1 oz/30 g) bread, 1 medium apple and 3 oz (90 g) grapes
Men: Add extra 1 oz (30 g) ham at Evening Meal
Teenagers: Add ½ pint (300 ml) skim milk

DAY 5

MORNING MEAL
½ medium grapefruit, grilled and sprinkled with ½ teaspoon
    (2.5 ml) brown sugar and pinch of cinnamon
¾ oz (20 g) muesli with 5 fl oz (150 ml) skim milk
tea or coffee

MIDDAY MEAL
Cheddar bap made with 1 (2-oz/60-g) bap spread with 2
    teaspoons (10 ml) margarine and filled with 2 oz (60 g) grated
    Cheddar cheese, lettuce and tomato slices
1 medium banana
tea or coffee

EVENING MEAL
Piquant Lemon Sole (page 153)
3 oz (90 g) steamed courgettes
3 oz (90 g) cooked spring greens
2 oz (60 g) vanilla ice cream
tea or coffee

SNACKS OR DRINKS AT PLANNED TIMES
15 fl oz (450 ml) skim milk

Serving Information
Men and Teenagers: Add 2 digestive biscuits and 2 small
    tangerines
Teenagers: Add 5 fl oz (150 ml) natural yogurt

DAY 2

MORNING MEAL
4 fl oz (120 ml) grapefruit juice
¾ oz (20 g) cornflakes served with 5 fl oz (150 ml) skim milk
tea or coffee

MIDDAY MEAL
cottage cheese salad made with 5 oz (150 g) cottage cheese
  mixed with 2 spring onions, diced, and 2 tablespoons (30 ml)
  diced celery, served on shredded lettuce with sliced tomato
  with 2 teaspoons (10 ml) salad cream
1 slice (1 oz/30 g) bread
1 teaspoon (5 ml) margarine
1 medium apple
tea or coffee

EVENING MEAL
Savoury Beans (page 166)
3 oz (90 g) poached mushrooms
2 canned pear halves
tea or coffee

SNACKS OR DRINKS AT PLANNED TIMES
15 fl oz (450 ml) skim milk

Serving Information
Men and Teenagers: Add extra 2 slices (2 oz/60 g) bread and 1
  medium orange
Teenagers: Add 5 fl oz (150 ml) natural yogurt

DAY 3

MORNING MEAL
1 medium orange, peeled and diced with 1 teaspoon (5 ml)
  honey
1 oz (30 g) Cheddar cheese grilled on 1 slice (1 oz/30 g)
  wholemeal bread, toasted
tea or coffee

MIDDAY MEAL
egg salad made with 2 hard-boiled eggs, sliced and arranged on
  shredded lettuce with sliced tomato and cucumber, chopped,
  with 2 teaspoons (10 ml) salad cream
¾ oz (20 g) crispbread
1 teaspoon (5 ml) margarine
1 medium apple
tea or coffee

EVENING MEAL
3-4 oz (90-120 g) grilled lamb's liver
3 oz (90 g) onion, cut in rings and sauteed in 1 teaspoon (5 ml)
  vegetable oil
3 oz (90 g) steamed carrots
2 oz (60 g) cooked noodles
1 medium apple
tea or coffee

SNACKS OR DRINKS AT PLANNED TIMES
½ pint (300 ml) skim milk, 5 fl oz (150 ml) natural yogurt

Serving Information
Men and Teenagers: Add extra 2 oz (60 g) noodles, 1 digestive
  biscuit, 1 medium apple
Teenagers: Add ½ pint (300 ml) skim milk

DAY 6

MORNING MEAL
4 fl oz (120 ml) orange juice
2½ oz (75 g) curd cheese mixed with 1 teaspoon (5 ml) chopped
  chives and spread on 1 slice (1 oz/30 g) brown bread, toasted
tea or coffee

MIDDAY MEAL
4 fish fingers, breadcrumbed, spread with 1 teaspoon (5 ml)
  margarine, and grilled
3 oz (90 g) cooked peas
3 oz (90 g) canned baked beans
4 oz (120 g) canned fruit cocktail
tea or coffee

EVENING MEAL
3-4 oz (90-120 g) grilled steak
3 oz (90 g) steamed broccoli
3 oz (90 g) cooked carrots dotted with 2 teaspoons (10 ml)
  margarine
1 medium apple
tea or coffee

SNACKS OR DRINKS AT PLANNED TIMES
½ pint (300 ml) skim milk, 5 fl oz (150 ml) natural yogurt

Serving Information
Men and Teenagers: Add extra 3 oz (90 g) baked beans, 1 slice (1
  oz/30 g) bread and 1 medium banana
Teenagers: Add ½ pint (300 ml) skim milk

DAY 7

MORNING MEAL
4 fl oz (120 ml) orange juice
¾ oz (20 g) wheat flakes served with 5 fl oz (150 ml) skim milk
tea or coffee

MIDDAY MEAL
Orange Lamb with Rosemary (page 139)
3 oz (90 g) shredded and steamed spring greens
2 oz (60 g) boiled rice
6 oz (180 g) grapes
tea or coffee

EVENING MEAL
3-4 oz (90-120 g) canned salmon with mixed salad of lettuce,
  tomatoes and cucumber, and 3 oz (90 g) diced beetroot with 2
  teaspoons (10 ml) mayonnaise
1 digestive biscuit crumbled into 5 fl oz (150 ml) natural yogurt
  with 2 tablespoons (30 ml) sultanas
tea or coffee

SNACKS OR DRINKS AT PLANNED TIMES
5 fl oz (150 ml) skim milk

Serving Information
Men and Teenagers: Add extra 2 oz (60 g) boiled rice and extra
  digestive biscuit; add 8 oz (240 g) fresh fruit salad
Teenagers: Add ½ pint (300 ml) skim milk

WEEK 16

This week sees three great religious observances – Good Friday, Easter Sunday and the Jewish Passover.

We suggest a fish dish for Good Friday – cod poached in a well-flavoured sauce, with French beans and tomato. It's far removed from plain boiled cod!

On Easter Sunday, with the family at home perhaps, enjoy roast beef plus a variety of trimmings followed by a simple pudding.

The alternatives for our Jewish readers include Matzo Brei, Mock Kishka and a lovely sweet dish – Fruited Matzo Kugel.

It's interesting to note that Easter and Passover share one symbol – the egg. New birth, new life, the joy of the new season is reflected in the foods of this festival week.

DAY 1

MORNING MEAL
4 fl oz (120 ml) orange juice
Matzo Brei (page 119)
tea or coffee

MIDDAY MEAL
5 oz (150 g) quark cheese
green salad with sliced tomato and cucumber
1 teaspoon (5 ml) mayonnaise
1 slice (1 oz/30 g) wholemeal bread
1 medium orange
mineral water with twist of lemon
tea or coffee

EVENING MEAL
3-4 oz (90-120 g) grilled herring with **Dijon-Herb Dressing** (page 182)
3 oz (90 g) mushrooms sauteed in ½ teaspoon (2.5 ml) oil
3 oz (90 g) cooked carrot slices
5 fl oz (150 ml) natural yogurt
tea or coffee

SNACKS OR DRINKS AT PLANNED TIMES
½ pint (300 ml) skim milk, 2 oz (60 g) vanilla ice cream with 4 oz (120 g) canned mandarin oranges

Serving Information
Men and Teenagers: Add 4 fl oz (120 ml) orange juice, 1½-oz (45-g) scone with 2 teaspoons (10 ml) low-calorie jam, 4 oz (120 g) canned mandarin oranges
Teenagers: Add ½ pint (300 ml) skim milk

DAY 4

MORNING MEAL
4 oz (120 g) grapefruit sections
2½ oz (75 g) soft cheese
1 slice (1 oz/30 g) currant bread
1 teaspoon (5 ml) margarine
tea or coffee

MIDDAY MEAL
3-4 oz (90-120 g) sliced roast turkey or chicken
1 medium tomato, sliced
shredded lettuce
1 slice (1 oz/30 g) wholemeal bread
1 teaspoon (5 ml) margarine
4 oz (120 g) fruit salad □ tea or coffee

EVENING MEAL
3-4 oz (90-120 g) grilled steak
3-oz (90-g) baked jacket potato with 1 teaspoon (5 ml) margarine
3 oz (90 g) cooked onion
3 oz (90 g) steamed spinach
green salad with lemon juice and herbs
sparkling mineral water with twist of lemon
tea or coffee

SNACKS OR DRINKS AT PLANNED TIMES
5 oz (150 g) raspberries, 5 fl oz (150 ml) natural yogurt, ½ pint (300 ml) skim milk

Serving Information
Men and Teenagers: Add 4 fl oz (120 ml) orange juice, 1 slice (1 oz/30 g) wholemeal bread
Teenagers: Add 5 fl oz (150 ml) natural yogurt

DAY 5

MORNING MEAL
2½ fl oz (75 ml) apple juice
1 oz (30 g) Cheddar cheese
1 slice (1 oz/30 g) wholemeal bread
tea or coffee

MIDDAY MEAL
Poached Cod with French Beans and Tomato (page 154)
3 oz (90 g) steamed courgette slices
shredded lettuce with sliced radishes and 1 teaspoon (5 ml) mayonnaise
1 slice (1 oz/30 g) wholemeal bread
1 medium orange
tea or coffee

EVENING MEAL
Vegetable-Cheese Platter (page 118)
sliced cucumber on lettuce leaves with 1 teaspoon (5 ml) imitation bacon bits
1 teaspoon (5 ml) mayonnaise
½ pint (300 ml) lager or cider
tea or coffee

SNACKS OR DRINKS AT PLANNED TIMES
5 fl oz (150 ml) natural yogurt, 7½ fl oz (225 ml) skim milk, 1 medium apple

Serving Information
Men and Teenagers: Add 2½ fl oz (75 ml) apple juice, 2-oz (60-g) bread roll
Teenagers: Add ½ pint (300 ml) skim milk

DAY 2

MORNING MEAL
4 fl oz (120 ml) orange juice
¾ oz (20 g) instant cereal made with 5 fl oz (150 ml) hot skim milk
tea or coffee

MIDDAY MEAL
3-4 oz (90-120 g) grilled chicken
3 oz (90 g) steamed green beans
green salad with sliced tomato and **Savory Vinaigrette** (page 183)
1 teaspoon (5 ml) imitation bacon bits
Mock Kishka (page 174)
1 medium apple □ tea or coffee

EVENING MEAL
Ham with Rice and Water Chestnuts (page 151)
3 oz (90 g) steamed beansprouts
3 oz (90 g) cooked carrots
tea or coffee

SNACKS OR DRINKS AT PLANNED TIMES
½ pint (300 ml) skim milk, **Apricot Frappe** (page 195)
 1 digestive biscuit

Serving Information
Men and Teenagers: Add 4 fl oz (120 ml) orange juice, 1
 digestive biscuit and 4 oz (120 g) canned sliced peaches
Men: Add 1 oz (30 g) grilled chicken at Midday Meal
Teenagers: Add ½ pint (300 ml) skim milk

DAY 3

MORNING MEAL
Fruited Matzo Kugel (page 175)
tea or coffee

MIDDAY MEAL
3-4 oz (90-120 g) canned tuna
Curried Cole Slaw (page 178)
3 oz (90 g) whole kernel sweet corn
1 medium orange
tea or coffee

EVENING MEAL
3-4 oz (90-120 g) grilled veal
3 oz (90 g) steamed mange tout peas
1 medium tomato, sliced
green salad with 1 teaspoon (5 ml) vegetable oil, plus wine
 vinegar
tea or coffee

SNACKS OR DRINKS AT PLANNED TIMES
Pear Frozen Yogurt (page 00) ½ pint (300 ml) skim milk

Serving Information
Men and Teenagers: Add ½ medium grapefruit, 1½-oz (45-g)
 scone, toasted and spread with 2 teaspoons (10 ml) low-
 calorie raspberry jam
Teenagers: Add ½ pint (300 ml) skim milk

DAY 6

MORNING MEAL
½ medium banana, sliced
¾ oz (20 g) ready-to-eat cereal
5 fl oz (150 ml) skim milk
tea or coffee

MIDDAY MEAL
3-4 oz (90-120 g) grilled chicken livers with 1 slice lean back
 bacon, grilled
1 medium tomato, grilled
1-oz (30-g) wholemeal roll
2 teaspoons (10 ml) low-fat spread
4 oz (120 g) fruit salad
tea or coffee

EVENING MEAL
Chicken Capri with Potatoes (page 134)
3 oz (90 g) steamed courgettes
green salad with 2 teaspoons (10 ml) low-calorie mayonnaise
sparkling mineral water with sprig of mint
tea or coffee

SNACKS OR DRINKS AT PLANNED TIMES
1 medium apple, 5 fl oz (150 ml) natural yogurt, 5 fl oz (150 ml)
 skim milk

Serving Information
Men and Teenagers: Add ½ medium banana, 1 digestive biscuit
Teenagers: Add ½ pint (300 ml) skim milk

DAY 7

MORNING MEAL
Swedish Apple Bake (page 186)
tea or coffee

MIDDAY MEAL
3-4 oz (90-120 g) sliced roast beef
1 medium tomato, sliced and 3 green pepper rings on lettuce
 with 1 teaspoon (5 ml) mayonnaise
1 slice (1 oz/30 g) wholemeal bread
4 oz (120 g) canned pineapple chunks
tea or coffee

EVENING MEAL
3-4 oz (90-120 g) grilled sole with lemon wedge
3 oz (90 g) steamed carrots and 3 oz (90 g) cooked peas dotted
 with 1 teaspoon (5 ml) margarine
green salad with **Garlic Vinaigrette** (page 183)
2-inch (5-cm) wedge honeydew melon
tea or coffee

SNACKS OR DRINKS AT PLANNED TIMES
5 fl oz (150 ml) natural yogurt, ½ pint (300 ml) skim milk,
 1 digestive biscuit

Serving Information
Men and Teenagers: Add 4 fl oz (120 ml) grapefruit juice,
 1 digestive biscuit
Teenagers: Add ½ pint (300 ml) skim milk

WEEK 17

Easter Monday is a bank holiday and perhaps you will be going out for the day. We've made the midday and evening meals interchangeable so that you can take a picnic if you wish. The Gypsy Cheese Salad is quickly put together and easily portable.

Another portable meal included this week is Lunch Box Fish and Cheese. In this recipe the tuna fish and Cheddar cheese and lettuce are packed neatly into a 'pocket' of pitta bread – a very good way to transport one's food!

You will see that courgettes feature on Day 5. Courgettes (also called zucchini) are really miniature marrows. They differ from their big brothers in that they are flavoursome and crisp. They also absorb well the flavour of the ingredients cooked with them and they have the property of tenderising meat, too. Our recipe combines them deliciously with tomato, garlic and basil – very Italian.

DAY 1

MORNING MEAL
½ medium grapefruit
1 egg, scrambled with chives in 1 teaspoon (5 ml) low-fat spread
1 medium grilled tomato
1 (2-oz/60-g) hot-cross bus
2 teaspoons (10 ml) low-fat spread
tea or coffee

MIDDAY MEAL
3-4 oz (90-120 g) roast chicken
3-oz (90-g) baked jacket potato with 1 teaspoon (5 ml) low-fat spread
Cauliflower with Mushroom Sauce (page 171)
Baked Apple (page 188)
4 fl oz (120 ml) white wine
tea or coffee

EVENING MEAL
Gypsy Cheese Salad (page 122)
4 oz (120 g) canned mandarin oranges topped with 5 fl oz (150 ml) natural yogurt, sprinkled with pinch cinnamon
tea or coffee

SNACKS OR DRINKS AT PLANNED TIMES
8 fl oz (240 ml) skim milk

Serving Information
Men and Teenagers: Add 3-oz (90-g) baked jacket potato at Midday Meal; 1 slice (1 oz/30 g) wholemeal bread at Evening Meal; 1 medium apple
Teenagers: Add 5 fl oz (150 ml) natural yogurt

DAY 4

MORNING MEAL
½ medium banana, sliced
¾ oz (20 g) instant cereal
5 fl oz (150 ml) hot skim milk
1 slice (1 oz/30 g) wholemeal bread
2 teaspoons (10 ml) low-fat spread
½ teaspoon (2.5 ml) honey ☐ tea or coffee

MIDDAY MEAL
8 fl oz (240 ml) tomato juice
3-4 oz (90-120 g) liver sausage
mixed salad with 3 oz (90 g) diced beetroot
2 teaspoons (10 ml) low-calorie mayonnaise
tea or coffee

EVENING MEAL
3-4 oz (90-120 g) roast turkey
3 oz (90 g) steamed white cabbage
3 oz (90 g) cooked baby carrots
1 medium baked onion
3 oz (90 g) sweet corn
4 oz (120 g) canned pineapple
tea or coffee

SNACKS OR DRINKS AT PLANNED TIMES
1 slice (1 oz/30 g) currant bread, 1 teaspoon (5 ml) margarine, 5 fl oz (150 ml) natural yogurt, 5 fl oz (150 ml) skim milk

Serving Information
Men and Teenagers: Add 1 medium apple, 3 oz (90 g) grapes, 3 oz (90 g) sweet corn at Evening Meal and 1 digestive biscuit
Teenagers: Add ½ pint (300 ml) skim milk

DAY 5

MORNING MEAL
4 oz (120 g) canned peaches, chopped and combined with 2½ oz (75 g) quark or cottage cheese
1 slice (1 oz/30 g) currant bread
1 teaspoon (5 ml) low-fat spread
tea or coffee

MIDDAY MEAL
3 tablespoons (45 ml) peanut butter
¾ oz (20 g) crispbread
1 medium tomato, sliced with onion rings
1 medium apple
tea or coffee

EVENING MEAL
3-4 oz (90-120 g) poached cod
3 oz (90 g) steamed spinach
Courgettes Italian Style (page 170)
2 oz (60 g) cooked pasta shells
1 teaspoon (5 ml) low-fat spread
1 medium orange
tea or coffee

SNACKS OR DRINKS AT PLANNED TIMES
5 fl oz (150 ml) natural yogurt, ½ pint (300 ml) skim milk

Serving Information
Men and Teenagers: Add 1 medium apple and 1 medium orange; ¾ oz (20 g) crispbread; 2 oz (60 g) cooked pasta shells at Evening Meal
Teenagers: Add 5 fl oz (150 ml) natural yogurt

DAY 2

MORNING MEAL
4 fl oz (120 ml) orange juice
¾ oz (20 g) porridge oats cooked with water and 1 tablespoon
(15 ml) raisins
5 fl oz (150 ml) skim milk □ tea or coffee

MIDDAY MEAL
3-4 oz (90-120 g) grilled plaice with 1 teaspoon (5 ml) margarine
3 oz (90 g) steamed green beans
1 medium grilled tomato
green salad with **Lemon Salad Dressing** (page 182)
1 slice (1 oz/30 g) wholemeal bread □ tea or coffee

EVENING MEAL
Grilled Ham Steak with Pineapple (page 139)
3 oz (90 g) boiled swede
3 oz (90 g) boiled potato, mashed together with 3 teaspoons
(15 ml) low-fat spread
3 oz (90 g) cooked carrots
4 oz (120 g) canned sliced peaches topped with 1 teaspoon
(5 ml) toasted coconut □ tea or coffee

SNACKS OR DRINKS AT PLANNED TIMES
5 fl oz (150 ml) natural yogurt, 5 fl oz (150 ml) skim milk,
1 digestive biscuit

Serving Information
Men and Teenagers: Add 1 slice (1 oz/30 g) wholemeal bread
and 1 digestive biscuit, 4 fl oz (120 ml) orange juice
Men: Add 1 oz (30 g) ham at Midday Meal
Teenagers: Add ½ pint (300 ml) skim milk

DAY 3

MORNING MEAL
½ medium grapefruit
2½ oz (75 g) cottage cheese
1 slice (1 oz/30 g) wholemeal bread
2 teaspoons (10 ml) low-fat spread
tea or coffee

MIDDAY MEAL
Lunch Box Fish and Cheese (page 162)
Curried Cole Slaw (page 178)
3 oz (90 g) white grapes
tea or coffee

EVENING MEAL
3-4 oz (90-120 g) grilled veal chop
3 oz (90 g) steamed broccoli with 1 teaspoon (5 ml) margarine
mixed green salad with 1 teaspoon (5 ml) vegetable oil
1 glass sparkling mineral water with twist lemon
tea or coffee

SNACKS OR DRINKS AT PLANNED TIMES
½ medium banana sliced into 5 fl oz (150 ml) natural yogurt,
½ pint (300 ml) skim milk

Serving Information
Men and Teenagers: Add 3 oz (90 g) grapes, ½ medium banana,
1 slice (1 oz/30 g) wholemeal bread and 1 digestive biscuit
Teenagers: Add 5 fl oz (150 ml) natural yogurt

DAY 6

MORNING MEAL
1 medium apple
1 oz (30 g) Edam cheese
1 slice (1 oz/30 g) wholemeal bread
2 teaspoons (10 ml) low-fat spread □ tea or coffee

MIDDAY MEAL
Cream of Cauliflower Soup (page 115)
4 oz (120 g) tuna fish, drained
mixed green salad with **Oregano Vinaigrette** (page 183)
1 medium orange, diced
5 fl oz (150 ml) natural yogurt □ tea or coffee

EVENING MEAL
Lamb's Liver Creole (page 143)
3 oz (90 g) cooked peas
3 oz (90 g) cooked cauliflower
2 oz (60 g) cooked rice
6 canned apricot halves
2 oz (60 g) vanilla ice cream □ tea or coffee

SNACKS OR DRINKS AT PLANNED TIMES
7½ fl oz (225 ml) skim milk, 2 cream crackers, 2 teaspoons
(10 ml) low-fat spread, 1 teaspoon (5 ml) grated Parmesan
cheese, low-calorie fizzy drink

Serving Information
Men and Teenagers: Add 1 medium banana; 2 oz (60 g) cooked
rice at Evening Meal; 1 digestive biscuit
Teenagers: Add ½ pint (300 ml) skim milk

DAY 7

MORNING MEAL
Swedish Apple Bake (page 186)
5 fl oz (150 ml) natural yogurt
tea or coffee

MIDDAY MEAL
3-4 oz (90-120 g) roast beef
3 oz (90 g) cooked parsnips
3 oz (90 g) steamed savoy cabbage
3 oz (90 g) cooked carrots
1 teaspoon (5 ml) low-fat spread
2 medium plums
tea or coffee

EVENING MEAL
1½ hard-boiled eggs
1 medium tomato
mixed green salad
1 teaspoon (5 ml) low-calorie mayonnaise
Profiteroles and Chocolate Sauce (page 194)
tea or coffee

SNACKS OR DRINKS AT PLANNED TIMES
¾-oz (20-g) crumpet, 2 teaspoons (10 ml) low-fat spread, ½ pint
(300 ml) skim milk, 1 medium orange

Serving Information
Men and Teenagers: Add 3 oz (90 g) boiled potatoes at Midday
Meal; 1 digestive biscuit, 2 medium plums
Teenagers: Add ½ pint (300 ml) skim milk

WEEK 18

After the busy holiday period you will probably enjoy a relaxed week. You will find these meals quick and easy to prepare. All the decisions have been taken for you; the grilling and steaming and roasting are simple processes and there are several cold meals. There are no recipes this week. Take a little rest!

Spinach and broccoli are included among the vegetables. Perhaps you think of spinach as the producer of splendid muscles. Certainly it's a good nourishing food and if it's not overcooked the leaves contain a high level of iron and potassium. It needs only one inch of boiling salted water and four minutes over a high heat to reach the peak of delicious flavour.

Broccoli should be lightly cooked until it is tender and crisp; about eight minutes only. It's also very good served cold – cook it first, dress it with a vinaigrette while still warm and then leave to cool. This makes it an unusual and delicious ingredient in a salad.

DAY 1

MORNING MEAL
4 fl oz (120 ml) orange juice
¾ oz (20 g) cornflakes
5 fl oz (150 ml) skim milk
tea or coffee

MIDDAY MEAL
3-4 oz (90-120 g) grilled cod
3 oz (90 g) cooked broccoli
lettuce, celery and grated carrots
1 teaspoon (5 ml) mayonnaise
1 slice (1 oz/30 g) wholemeal bread
1 medium apple
tea or coffee

EVENING MEAL
3-4 oz (90-120 g) roast chicken
3 oz (90 g) cooked spinach
3 oz (90 g) steamed potatoes
green salad
2 teaspoons (10 ml) vegetable oil with vinegar and herbs
tea or coffee

SNACKS OR DRINKS AT PLANNED TIMES
1 medium orange, 5 fl oz (150 ml) natural yogurt, 5 fl oz (150 ml) skim milk

Serving Information
Men and Teenagers: Add 3 oz (90 g) sweet corn to Midday Meal; 3 oz (90 g) potato to Evening Meal; 4 fl oz (120 ml) orange juice
Teenagers: Add ½ pint (300 ml) skim milk

DAY 4

MORNING MEAL
1 medium orange
¾ oz (20 g) muesli
5 fl oz (150 ml) skim milk □ tea or coffee

MIDDAY MEAL
3-4 oz (90-120 g) mussels
lettuce with celery and cucumber
2 teaspoons (10 ml) salad cream
1 oz (30 g) French bread
1 medium portion stewed rhubarb
tea or coffee

EVENING MEAL
3-4 oz (90-120 g) roast chicken
3 oz (90 g) steamed potatoes
3 oz (90 g) steamed broccoli
2 teaspoons (10 ml) low-fat spread
green salad
1 teaspoon (5 ml) vegetable oil with vinegar and herbs
4 oz (120 g) canned fruit cocktail
tea or coffee

SNACKS OR DRINKS AT PLANNED TIMES
½ medium banana, 5 fl oz (150 ml) natural yogurt, 5 fl oz (150 ml) skim milk

Serving Information
Men and Teenagers: Add extra ¾ oz (20 g) muesli at Morning Meal; 1 oz (30 g) French bread at Midday Meal; ½ medium banana
Teenagers: Add ½ pint (300 ml) skim milk

DAY 5

MORNING MEAL
8 fl oz (240 ml) tomato juice
1 oz (30 g) Edam cheese
1 slice (1 oz/30 g) wholemeal bread
tea or coffee

MIDDAY MEAL
3-4 oz (90-120 g) cold roast chicken
lettuce with cress and onion
1 medium tomato
2 teaspoons (10 ml) mayonnaise
2 cream crackers
1 medium apple
tea or coffee

EVENING MEAL
3-4 oz (90-120 g) roast lamb
3 oz (90 g) steamed carrots
3 oz (90 g) steamed cauliflower
1 teaspoon (5 ml) margarine
tea or coffee

SNACKS OR DRINKS AT PLANNED TIMES
5 fl oz (150 ml) natural yogurt, ½ pint (300 ml) skim milk, 4 oz (120 g) canned peaches

Serving Information
Men and Teenagers: Add 6 oz (180 g) steamed potatoes at Evening Meal; ½ medium grapefruit
Teenagers: Add ½ pint (300 ml) skim milk

DAY 2

MORNING MEAL
½ medium grapefruit
1 oz (30 g) Cheddar cheese
1 slice (1 oz/30 g) bread
tea or coffee

MIDDAY MEAL
3-4 oz (90-120 g) cold roast chicken
cucumber slices with celery
1 teaspoon (5 ml) mayonnaise
1 oz (30 g) French bread
tea or coffee

EVENING MEAL
3-4 oz (90-120 g) grilled lamb's liver
3 oz (90 g) steamed broccoli
2 teaspoons (10 ml) low-fat spread
green salad
2 teaspoons (10 ml) salad cream
1 medium orange
tea or coffee

SNACKS OR DRINKS AT PLANNED TIMES
½ medium banana, ½ pint (300 ml) skim milk, 5 fl oz (150 ml)
   natural yogurt

Serving Information
Men and Teenagers: Add 1 oz (30 g) French bread at Midday
   Meal; 3 oz (90 g) cooked noodles at Evening Meal; ½ medium
   banana
Teenagers: Add ½ pint (300 ml) skim milk

DAY 3

MORNING MEAL
4 fl oz (120 ml) orange juice
1 boiled egg
1 slice (1 oz/30 g) wholemeal bread
1 teaspoon (5 ml) margarine
tea or coffee

MIDDAY MEAL
5 oz (150 g) cottage cheese
lettuce with sliced tomato
2 cream crackers
4 oz (120 g) canned fruit cocktail
tea or coffee

EVENING MEAL
3-4 oz (90-120 g) steamed plaice
3 oz (90 g) steamed green beans
2 teaspoons (10 ml) low-fat spread
green salad with 1 teaspoon (5 ml) vegetable oil and wine
   vinegar
tea or coffee

SNACKS OR DRINKS AT PLANNED TIMES
½ pint (300 ml) skim milk, 5 fl oz (150 ml) natural yogurt, 1
   medium apple

Serving Information
Men and Teenagers: Add 6 oz (180 g) steamed potato at
   Evening Meal; 4 oz (120 g) canned fruit cocktail
Teenagers: Add ½ pint (300 ml) skim milk

DAY 6

MORNING MEAL
½ medium grapefruit
1 poached egg
1 slice (1 oz/30 g) wholemeal bread
1 teaspoon (5 ml) margarine
tea or coffee

MIDDAY MEAL
7-8 oz (210-240 g) baked beans
3 oz (90 g) poached mushrooms
1 slice (1 oz/30 g) wholemeal bread
1 teaspoon (5 ml) margarine
tea or coffee

EVENING MEAL
3-4 oz (90-120 g) peeled prawns
lettuce with tomato, onion and cucumber
2 teaspoons (10 ml) salad cream
3 oz (90 g) grapes
tea or coffee

SNACKS OR DRINKS AT PLANNED TIMES
4 oz (120 g) fruit cocktail, 5 fl oz (150 ml) natural yogurt, ½ pint
   (300 ml) skim milk

Serving Information
Men and Teenagers: Add 3 oz (90 g) diced cooked potato; 3 oz
   (90 g) canned sweet corn at Evening Meal; 3 oz (90 g) grapes
Teenagers: Add ½ pint (300 ml) skim milk

DAY 7

MORNING MEAL
3 oz (90 g) grapes
¾ oz (20 g) porridge oats cooked with water
5 fl oz (150 ml) skim milk
tea or coffee

MIDDAY MEAL
3-4 oz (90-120 g) roast chicken
3 oz (90 g) steamed green beans
3 oz (90 g) steamed carrots
2 teaspoons (10 ml) low-fat spread
green salad
1 teaspoon (5 ml) vegetable oil with vinegar and herbs
tea or coffee

EVENING MEAL
2 hard-boiled eggs
lettuce with celery and grated carrot.
1 teaspoon (5 ml) mayonnaise
2-oz (60-g) bread roll
4 oz (120 g) canned peaches
tea or coffee

SNACKS OR DRINKS AT PLANNED TIMES
1 medium orange, 5 fl oz (150 ml) skim milk, 5 fl oz (150 ml)
   natural yogurt

Serving Information
Men and Teenagers: Add 6 oz (180 g) steamed potatoes at
   Midday Meal; 4 oz (120 g) canned peaches
Teenagers: Add ½ pint (300 ml) skim milk

WEEK 19

The merry month of May brings the May Bank Holiday and historic echoes of May Queens, Maypoles and the prospect of summer. The Morris dancers used to welcome the sun at five-o'-clock on May morning and young girls believed that if they rose early to wash their faces in the morning dew, their complexions would improve dramatically. Perhaps it's safer to rely on sound dietary principles to produce a clear skin, rather than dew!

Tarragon is used this week with chicken livers. Tarragon is an important culinary herb, much used in French cuisine. Its flavour is a combination of bitter and sweet, with a 'tang' which is overpowering if you use too much. You can use it fresh or dried and a sprig of tarragon in the vinegar bottle produces a very special flavour in salad dressings.

DAY 1

MORNING MEAL
4 oz (120 g) canned sliced peaches
2½ oz (75 g) curd cheese
¾ oz (20 g) crispbread
1 teaspoon (5 ml) margarine
tea or coffee

MIDDAY MEAL
3-4 oz (90-120 g) canned salmon
sliced tomato and onion rings on lettuce with 1 teaspoon (5 ml) mayonnaise
1 slice (1 oz/30 g) rye bread, toasted
5 fl oz (150 ml) natural yogurt with 2 teaspoons (10 ml) low-calorie jam □ tea or coffee

EVENING MEAL
'Re-fried' Beans (page 167)
3 oz (90 g) steamed green beans
1 slice (1 oz/30 g) brown bread
4 fl oz (120 ml) orange juice
tea or coffee

SNACKS OR DRINKS AT PLANNED TIMES
Minted Passion Cooler (page 190) 5 fl oz (150 ml) skim milk

Serving Information
Men and Teenagers: Add 1 slice (1 oz/30 g) rye bread, 1 digestive biscuit and 4 oz (120 g) cherries
Men: Add 1 oz (30 g) canned baked beans to salad at Midday Meal
Teenagers: Add ½ pint (300 ml) skim milk

DAY 4

MORNING MEAL
4 fl oz (120 ml) grapefruit juice
1 oz (30 g) Cheddar cheese, grilled on 1 slice (1 oz/30 g) wholemeal bread □ tea or coffee

MIDDAY MEAL
3 oz (90 g) boiled knackwurst with 1 teaspoon (5 ml) French mustard
3 oz (90 g) sauerkraut
3 oz (90 g) cooked peas dotted with 1½ teaspoons (7.5 ml) margarine
4 oz (120 g) canned mandarin orange sections
½ pint (300 ml) lager or cider
tea or coffee

EVENING MEAL
3-4 oz (90-120 g) grilled veal steak
3 oz (90 g) poached sliced courgettes, dotted with 1 teaspoon (5 ml) margarine
2 oz (60 g) cooked noodles
green salad with **Dijon-Herb Dressing** (page 182)
1 medium peach
tea or coffee

SNACKS OR DRINKS AT PLANNED TIMES
5 fl oz (150 ml) natural yogurt, ½ pint (300 ml) skim milk

Serving Information
Men and Teenagers: Add 1 x 2-oz (60-g) bread roll, 4 oz (120 g) canned mandarin orange sections
Men: Add 1 oz (30 g) boiled knackwurst at Midday Meal
Teenagers: Add ½ pint (300 ml) skim milk

DAY 5

MORNING MEAL
½ medium banana, sliced
¾ oz (20 g) cornflakes
5 fl oz (150 ml) skim milk
tea or coffee

MIDDAY MEAL
Poached Halibut Parmesan (page 162)
3 oz (90 g) steamed green beans
3 oz (90 g) steamed cauliflower
3 oz (90 g) boiled potatoes
5 oz (150 g) strawberries
tea or coffee

EVENING MEAL
2-egg omelette with mixed fresh herbs cooked in 1½ teaspoons (7.5 ml) vegetable oil with 3 oz (90 g) baked beans
1 medium apple
tea or coffee

SNACKS OR DRINKS AT PLANNED TIMES
15 fl oz (450 ml) skim milk

Serving Information
Men and Teenagers: Add extra 3 oz (90 g) boiled potatoes at Evening Meal; 1 medium peach
Teenagers: Add ½ pint (300 ml) skim milk

DAY 2

MORNING MEAL
4 oz (120 g) canned grapefruit sections
¾ oz (20 g) cornflakes
5 fl oz (150 ml) skim milk
tea or coffee

MIDDAY MEAL
Tarragon Chicken Livers (page 143)
3 oz (90 g) cooked sliced courgettes
green salad with **Basic Vinaigrette** (page 183)
1 medium pear
tea or coffee

EVENING MEAL
3-4 oz (90-120 g) grilled Pacific prawns
6 medium steamed asparagus spears
1 medium tomato, halved and grilled
1 slice (1 oz/30 g) wholemeal bread
1 teaspoon (5 ml) margarine
4 fl oz (120 ml) white wine
tea or coffee

SNACKS OR DRINKS AT PLANNED TIMES
15 fl oz (450 ml) skim milk, 1 medium apple

Serving Information
Men and Teenagers: Add 1 slice (1 oz/30 g) bread and 1 medium
  pear
Teenagers: Add ½ pint (300 ml) skim milk

DAY 3

MORNING MEAL
2½ fl oz (75 ml) apple juice
1 scrambled egg
1 slice (1 oz/30 g) bread, toasted
1 teaspoon (5 ml) margarine
tea or coffee

MIDDAY MEAL
3-4 oz (90-120 g) roast chicken
3 oz (90 g) cooked peas
2 oz (60 g) cooked rice, with 2 teaspoons (10 ml) margarine
1 medium pear
tea or coffee

EVENING MEAL
3-4 oz (90-120 g) grilled plaice
3 oz (90 g) steamed spinach
3 oz (90 g) steamed sliced carrots
5 oz (150 g) gooseberries
tea or coffee

SNACKS OR DRINKS AT PLANNED TIMES
¾ oz (20 g) crispbread with 2 teaspoons (10 ml) low-calorie jam,
  5 fl oz (150 ml) natural yogurt, ½ pint (300 ml) skim milk

Serving Information
Men and Teenagers: Add 2½ fl oz (75 ml) apple juice, 1 medium
  peach and 2-oz (60-g) bread roll
Teenagers: Add ½ pint (300 ml) skim milk

DAY 6

MORNING MEAL
1 medium pear
1 oz (30 g) Edam cheese
¾ oz (20 g) crispbread
tea or coffee

MIDDAY MEAL
5 oz (150 g) cottage cheese with mixed salad of lettuce,
  watercress, sliced tomatoes and cucumber
1 tablespoon (15 ml) mayonnaise
2 medium plums
tea or coffee

EVENING MEAL
3-4 oz (90-120 g) grilled beefburger
3 oz (90 g) cooked green beans
1 medium tomato, halved and grilled
3 oz (90 g) boiled potatoes
1 medium orange
tea or coffee

SNACKS OR DRINKS AT PLANNED TIMES
5 fl oz (150 ml) natural yogurt, ½ pint (300 ml) skim milk

Serving Information
Men and Teenagers: Add 1 slice (1 oz/30 g) wholemeal bread,
  1 medium apple, 1 digestive biscuit
Teenagers: Add ½ pint (300 ml) skim milk

DAY 7

MORNING MEAL
½ medium grapefruit
¾ oz (20 g) puffed rice
5 fl oz (150 ml) skim milk □ tea or coffee

MIDDAY MEAL
3-4 oz (90-120 g) roast leg of lamb
3-oz (90-g) baked jacket potato with 2½ fl oz (75 ml) natural
  yogurt and chopped chives
3 oz (90 g) cooked green beans
3 oz (90 g) cooked cauliflower
2 teaspoons (10 ml) margarine
4 oz (120 g) canned peach slices and 2½ fl oz (75 ml) natural
  yogurt □ tea or coffee

EVENING MEAL
1 hard-boiled egg with 2 oz (60 g) sardines
1 medium tomato
3 oz (90 g) cooked beetroot
sliced cucumber and grated carrot on lettuce with 1 teaspoon
  (5 ml) low-calorie mayonnaise
1 oz (30 g) French bread with 1 teaspoon (5 ml) low-fat spread
4 oz (120 g) stewed apple □ tea or coffee

SNACKS OR DRINKS AT PLANNED TIMES
5 fl oz (150 ml) skim milk

Serving Information
Men and Teenagers: Add extra 3-oz (90-g) baked jacket potato
  at Evening Meal; 1 slice (1 oz/30 g) wholemeal bread, and 4 oz
  (120 g) stewed apple
Teenagers: Add ½ pint (300 ml) skim milk

WEEK 20

The bushy nutmeg tree (**Myristica fragrans**) grows up to forty feet in height and is now cultivated in Indonesia and Malaysia. The fruit, when ripe, is like a peach in appearance. Its outer husk is removed, then the fibrous fruit (the mace), and the little brown nutmeg lies at the centre. They are dried slowly and exported to be sold both whole and ground. We associate it with sweet dishes – the brown topping of a rice-pudding, for instance – but it is delicious, too, in vegetable dishes and with eggs. Try the tasty Spinach Frittata – an Italian omelette – this week.

DAY 1

MORNING MEAL
½ medium cantaloupe melon
¾ oz (20 g) cornflakes
5 fl oz (150 ml) skim milk
tea or coffee

MIDDAY MEAL
Macaroni-Cheese Salad (page 122)
3 oz (90 g) cooked cold peas
green salad with **Dijon-Herb Dressing** (page 182)
1 medium peach
sparkling mineral water with sprig of mint
tea or coffee

EVENING MEAL
3-4 oz (90-120 g) grilled beefburger
3 oz (90 g) onion rings, grilled
3 oz (90 g) steamed broccoli
1 tablespoon (15 ml) tomato relish
3 oz (90 g) boiled potatoes dotted with 1½ teaspoons (7.5 ml) margarine
5 oz (150 g) strawberries
tea or coffee

SNACKS OR DRINKS AT PLANNED TIMES
12½ fl oz (375 ml) skim milk

Serving Information
Men and Teenagers: Add 3 oz (90 g) grapes, 3 oz (90 g) boiled potatoes, 1 digestive biscuit
Teenagers: Add 5 fl oz (150 ml) natural yogurt

DAY 4

MORNING MEAL
1 medium orange
¾ oz (20 g) porridge oats, cooked with water
5 fl oz (150 ml) skim milk
tea or coffee

MIDDAY MEAL
Spinach Frittata (page 126)
green salad with 1 teaspoon (5 ml) vegetable oil, mixed with vinegar
1 slice (1 oz/30 g) wholemeal bread
1 teaspoon (5 ml) low-fat spread
1 medium portion stewed rhubarb
2 oz (60 g) vanilla ice cream
tea or coffee

EVENING MEAL
8 fl oz (240 ml) tomato juice
3-4 oz (90-120 g) grilled mackerel
3 oz (90 g) steamed courgettes
3 oz (90 g) steamed cauliflower
3 oz (90 g) boiled potatoes
4 oz (120 g) canned peach slices
tea or coffee

SNACKS OR DRINKS AT PLANNED TIMES
15 fl oz (450 ml) skim milk

Serving Information
Men and Teenagers: Add 4 fl oz (120 ml) orange juice, ¾ oz (20 g) porridge oats, 1 digestive biscuit
Teenagers: Add 5 fl oz (150 ml) natural yogurt

DAY 5

MORNING MEAL
4 fl oz (120 ml) orange juice
1 oz (30 g) Cheddar cheese grilled on 1 slice (1 oz/30 g) bread, toasted
tea or coffee

MIDDAY MEAL
3-4 oz (90-120 g) cold cooked chicken
radishes, sliced with sliced chicory and 2 teaspoons (10 ml) salad cream
5 fl oz (150 ml) natural yogurt with 5 oz (150 g) strawberries and 1 digestive biscuit
tea or coffee

EVENING MEAL
Rock Fish Kebabs (page 159)
3 oz (90 g) cooked spinach dotted with 2 teaspoons (10 ml) margarine
3 oz (90 g) steamed carrots
1 medium orange
tea or coffee

SNACKS OR DRINKS AT PLANNED TIMES
½ pint (300 ml) skim milk

Serving Information
Men and Teenagers: Add 1 medium apple, 2 digestive biscuits
Teenagers: Add ½ pint (300 ml) skim milk

DAY 2

MORNING MEAL
4 fl oz (120 ml) orange juice
1 poached egg
1 slice (1 oz/30 g) wholemeal bread, toasted
1 teaspoon (5 ml) margarine
tea or coffee

MIDDAY MEAL
3-4 oz (90-120 g) sliced cooked chicken on shredded lettuce
leaves with 2-3 small tomatoes, halved, and 2-3 spring onions,
diced
2 teaspoons (10 ml) low-calorie mayonnaise
½ medium banana, sliced into 1 serving **Custard** (page 191)
tea or coffee

EVENING MEAL
3-4 oz (90-120 g) grilled haddock, dotted with 1 teaspoon (5 ml)
margarine
3 oz (90 g) cooked peas
3 oz (90 g) steamed carrots
3 oz (90 g) boiled potatoes
4 oz (120 g) fruit salad
tea or coffee

SNACKS OR DRINKS AT PLANNED TIMES
5 fl oz (150 ml) natural yogurt, 5 fl oz (150 ml) skim milk

Serving Information
Men and Teenagers: Add ½ medium banana, 1½-oz (45-g)
crumpet, toasted with 2 teaspoons (10 ml) low-calorie jam
Teenagers: Add ½ pint (300 ml) skim milk

DAY 3

MORNING MEAL
½ medium grapefruit
Cinnamon-Cheese Toast (page 123)
tea or coffee

MIDDAY MEAL
3-4 oz (90-120 g) peeled shrimps on shredded lettuce, diced
cucumber and sliced tomatoes, with 4 teaspoons (20 ml)
low-calorie mayonnaise
3 oz (90 g) whole kernel sweet corn
3 oz (90 g) grapes
sparkling low-calorie lemonade
tea or coffee

EVENING MEAL
3-4 oz (90-120 g) grilled liver
3 oz (90 g) sliced steamed onion
3 oz (90 g) poached mushrooms
1 medium tomato, halved and grilled dotted with 1 teaspoon
(5 ml) margarine
1 medium apple
tea or coffee

SNACKS OR DRINKS AT PLANNED TIMES
5 fl oz (150 ml) natural yogurt, ½ pint (300 ml) skim milk

Serving Information
Men and Teenagers: Add 1 medium orange, 3 oz (90 g) boiled
potatoes, 1 slice (1 oz/30 g) bread
Teenagers: Add ½ pint (300 ml) skim milk

DAY 6

MORNING MEAL
½ medium grapefruit
¾ oz (20 g) wheat flakes
5 fl oz (150 ml) skim milk
tea or coffee

MIDDAY MEAL
3 tablespoons (45 ml) peanut butter
2-oz (60-g) wholemeal bread roll
celery and cucumber sticks
1 medium apple
tea or coffee

EVENING MEAL
3-4 oz (90-120 g) grilled steak
3 oz (90 g) poached mushrooms
3 oz (90 g) cooked peas
1 medium tomato, halved and grilled with 1 teaspoon (5 ml)
margarine
4 oz (120 g) fruit salad
tea or coffee

SNACKS OR DRINKS AT PLANNED TIMES
15 fl oz (450 ml) skim milk

Serving Information
Men and Teenagers: Add 4 oz (120 g) fruit salad, ¾ oz (20 g)
wheat flakes, 3 oz (90 g) boiled potatoes
Teenagers: Add 5 fl oz (150 ml) natural yogurt

DAY 7

MORNING MEAL
4 fl oz (120 ml) orange juice
1 boiled egg
1 slice (1 oz/30 g) wholemeal bread, toasted
1 teaspoon (5 ml) margarine ☐ tea or coffee

MIDDAY MEAL
3-4 oz (90-120 g) roast beef
3 oz (90 g) baked onion
3 oz (90 g) steamed broccoli
3 oz (90 g) cooked carrots
3-oz (90-g) baked jacket potato
1 teaspoon (5 ml) margarine
Gravy (page 182)
4 oz (120 g) canned pineapple
4 fl oz (120 ml) red wine
tea or coffee

EVENING MEAL
3-4 oz (90-120 g) tuna with mixed salad of lettuce, tomato,
cucumber, spring onions, and watercress
2 teaspoons (10 ml) salad cream
1 medium apple
tea or coffee

SNACKS OR DRINKS AT PLANNED TIMES
5 fl oz (150 ml) natural yogurt, ½ pint (300 ml) skim milk

Serving Information
Men and Teenagers: Add 1 medium peach; 4 oz (120 g) cooked
rice at Evening Meal
Teenagers: Add ½ pint (300 ml) skim milk

WEEK 21

You will sometimes like to 'cook ahead' and have time to spend on other things. Several of this week's recipes allow you to do this. The Minted Carrots will keep covered in the refrigerator for up to a week. The Broccoli Quiche can be cooked in advance and reheated when you are ready to use it.

Calamari may be new to you. It's a member of the squid family and is cooked here with tomatoes and onion and served with spaghetti – definitely different!

Chinese-Style Pancakes contain no flour but consist of a delicious mixture of rice and vegetables stirred into beaten eggs and cooked like an omelette. A thickened soy sauce adds flavour to this tasty pancake.

DAY 1

MORNING MEAL
4 oz (120 g) canned grapefruit sections
¾ oz (20 g) ready-to-eat cereal
5 fl oz (150 ml) skim milk
tea or coffee

MIDDAY MEAL
Chinese-Style Pancakes (page 118)
3 oz (90 g) steamed green beans
1 slice (1 oz/30 g) wholemeal bread
1 teaspoon (5 ml) margarine
4 oz (120 g) cherries
tea or coffee

EVENING MEAL
3-4 oz (90-120 g) grilled veal escalope
3 oz (90 g) cooked peas
1 teaspoon (5 ml) margarine
Minted Carrots (page 170)
1 medium portion stewed rhubarb with 2 oz (60 g) vanilla ice cream
tea or coffee

SNACKS OR DRINKS AT PLANNED TIMES
2½ fl oz (75 ml) natural yogurt with 2½ oz (75 g) strawberries, ½ pint (300 ml) skim milk

Serving Information
Men and Teenagers: Add 4 oz (120 g) cherries, 1½-oz (45-g) scone with 2 teaspoons (10 ml) low-calorie jam
Teenagers: Add 5 fl oz (150 ml) natural yogurt

DAY 4

MORNING MEAL
8 fl oz (240 ml) tomato juice
2½ oz (75 g) cottage cheese
¾ oz (20 g) crispbread
tea or coffee

MIDDAY MEAL
Sardine Salad (page 156)
1 medium tomato, sliced
2 water biscuits
1 teaspoon (5 ml) low-fat spread
4 oz (120 g) cherries
tea or coffee

EVENING MEAL
3-4 oz (90-120 g) grilled chicken breast
3 oz (90 g) cooked butter beans
3 oz (90 g) steamed carrots
1 medium tomato, halved and grilled
1 teaspoon (5 ml) margarine
½ medium banana
Custard (page 191)

SNACKS OR DRINKS AT PLANNED TIMES
15 fl oz (450 ml) skim milk

Serving Information
Men and Teenagers: Add ½ medium banana, 3 oz (90 g) cooked butter beans, 1-oz (30-g) scotch pancake with 1 teaspoon (5 ml) low-calorie jam
Teenagers: Add 5 fl oz (150 ml) natural yogurt

DAY 5

MORNING MEAL
Oatmeal with Spiced Fruit Ambrosia (page 176)
tea or coffee

MIDDAY MEAL
3 tablespoons (45 ml) crunchy peanut butter on 1 slice (1 oz/30 g) wholemeal bread, toasted
2-3 celery sticks
1 medium peach
low-calorie sparkling lemonade
tea or coffee

EVENING MEAL
Lamb Burgers (page 138)
3 oz (90 g) steamed courgettes
green salad with wine vinegar
5 oz (150 g) gooseberries
sparkling mineral water with lemon slice
tea or coffee

SNACKS OR DRINKS AT PLANNED TIMES
5 fl oz (150 ml) natural yogurt, 5 fl oz (150 ml) skim milk

Serving Information
Men and Teenagers: Add 1 medium orange, 1 slice (1 oz/30 g) wholemeal bread, 1 digestive biscuit
Teenagers: Add ½ pint (300 ml) skim milk

DAY 2

MORNING MEAL
3 medium apricots, stewed with 1 teaspoon (5 ml) honey
2½ oz (75 g) curd cheese
1 slice (1 oz/30 g) wholemeal bread, toasted
tea or coffee

MIDDAY MEAL
3-4 oz (90-120 g) grilled chicken livers
Bean Salad (page 179)
1 slice (1 oz/30 g) wholemeal bread
1 teaspoon (5 ml) margarine
1 medium peach
tea or coffee

EVENING MEAL
3 oz (90 g) smoked mackerel
sliced tomato and onion rings with 1 teaspoon (5 ml) oil mixed
    with lemon juice
Curried Cole Slaw (page 178)
5 oz (150 g) strawberries
tea or coffee

SNACKS OR DRINKS AT PLANNED TIMES
5 fl oz (150 ml) natural yogurt, ½ pint (300 ml) skim milk

Serving Information
Men and Teenagers: Add 1 medium apple, 3 oz (90 g) baked
    beans, 1 digestive biscuit
Men: Add 1 oz (30 g) smoked mackerel at Evening Meal
Teenagers: Add ½ pint (300 ml) skim milk

DAY 3

MORNING MEAL
4 fl oz (120 ml) grapefruit juice
¾ oz (20 g) porridge oats cooked with water
5 fl oz (150 ml) skim milk
tea or coffee

MIDDAY MEAL
Broccoli Quiche (page 120)
mixed salad of shredded lettuce, sliced tomatoes and cucumber
    with ½ hard-boiled egg and 2 teaspoons (10 ml) low-calorie
    mayonnaise
¾ oz (20 g) melba toast
5 oz (150 g) strawberries with 2½ fl oz (75 ml) natural yogurt
sparkling mineral water with lemon slice
tea or coffee

EVENING MEAL
½ medium cantaloupe melon
3-4 oz (90-120 g) grilled steak
3 oz (90 g) boiled potatoes
3 oz (90 g) poached mushrooms
3 oz (90 g) cooked peas
2 teaspoons (10 ml) low-fat spread
tea or coffee

SNACKS OR DRINKS AT PLANNED TIMES
7 fl oz (210 ml) skim milk, 1 medium peach

Serving Information
Men and Teenagers: Add 4 fl oz (120 ml) grapefruit juice, ¾ oz
    (20 g) porridge oats, 3 oz (90 g) boiled potatoes
Teenagers: Add 5 fl oz (150 ml) natural yogurt

DAY 6

MORNING MEAL
4 oz (120 g) orange sections
1 egg scrambled in 1 teaspoon (5 ml) margarine, on 1 slice
    (1 oz/30 g) bread, toasted
tea or coffee

MIDDAY MEAL
3-4 oz (90-120 g) cold sliced chicken on shredded lettuce with
    sliced tomatoes and sliced cucumber
2-3 spring onions
3 oz (90 g) boiled beetroot
2 teaspoons (10 ml) salad cream
5 fl oz (150 ml) natural yogurt
1 medium peach
1 digestive biscuit
tea or coffee

EVENING MEAL
Calamari with Spaghetti (page 155)
3 oz (90 g) steamed green beans
3 oz (90 g) poached mushrooms
5 oz (150 g) strawberries
tea or coffee

SNACKS OR DRINKS AT PLANNED TIMES
½ pint (300 ml) skim milk

Serving Information
Men and Teenagers: Add 4 oz (120 g) orange sections; 4 oz
    (120 g) cooked spaghetti at Evening Meal
Teenagers: Add 5 fl oz (150 ml) natural yogurt

DAY 7

MORNING MEAL
4 fl oz (120 ml) orange juice
2½ oz (75 g) cottage cheese
1 slice (1 oz/30 g) wholemeal bread, toasted
tea or coffee

MIDDAY MEAL
3-4 oz (90-120 g) roast veal
3 oz (90 g) cooked peas
3 oz (90 g) steamed turnips
3 oz (90 g) boiled potatoes dotted with 1 teaspoon (5 ml)
    margarine
5 fl oz (150 ml) natural yogurt
5 oz (150 g) strawberries
4 fl oz (120 ml) white wine
tea or coffee

EVENING MEAL
3-4 oz (90-120 g) liver sausage
mixed salad of shredded lettuce with tomato, radishes,
    watercress, cucumber and spring onions
4 teaspoons (20 ml) salad cream
4 oz (120 g) fruit salad
tea or coffee

SNACKS OR DRINKS AT PLANNED TIMES
½ pint (300 ml) skim milk

Serving Information
Men and Teenagers: Add 4 fl oz (120 ml) orange juice, 4 water
    biscuits
Teenagers: Add ½ pint (300 ml) skim milk

WEEK 22

Bank Holidays offer you a chance to take a meal into the country or in the garden if the sun shines. Ham salad is an excellent picnic standby.

Macaroni with Cheese and Peanut Sauce is an interesting recipe. Peanut butter is, obviously, made from peanuts – a very popular and widely available nut. It is very nutritious.

Kedgeree (Day 7) is one of those recipes brought home from India in the days of the British Raj. In its native land it consisted of curried fish and rice served with hard-boiled eggs. We omit the curry and eggs and use smoked haddock to add flavour to the rice with grilled cheese and chopped chives, then serve it on a large mushroom to make a very satisfying breakfast.

DAY 1

MORNING MEAL
¾ oz (20 g) muesli and
1 medium apple, peeled cored and diced, served with 5 fl oz (150 ml) skim milk
tea or coffee

MIDDAY MEAL
ham salad made with 3 oz (90 g) ham with a salad of cucumber, tomato and lettuce
2 teaspoons (10 ml) low-calorie salad dressing
3 oz (90 g) sweet corn
2 cream crackers
1 medium peach
tea or coffee

EVENING MEAL
3-4 oz (90-120 g) fillet plaice dipped in 1 tablespoon (15 ml) seasoned flour and sauteed in 2 teaspoons (10 ml) vegetable oil
3 oz (90 g) cooked peas
3 oz (90 g) steamed carrots
1 medium orange
tea or coffee

SNACKS OR DRINKS AT PLANNED TIMES
15 fl oz (450 ml) skim milk

Serving Information
Men and Teenagers: Add extra 3 oz (90 g) sweet corn and 3 oz (90 g) boiled potatoes, 3 oz (90 g) grapes and 1 medium apple
Men: Add extra 1 oz (30 g) ham
Teenagers: Add ½ pint (300 ml) skim milk

DAY 4

MORNING MEAL
4 fl oz (120 ml) orange juice
1 oz (30 g) Cheddar cheese sliced and grilled on 1 slice (1 oz/30 g) bread, toasted
tea or coffee

MIDDAY MEAL
3-4 oz (90-120 g) sliced liver sausage with salad of sliced tomatoes and cucumber with 2 teaspoons (10 ml) vegetable oil mixed with cider vinegar
½ medium banana
tea or coffee

EVENING MEAL
4 breadcrumbed fish fingers sauteed in 1 teaspoon (5 ml) vegetable oil
3 oz (90 g) baked beans
1 medium tomato, halved and grilled
4 oz (120 g) canned mandarin sections
tea or coffee

SNACKS OR DRINKS AT PLANNED TIMES
5 fl oz (150 ml) natural yogurt, ½ pint (300 ml) skim milk

Serving Information
Men and Teenagers: Add 1 slice (1 oz/30 g) bread, 3 oz (90 g) baked beans, ½ medium banana
Teenagers: Add ½ pint (300 ml) skim milk

DAY 5

MORNING MEAL
4 fl oz (120 ml) orange juice
¾ oz (20 g) wheat flakes served with 5 fl oz (150 ml) skim milk
tea or coffee

MIDDAY MEAL
Layered Sandwich (page 174)
1 medium apple
tea or coffee

EVENING MEAL
3-4 oz (90-120 g) chicken breast cut into strips and sauteed in 2 teaspoons (10 ml) vegetable oil
3 oz (90 g) cooked peas
3 oz (90 g) steamed courgettes
1 medium orange
tea or coffee

SNACKS OR DRINKS AT PLANNED TIMES
15 fl oz (450 ml) skim milk

Serving Information
Men and Teenagers: Add 3 oz (90 g) boiled potatoes and 1 slice (1 oz/30 g) bread, 1 medium banana
Teenagers: Add 5 fl oz (150 ml) natural yogurt

DAY 2

MORNING MEAL
2-inch (5-cm) wedge honeydew melon
1 boiled egg
1 slice (1 oz/30 g) bread, toasted and spread with 2 teaspoons (10 ml) low-fat spread
tea or coffee

MIDDAY MEAL
3-4 oz (90-120 g) canned tuna with mixed green salad, with 2 teaspoons (10 ml) low-calorie mayonnaise
1 medium orange
tea or coffee

EVENING MEAL
3-4 oz (90-120 g) turkey breast
3-oz (90-g) baked jacket potato with 2 teaspoons (10 ml) low-fat spread
3 oz (90 g) steamed courgettes
1 tablespoon (15 ml) relish (any type)
3 oz (90 g) grapes
tea or coffee

SNACKS OR DRINKS AT PLANNED TIMES
5 fl oz (150 ml) natural yogurt, ½ pint (300 ml) skim milk

Serving Information
Men and Teenagers: Add 1 slice (1 oz/30 g) bread; 3-oz (90-g) baked jacket potato and 3 oz (90 g) grapes at Evening Meal
Teenagers: Add ½ pint (300 ml) skim milk

DAY 3

MORNING MEAL
¾ oz (20 g) cornflakes with ½ medium banana sliced and served with 5 fl oz (150 ml) skim milk
tea or coffee

MIDDAY MEAL
5 oz (150 g) cottage cheese mixed with 1 medium orange, peeled and diced
mixed green salad with 2 teaspoons (10 ml) mayonnaise
¾ oz (20 g) crispbread
1 teaspoon (5 ml) margarine
tea or coffee

EVENING MEAL
Liver and Noodle Casserole (page 144)
3 oz (90 g) cooked green beans
4 oz (120 g) canned pineapple
tea or coffee

SNACKS OR DRINKS AT PLANNED TIMES
15 fl oz (450 ml) skim milk

Serving Information
Men and Teenagers: Add extra ¾ oz (20 g) crispbread 2 oz (60 g) noodles, 4 oz (120 g) canned pineapple
Teenagers: Add 5 fl oz (150 ml) natural yogurt

DAY 6

MORNING MEAL
2 inch (5 cm) wedge honeydew melon
1 oz (30 g) canned sardines mashed with 2 teaspoons (10 ml) tomato ketchup on 1 slice (1 oz/30 g) bread, toasted
tea or coffee

MIDDAY MEAL
Macaroni with Cheese and Peanut Sauce (page 176)
mixed salad of lettuce, tomato, red pepper, spring onion with 2 teaspoons (10 ml) low-calorie salad dressing
2 medium plums
tea or coffee

EVENING MEAL
2-egg omelette cooked in 1 teaspoon (5 ml) vegetable oil, and filled with 3 oz (90 g) sliced and poached mushrooms
3 oz (90 g) cooked peas
mixed green salad with lemon juice
4 oz (120 g) canned fruit cocktail
tea or coffee

SNACKS OR DRINKS AT PLANNED TIMES
5 fl oz (150 ml) natural yogurt, 8 fl oz (240 ml) skim milk

Serving Information
Men and Teenagers: Add extra 2 oz (60 oz) cooked macaroni and 1 digestive biscuit, 4 oz (120 g) canned fruit cocktail
Teenagers: Add ½ pint (300 ml) skim milk

DAY 7

MORNING MEAL
1 medium orange
Kedgeree and Mushroom Grill (page 176)
tea or coffee

MIDDAY MEAL
3-4 oz (90-120 g) roast lamb
3-oz (90-g) baked jacket potato
2 teaspoons (10 ml) low-fat spread
3 oz (90 g) cooked peas
3 oz (90 g) steamed carrots
4 oz (120 g) canned peach slices
tea or coffee

EVENING MEAL
3-4 oz (90-120 g) peeled prawns on mixed green salad with 1 medium tomato, sliced, 2-3 onion rings, with 3 teaspoons (15 ml) salad cream
1 medium pear
tea or coffee

SNACKS OR DRINKS AT PLANNED TIMES
5 fl oz (150 ml) natural yogurt, ½ pint (300 ml) skim milk

Serving Information
Men and Teenagers: Add extra 3-oz (90-g) baked jacket potato and 3 oz (90 g) baked beans, 1 medium banana
Teenagers: Add ½ pint (300 ml) skim milk

WEEK 23

Ginger is usually associated with biscuits and parkin and ginger beer but this week we flavour grilled chicken with it. The fresh ginger root has a very special flavour – more pungent than the ground form which we buy in small packs from the grocer.

It's a very ancient spice, enjoyed by the Greeks and the Romans and even mentioned by the Chinese philosopher, Confucius (551-479 BC). Indian cookery has always included it, considering it to be an aid to digestion and a protection against disease. It's an excellent ingredient in all curry powders and pastes, and leads to the brow-mopping which follows the consumption of any specially 'hot' curried dish.

The description 'Florentine' applied to any dish means that it contains cooked spinach, and on Day 2 we suggest Fillet of Sole Florentine for your midday meal.

DAY 1

MORNING MEAL
½ medium grapefruit
¾ oz (20 g) ready-to-eat cereal
5 fl oz (150 ml) skim milk
tea or coffee

MIDDAY MEAL
Baked Cheese Souffle (page 116)
green salad with **Cider Vinaigrette** (page 183)
¾ oz (20 g) crispbread
1 teaspoon (5 ml) margarine
2-inch (5-cm) wedge honeydew melon
tea or coffee

EVENING MEAL
Ginger-Grilled Chicken (page 130)
3 oz (90 g) steamed mange tout peas
3 oz (90 g) steamed carrots
green salad with **Dijon Herb Dressing** (page 182)
1-oz (30-g) bread roll
1 teaspoon (5 ml) low-fat spread
4 fl oz (120 ml) white wine
tea or coffee

SNACKS OR DRINKS AT PLANNED TIMES
Tropical Shake (page 194), 5 fl oz (150 ml) skim milk

Serving Information
Men and Teenagers: Add 5 oz (150 g) strawberries, 2 digestive biscuits
Teenagers: Add ½ pint (300 ml) skim milk

DAY 4

MORNING MEAL
2-inch (5-cm) wedge honeydew melon
¾ oz (20 g) cornflakes
5 fl oz (150 ml) skim milk □ tea or coffee

MIDDAY MEAL
3-4 oz (90-120 g) grilled lamb's liver
3 oz (90 g) steamed spinach
3 oz (90 g) steamed mushrooms
shredded lettuce with cider vinegar
1-oz (30-g) bread roll
2 teaspoons (10 ml) low-fat spread
5 oz (150 g) strawberries
soda water with slice of lemon □ tea or coffee

EVENING MEAL
3-4 oz (90-120 g) roast lamb
3 oz (90 g) cooked sliced carrots
3 oz (90 g) cooked green beans
Braised Leek Salad (page 178)
5 oz (150 g) raspberries
tea or coffee

SNACKS OR DRINKS AT PLANNED TIMES
1½-oz (45-g) scone with 2 teaspoons (10 ml) low-calorie strawberry jam, 5 fl oz (150 ml) natural yogurt, 5 fl oz (150 ml) skim milk

Serving Information
Men and Teenagers: Add 1 medium apple, 1½-oz (45-g) scone
Teenagers: Add ½ pint (300 ml) skim milk

DAY 5

MORNING MEAL
4 fl oz (120 ml) orange juice
1 scrambled egg with chives
1 slice (1 oz/30 g) wholemeal bread, toasted
1 teaspoon (5 ml) margarine
tea or coffee

MIDDAY MEAL
3-4 oz (90-120 g) tuna
mixed salad of lettuce, tomato and cucumber, with 3 teaspoons (15 ml) low-calorie mayonnaise
1 medium peach
tea or coffee

EVENING MEAL
3-4 oz (90-120 g) grilled chicken
3 oz (90 g) boiled new potatoes
3 oz (90 g) cooked peas dotted with 1 teaspoon (5 ml) low-fat spread
4 oz (120 g) canned fruit cocktail
tea or coffee

SNACKS OR DRINKS AT PLANNED TIMES
2 oz (60 g) vanilla ice cream, 5 fl oz (150 ml) natural yogurt, ½ pint (300 ml) skim milk

Serving Information
Men and Teenagers: Add 4 fl oz (120 ml) orange juice, 3 oz (90 g) boiled new potatoes, 1 digestive biscuit
Teenagers: Add ½ pint (300 ml) skim milk

DAY 2

MORNING MEAL
4 fl oz (120 ml) orange juice
1 oz (30 g) Cheshire cheese
1 slice (1 oz/30 g) wholemeal bread, toasted
1 teaspoon (5 ml) low-fat spread
tea or coffee

MIDDAY MEAL
Fillet of Sole Florentine (page 159)
3 oz (90 g) cooked green beans
4 oz (120 g) canned fruit cocktail
tea or coffee

EVENING MEAL
3 oz (90 g) lean ham
mixed salad with lettuce, tomatoes and cucumber, with 1½
    teaspoons (7.5 ml) vegetable oil and wine vinegar
2 cream crackers
1 medium apple
tea or coffee

SNACKS OR DRINKS AT PLANNED TIMES
5 fl oz (150 ml) natural yogurt, ½ pint (300 ml) skim milk

Serving Information
Men and Teenagers: Add 4 fl oz (120 ml) orange juice, 1 slice (1
    oz/30 g) wholemeal bread, 1 digestive biscuit
Men: Add 1 oz (30 g) lean ham at Evening Meal
Teenagers: Add ½ pint (300 ml) skim milk

DAY 3

MORNING MEAL
5 oz (150 g) strawberries
1 boiled egg
1 slice (1 oz/30 g) wholemeal bread, toasted
1 teaspoon (5 ml) margarine
tea or coffee

MIDDAY MEAL
3-4 oz (90-120 g) sliced roast turkey breast
tomato slices and green pepper rings on lettuce
1 oz (30 g) pitta bread
1 teaspoon (5 ml) mayonnaise
½ medium banana
tea or coffee

EVENING MEAL
3-4 oz (90-120 g) grilled veal steak
3-oz (90-g) baked jacket potato with 1 teaspoon (5 ml) margarine
3 oz (90 g) steamed broccoli
Curried Cole Slaw (page 178)
4 fl oz (120 ml) white wine
tea or coffee

SNACKS OR DRINKS AT PLANNED TIMES
1 medium kiwi fruit, 1 pint (600 ml) skim milk

Serving Information
Men and Teenagers: Add 5 oz (150 g) strawberries, 2-oz (60-g)
    wholemeal roll with 2 teaspoons (10 ml) low-calorie jam
Teenagers: Add ½ pint (300 ml) skim milk

DAY 6

MORNING MEAL
4 fl oz (120 ml) grapefruit juice
1 boiled egg
1 slice (1 oz/30 g) wholemeal bread, toasted
2 teaspoons (10 ml) low-fat spread
tea or coffee

MIDDAY MEAL
2½ oz (75 g) cottage cheese
1 oz (30 g) Cheddar cheese, grated
2 cream crackers
chicory and watercress salad with 1 teaspoon (5 ml) vegetable
    oil and cider vinegar
4 oz (120 g) canned peach slices
mineral water with mint sprig
tea or coffee

EVENING MEAL
3-4 oz (90-120 g) grilled fillet of plaice
3 oz (90 g) steamed carrots
3 oz (90 g) steamed courgettes dotted with 1 teaspoon (5 ml)
    margarine
Pear Frozen Yogurt (page 195)
tea or coffee

SNACKS OR DRINKS AT PLANNED TIMES
10 fl oz (300 ml) skim milk

Serving Information
Men and Teenagers: Add 5 fl oz (150 ml) apple juice, 2 digestive
    biscuits
Teenagers: Add ½ pint (300 ml) skim milk

DAY 7

MORNING MEAL
2½ fl oz (75 ml) apple juice
¾ oz (20 g) wheat flakes
5 fl oz (150 ml) skim milk □ tea or coffee

MIDDAY MEAL
Sauteed Chick Peas Italian Style (page 166)
2 oz (60 g) cooked brown rice
3 oz (90 g) cooked spinach
green salad with 1 teaspoon (5 ml) mayonnaise
4 oz (120 g) cherries
tea or coffee

EVENING MEAL
3-4 oz (90-120 g) grilled beef steak
3 oz (90 g) boiled potatoes dotted with 1 teaspoon (5 ml) low-fat
    spread
3 oz (90 g) steamed onion rings
3 oz (90 g) poached mushrooms
1 medium tomato, halved and grilled
5 oz (150 g) strawberries
tea or coffee

SNACKS OR DRINKS AT PLANNED TIMES
15 fl oz (450 ml) skim milk

Serving Information
Men and Teenagers: Add 2 oz (60 g) French bread, 4 oz (120 g)
    cherries
Men: Add ½ oz (15 g) grated Cheddar cheese to salad at Midday
    Meal
Teenagers: Add ½ pint (300 ml) skim milk

WEEK 24

This week we include some unusual vegetable dishes. The idea of Curried Vegetables may be new to you, and this recipe is interesting because in effect, you make your own curry sauce, and that has quite a different taste from the commercial variety. The ingredients have such evocative names – coriander, turmeric, cumin – you can smell that distinct aroma as you read them. This dish can be used as a starter to the meal or served with the meat of the main course.

Red Salad sounds colourful and is based on a Russian tomato dish. It looks splendid when served with fish, as on Day 5.

Risotto is an Italian rice speciality. In our version a variety of vegetables, cooked in stock, are poured over the rice and cheese is added to make a complete meal.

DAY 1

MORNING MEAL
2½ oz (75 g) cottage cheese
4 oz (120 g) canned sliced peaches
1 slice (1 oz/30 g) currant bread □ tea or coffee

MIDDAY MEAL
3-4 oz (90-120 g) cold roast lamb with **Mint Sauce** (page 182)
3 oz (90 g) sweet corn
green salad with 1 teaspoon (5 ml) mayonnaise
1 medium orange, sliced into 5 fl oz (150 ml) natural yogurt
tea or coffee

EVENING MEAL
3-4 oz (90-120 g) grilled lamb's liver
1 oz (30 g) lean grilled back bacon
3 oz (90 g) cooked green beans
3 oz (90 g) cooked cauliflower
3 oz (90 g) cooked carrots
2 teaspoons (10 ml) margarine
tapioca pudding made with 3 teaspoons (15 ml) tapioca, 5 fl oz (150 ml) skim milk and artificial sweetener to taste
2 tablespoons (30 ml) raisins
tea or coffee

SNACKS OR DRINKS AT PLANNED TIMES
5 fl oz (150 ml) skim milk

Serving Information
Men and Teenagers: Add extra 1 slice (1 oz/30 g) currant bread at Morning Meal; 1 digestive biscuit, 6 oz (180 g) grapes
Teenagers: Add ½ pint (300 ml) skim milk

DAY 4

MORNING MEAL
4 fl oz (120 ml) orange juice
¾ oz (20 g) cornflakes
5 fl oz (150 ml) skim milk
tea or coffee

MIDDAY MEAL
Curried Vegetables (page 170)
3-4 oz (90-120 g) chicken, grilled with lemon juice and tandoori spice
4 oz (120 g) canned pineapple with 5 fl oz (150 ml) natural yogurt
tea or coffee

EVENING MEAL
3 oz (90 g) grilled kipper fillets
2 slices (1 oz/30 g each) wholemeal bread
3 teaspoons (15 ml) margarine
1 teaspoon (5 ml) golden syrup
1 medium pear
tea or coffee

SNACKS OR DRINKS AT PLANNED TIMES
5 fl oz (150 ml) skim milk

Serving Information
Men and Teenagers: Add extra ¾ oz (20 g) cornflakes at Morning Meal and 1 medium banana, sliced
Men: Add extra 1-oz (30-g) kipper at Evening Meal
Teenagers: Add ½ pint (300 ml) skim milk

DAY 5

MORNING MEAL
2½ oz (75 g) cottage cheese
2 slices canned pineapple
¾ oz (20 g) crispbread
tea or coffee

MIDDAY MEAL
2 hard-boiled eggs, sliced on green salad with lemon juice
1 medium tomato, sliced
3 oz (90 g) cooked beetroot
1 medium apple
tea or coffee

EVENING MEAL
Red Salad (page 172)
6 oz (180 g) boil-in-the-bag fish in sauce (any type)
4 oz (120 g) cooked rice
3 oz (90 g) cooked broccoli
1 medium orange
tea or coffee

SNACKS OR DRINKS AT PLANNED TIMES
15 fl oz (450 ml) skim milk

Serving Information
Men and Teenagers: Add 2 slices (2 oz/60 g) wholemeal bread at Midday Meal; 2 slices canned pineapple
Teenagers: Add 5 fl oz (150 ml) natural yogurt

DAY 2

MORNING MEAL
¾ oz (20 g) bran flakes
2 tablespoons (30 ml) raisins
5 fl oz (150 ml) skim milk
2 medium tomatoes, grilled on 1 slice (1 oz/30 g) bread, toasted
1 teaspoon (5 ml) margarine ☐ tea or coffee

MIDDAY MEAL
2½ oz (75 g) cottage cheese and 1 oz (30 g) Cheddar cheese,
    mixed, grilled on 1 slice (1 oz/30 g) wholemeal bread
2 pickled onions
Worcestershire sauce
2 sticks celery
5 fl oz (150 ml) natural yogurt with 1 medium portion of stewed
    rhubarb ☐ tea or coffee

EVENING MEAL
3-4 oz (90-120 g) cold roast chicken
Green Vegetable Salad (page 171)
2 teaspoons (10 ml) mayonnaise
1 medium orange
tea or coffee

SNACKS OR DRINKS AT PLANNED TIMES
5 fl oz (150 ml) skim milk, 1 digestive biscuit, 3 oz (90 g) grapes

Serving Information
Men and Teenagers: Add 2-oz (60-g) Scotch pancake;
    1½ teaspoons (7.5 ml) strawberry jam; 2 tablespoons (30 ml)
    raisins at Morning Meal and 3 oz (90 g) grapes
Teenagers: Add ½ pint (300 ml) skim milk

DAY 3

MORNING MEAL
½ medium grapefruit
1 poached egg on ¾-oz (20-g) crumpet
2 teaspoons (10 ml) low-fat spread
tea or coffee

MIDDAY MEAL
3-4 oz (90-120 g) cockles
green salad
1 medium tomato
1 teaspoon (5 ml) low-calorie mayonnaise
¾ oz (20 g) crispbread
4 oz (120 g) canned peach slices ☐ tea or coffee

EVENING MEAL
3 oz (90 g) grilled frankfurters
Savoury Cabbage (page 171)
3 oz (90 g) boiled potatoes
½ pint (300 ml) lager
5 fl oz (150 ml) natural yogurt with rum flavouring and 2
    tablespoons (30 ml) raisins ☐ tea or coffee

SNACKS OR DRINKS AT PLANNED TIMES
½ pint (300 ml) skim milk

Serving Information
Men and Teenagers: Add ¾-oz (20-g) crumpet at Morning
    Meal; 3 oz (90 g) boiled potatoes at Evening Meal; 1 medium
    banana
Men: Add extra 1-oz (30-g) frankfurter at Evening Meal
Teenagers: Add ½ pint (300 ml) skim milk

DAY 6

MORNING MEAL
2-inch (5-cm) wedge honeydew melon
¾ oz (20 g) muesli
5 fl oz (150 ml) skim milk
tea or coffee

MIDDAY MEAL
7-8 oz (210-240 g) baked beans, heated with 2 tablespoons (30
    ml) sultanas and curry powder to taste, on 1 slice (1 oz/30 g)
    bread, toasted
2 teaspoons (10 ml) low-fat spread
green salad with 1 medium tomato, sliced
2 teaspoons (10 ml) mayonnaise
tea or coffee

EVENING MEAL
Cheese and Vegetable Risotto (page 123)
5 fl oz (150 ml) natural yogurt with 2 teaspoons (10 ml) low-
    calorie raspberry jam
tea or coffee

SNACKS OR DRINKS AT PLANNED TIMES
1 digestive biscuit, 5 fl oz (150 ml) skim milk

Serving Information
Men and Teenagers: Add ¾ oz (20 g) muesli at Morning Meal; 1
    slice (1 oz/30 g) bread at Midday Meal; 1 medium banana
Teenagers: Add ½ pint (300 ml) skim milk

DAY 7

MORNING MEAL
½ medium grapefruit
1 egg, scrambled with 2 teaspoons (10 ml) low-fat spread
1 slice (1 oz/30 g) bread
2 medium grilled tomatoes
tea or coffee

MIDDAY MEAL
2-inch (5-cm) wedge honeydew melon
3-4 oz (90-120 g) grilled salmon
3 oz (90 g) cooked new potatoes
3 oz (90 g) cooked peas
2 teaspoons (10 ml) low-fat spread
cucumber salad with 2½ fl oz (75 ml) natural yogurt and chopped
    pickled cucumber
4 fl oz (120 ml) white wine
2½ fl oz (75 ml) natural yogurt with 5 oz (150 g) raspberries
tea or coffee

EVENING MEAL
Swiss Cheese Bake (page 123)
tea or coffee

SNACKS OR DRINKS AT PLANNED TIMES
½ pint (300 ml) skim milk

Serving Information
Men and Teenagers: Add 3 oz (90 g) cooked potatoes at Midday
    Meal; 1-oz (30-g) Scotch pancake with 2 teaspoons (10 ml)
    strawberry jam, 6 oz (180 g) grapes
Men: Add ½ oz (15 g) ham at Evening Meal
Teenagers: Add ½ pint (300 ml) skim milk

WEEK 25

The concept of combining fruit with meat is not a new one. We've had apple sauce with pork, oranges with duck, for years. But you may find Day 7's midday meal a new idea – roast beef served with Spicy Plum Sauce. It's actually a Polish recipe and we've adapted it to conform to our Food Plan. The slightly tart taste and smooth consistency of the plum sauce are a surprising complement to the beef's texture and flavour.

'Provencal' used as part of the name of a dish indicates that it contains oil, tomatoes and garlic. Our Chicken Provencal has all these and olives and mushrooms and wine as well. It's still within the capabilities of the 'plain cook' and yet gives a truly gourmet impression.

DAY 1

MORNING MEAL
½ medium grapefruit
1 boiled egg
1 slice (1 oz/30 g) wholemeal bread
2 teaspoons (10 ml) low-fat spread
tea or coffee

MIDDAY MEAL
Liver Pate (page 146)
mixed green salad tossed with **Basic Vinaigrette** (page 183)
tea or coffee

EVENING MEAL
Beef Pie (page 147)
3 oz (90 g) steamed carrots
Baked Spiced Pear (page 188)
tea or coffee

SNACKS OR DRINKS AT PLANNED TIMES
½ pint (300 ml) skim milk, 5 fl oz (150 ml) natural yogurt

Serving Information
Men and Teenagers: Add 1-oz (30-g) bread roll, 1 medium
   orange
Teenagers: Add 5 fl oz (150 ml) natural yogurt

DAY 4

MORNING MEAL
½ medium banana, sliced with ¾ oz (20 g) cornflakes
5 fl oz (150 ml) skim milk
tea or coffee

MIDDAY MEAL
Cauliflower and Courgette Soup (page 110)
2½ oz (75 g) cottage cheese sprinkled with chives
1 oz (30 g) grated Edam cheese served on shredded iceberg
   lettuce
4 cream crackers
4 teaspoons (20 ml) low-fat spread
1 medium apple
tea or coffee

EVENING MEAL
½ medium grapefruit
3-4 oz (90-120 g) roast chicken
1 oz (30 g) grilled lean bacon
3 oz (90 g) steamed fennel
3 oz (90 g) steamed courgettes
3-oz (90-g) baked jacket potato
2 teaspoons (10 ml) low-fat spread
tea or coffee

SNACKS OR DRINKS AT PLANNED TIMES
15 fl oz (450 ml) skim milk

Serving Information
Men and Teenagers: Add 3-oz (90-g) baked jacket potato, 1
   medium apple
Teenagers: Add 5 fl oz (150 ml) natural yogurt

DAY 5

MORNING MEAL
½ medium grapefruit
2½ oz (75 g) cottage cheese grilled on 1 slice (1 oz/30 g)
   wholemeal bread, toasted
tea or coffee

MIDDAY MEAL
mackerel salad
   toss together in lemon juice, 3-4 oz (90-120 g) canned drained
   mackerel fillets, flaked, 3 oz (90 g) canned French beans, 3 oz
   (90 g) canned peas, 1½ oz (45 g) sweet corn, 1½ oz (45 g) red
   pepper, seeded and sliced
1 slice (1 oz/30 g) wholemeal bread
tea or coffee

EVENING MEAL
2-inch (5-cm) wedge honeydew melon
Baked Prawns Thermidor (page 155)
3 oz (90 g) steamed broccoli
3 oz (90 g) steamed carrots
2 small satsumas
tea or coffee

SNACKS OR DRINKS AT PLANNED TIMES
5 fl oz (150 ml) natural yogurt, 7½ fl oz (225 ml) skim milk

Serving Information
Men and Teenagers: Add 1 slice (1 oz/30 g) wholemeal bread, 1
   medium apple, 2 small satsumas
Teenagers: Add ½ pint (300 ml) skim milk

DAY 2

MORNING MEAL
½ medium grapefruit
1 oz (30 g) grated Cheddar cheese, grilled on 1 slice (1 oz/30 g) wholemeal bread, toasted
tea or coffee

MIDDAY MEAL
1 poached egg, served on 6 oz (180 g) steamed spinach dotted with 2 teaspoons (10 ml) low-fat spread
2½ oz (75 g) quark or cottage cheese mixed with 4 oz (120 g) canned apricots, diced
1 digestive biscuit
tea or coffee

EVENING MEAL
Chicken Provencale (page 132)
2 oz (60 g) cooked pasta shells
3 oz (90 g) steamed French beans
2 teaspoons (10 ml) low-fat spread
¼ small fresh pineapple
4 fl oz (120 ml) white wine
tea or coffee

SNACKS OR DRINKS AT PLANNED TIMES
½ pint (300 ml) skim milk, 5 fl oz (150 ml) natural yogurt

Serving Information
Men and Teenagers: Add 1 digestive biscuit and 1 medium apple
Teenagers: Add ½ pint (300 ml) skim milk

DAY 3

MORNING MEAL
4 fl oz (120 ml) orange juice
¾ oz (20 g) muesli
5 fl oz (150 ml) skim milk
tea or coffee

MIDDAY MEAL
3-4 oz (90-120 g) cooked, flaked cod, 1 diced celery stick, 3 oz (90 g) canned green beans, drained and chopped, 1½ oz (45 g) seeded and diced red pepper, 2 oz (60 g) cooked pasta shells, 2 teaspoons (10 ml) olive oil
3 oz (90 g) grapes
tea or coffee

EVENING MEAL
3-4 oz (90-120 g) grilled lamb chop
3-oz (90-g) boiled potato mashed with 2 teaspoons (10 ml) low-fat spread
3 oz (90 g) steamed cauliflower
1 medium grilled tomato
½ medium banana, sliced, sprinkled with pinch cinnamon
tea or coffee

SNACKS OR DRINKS AT PLANNED TIMES
15 fl oz (450 ml) skim milk, 2 cream crackers topped with 2 teaspoons (10 ml) grated cheese

Serving Information
Men and Teenagers: Add 3-oz (90-g) mashed potato, 3 oz (90 g) grapes, ½ medium banana
Teenagers: Add 5 fl oz (150 ml) natural yogurt

DAY 6

MORNING MEAL
2 tablespoons (30 ml) raisins mixed with ¾ oz (20 g) porridge oats cooked with water
5 fl oz (150 ml) skim milk
tea or coffee

MIDDAY MEAL
2-egg omelette cooked in 1½ teaspoons (7.5 ml) vegetable oil and filled with 3 oz (90 g) skinned and diced tomatoes
3 oz (90 g) cooked peas
1 slice (1 oz/30 g) wholemeal bread
1 medium orange

EVENING MEAL
Italian Veal and Peppers (page 127)
2 oz (60 g) cooked pasta shells
3 oz (90 g) cooked broccoli
4 oz (120 g) canned peaches
2 oz (60 g) vanilla ice cream
tea or coffee

SNACKS OR DRINKS AT PLANNED TIMES
15 fl oz (450 ml) skim milk

Serving Information
Men and Teenagers: Add 2 oz (60 g) cooked pasta shells, 1 medium orange
Teenagers: Add 5 fl oz (150 ml) natural yogurt

DAY 7

MORNING MEAL
1 medium orange sliced with ¾ oz (20 g) muesli
5 fl oz (150 ml) skim milk
tea or coffee

MIDDAY MEAL
3-4 oz (90-120 g) lean roast beef with **Spicy Plum Sauce** (page 184)
3 oz (90 g) steamed courgettes
3 oz (90 g) steamed parsnips
3 oz (90 g) roast potato cooked with 2 teaspoons (10 ml) vegetable oil
Pear Frozen Yogurt (page 195)
tea or coffee

EVENING MEAL
Danish sandwich
2 slices (2 oz/60 g) rye bread, spread with 2 teaspoons (10 ml) low-calorie mayonnaise, topped with lettuce, tomato and cucumber slices and 3-4oz (90-120 g) canned brisling
tea or coffee

SNACKS OR DRINKS AT PLANNED TIMES
5 fl oz (150 ml) skim milk

Serving Information
Men and Teenagers: Add 1 digestive biscuit, 1 medium orange, 2 small satsumas
Teenagers: Add ½ pint (300 ml) skim milk

WEEK 26

Tomatoes are such a familiar vegetable – although they used to be known as a fruit, the 'love-apple' of the 16th century. They were regarded with some suspicion at first and the pips were even thought to be a cause of appendicitis. But by the 19th century they were accepted in Britain as a useful food and became widely cultivated.

The tomatoes grown in the Mediterranean regions have a colour and taste which differs from our home product, although the taste of our local varieties is intensified by length of cooking as in a sauce or puree. The canned tomatoes, usually from Italy, make an excellent substitute in cooked dishes when fresh varieties are expensive or not available.

We enjoy the tomato raw in salads for both its colour and its taste and the flavour can be wonderfully enhanced by the addition of a little basil – that useful herb. Our recipe for Tomato Stuffed with Herb Cheese (Day 1) uses onion, parsley and dill to pep up the flavour.

DAY 1

MORNING MEAL
1 medium orange
¾ oz (20 g) ready-to-eat cereal
5 fl oz (150 ml) skim milk
tea or coffee

MIDDAY MEAL
Tomato Stuffed with Herb Cheese (page 126)
1 slice (1 oz/30 g) rye bread
1 teaspoon (5 ml) margarine
½ medium banana, sliced and set in 5 fl oz (150 ml) lemon jelly
tea or coffee

EVENING MEAL
3-4 oz (90-120 g) grilled lamb chop
3 oz (90 g) cooked carrots
3 oz (90 g) cooked broad beans
green salad with **Basic Vinaigrette** (page 183)
1-oz (30-g) bread roll
1 teaspoon (5 ml) margarine
4 oz (120 g) cherries
tea or coffee

SNACKS OR DRINKS AT PLANNED TIMES
15 fl oz (450 ml) skim milk

Serving Information
Men and Teenagers: Add ½ medium banana, ¾ oz (20 g) ready-to-eat cereal, 3 oz (90 g) boiled potatoes
Teenagers: Add 5 fl oz (150 ml) natural yogurt

DAY 4

MORNING MEAL
½ medium banana sliced on ¾ oz (20 g) muesli with 5 fl oz (150 ml) skim milk
tea or coffee

MIDDAY MEAL
3-4 oz (90-120 g) grilled chicken livers
3 oz (90 g) steamed onion rings
3 oz (90 g) steamed broccoli dotted with 1 teaspoon (5 ml) margarine
3 oz (90 g) baked beans
5 oz (150 g) fresh blackcurrants with 1½ teaspoons (7.5 ml) sugar
tea or coffee

EVENING MEAL
3-4 oz (90-120 g) grilled plaice with 2 teaspoons (10 ml) low-calorie seafood dressing
3 oz (90 g) whole kernel sweet corn
1 teaspoon (5 ml) margarine
3 oz (90 g) steamed spinach
5 oz (150 g) raspberries
tea or coffee

SNACKS OR DRINKS AT PLANNED TIMES
2 water biscuits with 2 teaspoons (10 ml) low-fat spread
15 fl oz (450 ml) skim milk

Serving Information
Men and Teenagers: Add ½ medium banana, 3 oz (90 g) baked beans, 3 oz (90 g) whole kernel sweet corn
Teenagers: Add 5 fl oz (150 ml) natural yogurt

DAY 5

MORNING MEAL
4 fl oz (120 ml) orange juice
1 boiled egg
1 slice (1 oz/30 g) wholemeal bread, toasted
1 teaspoon (5 ml) margarine □ tea or coffee

MIDDAY MEAL
5 oz (150 g) cottage cheese with mixed salad of shredded lettuce, 1 medium tomato sliced, 2-inch (5-cm) chunk cucumber diced, 2-3 spring onions, 2 teaspoons (10 ml) salad cream
2 water biscuits
5 oz (150 g) strawberries
5 fl oz (150 ml) natural yogurt
tea or coffee

EVENING MEAL
3-4 oz (90-120 g) grilled steak
1 medium tomato, halved and grilled
3 oz (90 g) cooked peas
3 oz (90 g) steamed broccoli dotted with 1 teaspoon (5 ml) margarine
5 oz (150 g) dessert gooseberries
tea or coffee

SNACKS OR DRINKS AT PLANNED TIMES
½ pint (300 ml) skim milk

Serving Information
Men and Teenagers: Add 4 fl oz (120 ml) orange juice, 1½-oz (45-g) scone with 2 teaspoons (10 ml) low-calorie jam
Teenagers: Add ½ pint (300 ml) skim milk

DAY 2

MORNING MEAL
2½ fl oz (75 ml) apple juice
1 egg, scrambled in 1 teaspoon (5 ml) margarine
1 slice (1 oz/30 g) wholemeal bread
tea or coffee

MIDDAY MEAL
3-4 oz (90-120 g) cooked chicken
3 oz (90 g) steamed marrow
3 oz (90 g) steamed whole baby carrots dotted with 1 teaspoon
   (5 ml) margarine
green salad with **Russian Dressing** (page 184)
1 medium peach
tea or coffee

EVENING MEAL
3-4 oz (90-120 g) grilled trout with 2 teaspoons (10 ml)
   horseradish relish
2 oz (60 g) cooked noodles
3 oz (90 g) poached courgettes
3 oz (90 g) cooked peas
5 oz (150 g) strawberries with 2½ fl oz (75 ml) natural yogurt
tea or coffee

SNACKS OR DRINKS AT PLANNED TIMES
15 fl oz (450 ml) skim milk

Serving Information
Men and Teenagers: Add 2½ fl oz (75 ml) apple juice; 4 oz
   (120 g) cooked noodles at Evening Meal
Teenagers: Add 5 fl oz (150 ml) natural yogurt

DAY 3

MORNING MEAL
½ medium grapefruit
2½ oz (75 g) cottage cheese
1 slice (1 oz/30 g) wholemeal bread
tea or coffee

MIDDAY MEAL
3-4 oz (90-120 g) poached salmon
3 oz (90 g) steamed asparagus
Cucumber and Tomato Salad (page 179)
4 oz (120 g) apple, stewed
2 oz (60 g) vanilla ice cream
tea or coffee

EVENING MEAL
Mexican Beef Patties (page 142)
3 oz (90 g) hot cooked beetroot
3 oz (90 g) steamed green beans
3 oz (90 g) boiled potatoes dotted with 1½ teaspoons (7.5 ml)
   margarine
4 oz (120 g) canned mandarin oranges
tea or coffee

SNACKS OR DRINKS AT PLANNED TIMES
5 fl oz (150 ml) natural yogurt, ½ pint (300 ml) skim milk

Serving Information
Men and Teenagers: Add 1 medium peach, 1½-oz (45-g) scone,
   split and spread with 2 teaspoons (10 ml) low-calorie jam
Teenagers: Add 5 fl oz (150 ml) natural yogurt

DAY 6

MORNING MEAL
3 medium apricots, stoned and diced on ¾ oz (20 g) ready-to-eat
   cereal
5 fl oz (150 ml) skim milk
tea or coffee

MIDDAY MEAL
Mushroom Omelette (page 120)
green salad with green pepper rings and **Cider Vinaigrette**
   (page 183)
1 slice (1 oz/30 g) wholemeal bread with 1 teaspoon (5 ml)
   margarine
5 oz (150 g) strawberries with 3 tablespoons (45 ml) single
   cream
tea or coffee

EVENING MEAL
3-4 oz (90-120 g) grilled veal chop
3 oz (90 g) cooked broad beans
3 oz (90 g) cooked carrots
3 oz (90 g) boiled potatoes
4 oz (120 g) black cherries
tea or coffee

SNACKS OR DRINKS AT PLANNED TIMES
15 fl oz (450 ml) skim milk

Serving Information
Men and Teenagers: Add 4 oz (120 g) cherries, ¾ oz (20 g)
   ready-to-eat cereal, 3 oz (90 g) boiled potatoes
Teenagers: Add 5 fl oz (150 ml) natural yogurt

DAY 7

MORNING MEAL
4 fl oz (120 ml) orange juice
1 oz (30 g) Cheddar cheese, sliced and grilled on 1 slice
   (1 oz/30 g) bread, toasted
tea or coffee

MIDDAY MEAL
Mackerel Patties (page 163)
3 oz (90 g) steamed courgettes
3 oz (90 g) hot cooked beetroot
green salad with ½ teaspoon (2.5 ml) oil with wine vinegar
1 medium peach
tea or coffee

EVENING MEAL
Sesame Chicken with Green Beans (page 131)
3 oz (90 g) steamed sliced carrots
shredded lettuce with green pepper rings and lemon juice
5 oz (150 g) redcurrants stewed with artificial sweetener to taste
tea or coffee

SNACKS OR DRINKS AT PLANNED TIMES
5 fl oz (150 ml) natural yogurt, ½ pint (300 ml) skim milk

Serving Information
Men and Teenagers: Add 4 fl oz (120 ml) orange juice, 3 oz (90 g)
   baked beans, 1 slice (1 oz/30 g) wholemeal bread
Teenagers: Add ½ pint (300 ml) skim milk

WEEK 27

Oregano is a native of the Mediterranean regions and can also be found growing wild in chalky areas of England. It is easily cultivated and grows to a height of two feet. It has clusters of lavender-coloured flowers. The taste of oregano is slightly bitter and it combines well with parsley and chives. It's a vital ingredient in Mediterranean cooking – spaghetti bolognese and pizza are not the same without it.

Kebabs also feature in this week's menu. This method of cooking uses pieces of fish or meat threaded onto a skewer between pieces of vegetable. They are then grilled and served on a bed of rice. Extra flavour is added by marinading the meat or fish first and basting the kebabs with the marinade while grilling.

DAY 1

MORNING MEAL
4 fl oz (120 ml) grapefruit juice
¾ oz (20 g) cornflakes
5 fl oz (150 ml) skim milk
tea or coffee

MIDDAY MEAL
fruit and cheese salad made with 2½ oz (75 g) cottage cheese, 2 tablespoons (30 ml) raisins, tossed together and served on shredded lettuce
¾ oz (20 g) crispbread
2 teaspoons (10 ml) low-fat spread
tea or coffee

EVENING MEAL
6 oz (180 g) boil-in-the-bag fish in sauce (any type)
3 oz (90 g) cooked peas
3 oz (90 g) cooked carrots dotted with 2 teaspoons (10 ml) low-fat spread
Rice Pudding (page 190)
tea or coffee

SNACKS OR DRINKS AT PLANNED TIMES
¾ oz (20 g) crispbread, 2 teaspoons (10 ml) low-fat spread, 2 teaspoons (10 ml) low-calorie jam, 11 fl oz (330 ml) skim milk

Serving Information
Men and Teenagers: Add 3 oz (90 g) boiled potatoes at Evening Meal; 2 small satsumas
Teenagers: Add ½ pint (300 ml) skim milk

DAY 4

MORNING MEAL
1 medium orange
2½ oz (75 g) cottage cheese lightly grilled on 1 slice (1 oz/30 g) wholemeal bread, toasted
tea or coffee

MIDDAY MEAL
Toss together, 3-4 oz (90-120 g) cold cooked chicken, diced, 3 oz (90 g) canned, red kidney beans, 1 diced celery stick, 1 medium grated carrot, 1 medium grated apple, sprinkled with lemon juice, 4 teaspoons (20 ml) salad cream
tea or coffee

EVENING MEAL
Lamb Kebabs (page 136)
2 oz (60 g) hot cooked rice
1 medium tomato, sliced with onion rings and **Basic Vinaigrette** (page 183)
2 canned pear halves
2 oz (60 g) vanilla ice cream
tea or coffee

SNACKS OR DRINKS AT PLANNED TIMES
15 fl oz (450 ml) skim milk

Serving Information
Men and Teenagers: Add 2 oz (60 g) cooked rice at Evening Meal; 1 medium orange
Teenagers: Add 5 fl oz (150 ml) natural yogurt

DAY 5

MORNING MEAL
2 tablespoons (30 ml) raisins mixed with ¾ oz (20 g) porridge oats cooked with water
5 fl oz (150 ml) skim milk
tea or coffee

MIDDAY MEAL
toss together, 2 oz (60 g) drained sardines, 1 hard-boiled egg, sliced, 1 medium sliced tomato, onion rings, with 2 teaspoons (10 ml) mayonnaise, tucked into 1 x 2-oz (60-g) pitta bread
tea or coffee

EVENING MEAL
4 oz (120 g) canned grapefruit sections
3-4 oz (90-120 g) trout, grilled
Chinese Cabbage and Tomato Medley (page 171)
1 slice (1oz/30 g) wholemeal bread
tea or coffee

SNACKS OR DRINKS AT PLANNED TIMES
5 oz (150 g) frozen blackberries, defrosted and added to 5 fl oz (150 ml) natural yogurt, 5 fl oz (150 ml) skim milk

Serving Information
Men and Teenagers: Add 3-oz (90-g) boiled potato at Evening Meal, 3 oz (90 g) grapes
Teenagers: Add ½ pint (300 ml) skim milk

DAY 2

MORNING MEAL
4 fl oz (120 ml) grapefruit juice
1 tablespoon (15 ml) peanut butter spread on 1 slice (1 oz/30 g) wholemeal bread, toasted
tea or coffee

MIDDAY MEAL
celery and bean soup made with 6 oz (180 g) canned celery and 6 fl oz (180 ml) beef stock made with ½ stock cube. Bring to the boil and puree in blender. Reheat, adding 3 oz (90 g) canned red kidney beans
Pineapple Cheese Cake (page 190)
tea or coffee

EVENING MEAL
2-inch (5-cm) wedge honeydew melon
3-4 oz (90-120 g) grilled lamb's liver
1 oz (30 g) grilled lean bacon
3 oz (90 g) steamed broccoli
1 small satsuma
tea or coffee

SNACKS OR DRINKS AT PLANNED TIMES
5 fl oz (150 ml) skim milk, 5 fl oz (150 ml) natural yogurt

Serving Information
Men and Teenagers: Add 1 slice (1 oz/30 g) wholemeal bread, 2 small satsumas, 1 medium apple
Teenagers: Add 5 fl oz (150 ml) natural yogurt

DAY 3

MORNING MEAL
2-inch (5-cm) wedge honeydew melon
¾ oz (20 g) cornflakes
5 fl oz (150 ml) skim milk
tea or coffee

MIDDAY MEAL
mixed green salad with 2 hard-boiled eggs, sliced, 1 tablespoon (15 ml) mayonnaise
1 medium apple
1 digestive biscuit
tea or coffee

EVENING MEAL
4 oz (120 g) roast chicken
3 oz (90 g) cooked peas
6 canned apricot halves
tea or coffee

SNACKS OR DRINKS AT PLANNED TIMES
2 digestive biscuits, 5 fl oz (150 ml) skim milk, 5 fl oz (150 ml) natural yogurt

Serving Information
Men and Teenagers: Add 1 digestive biscuit, 3 oz (90 g) canned whole kernel sweet corn, 1 medium apple
Teenagers: Add ½ pint (300 ml) skim milk

DAY 6

MORNING MEAL
3 oz (90 g) grapes
¾ oz (20 g) muesli
5 fl oz (150 ml) skim milk
tea or coffee

MIDDAY MEAL
3-4 oz (90-120 g) grilled beefburger
2-oz (60-g) bap
2 teaspoons (10 ml) low-fat spread
2 teaspoons (10 ml) tomato ketchup
tea or coffee

EVENING MEAL
Chicken Greek Style (page 00)
3 oz (90 g) steamed green beans
3 oz (90 g) steamed cauliflower
1 teaspoon (5 ml) low-fat spread
1 medium orange
tea or coffee

SNACKS OR DRINKS AT PLANNED TIMES
1 oz (30 g) French bread, **Turkish Chilled Tomato Soup** (page 194), 5 fl oz (150 ml) skim milk

Serving Information
Men and Teenagers: Add 1 slice (1 oz/30 g) currant bread, 3-oz (90-g) baked jacket potato at Evening Meal; 1 medium orange
Teenagers: Add 5 fl oz (150 ml) natural yogurt

DAY 7

MORNING MEAL
4 oz (120 g) sliced canned peaches
2½ oz (75 g) cottage cheese
1 slice (1 oz/30 g) wholemeal bread, toasted
tea or coffee

MIDDAY MEAL
3-4 oz (90-120 g) roast turkey breast
Fennel with Parmesan Cheese (page 172)
3 oz (90 g) cooked parsnips
3 oz (90 g) cooked carrots
3-oz (90-g) baked jacket potato
2 teaspoons (10 ml) low-fat spread
4 fl oz (120 ml) white wine
Cherry Tarts (page 187)
tea or coffee

EVENING MEAL
Salmon Salad (page 162)
1 medium orange
5 fl oz (150 ml) natural yogurt
tea or coffee

SNACKS OR DRINKS AT PLANNED TIMES
½ pint (300 ml) skim milk, 1 can low-calorie fizzy drink

Serving Information
Men and Teenagers: Add 3-oz (90-g) baked jacket potato at Midday Meal; 1 medium apple
Teenagers: Add 5 fl oz (150 ml) natural yogurt

WEEK 28

We've provided five cold midday meals this week, so that if the children are on holiday from school you can eat a picnic while on a day's outing. The notion of sandwiches as the only acceptable picnic meal is soon overturned when you realise how easy it is to pack salad plus fish or cheese or cold meat into a plastic container – perhaps one that you originally bought filled with cottage cheese or something similar. Add some fruit and bread and a drink and you will be well nourished and satisfied and still within your food plan requirements. Perhaps the children could pack and prepare these picnic meals themselves – it's very easy to do so from ingredients washed and assembled by an adult. It's very good for the young to learn about food and nutrition in this simple way.

DAY 1

MORNING MEAL
4 fl oz (120 ml) orange juice
¾ oz (20 g) cornflakes with 5 fl oz (150 ml) skim milk
tea or coffee

MIDDAY MEAL
Cheddar salad made with 2 oz (60 g) Cheddar cheese grated
    over green salad with 4 teaspoons (20 ml) salad cream
1 slice (1 oz/30 g) bread
1 teaspoon (5 ml) low-fat spread
1 medium orange
tea or coffee

EVENING MEAL
Sausages in Tomato Sauce with Rice (page 151)
3 oz (90 g) sliced cooked green beans dotted with 1 teaspoon
    (5 ml) low-fat spread
4 oz (120 g) pineapple chunks
tea or coffee

SNACKS OR DRINKS AT PLANNED TIMES
15 fl oz (450 ml) skim milk

Serving Information
Men and Teenagers: Add extra 1 slice (1 oz/30 g) bread and 2 oz
    (60 g) cooked rice, 4 oz (120 g) canned pineapple chunks
Teenagers: Add ½ pint (300 ml) skim milk

DAY 4

MORNING MEAL
1 medium orange
1 boiled egg
1 slice (1 oz/30 g) bread, toasted, spread with 2 teaspoons
    (10 ml) low-fat spread
tea or coffee

MIDDAY MEAL
3-4 oz (90-120 g) fresh crab
green salad dressed with 1 tablespoon (15 ml) low-calorie salad
    dressing
¾ oz (20 g) crispbread
1 medium apple
tea or coffee

EVENING MEAL
5-6 oz (150-180 g) uncooked liver, sliced,
    3 oz (90 g) onion, sliced, sauteed in 2 teaspoons (10 ml)
    vegetable oil
1 oz (30 g) lean back bacon grilled until crisp
3 oz (90 g) steamed carrots
½ medium banana
tea or coffee

SNACKS OR DRINKS AT PLANNED TIMES
½ pint (300 ml) skim milk, 5 fl oz (150 ml) natural yogurt

Serving Information
Men and Teenagers: Add 3-oz (90-g) boiled potato,
    1 digestive biscuit, 1 medium orange
Teenagers: Add ½ pint (300 ml) skim milk

DAY 5

MORNING MEAL
4 fl oz (120 ml) grapefruit juice
1 tablespoon (15 ml) crunchy peanut butter spread on ¾ oz
    (20 g) crispbread
tea or coffee

MIDDAY MEAL
cottage cheese salad made with 5 oz (150 g) cottage cheese
    mixed with 3 oz (90 g) diced cucumber, 3 oz (90 g) diced red
    pepper and celery
2 tablespoons (30 ml) raisins and 2 teaspoons (10 ml) salad
    cream
tea or coffee

EVENING MEAL
Savoury Mince with Noodles (page 139)
mixed green salad with lemon juice
3 oz (90 g) grapes
tea or coffee

SNACKS OR DRINKS AT PLANNED TIMES
½ pint (300 ml) skim milk, 5 fl oz (150 ml) natural yogurt

Serving Information
Men and Teenagers: Add 1 slice (1 oz/30 g) bread, 2 oz (60 g)
    cooked noodles and 4 fl oz (120 ml) grapefruit juice
Teenagers: Add ½ pint (300 ml) skim milk

DAY 2

MORNING MEAL
4 fl oz (120 ml) orange juice
1 egg, scrambled in 1 teaspoon (5 ml) low-fat spread
1 slice (1 oz/30 g) bread, toasted
1 teaspoon (5 ml) low-fat spread
tea or coffee

MIDDAY MEAL
salmon salad made with 3-4 oz (90-120 g) canned salmon on
mixed salad with 2 teaspoons (10 ml) salad cream
3 oz (90 g) cooked beetroot
¾ oz (20 g) crispbread spread with 2 teaspoons (10 ml) low-fat
spread
1 medium apple
tea or coffee

EVENING MEAL
3-4 oz (90-120 g) roast chicken
3 oz (90 g) steamed Brussels sprouts
3 oz (90 g) cooked carrots
6 canned apricot halves
tea or coffee

SNACKS OR DRINKS AT PLANNED TIMES
½ pint (300 ml) skim milk, 5 fl oz (150 ml) natural yogurt

Serving Information
Men and Teenagers: Add extra ¾ oz (20 g) crispbread, 3-oz
(90-g) baked jacket potato, 1 medium apple
Teenagers: Add ½ pint (300 ml) skim milk

DAY 3

MORNING MEAL
½ medium banana sliced over ¾ oz (20 g) muesli with 5 fl oz
(150 ml) skim milk
tea or coffee

MIDDAY MEAL
3-4 oz (90-120 g) cooked chicken and green salad
dressed with 2 teaspoons (10 ml) low-calorie mayonnaise
2 cream crackers with 2 teaspoons (10 ml) low-fat spread
1 medium orange
tea or coffee

EVENING MEAL
1 portion (6 oz/180 g) boil-in-bag fish in sauce (any type)
3 oz (90 g) cooked peas
3 oz (90 g) boiled potatoes dotted with 2 teaspoons (10 ml)
low-fat spread
4 oz (120 g) canned peach slices
tea or coffee

SNACKS OR DRINKS AT PLANNED TIMES
15 fl oz (450 ml) skim milk

Serving Information
Men and Teenagers: Add extra 2 cream crackers at Midday
Meal; 3 oz (90 g) boiled potatoes, 1 medium apple
Teenagers: Add ½ pint (300 ml) skim milk

DAY 6

MORNING MEAL
½ medium grapefruit
¾ oz (20 g) porridge oats cooked with water and served with
5 fl oz (150 ml) skim milk
tea or coffee

MIDDAY MEAL
8 fl oz (240 ml) tomato juice
7-8 oz (210-240 g) baked beans served on 1 slice (1 oz/30 g)
bread toasted and spread with 2 teaspoons (10 ml) low-fat
spread
1 medium grilled tomato
2 oz (60 g) vanilla ice cream
tea or coffee

EVENING MEAL
Baked Hake Steak (page 156)
3 oz (90 g) steamed carrots
3 oz (90 g) cooked peas
3 oz (90 g) boiled potatoes dotted with 2 teaspoons (10 ml)
low-fat spread
½ medium banana
tea or coffee

SNACKS OR DRINKS AT PLANNED TIMES
15 fl oz (450 ml) skim milk

Serving Information
Men and Teenagers: Add 1 slice (1 oz/30 g) bread and 3 oz (90 g)
boiled potatoes, 1 medium apple, ½ medium banana
Teenagers: Add ½ pint (300 ml) skim milk

DAY 7

MORNING MEAL
½ medium grapefruit
1 oz (30 g) Cheddar cheese sliced and grilled on 1 slice (1 oz/30 g)
bread, toasted □ tea or coffee

MIDDAY MEAL
3-4 oz (90-120 g) lean roast pork
3 oz (90 g) braised leeks
3 oz (90 g) steamed Brussels sprouts
3-oz (90-g) baked jacket potato with 2 teaspoons (10 ml) low-fat
spread
Apple Meringue (page 195)
4 fl oz (120 ml) white wine □ tea or coffee

EVENING MEAL
2-egg omelette cooked in 2 teaspoons (10 ml) vegetable oil and
filled with 1 medium tomato, chopped
3 oz (90 g) poached mushrooms
green salad with lemon juice
1 medium orange □ tea or coffee

SNACKS OR DRINKS AT PLANNED TIMES
½ pint (300 ml) skim milk, 5 fl oz (150 ml) natural yogurt

Serving Information
Men and Teenagers: Add extra 3-oz (90-g) baked jacket potato,
1 slice (1 oz/30 g) bread, ½ medium grapefruit
Teenagers: Add ½ pint (300 ml) skim milk

WEEK 29

This is Budget Week. Perhaps you are just going on or just returning from holiday. Expenses mount up in a frightening fashion at such times and so here is a chance to pull the purse-strings tight while still eating well. Fish cakes are tasty and cheap. Beefburgers are one of the least expensive ways of using beef, and liver is a splendidly nutritious, economical food. The omelette uses only two eggs and sausages are a good old standby for hard-up days.

A Fruit Sundae is a delicious treat to find on a weight-reducing plan. It sounds too good to be true – ice cream with fruit and even chocolate sauce! – yet it's calculated very carefully within your weekly food intake, so go ahead, feel sinful and enjoy it!

DAY 1

MORNING MEAL
½ medium grapefruit
1 oz (30 g) lean back bacon
3 oz (90 g) baked beans
1 slice (1 oz/30 g) bread, toasted
1 teaspoon (5 ml) low-fat spread
tea or coffee

MIDDAY MEAL
2 oz (60 g) Cheddar cheese
2 teaspoons (10 ml) relish, any flavour
2 celery sticks
green salad with lemon juice
2 cream crackers
½ medium banana
tea or coffee

EVENING MEAL
3 breadcrumbed fish cakes, grilled with 3 teaspoons (15 ml) low-fat spread
3 oz (90 g) steamed carrots
3 oz (90 g) steamed cauliflower dotted with 2 teaspoons (10 ml) low-fat spread
3 oz (90 g) grapes □ tea or coffee

SNACKS OR DRINKS AT PLANNED TIMES
½ pint (300 ml) skim milk, 5 fl oz (150 ml) natural yogurt

Serving Information
Men and Teenagers: Add extra 2 cream crackers at Midday Meal; 1 medium apple, ¾-oz (20-g) scone with 1 teaspoon (5 ml) jam
Teenagers: Add ½ pint (300 ml) skim milk

DAY 4

MORNING MEAL
4 fl oz (120 ml) orange juice
¾ oz (20 g) cornflakes
5 fl oz (150 ml) skim milk
tea or coffee

MIDDAY MEAL
3-4 oz (90-120 g) canned tuna
3 oz (90 g) canned whole kernel sweet corn
sliced cucumber and onion rings with 4 teaspoons (20 ml) low-calorie mayonnaise and 1 tablespoon (15 ml) wine vinegar
4 oz (120 g) canned peach slices
tea or coffee

EVENING MEAL
Casseroled Liver (page 147)
1 medium apple
tea or coffee

SNACKS OR DRINKS AT PLANNED TIMES
5 fl oz (150 ml) skim milk, 5 fl oz (150 ml) natural yogurt

Serving Information
Men and Teenagers: Add extra 3 oz (90 g) canned whole kernel sweet corn at Midday Meal and 3-oz (90-g) baked jacket potato at Evening Meal, 1 medium pear
Teenagers: Add ½ pint (300 ml) skim milk

DAY 5

MORNING MEAL
¾ oz (20 g) bran flakes with 2 tablespoons (30 ml) sultanas
5 fl oz (150 ml) skim milk
tea or coffee

MIDDAY MEAL
2-egg omelette cooked in 2 teaspoons (10 ml) vegetable oil
3 oz (90 g) poached mushrooms
1-oz (30-g) bread roll
1 medium orange
tea or coffee

EVENING MEAL
3-4 oz (90-120 g) grilled beef sausages
3 oz (90 g) baked beans
3 oz (90 g) grilled tomatoes
4 oz (120 g) canned fruit cocktail
tea or coffee

SNACKS OR DRINKS AT PLANNED TIMES
5 fl oz (150 ml) skim milk, 5 fl oz (150 ml) natural yogurt

Serving Information
Men and Teenagers: Add 1-oz (30-g) bread roll at Midday Meal; 3 oz (90 g) baked beans and 4 oz (120 g) fruit cocktail at Evening Meal
Teenagers: Add ½ pint (300 ml) skim milk

MORNING MEAL
4 fl oz (120 ml) orange juice
¾ oz (20 g) muesli with 5 fl oz (150 ml) skim milk
tea or coffee

MIDDAY MEAL
2 slices (2 oz/60 g) wholemeal bread spread with 2 teaspoons
   (10 ml) low-fat spread, with 4 oz (120 g) sardines
3-oz (90-g) tomato, sliced
cucumber and onion rings
1 teaspoon (5 ml) low-calorie mayonnaise
1 medium pear
tea or coffee

EVENING MEAL
Pork Chops with Orange Slices (page 142)
3 oz (90 g) finely shredded cabbage, sauteed in 3 teaspoons
   (15 ml) low-fat spread
3 oz (90 g) cooked parsnips
2 oz (60 g) vanilla ice cream
tea or coffee

SNACKS OR DRINKS AT PLANNED TIMES
5 fl oz (150 ml) skim milk and 5 fl oz (150 ml) natural yogurt

Serving Information
Men and Teenagers: Add 4 oz (120 g) cooked noodles at
   Evening Meal and 2 tablespoons (30 ml) raisins
Teenagers: Add ½ pint (300 ml) skim milk

MORNING MEAL
½ medium grapefruit
1 boiled egg
1 slice (1 oz/30 g) wholemeal bread, toasted
1 teaspoon (5 ml) low-fat spread
tea or coffee

MIDDAY MEAL
3-4 oz (90-120 g) cooked chicken
2 sticks celery, chopped, mixed with 1 medium red apple, cored
   and chopped and 4 teaspoons (20 ml) salad cream
green salad with lemon juice
1-oz (30-g) bread roll
tea or coffee

EVENING MEAL
3-4 oz (90-120 g) grilled beefburger
3 oz (90 g) grilled sliced onion
3 oz (90 g) cooked peas
1 teaspoon (5 ml) low-fat spread
½ medium banana
tea or coffee

SNACKS OR DRINKS AT PLANNED TIMES
5 fl oz (150 ml) natural unsweetened yogurt, ½ pint (300 ml)
   skim milk

Serving Information
Men and Teenagers: Add 2-oz (60-g) hamburger bap at Evening
   Meal and ½ medium banana
Teenagers: Add ½ pint (300 ml) skim milk

MORNING MEAL
4 fl oz (120 ml) orange juice
1 oz (30 g) Cheddar cheese, grilled on 1 slice (1 oz/30 g) bread
tea or coffee

MIDDAY MEAL
5 oz (150 g) cottage cheese
6 oz (180 g) finely shredded cabbage, grated carrot and thinly
   sliced onion, with 4 teaspoons (20 ml) salad cream
tea or coffee

EVENING MEAL
Cod Baked in Foil (page 163)
3 oz (90 g) cooked green beans
2 oz (60 g) cooked rice
1 medium banana
tea or coffee

SNACKS OR DRINKS AT PLANNED TIMES
½ pint (300 ml) skim milk, 5 fl oz (150 ml) natural yogurt

Serving Information
Men and Teenagers: Add extra 2 oz (60 g) cooked rice at Evening
   Meal; 1 digestive biscuit and 3 oz grapes
Teenagers: Add ½ pint (300 ml) skim milk

MORNING MEAL
½ medium grapefruit
1 egg, scrambled in 1 teaspoon (5 ml) low-fat spread
1 small grilled tomato
1 slice (1 oz/30 g) bread, toasted
1 teaspoon (5 ml) low-fat spread
½ teaspoon (2.5 ml) marmalade □ tea or coffee

MIDDAY MEAL
3-4 oz (90-120 g) cooked chicken
3 oz (90 g) cooked Brussels sprouts
3 oz (90 g) steamed carrots
3-oz (90-g) baked jacket potato
2 teaspoons (10 ml) low-fat spread
Fruit Sundae (page 196)
tea or coffee

EVENING MEAL
3-4 oz (90-120 g) canned salmon
3 oz (90 g) sliced tomatoes
green salad
2 teaspoons (10 ml) salad cream
tea or coffee

SNACKS OR DRINKS AT PLANNED TIMES
½ pint (300 ml) skim milk, 5 fl oz (150 ml) natural yogurt

Serving Information
Men and Teenagers: Add extra 3-oz (90-g) baked jacket potato
   at Midday Meal, 1-oz (30-g) bread roll at Evening Meal and
   1 medium orange
Teenagers: Add ½ pint (300 ml) skim milk

WEEK 30

Did you know that over 100 different varieties of fish are offered for sale in the United Kingdom? They all appear in their seasons. Fresh fish may be scarce in the winter but frozen fish is available at all times and can be found in the freezers of most supermarkets.

Fish is an excellent source of good quality protein, low in fat and low in calories. It can be cooked in so many ways and is so easily digested that even the most 'picky' appetite can be pleased.

We have avoided good old cod and give you recipes for fish dishes which are probably less familiar.

Skate is a white sea-fish, and we eat only the wings or fins. Its flesh is cut into pieces and cooked in a stock – 'court bouillon'. We suggest that you serve it with a piquant lemon sauce.

The herring is a versatile and inexpensive fish. It can be cooked in a dozen different ways but is particularly tasty when 'soused' – cooked in a spicy mixture. It improves with keeping and so is a useful standby.

The mackerel has a rich pinkish flesh and needs a sharp flavour to enhance it. You will find that our 'Piquant Stuffing' does just that.

The kipper is a cured and smoked herring – full of flavour and very economical. Our pate is quick and easy to make and very good to eat.

DAY 1

MORNING MEAL
1 medium apple, diced into ¾ oz (20 g) muesli
5 fl oz (150 ml) skim milk □ tea or coffee

MIDDAY MEAL
1 egg, scrambled in 1 teaspoon (5 ml) margarine, cooled and topped with 2 oz (60 g) peeled prawns, 1 teaspoon (5 ml) low-calorie mayonnaise and served on 1 slice (1 oz/30 g) wholemeal bread with 1 teaspoon (5 ml) low-fat spread
green salad with lemon juice
½ pint (300 ml) lager
2 medium plums
tea or coffee

EVENING MEAL
1½-2 oz (45-60 g) all-beef burger served on 6 oz (180 g) steamed spinach and topped with 1 oz (30 g) melted Cheddar cheese
1 teaspoon (5 ml) French mustard
2 medium grilled tomatoes
4 fl oz (120 ml) orange juice
tea or coffee

SNACKS OR DRINKS AT PLANNED TIMES
5 fl oz (150 ml) skim milk, 5 fl oz (150 ml) natural yogurt, 1½-oz (45-g) muffin with 2 teaspoons (10 ml) low-fat spread, 1½ teaspoons (7.5 ml) raspberry jam

Serving Information
Men and Teenagers: Add ¾ oz (20 g) muesli at Morning Meal; 1 digestive biscuit, 4 fl oz (120 ml) orange juice
Teenagers: Add ½ pint (300 ml) skim milk

DAY 4

MORNING MEAL
½ medium banana
¾ oz (20 g) bran flakes
5 fl oz (150 ml) skim milk
tea or coffee

MIDDAY MEAL
2-egg omelette cooked in 1 teaspoon (5 ml) vegetable oil and filled with 3 oz (90 g) steamed mushrooms
green salad with lemon juice
1 oz (30 g) French bread with 2 teaspoons (10 ml) low-fat spread
5 oz (150 g) strawberries with 5 fl oz (150 ml) natural yogurt
tea or coffee

EVENING MEAL
3-4 oz (90-120 g) grilled chicken seasoned with barbecue spice and lemon juice
small tomatoes, onions, mushrooms, and 1-inch (2.5-cm) cubes green pepper skewered alternately and grilled with 1 teaspoon (5 ml) vegetable oil and garlic salt
4 oz (120 g) steamed rice
2-inch (5-cm) wedge honeydew melon
tea or coffee

SNACKS OR DRINKS AT PLANNED TIMES
5 fl oz (150 ml) skim milk

Serving Information
Men and Teenagers: Add ¾ oz (20 g) bran flakes and ½ medium banana at Morning Meal; 1 oz (30 g) French bread at Midday Meal; 2-inch (5-cm) wedge honeydew melon
Teenagers: Add ½ pint (300 ml) skim milk

DAY 5

MORNING MEAL
1 tablespoon (15 ml) peanut butter
½ medium banana and 1 teaspoon (5 ml) raspberry jam on 1 slice (1 oz/30 g) wholemeal bread
tea or coffee

MIDDAY MEAL
2 oz (60 g) Cheddar cheese grated finely over green salad with 1 medium sliced tomato, 3 oz (90 g) cooked beetroot
2 teaspoons (10 ml) low-calorie mayonnaise
4 oz (120 g) stewed apple with 2½ fl oz (75 ml) natural yogurt
tea or coffee

EVENING MEAL
3-4 oz (90-120 g) grilled plaice
6-oz (180-g) baked jacket potato with 2½ fl oz (75 ml) natural yogurt and chopped chives
3 oz (90 g) steamed cauliflower
3 oz (90 g) steamed courgettes
2 teaspoons (10 ml) low-fat spread
4 fl oz (120 ml) orange juice
tea or coffee

SNACKS OR DRINKS AT PLANNED TIMES
½ pint (300 ml) skim milk

Serving Information
Men and Teenagers: Add 3 oz (90 g) canned whole kernel sweet corn and 2 cream crackers at Midday Meal; 4 fl oz (120 ml) orange juice
Teenagers: Add ½ pint (300 ml) skim milk

MORNING MEAL
5 oz (150 g) blackberries on 2½ oz (75 g) cottage cheese
1 slice (1 oz/30 g) wholemeal bread
1 teaspoon (5 ml) margarine □ tea or coffee

MIDDAY MEAL
7-8 oz (210-240 g) baked beans on 1 slice (1 oz/30 g) bread, toasted
2 teaspoons (10 ml) low-fat spread
3 oz (90 g) steamed mushrooms
4 oz (120 g) canned peach slices
5 fl oz (150 ml) natural yogurt
tea or coffee

EVENING MEAL
Skate with Lemon Sauce (page 156)
3 oz (90 g) boiled potatoes, mashed with 1 teaspoon (5 ml) low-fat spread
3 oz (90 g) cooked green beans
3 oz (90 g) cooked carrots
2-inch (5-cm) wedge honeydew melon
4 fl oz (120 ml) white wine
tea or coffee

SNACKS OR DRINKS AT PLANNED TIMES
½ pint (300 ml) skim milk

Serving Information
Men and Teenagers: Add 1 slice (1 oz/30 g) bread, toasted, at Midday Meal; 3 oz (90 g) potatoes at Evening Meal; 1 medium apple and 2 medium plums
Teenagers: Add ½ pint (300 ml) skim milk

MORNING MEAL
2 tablespoons (30 ml) raisins
¾ oz (20 g) porridge oats cooked with water and served with 5 fl oz (150 ml) skim milk
tea or coffee

MIDDAY MEAL
Soused Herring (page 158)
6 oz (180 g) cooked potatoes, diced and mixed with 4 teaspoons (20 ml) low-calorie mayonnaise and 2 tablespoons (30 ml) chopped chives
3 oz (90 g) cooked beetroot with onion rings and wine vinegar
8 fl oz (240 ml) tomato juice with ice and lemon wedge
tea or coffee

EVENING MEAL
3-4 oz (90-120 g) grilled lamb chop
3 oz (90 g) cooked runner beans
3 oz (90 g) cooked courgettes
1 medium grilled tomato
1 teaspoon (5 ml) margarine
2 medium plums stewed with **Custard** (page 191)
tea or coffee

SNACKS OR DRINKS AT PLANNED TIMES
½ pint (300 ml) skim milk, 1 digestive biscuit

Serving Information
Men and Teenagers: Add ¾ oz (20 g) porridge oats at Morning Meal; 3 oz (90 g) canned whole kernel sweet corn at Evening Meal; 4 medium stewed plums at Evening Meal
Teenagers: Add ½ pint (300 ml) skim milk

MORNING MEAL
4 oz (120 g) canned apricots
¾ oz (20 g) wheat flakes with 5 fl oz (150 ml) skim milk
tea or coffee

MIDDAY MEAL
8 fl oz (240 ml) tomato juice
4 breadcrumbed fish fingers, grilled
3 oz (90 g) canned whole kernel sweet corn
3 oz (90 g) baked beans
2 medium tomatoes, grilled
tea or coffee

EVENING MEAL
5-6 oz (150-180 g) lamb's liver, sauteed in 1 teaspoon (5 ml) vegetable oil with 1 medium onion, sliced
3 oz (90 g) steamed runner beans
3 oz (90 g) steamed marrow
3 oz (90 g) steamed potatoes
2 teaspoons (10 ml) margarine
2½ oz (75 g) blackberries and 2 oz (60 g) apples, stewed, with 5 fl oz (150 ml) natural yogurt □ tea or coffee

SNACKS OR DRINKS AT PLANNED TIMES
5 fl oz (150 ml) skim milk

Serving Information
Men and Teenagers: Add ¾ oz (20 g) wheat flakes at Morning Meal; 3 oz (90 g) steamed potatoes at Evening Meal; 4 oz (120 g) canned apricots
Teenagers: Add ½ pint (300 ml) skim milk

MORNING MEAL
4 fl oz (120 ml) orange juice
1 egg scrambled in 1 teaspoon (5 ml) low-fat spread
1 oz (30 g) lean back bacon, grilled
¾ oz (20 g) crispbread
1 teaspoon (5 ml) marmalade □ tea or coffee

MIDDAY MEAL
2-inch (5-cm) wedge honeydew melon
3-4 oz (90-120 g) roast beef
2 teaspoons (10 ml) horseradish relish
3 oz (90 g) steamed turnips
3 oz (90 g) steamed carrots
3 oz (90 g) steamed runner beans
4 oz (120 g) fresh fruit salad □ tea or coffee

EVENING MEAL
Kipper Pate (page 156) and green salad with lemon juice
¾ oz (20 g) crispbread
¾ oz (20 g) scone with 2 teaspoons (10 ml) low-calorie strawberry jam
1 teaspoon (5 ml) low-fat spread □ tea or coffee

SNACKS OR DRINKS AT PLANNED TIMES
5 fl oz (150 ml) natural yogurt, with coffee flavouring, 5 fl oz (150 ml) skim milk

Serving Information
Men and Teenagers: Add 3 oz (90 g) steamed potatoes at Midday Meal; 4 oz (120 g) fresh fruit salad
Men: Add ½ oz (15 g) Cheddar cheese and 2 cream crackers
Teenagers: Add ½ pint (300 ml) skim milk

WEEK 31

Parsley is all too often dismissed as the bit of green which decorates a pile of sandwiches or a plate of fish, but it is actually a most valuable and versatile herb. The ancient Greeks used it in funeral rites and the Romans regarded it as a safeguard against intoxication and wore garlands of it to ward off the effects of wine. It has a sweet flavour which goes well with fish and is good in casseroles and vegetable dishes. You can grow it in shady, moist conditions but it needs help with germination – soaking the seeds first in lukewarm water can do the trick.

We suggest Parsley Soup as a slightly unusual use of this healthy herb.

DAY 1

MORNING MEAL
½ medium grapefruit
1 poached egg
1 slice (1 oz/30 g) bread, toasted
1 teaspoon (5 ml) margarine
tea or coffee

MIDDAY MEAL
Chick Pea Croquettes (page 165)
1 medium tomato, halved and grilled
green salad with onion and pepper rings
1 teaspoon (5 ml) vegetable oil with wine vinegar
1-oz (30-g) pitta bread
4 oz (120 g) fruit salad
tea or coffee

EVENING MEAL
3-4 oz (90-120 g) baked hake
3 oz (90 g) steamed carrots
3 oz (90 g) steamed courgettes
green salad with **Basic Vinaigrette** (page 183)
1 medium peach
tea or coffee

SNACKS OR DRINKS AT PLANNED TIMES
½ pint (300 ml) skim milk

Serving Information
Men and Teenagers: Add 4 oz (120 g) fruit salad, 1½-oz (45-g) scone with 2 teaspoons (10 ml) low-calorie jam
Men: Add ½ oz (15 g) grated Cheddar cheese at Midday Meal
Teenagers: Add 5 fl oz (150 ml) natural yogurt

DAY 4

MORNING MEAL
Oatmeal with Spiced Fruit Ambrosia (page 176)
tea or coffee

MIDDAY MEAL
3-4 oz (90-120 g) grilled liver
3 oz (90 g) steamed mushrooms
3 oz (90 g) cooked peas
2 oz (60 g) boiled rice
1 teaspoon (5 ml) margarine
sliced tomatoes and onion rings
Dijon-Herb Dressing (page 182)
2 canned pear halves
tea or coffee

EVENING MEAL
3-4 oz (90-120 g) grilled veal chop
3 oz (90 g) steamed green beans
3 oz (90 g) steamed carrots
3 oz (90 g) boiled potatoes
3 teaspoons (15 ml) low-fat spread
1 medium orange
tea or coffee

SNACKS OR DRINKS AT PLANNED TIMES
15 fl oz (450 ml) skim milk

Serving Information
Men and Teenagers: Add 4 fl oz (120 ml) orange juice, 2-oz (60-g) bread roll
Teenagers: Add ½ pint (300 ml) skim milk

DAY 5

MORNING MEAL
2½ fl oz (75 ml) apple juice
1 oz (30 g) Cheddar cheese
grilled on 1 slice (1 oz/30 g) bread, toasted
tea or coffee

MIDDAY MEAL
Salmon Salad (page 162) on shredded lettuce
3 oz (90 g) canned sweet corn
1 medium peach
tea or coffee

EVENING MEAL
Steak Pizzaiola with Spanish Sauce (page 139)
3 oz (90 g) steamed broccoli
mixed salad with shredded lettuce, sliced tomatoes, green pepper and onion rings
Savory Vinaigrette (page 183)
5 oz (150 g) blackcurrants, stewed
½ pint (300 ml) beer or cider
tea or coffee

SNACKS OR DRINKS AT PLANNED TIMES
5 fl oz (150 ml) natural yogurt, ½ pint (300 ml) skim milk

Serving Information
Men and Teenagers: Add 2½ fl oz (75 ml) apple juice, 3 oz (90 g) sweet corn and 3 oz (90 g) boiled potatoes
Teenagers: Add ½ pint (300 ml) skim milk

MORNING MEAL
½ medium banana, sliced on ¾ oz (20 g) cornflakes with 5 fl oz (150 ml) skim milk
tea or coffee

MIDDAY MEAL
Peach and Cottage Cheese Mould (page 126)
1 medium tomato sliced with onion rings
Basic Vinaigrette (page 183)
2 cream crackers
1 teaspoon (5 ml) margarine
Lemonade (page 188)
tea or coffee

EVENING MEAL
3-4 oz (90-120 g) grilled lamb chop
3 oz (90 g) cooked peas
3 oz (90 g) steamed green beans
3 oz (90 g) boiled potatoes
2 teaspoons (10 ml) margarine
5 oz (150 g) strawberries
tea or coffee

SNACKS OR DRINKS AT PLANNED TIMES
12½ fl oz (375 ml) skim milk

Serving Information
Men and Teenagers: Add ½ medium banana and 2 digestive biscuits
Teenagers: Add ½ pint (300 ml) skim milk

MORNING MEAL
4 fl oz (120 ml) orange juice
1 egg, scrambled in 1 teaspoon (5 ml) low-fat spread
1 slice (1 oz/30 g) bread, toasted
tea or coffee

MIDDAY MEAL
Parsley Soup (page 175)
3-4 oz (90-120 g) cooked chicken
mixed salad with shredded lettuce, sliced cucumber and tomato
2 teaspoons (10 ml) salad cream
2 cream crackers
2 medium plums
tea or coffee

EVENING MEAL
3-4 oz (90-120 g) grilled haddock dotted with 1 teaspoon (5 ml) low-fat spread
Savoury Grilled Tomatoes (page 172)
3 oz (90 g) steamed cauliflower
green salad with **Russian Dressing** (page 184)
5 oz (150 g) strawberries
4 fl oz (120 ml) wine
tea or coffee

SNACKS OR DRINKS AT PLANNED TIMES
5 fl oz (150 ml) natural yogurt, ½ pint (300 ml) skim milk

Serving Information
Men and Teenagers: Add 5 oz (150 g) strawberries, 1½-oz (45-g) crumpet with 2 teaspoons (10 ml) low-calorie jam
Teenagers: Add ½ pint (300 ml) skim milk

MORNING MEAL
1 medium peach, sliced
¾ oz (20 g) wheat flakes
5 fl oz (150 ml) skim milk
tea or coffee

MIDDAY MEAL
3 tablespoons (45 ml) peanut butter on 2 slices (1 oz/30 g each) wholemeal bread, toasted, with 3 oz (90 g) cucumber, cut into sticks
1 medium orange
tea or coffee

EVENING MEAL
Crepes Divan (page 124)
3 oz (90 g) steamed courgettes, sliced
4 fl oz (120 ml) white wine
Baked Apple (page 188)
tea or coffee

SNACKS OR DRINKS AT PLANNED TIMES
12½ fl oz (375 ml) skim milk

Serving Information
Men and Teenagers: Add 1 medium orange, 2-oz (60-g) scotch pancake with 2 teaspoons (10 ml) low-calorie jam
Teenagers: Add 5 fl oz (150 ml) natural yogurt

MORNING MEAL
Honey-Stewed Prunes (page 192)
1 egg, cooked in 1 teaspoon (5 ml) oil on 1 slice (1 oz/30 g) bread, toasted with 1 medium tomato, halved and grilled
tea or coffee

MIDDAY MEAL
3-4 oz (90-120 g) roast beef
3 oz (90 g) boiled potatoes
3 oz (90 g) steamed cabbage, shredded
3 oz (90 g) steamed carrots and turnips, diced, dotted with 1 teaspoon (5 ml) margarine
5 oz (150 g) gooseberries, stewed, served with 3 tablespoons (45 ml) single cream
tea or coffee

EVENING MEAL
8 fl oz (240 ml) tomato juice
3-4 oz (90-120 g) canned sardines with mixed salad of shredded lettuce, tomatoes, cucumber and spring onion
3 oz (90 g) boiled beetroot
2 teaspoons (10 ml) salad cream
1 medium portion stewed rhubarb
tea or coffee

SNACKS OR DRINKS AT PLANNED TIMES
5 fl oz (150 ml) natural yogurt, ½ pint (300 ml) skim milk

Serving Information
Men and Teenagers: Add 1 medium peach, 2 digestive biscuits
Teenagers: Add ½ pint (300 ml) skim milk

WEEK 32

Pasta is now a familiar and useful part of any cook's vocabulary. In its uncooked state it's either dried and brittle or fresh and soft, made from fine semolina mixed with water. It has long formed the staple diet of the Italians. We all know macaroni and spaghetti but many, many more forms can now be found; indeed there are over a hundred different shapes available. Some pasta is enriched by the addition of egg at the early mixing stage.

All pasta should be cooked in lots of boiling, salted water until it reaches the 'al dente' stage – soft but firm to the teeth.

Because pasta itself has little taste it is always combined with a highly flavoured sauce. Our recipe (Day 6) uses two cheeses – Danish Blue plus curd cheese with garlic, thyme, oregano and parsley to produce a very savoury dish.

DAY 1

MORNING MEAL
1 medium orange
1 oz (30 g) Edam cheese
1 slice (1 oz/30 g) wholemeal bread, toasted
tea or coffee

MIDDAY MEAL
3-4 oz (90-120 g) sliced roast chicken
1 medium tomato, sliced on shredded lettuce with sliced radishes and spring onion
2 teaspoons (10 ml) salad cream
1 slice (1 oz/30 g) wholemeal bread
5 oz (150 g) gooseberries, stewed with 1½ teaspoons (7.5 ml) honey
tea or coffee

EVENING MEAL
5-6 oz (150-180 g) uncooked chicken livers sauteed in 1 teaspoon (5 ml) oil with 2 oz (60 g) sliced onion
3 oz (90 g) steamed carrots dotted with 1 teaspoon (5 ml) margarine
4 oz (120 g) fruit salad
tea or coffee

SNACKS OR DRINKS AT PLANNED TIMES
5 fl oz (150 ml) natural yogurt, ½ pint (300 ml) skim milk

Serving Information
Men and Teenagers: Add 3 medium apricots, 1 medium corn on the cob, 1 digestive biscuit
Teenagers: Add ½ pint (300 ml) skim milk

DAY 4

MORNING MEAL
½ medium cantaloupe melon
1 egg, scrambled in 1 teaspoon (5 ml) margarine
1 slice (1 oz/30 g) bread, toasted
tea or coffee

MIDDAY MEAL
sardine open sandwich made with 3-4 oz (90-120 g) sardines on 1 slice (1 oz/30 g) wholemeal bread, topped with tomato and cucumber slices with 2 teaspoons (10 ml) low-calorie mayonnaise
1 medium plum
tea or coffee

EVENING MEAL
Sweet and Sour Chicken Stir-Fry (page 131)
3 oz (90 g) cooked sliced courgettes
3 oz (90 g) steamed cauliflower
4 oz (120 g) apple, stewed, with 5 fl oz (150 ml) natural yogurt
tea or coffee

SNACKS OR DRINKS AT PLANNED TIMES
½ pint (300 ml) skim milk

Serving Information
Men and Teenagers: Add 2 medium plums, 4 oz (120 g) cooked pasta
Teenagers: Add ½ pint (300 ml) skim milk

DAY 5

MORNING MEAL
4 fl oz (120 ml) orange juice
2½ oz (75 g) cottage cheese
¾ oz (20 g) melba toast
tea or coffee

MIDDAY MEAL
Egg Salad (page 123)
green salad with lemon juice
¾ oz (20 g) melba toast
4 oz (120 g) fruit salad
tea or coffee

EVENING MEAL
Green Bean and Red Cabbage Starter (page 114)
3-4 oz (90-120 g) grilled mackerel
1 medium tomato, grilled
5 oz (150 g) strawberries
2 oz (60 g) vanilla ice cream
tea or coffee

SNACKS OR DRINKS AT PLANNED TIMES
5 fl oz (150 ml) natural yogurt, ½ pint (300 ml) skim milk

Serving Information
Men and Teenagers: Add 4 oz (120 g) fruit salad, 4 cream crackers
Teenagers: Add ½ pint (300 ml) skim milk

MORNING MEAL
2½ fl oz (75 ml) pineapple juice
1 boiled egg
1 slice (1 oz/30 g) wholemeal bread, toasted
1 teaspoon (5 ml) margarine
tea or coffee

MIDDAY MEAL
3-4 oz (90-120 g) canned tuna in brine with mixed salad of
    shredded lettuce, sliced tomatoes and cucumber with 3 oz
    (90 g) cooked beetroot
2 teaspoons (10 ml) salad cream
2 water biscuits
5 oz (150 g) blackberries with 5 fl oz (150 ml) natural yogurt
tea or coffee

EVENING MEAL
8 fl oz (240 ml) tomato juice
Sesame Chicken with Green Beans (page 131)
3 oz (90 g) steamed marrow
tea or coffee

SNACKS OR DRINKS AT PLANNED TIMES
½ pint (300 ml) skim milk

Serving Information
Men and Teenagers: Add 2½ fl oz (75 ml) pineapple juice and
    3 oz (90 g) boiled potatoes, 1 slice (1 oz/30 g) wholemeal
    bread spread with 2 teaspoons (10 ml) low-calorie jam
Teenagers: Add ½ pint (300 ml) skim milk

MORNING MEAL
1 medium orange
Cinnamon-Cheese Toast (page 123)
tea or coffee

MIDDAY MEAL
3-4 oz (90-120 g) liver sausage with mixed green salad of lettuce,
    watercress, mustard and cress, spring onion and cucumber
3 oz (90 g) whole kernel sweet corn
2 teaspoons (10 ml) salad cream
2 medium plums
tea or coffee

EVENING MEAL
3-4 oz (90-120 g) Pacific prawns brushed with 1 teaspoon (5 ml)
    vegetable oil and grilled
3 oz (90 g) cooked peas
1 medium tomato, halved and grilled
3 oz (90 g) poached mushrooms dotted with 1 teaspoon (5 ml)
    margarine
4 oz (120 g) fruit salad
4 fl oz (120 ml) wine
tea or coffee

SNACKS OR DRINKS AT PLANNED TIMES
5 fl oz (150 ml) natural yogurt, ½ pint (300 ml) skim milk

Serving Information
Men and Teenagers: Add 2 medium plums, 3 oz (90 g) whole
    kernel sweet corn, 1 digestive biscuit
Teenagers: Add ½ pint (300 ml) skim milk

MORNING MEAL
4 fl oz (120 ml) orange juice
¾ oz (20 g) cornflakes
5 fl oz (150 ml) skim milk
tea or coffee

MIDDAY MEAL
Spaghetti Cheese with Herbs (page 124)
mixed salad of shredded lettuce, sliced tomatoes and cucumber
3 oz (90 g) cooked beetroot
2 teaspoons (10 ml) salad cream
5 oz (150 g) blackcurrants, stewed and served with 3
    tablespoons (45 ml) single cream
tea or coffee

EVENING MEAL
Oven-Baked Burgers (page 148)
3 oz (90 g) steamed courgettes
3 oz (90 g) steamed carrots
1 medium tomato, sliced, sprinkled with 1 teaspoon (5 ml) oil
    and wine vinegar
1 (2-oz/60-g) wholemeal bap
4 oz (120 g) fruit salad
tea or coffee

SNACKS OR DRINKS AT PLANNED TIMES
5 fl oz (150 ml) natural yogurt, 5 fl oz (150 ml) skim milk

Serving Information
Men and Teenagers: Add 4 fl oz (120 ml) orange juice, 1½-oz
    (45-g) scone with 2 teaspoons (10 ml) low-calorie jam
Teenagers: Add ½ pint (300 ml) skim milk

MORNING MEAL
4 fl oz (120 ml) orange juice
¾ oz (20 g) wheat flakes
5 fl oz (150 ml) skim milk
tea or coffee

MIDDAY MEAL
3-4 oz (90-120 g) grilled beef steak
1 medium tomato, halved and grilled
3 oz (90 g) cooked green beans
3 oz (90 g) cooked potatoes
1 teaspoon (5 ml) margarine
1 medium peach
tea or coffee

EVENING MEAL
8 fl oz (240 ml) tomato juice
Fish and Rice Salad (page 155)
mixed salad of shredded lettuce, sliced tomato and cucumber,
    spring onion and 2 oz (60 g) cooked beetroot
2 teaspoons (10 ml) salad cream
1 medium portion stewed rhubarb
tea or coffee

SNACKS OR DRINKS AT PLANNED TIMES
15 fl oz (450 ml) skim milk

Serving Information
Men and Teenagers: Add 4 fl oz (120 ml) orange juice,
    2 digestive biscuits
Men: Add extra 1 oz (30 g) smoked fish at Evening Meal
Teenagers: Add 5 fl oz (150 ml) natural yogurt

WEEK 33

Cold soups probably do not come to mind, in our climate, so readily as the warming hearty brews which we enjoy on chilly winter days. But in warmer parts of the world, cold savoury soups are a welcome item on the menu.

We suggest Gazpacho this week – hoping for a hot August spell. It's a cold vegetable soup, so full of summer's bounty that it could well be called a liquid salad. The original recipe comes from Spain – the Andalusian region. It is made from cucumbers, onions, tomatoes and green peppers with lemon juice and oil and, sometimes, breadcrumbs. It is highly seasoned and must be served chilled, with ice cubes actually added to the soup, or with each individual bowl sitting on a bed of crushed ice. Dishes of chopped vegetables are served with the soup, so that diners can add them as they wish to their own bowls.

DAY 1

MORNING MEAL
2-inch (5-cm) wedge honeydew melon
1 oz (30 g) Cheddar cheese, grated and grilled on 1 slice (1 oz/30 g) bread
tea or coffee

MIDDAY MEAL
Ginger-Grilled Chicken (page 130)
3 oz (90 g) cooked peas
3 oz (90 g) steamed whole green beans
green salad with red pepper rings
2 teaspoons (10 ml) mayonnaise
1 medium orange, peeled and diced
Custard (page 191)
tea or coffee

EVENING MEAL
cheese omelette made with 1 egg and 1 oz (30 g) Cheddar cheese, cooked in 2 teaspoons (10 ml) vegetable oil
3 oz (90 g) baked beans
3 oz (90 g) cooked spinach dotted with 1 teaspoon (5 ml) margarine
5 oz (150 g) blackcurrants
tea or coffee

SNACKS OR DRINKS AT PLANNED TIMES
15 fl oz (450 ml) skim milk

Serving Information
Men and Teenagers: Add 1 medium apple, 3 oz (90 g) baked beans, 1 slice (1 oz/30 g) bread, toasted
Teenagers: Add 5 fl oz (150 ml) natural yogurt

DAY 4

MORNING MEAL
1 medium orange
2½ oz (75 g) cottage cheese
¾ oz (20 g) crispbread
tea or coffee

MIDDAY MEAL
3-4 oz (90-120 g) grilled liver
3 oz (90 g) diced onion, sauteed in 1 teaspoon (5 ml) margarine
3 oz (90 g) steamed broccoli
3 oz (90 g) poached mushrooms
2 oz (60 g) cooked pasta shells
4 oz (120 g) canned peach slices and 2½ fl oz (75 ml) natural yogurt
tea or coffee

EVENING MEAL
3-4 oz (90-120 g) grilled chicken
3 oz (90 g) steamed cauliflower
3 oz (90 g) steamed green beans dotted with 2 teaspoons (10 ml) margarine
2½ fl oz (75 ml) natural yogurt with 4 oz (120 g) canned mandarin orange sections
tea or coffee

SNACKS OR DRINKS AT PLANNED TIMES
½ pint (300 ml) skim milk

Serving Information
Men and Teenagers: Add 5 oz (150 g) blackberries, 2 oz (60 g) cooked pasta, 1 digestive biscuit
Teenagers: Add 5 fl oz (150 ml) natural yogurt

DAY 5

MORNING MEAL
2½ fl oz (75 ml) apple juice
1 oz (30 g) Edam cheese sliced on ¾ oz (20 g) melba toast
tea or coffee

MIDDAY MEAL
Gazpacho (page 115)
3-4 oz (90-120 g) tuna
mixed salad of lettuce, tomato, radishes and spring onions
3 teaspoons (15 ml) salad cream
1 medium plum
tea or coffee

EVENING MEAL
3-4 oz (90-120 g) grilled pork chop
2 oz (60 g) cooked noodles
3 oz (90 g) steamed cabbage
3 oz (90 g) steamed carrots
2 teaspoons (10 ml) tomato relish
5 fl oz (150 ml) natural yogurt with 4 oz (120 g) fruit salad
tea or coffee

SNACKS OR DRINKS AT PLANNED TIMES
½ pint (300 ml) skim milk

Serving Information
Men and Teenagers: Add 2½ fl oz (75 ml) apple juice, 4 oz (120 g) cooked noodles
Teenagers: Add 5 fl oz (150 ml) natural yogurt

DAY 2

MORNING MEAL
½ medium grapefruit
¾ oz (20 g) ready-to-eat cereal
5 fl oz (150 ml) skim milk
tea or coffee

MIDDAY MEAL
5 oz (150 g) cottage cheese
1 medium tomato, sliced onto shredded lettuce with sliced
    cucumber and radishes
Cider Vinaigrette (page 183)
1 slice (1 oz/30 g) wholemeal bread
1 teaspoon (5 ml) margarine
4 oz (120 g) canned apricot halves
tea or coffee

EVENING MEAL
Frankfurter Stir-Fry (page 151)
3 oz (90 g) steamed courgettes
green salad with **Dijon-Herb Dressing** (page 182)
3 oz (90 g) boiled potatoes
tea or coffee

SNACKS OR DRINKS AT PLANNED TIMES
15 fl oz (450 ml) skim milk

Serving Information
Men and Teenagers: Add 1 medium apple, 3 oz (90 g) boiled
    potatoes, 1 digestive biscuit
Men: Add 1 oz (30 g) Frankfurter at Evening Meal
Teenagers: Add 5 fl oz (150 ml) natural yogurt

DAY 3

MORNING MEAL
5 oz (150 g) strawberries
¾ oz (20 g) muesli
5 fl oz (150 ml) skim milk □ tea or coffee

MIDDAY MEAL
egg and cheese salad made with 1 hard-boiled egg, chopped,
    and 1 oz (30 g) Cheddar cheese grated, piled onto shredded
    lettuce with 1 medium tomato, sliced, and 2-inch (5-cm)
    chunk cucumber, sliced
2 teaspoons (10 ml) salad cream
3 oz (90 g) baked beans
1 medium apple
tea or coffee

EVENING MEAL
3-4 oz (90-120 g) grilled sole with 2 teaspoons (10 ml)
    mayonnaise mixed with 1 teaspoon (5 ml) chopped capers
    (optional)
2 oz (60 g) cooked rice
3 oz (90 g) cooked carrots and turnips
3 oz (90 g) cooked broad beans
Baked Apple (page 188) with 2 oz (60 g) vanilla ice cream
tea or coffee

SNACKS OR DRINKS AT PLANNED TIMES
15 fl oz (450 ml) skim milk

Serving Information
Men and Teenagers: Add 1 medium orange, 3 oz (90 g) baked
    beans, 2 oz (60 g) cooked rice
Teenagers: Add 5 fl oz (150 ml) natural yogurt

DAY 6

MORNING MEAL
½ medium banana sliced on ¾ oz (20 g) ready-to-eat cereal
5 fl oz (150 ml) skim milk
tea or coffee

MIDDAY MEAL
3-4 oz (90-120 g) cold roast turkey
celery sticks and cucumber sticks with bean sprouts
Cider Vinaigrette (page 183)
3 oz (90 g) butter beans
2-inch (5-cm) wedge honeydew melon
½ pint (300 ml) beer or cider
tea or coffee

EVENING MEAL
3-4 oz (90-120 g) grilled mackerel
2 teaspoons (10 ml) cucumber relish
1 medium tomato, halved and grilled
3 oz (90 g) mushrooms, sauteed in 2 teaspoons (10 ml)
    vegetable oil
3 oz (90 g) boiled potatoes
2-oz (60-g) apple stewed with 2½ oz (75 g) blackberries
tea or coffee

SNACKS OR DRINKS AT PLANNED TIMES
15 fl oz (450 ml) skim milk

Serving Information
Men and Teenagers: Add ½ medium banana, 3 oz (90 g) butter
    beans, 3 oz (90 g) boiled potatoes
Teenagers: Add 5 fl oz (150 ml) natural yogurt

DAY 7

MORNING MEAL
2½ fl oz (75 ml) apple juice
1 oz (30 g) smoked salmon with lemon wedge
1 slice (1 oz/30 g) wholemeal bread
1 teaspoon (5 ml) margarine □ tea or coffee

MIDDAY MEAL
3-4 oz (90-120 g) dressed crab with mixed salad of lettuce,
    tomato, cucumber, spring onions and celery
3 oz (90 g) cooked beetroot
2 teaspoons (10 ml) low-calorie mayonnaise
Baked Apple (page 188)
Custard (page 191)
tea or coffee

EVENING MEAL
2-inch (5-cm) wedge honeydew melon
tomato omelette made with 2 eggs and 3 oz (90 g) tomatoes,
    skinned and chopped, cooked in 1 teaspoon (5 ml) vegetable
    oil
3 oz (90 g) baked beans
green salad with lemon juice
4 fl oz (120 ml) white wine
tea or coffee

SNACKS OR DRINKS AT PLANNED TIMES
15 fl oz (450 ml) skim milk

Serving Information
Men and Teenagers: Add 2½ fl oz (75 ml) apple juice, 3 oz (90 g)
    baked beans, 1 slice (1 oz/30 g) bread, toasted
Teenagers: Add 5 fl oz (150 ml) natural yogurt

WEEK 34

The second crop of strawberries – always cheaper than the early offerings – should be in the shops now and we suggest that you use them as your 'sweet treat' on Day 3. These sweet and juicy, rosy fruits are the essence of summer days and festivals, associated with Wimbledon and Henley and sunny picnics.

Another fruit included this week is the prune, but forget childhood memories of wrinkled prunes and custard. We have stewed them gently in a honey-sweetened liquid and you will find this very eatable! The prune is a dried plum – very nutritious – and it needs to be soaked before cooking to achieve the plump, shiny shape we like to see.

Mint Sauce accompanies the lamb on Day 7. You probably know the garden mint which is very common in this country (spearmint) but there are several others – apple mint, water mint, peppermint, eau de cologne mint. Records show that mint sauce was being made as far back as in the third century and it was certainly used by the Egyptians, the Greeks and the Romans.

DAY 1

MORNING MEAL
½ medium banana, sliced
¾ oz (20 g) muesli
5 fl oz (150 ml) skim milk
tea or coffee

MIDDAY MEAL
5 oz (150 g) cottage cheese, tomato and lettuce salad with 1 teaspoon (5 ml) salad cream
2 cream crackers
1 teaspoon (5 ml) low-fat spread
1 medium orange
tea or coffee

EVENING MEAL
Sole Veronique (page 158)
3 oz (90 g) steamed carrots
2 oz (60 g) boiled rice dotted with 1 teaspoon (5 ml) low-fat spread
1 medium portion stewed rhubarb
tea or coffee

SNACKS OR DRINKS AT PLANNED TIMES
12½ fl oz (375 ml) skim milk

Serving Information
Men and Teenagers: Add ½ medium banana, 2 slices (1 oz/30 g each) currant bread with 2 teaspoons (10 ml) low-calorie jam
Teenagers: Add 5 fl oz (150 ml) natural yogurt

DAY 4

MORNING MEAL
4 fl oz (120 ml) grapefruit juice
1 oz (30 g) Cheddar cheese
¾ oz (20 g) crispbread
tea or coffee

MIDDAY MEAL
pitta pocket made with 1-oz (30-g) pitta bread, split open to form a pocket and filled with 3-4 oz (90-120 g) diced cooked chicken, 1 medium tomato, diced, chopped watercress and 1 teaspoon (5 ml) mayonnaise
2 medium plums
tea or coffee

EVENING MEAL
5-6 oz (150-180 g) uncooked chicken livers sauteed in 2 teaspoons (10 ml) vegetable oil with 3 oz (90 g) diced onion
3 oz (90 g) cooked peas
5 oz (150 g) gooseberries stewed with 1½ teaspoons (7.5 ml) honey
tea or coffee

SNACKS OR DRINKS AT PLANNED TIMES
5 fl oz (150 ml) natural yogurt, ½ pint (300 ml) skim milk

Serving Information
Men and Teenagers: Add 4 fl oz (120 ml) grapefruit juice, 1 oz (30 g) pitta bread, 3 oz (90 g) boiled potatoes
Teenagers: Add ½ pint (300 ml) skim milk

DAY 5

MORNING MEAL
2½ fl oz (75 ml) pineapple juice
1 egg, scrambled in 1 teaspoon (5 ml) margarine
1 slice (1 oz/30 g) wholemeal bread, toasted
tea or coffee

MIDDAY MEAL
3-4 oz (90-120 g) tuna
mixed salad of shredded lettuce, 1 medium tomato, sliced, 2 spring onions, sliced
2 oz (60 g) boiled beetroot
1 slice (1 oz/30 g) wholemeal bread
2 teaspoons (10 ml) margarine
1 medium orange
tea or coffee

EVENING MEAL
Pork Chili Burgers (page 142)
3 oz (90 g) boiled turnips
3 oz (90 g) cooked runner beans
4 oz (120 g) fruit salad
4 fl oz (120 ml) wine
tea or coffee

SNACKS OR DRINKS AT PLANNED TIMES
15 fl oz (450 ml) skim milk

Serving Information
Men and Teenagers: Add 2½ fl oz (75 ml) pineapple juice, 1 slice (1 oz/30 g) wholemeal bread, 3 oz (90 g) whole kernel sweet corn
Teenagers: Add 5 fl oz (150 ml) natural yogurt

DAY 2

MORNING MEAL
4 fl oz (120 ml) grapefruit juice
1 boiled egg
1 slice (1 oz/30 g) bread
1 teaspoon (5 ml) margarine
tea or coffee

MIDDAY MEAL
Baked Haddock (page 155)
3 oz (90 g) steamed spinach
1 medium tomato, halved and grilled
2 oz (60 g) cooked noodles dotted with 1 teaspoon (5 ml)
     margarine
½ medium banana, sliced with 5 fl oz (150 ml) natural yogurt
tea or coffee

EVENING MEAL
3 oz (90 g) lean ham slices grilled with 2 slices canned pineapple
3 oz (90 g) cooked peas
mixed green salad with lemon juice and seasoning salt
tea or coffee

SNACKS OR DRINKS AT PLANNED TIMES
½ pint (300 ml) skim milk

Serving Information
Men and Teenagers: Add ½ medium banana, 1½-oz (45-g)
     crumpet, toasted and spread with 1 teaspoon (5 ml) golden
     syrup
Men: Add extra 1 oz (30 g) ham at Evening Meal
Teenagers: Add ½ pint (300 ml) skim milk

DAY 3

MORNING MEAL
Honey-Stewed Prunes (page 192)
2½ oz (75 g) cottage cheese
¾ oz (20 g) crispbread
tea or coffee

MIDDAY MEAL
Mushroom Omelette (page 120)
mixed salad of shredded lettuce, sliced cucumber and tomato
2 teaspoons (10 ml) mayonnaise
5 oz (150 g) damsons, stewed with 1 teaspoon (5 ml) honey
tea or coffee

EVENING MEAL
3-4 oz (90-120 g) grilled mackerel with lemon slices and 2
     teaspoons (10 ml) low-calorie salad dressing
3 oz (90 g) steamed broccoli
3 oz (90 g) steamed carrots
3 oz (90 g) boiled potatoes
1 teaspoon (5 ml) margarine
5 oz (150 g) strawberries with 3 tablespoons (45 ml) single
     cream
tea or coffee

SNACKS OR DRINKS AT PLANNED TIMES
5 fl oz (150 ml) natural yogurt, ½ pint (300 ml) skim milk

Serving Information
Men and Teenagers: Add 1 medium pear, 3 oz (90 g) boiled
     potatoes, 1 digestive biscuit
Teenagers: Add ½ pint (300 ml) skim milk

DAY 6

MORNING MEAL
1 medium orange
1 oz (30 g) Cheddar cheese
1 slice (1 oz/30 g) wholemeal bread
tea or coffee

MIDDAY MEAL
3-4 oz (90-120 g) cooked chicken and green salad with
     Basic Vinaigrette (page 183)
1 medium tomato, halved and topped with chopped onion and
     parsley
3 oz (90 g) whole kernel sweet corn
5 oz (150 g) blackberries with 2 oz (60 g) vanilla ice cream
tea or coffee

EVENING MEAL
Trout with Mushroom Stuffing (page 152)
3 oz (90 g) steamed spinach
3 oz (90 g) steamed carrots dotted with 1 teaspoon (5 ml)
     margarine
1 medium peach
tea or coffee

SNACKS OR DRINKS AT PLANNED TIMES
5 fl oz (150 ml) natural yogurt, ½ pint (300 ml) skim milk

Serving Information
Men and Teenagers: Add 4 oz (120 g) fruit salad, 1½-oz (45-g)
     scone with 2 teaspoons (10 ml) low-calorie jam
Teenagers: Add ½ pint (300 ml) skim milk

DAY 7

MORNING MEAL
4 oz (120 g) fruit salad
¾ oz (20 g) cornflakes
5 fl oz (150 ml) skim milk
tea or coffee

MIDDAY MEAL
3-4 oz (90-120 g) roast lamb with **Mint Sauce** (page 182)
3 oz (90 g) boiled potatoes
3 oz (90 g) steamed green beans
3 oz (90 g) steamed courgettes dotted with 2 teaspoons (10 ml)
     margarine
5 oz (150 g) strawberries with 2½ fl oz (75 ml) natural yogurt
tea or coffee

EVENING MEAL
7-8 oz (210-240 g) baked beans, heated and served on 1 slice
     (1 oz/30 g) wholemeal bread, toasted and spread with 1
     teaspoon (5 ml) margarine
1 medium tomato, halved and grilled
3 oz (90 g) poached mushrooms
3 oz (90 g) grapes
tea or coffee

SNACKS OR DRINKS AT PLANNED TIMES
½ pint (300 ml) skim milk

Serving Information
Men and Teenagers: Add 4 oz (120 g) fruit salad, 2 digestive
     biscuits
Teenagers: Add 5 fl oz (150 ml) natural yogurt

WEEK 35

The barbecue is a splendid invention, introduced to us by our American cousins. The word itself seems to have come from the French 'barbqueue' meaning 'beard to tail' – a very ancient method of cooking a trussed animal over direct heat. We know it now as a method of outdoor cooking on a grid or rack over hot charcoal. There are all sorts of special barbecue equipment available on the market now, but a home-made version of a metal tray to hold the coals beneath a rack to hold the food, all supported by two sides of stacked bricks produces perfectly good results.

The food to be cooked is often improved by being marinaded first, and the addition of herbs and sauces helps to strengthen the taste. For instance, we suggest a mixture of tomatoes, paprika, chili, mustard and cumin to marinade the pork chops on Day 1, and lemon juice and garlic to spice up the chicken on Day 2.

If the weather fails you, all the barbecued dishes can be cooked indoors, under your grill.

DAY 1

MORNING MEAL
4 oz (120 g) canned grapefruit sections
¾ oz (20 g) wheat flakes
5 fl oz (150 ml) skim milk □ tea or coffee

MIDDAY MEAL
3-4 oz (90-120 g) fresh sardines, barbecued or grilled
1 oz (30 g) French bread
1 teaspoon (5 ml) margarine
1 medium tomato, sliced with onion rings
Apple Slaw (page 180)
3 oz (90 g) cherries with 2½ fl oz (75 ml) natural yogurt
tea or coffee

EVENING MEAL
Barbecued Pork Chops (page 143)
3 oz (90 g) cooked peas
3 oz (90 g) cooked sweet corn
3-oz (90-g) baked jacket potato with 2½ fl oz (75 ml) natural yogurt and chopped chives
mixed green salad with **Basic Vinaigrette** (page 183)
4 oz (120 g) fresh fruit salad
2 oz (60 g) vanilla ice cream
tea or coffee

SNACKS OR DRINKS AT PLANNED TIMES
5 fl oz (150 ml) skim milk

Serving Information
Men and Teenagers: Add 3-oz (90-g) baked jacket potato, 4 oz (120 g) cherries, 2½ fl oz (75 ml) apple juice
Teenagers: Add ½ pint (300 ml) skim milk

DAY 4

MORNING MEAL
5 oz (150 g) cooked chilled blackberries
¾ oz (20 g) cornflakes
5 fl oz (150 ml) natural yogurt □ tea or coffee

MIDDAY MEAL
5-6 oz (150-180 g) lamb's liver sauteed in 1 teaspoon (5 ml) olive oil
Courgette Basil (page 170)
watercress and lettuce tossed with **Lemon Salad Dressing** (page 182)
1 medium peach
tea or coffee

EVENING MEAL
3-4 oz (90-120 g) roast turkey breast
3 oz (90 g) steamed baby carrots with 1 teaspoon (5 ml) low-fat spread
3 oz (90 g) steamed runner beans
6 oz (180 g) baked jacket potato with 2½ fl oz (75 ml) natural yogurt sprinkled with fresh chopped chives
tea or coffee

SNACKS OR DRINKS AT PLANNED TIMES
5 fl oz (150 ml) skim milk, 8 fl oz (240 ml) tomato juice

Serving Information
Men and Teenagers: Add 2 cream crackers sprinkled with 2 teaspoons (10 ml) grated cheese, 1 digestive biscuit, 2 medium plums
Teenagers: Add ½ pint (300 ml) skim milk

DAY 5

MORNING MEAL
8 fl oz (240 ml) tomato juice
1 poached egg
1 slice (1 oz/30 g) wholemeal bread, toasted
1 teaspoon (5 ml) margarine □ tea or coffee

MIDDAY MEAL
3-4 oz (90-120 g) cold roast turkey, sliced
3 oz (90 g) beansprouts, 1 medium tomato, sliced, 3 oz (90 g) cooked beetroot
½ recipe **Yogurt Dressing** (page 182)
1 slice (1 oz/30 g) wholemeal bread
2 teaspoons (10 ml) low-fat spread □ tea or coffee

EVENING MEAL
2-inch (5-cm) wedge honeydew melon
Marinated Rump Steak (page 150)
3 oz (90 g) steamed marrow
3 oz (90 g) cooked celery hearts
1 medium grilled tomato
2 oz (60 g) cooked ribbon noodles
2 teaspoons (10 ml) low-fat spread
5 oz (150 g) cooked damsons, chilled
2½ fl oz (75 ml) natural yogurt □ tea or coffee

SNACKS OR DRINKS AT PLANNED TIMES
½ pint (300 ml) skim milk

Serving Information
Men and Teenagers: Add 2 oz (60 g) cooked noodles at Evening Meal; 1 medium banana
Teenagers: Add 5 fl oz (150 ml) natural yogurt

DAY 2

MORNING MEAL
2½ fl oz (75 ml) apple juice
1 boiled egg
1 slice (1 oz/30 g) wholemeal bread, toasted
2 teaspoons (10 ml) low-fat spread
tea or coffee

MIDDAY MEAL
3 oz (90 g) smoked mackerel fillets
1 medium tomato, sliced with onion rings on lettuce with
  1 teaspoon (5 ml) mayonnaise
1 oz (30 g) French bread
1 teaspoon (5 ml) margarine
5 oz (150 g) strawberries □ tea or coffee

EVENING MEAL
3-4 oz (90-120 g) grilled or barbecued chicken, seasoned with
  lemon juice, herbs and garlic salt
2 medium grilled tomatoes
3 oz (90 g) baked beans
Pineapple Sorbet (page 190)
tea or coffee

SNACKS OR DRINKS AT PLANNED TIMES
½ pint (300 ml) skim milk

Serving Information
Men and Teenagers: Add 1-oz (30-g) wholemeal bread roll, 3 oz
  (90 g) canned whole kernel sweet corn at Evening Meal,
  1 medium orange, 2 medium plums
Men: Add 1 oz (30 g) smoked mackerel at Midday Meal
Teenagers: Add 5 fl oz (150 ml) natural yogurt

DAY 3

MORNING MEAL
4 fl oz (120 ml) orange juice
Cinnamon-Cheese Toast (page 123)
tea or coffee

MIDDAY MEAL
2 poached eggs on 6 oz (180 g) steamed spinach
1-oz (30-g) wholemeal bread roll
2 teaspoons (10 ml) low-fat spread
2 medium plums
tea or coffee

EVENING MEAL
3-4 oz (90-120 g) scampi, brushed with 1 teaspoon (5 ml) corn oil
  and grilled or barbecued
2 oz (60 g) cooked rice
Chinese Cabbage and Tomato Medley (page 171)
dash soy sauce
tea or coffee

SNACKS OR DRINKS AT PLANNED TIMES
1 medium peach, sliced with 5 fl oz (150 ml) natural yogurt,
  ½ pint (300 ml) skim milk

Serving Information
Men and Teenagers: Add 4 oz (120 g) cooked rice at Evening
  Meal; 2 medium plums
Teenagers: Add ½ pint (300 ml) skim milk

DAY 6

MORNING MEAL
2-inch (5-cm) wedge honeydew melon
2½ oz (75 g) cottage cheese with 2 teaspoons (10 ml) low-
  calorie blackcurrant jam on 1 slice (1 oz/30 g) wholemeal
  bread, toasted
tea or coffee

MIDDAY MEAL
Chili-Cheese Rarebit (page 119)
mixed green salad with lemon juice
tea or coffee

EVENING MEAL
Chicken Kebabs (page 128)
mushroom and beansprout salad with 1 teaspoon (5 ml)
  vegetable oil and wine vinegar
1oz (30 g) French bread
1 teaspoon (5 ml) margarine
4 fl oz (120 ml) white wine
2 medium dessert plums
tea or coffee

SNACKS OR DRINKS AT PLANNED TIMES
5 fl oz (150 ml) skim milk, 5 fl oz (150 ml) natural yogurt with 5 oz
  (150 g) stewed blackberries, **Coconut-Coffee Mounds** (page
  192)

Serving Information
Men and Teenagers: Add 1 slice (1 oz/30 g) French bread,
  1 digestive biscuit, 1 medium banana
Teenagers: Add ½ pint (300 ml) skim milk

DAY 7

MORNING MEAL
4 fl oz (120 ml) orange juice
¾ oz (20 g) wheat flakes
5 fl oz (150 ml) skim milk □ tea or coffee

MIDDAY MEAL
Lemon-Minted Lamb (page 138)
3 oz (90 g) steamed French beans
3 oz (90 g) steamed courgettes
1 medium grilled tomato
3-oz (90-g) baked jacket potato
1 teaspoon (5 ml) low-fat spread
2½ oz (75 g) cooked blackberries
2 oz (60 g) cooked apple, sliced
2½ fl oz (75 ml) natural yogurt □ tea or coffee

EVENING MEAL
1 medium corn-on-the-cob, cooked
1 teaspoon (5 ml) low-fat spread
3-4 oz (90-120 g) grilled lemon sole or plaice with lemon juice
mixed green salad with **Basic Vinaigrette** (page 183)
1 medium peach
tea or coffee

SNACKS OR DRINKS AT PLANNED TIMES
½ pint (300 ml) skim milk

Serving Information
Men and Teenagers: Add 3-oz (90-g) baked jacket potato at
  Midday Meal; 1 digestive biscuit, 4 fl oz (120 ml) orange juice,
  2 medium dessert plums
Teenagers: Add 5 fl oz (150 ml) natural yogurt

WEEK 36

You will find references to steamed vegetables this week. Steaming is the best way to cook vegetables. It ensures that you don't end up with a water-sodden and overcooked mess to accompany your main course. The vegetables are placed in a perforated container which is then fitted over a pan in which a small amount of water is kept at a gentle boil. The food cooks in the steam which rises from the water. It keeps its colour and shape and flavour and retains all the nutrients which would have been lost in the water during more conventional cooking methods. Be sure to fit a lid over the steamer top to keep the steam in. If you don't possess a traditional steamer – (like a double saucepan but with the upper pan having a perforated base) you can use a metal colander or buy the inexpensive collapsible 'daisy' steamer which fits into any size of pan.

DAY 1

MORNING MEAL
½ medium cantaloupe melon
2½ oz (75 g) quark or cottage cheese
2 water biscuits
1 teaspoon (5 ml) margarine
tea or coffee

MIDDAY MEAL
open sandwich made with
    1 slice (1 oz/30 g) wholemeal bread with 1 teaspoon (5 ml) margarine, shredded lettuce topped with 3-4 oz (90-120 g) sardines, sliced tomatoes and 2 teaspoons (10 ml) low-calorie mayonnaise
1 medium apple
tea or coffee

EVENING MEAL
3-4 oz (90-120 g) grilled plaice with lemon juice
3 oz (90 g) steamed broccoli
3 oz (90 g) boiled carrots
Curried Coleslaw (page 178)
5 oz (150 g) strawberries
tea or coffee

SNACKS OR DRINKS AT PLANNED TIMES
5 fl oz (150 ml) natural yogurt, ½ pint (300 ml) skim milk

Serving Information
Men and Teenagers: Add 4 oz (120 g) fruit salad, 4 oz (120 g) boiled rice
Teenagers: Add ½ pint (300 ml) skim milk

DAY 4

MORNING MEAL
2½ fl oz (75 ml) apple juice
1 egg, scrambled in 1 teaspoon (5 ml) margarine
1 slice (1 oz/30 g) wholemeal bread, toasted
tea or coffee

MIDDAY MEAL
open cheese sandwich made
    with 1 slice (1 oz/30 g) wholemeal bread, 2 oz (60 g) grated Cheddar cheese, sliced tomatoes and watercress
1 medium orange
½ pint (300 ml) beer or cider
tea or coffee

EVENING MEAL
3-4 oz (90-120 g) roast chicken
3 oz (90 g) steamed swede
3 oz (90 g) steamed cabbage, dotted with 2 teaspoons (10 ml) margarine
4 oz (120 g) canned peach slices
tea or coffee

SNACKS OR DRINKS AT PLANNED TIMES
5 fl oz (150 ml) natural yogurt, ½ pint (300 ml) skim milk

Serving Information
Men and Teenagers: Add 2½ fl oz (75 ml) apple juice, 1 slice (1 oz/30 g) wholemeal bread, 2 oz (60 g) cooked noodles
Teenagers: Add ½ pint (300 ml) skim milk

DAY 5

MORNING MEAL
½ medium cantaloupe melon
¾ oz (20 g) porridge oats cooked with water
5 fl oz (150 ml) skim milk
tea or coffee

MIDDAY MEAL
5 oz (150 g) cottage cheese mixed with 3 oz (90 g) diced green pepper and 1 tablespoon (15 ml) diced onion
green salad with **Basic Vinaigrette** (page 183)
¾ oz (20 g) melba toast
1 medium peach
tea or coffee

EVENING MEAL
Chicken Livers Sauteed in Wine (page 144)
2 oz (60 g) cooked rice
3 oz (90 g) steamed asparagus
3 oz (90 g) steamed red pepper rings
2 medium plums
tea or coffee

SNACKS OR DRINKS AT PLANNED TIMES
15 fl oz (450 ml) skim milk

Serving Information
Men and Teenagers: Add 2 medium plums, 2 oz (60 g) cooked rice, 1 digestive biscuit
Teenagers: Add 5 fl oz (150 ml) natural yogurt

DAY 2

MORNING MEAL
2½ fl oz (75 ml) apple juice
¾ oz (20 g) oatmeal cooked with water
5 fl oz (150 ml) skim milk
tea and coffee

MIDDAY MEAL
3-4 oz (90-120 g) liver sausage
mixed salad made with shredded lettuce, sliced tomato and
    cucumber
1 slice (1 oz/30 g) wholemeal bread
Basic Vinaigrette (page 183)
5 oz (150 g) raspberries
tea or coffee

EVENING MEAL
3-4 oz (90-120 g) grilled chicken
1 oz (30 g) lean back bacon, grilled
3 oz (90 g) cooked peas
3 oz (90 g) cooked green beans
2 oz (60 g) boiled rice dotted with 2 teaspoons (10 ml) margarine
tea or coffee

SNACKS OR DRINKS AT PLANNED TIMES
15 fl oz (450 ml) skim milk, 1 medium orange

Serving Information
Men and Teenagers: Add 1 medium pear, 1½-oz (45-g) scone
    with 1 teaspoon (5 ml) honey
Teenagers: Add 5 fl oz (150 ml) natural yogurt

DAY 3

MORNING MEAL
½ medium grapefruit
¾ oz (20 g) cornflakes
5 fl oz (150 ml) skim milk
tea or coffee

MIDDAY MEAL
3-4 oz (90-120 g) salmon with mixed salad of lettuce,
    watercress, cucumber, radishes and tomatoes
2 teaspoons (10 ml) mayonnaise
1 slice (1 oz/30 g) bread
1 teaspoon (5 ml) margarine
1 medium pear
tea or coffee

EVENING MEAL
3-4 oz (90-120 g) grilled herring
3-oz (90-g) cooked mashed potato
3 oz (90 g) steamed spinach
3 oz (90 g) steamed courgettes
4 oz (120 g) fruit salad
tea or coffee

SNACKS OR DRINKS AT PLANNED TIMES
15 fl oz (450 ml) skim milk

Serving Information
Men and Teenagers: Add ½ medium grapefruit, 2 digestive
    biscuits
Teenagers: Add 5 fl oz (150 ml) natural yogurt

DAY 6

MORNING MEAL
½ medium grapefruit
1 tablespoon (15 ml) crunchy peanut butter
¾ oz (20 g) crispbread
tea or coffee

MIDDAY MEAL
French Omelette (page 120)
1 medium tomato, sliced
green salad with 2 teaspoons (10 ml) salad cream
1 slice (1 oz/30 g) bread
4 oz (120 g) canned peach slices
tea or coffee

EVENING MEAL
Cod-Vegetable Bake (page 154)
3 oz (90 g) steamed green beans
1 medium kiwi fruit
tea or coffee

SNACKS OR DRINKS AT PLANNED TIMES
5 fl oz (150 ml) natural yogurt, ½ pint (300 ml) skim milk

Serving Information
Men and Teenagers: Add 1 medium kiwi fruit, 3 oz (90 g) boiled
    potatoes, 1-oz (30-g) Scotch pancake with 2 teaspoons (10 ml)
    low-calorie jam
Teenagers: Add ½ pint (300 ml) skim milk

DAY 7

MORNING MEAL
½ medium grapefruit
1 egg, poached
1 slice (1 oz/30 g) brown bread, toasted
1 teaspoon (5 ml) margarine
tea or coffee

MIDDAY MEAL
3-4 oz (90-120 g) roast beef
3-oz (90-g) baked jacket potato
3 oz (90 g) cooked parsnips
3 oz (90 g) whole small onions, baked in 2 teaspoons (10 ml) oil
4 oz (120 g) fruit salad with 3 tablespoons (45 ml) single cream
tea or coffee

EVENING MEAL
3-4 oz (90-120 g) canned tuna
    with mixed salad of shredded lettuce, watercress and chicory,
    sliced tomatoes and cucumber
2 teaspoons (10 ml) low-calorie dressing
1 medium pear
tea or coffee

SNACKS OR DRINKS AT PLANNED TIMES
5 fl oz (150 ml) natural yogurt, ½ pint (300 ml) skim milk

Serving Information
Men and Teenagers: Add 4 oz (120 g) fruit salad, 3 oz (90 g)
    whole kernel sweet corn, 1 digestive biscuit
Teenagers: Add ½ pint (300 ml) skim milk

WEEK 37

The September crop of apples should be in the shops now – or in your garden if you're lucky enough to have fruit trees there. What a useful and versatile fruit the apple is. It can be eaten fresh, or cooked in one of a score of different ways. It makes a marvellous pudding or pie, accompanies savoury dishes as a piquant chutney or sauce. It is easily cooked and pureed, freezes well and can be dried. A crisp apple, eaten after a meal, cleanses the teeth and is said to kill off unhealthy germs in the stomach. We all know that 'an apple a day keeps the doctor away'. The most famous British dessert apple is the Cox's Orange Pippin and the Bramley is incomparably the finest cooking apple. Apples from France, Canada, Australia and New Zealand flood our shops of course, but there is little to beat the home-grown product.

DAY 1

MORNING MEAL
2-inch (5-cm) wedge honeydew melon
1 boiled egg
1 slice (1 oz/30 g) wholemeal bread, toasted
1 teaspoon (5 ml) margarine
tea or coffee

MIDDAY MEAL
prawn cocktail salad made with 3-4 oz (90-120 g) peeled prawns, shredded lettuce, sliced cucumber and 1 medium tomato, cut into quarters
2 teaspoons (10 ml) salad cream mixed with 1 teaspoon (5 ml) tomato ketchup and a dash of Worcestershire sauce
1 slice (1 oz/30 g) wholemeal bread
3 oz (90 g) grapes
tea or coffee

EVENING MEAL
Tomato Soup (page 111)
Crepes Divan (page 124)
3 oz (90 g) steamed whole green beans
4 oz (120 g) canned pineapple
4 fl oz (120 ml) white wine
tea or coffee

SNACKS OR DRINKS AT PLANNED TIMES
5 fl oz (150 ml) natural yogurt, 7½ fl oz (225 ml) skim milk

Serving Information
Men and Teenagers: Add 3 oz (90 g) grapes, 1 slice (1 oz/30 g) wholemeal bread, 2 oz (60 g) boiled rice
Teenagers: Add ½ pint (300 ml) skim milk

DAY 4

MORNING MEAL
½ medium grapefruit
¾ oz (20 g) cornflakes
5 fl oz (150 ml) skim milk
tea or coffee

MIDDAY MEAL
Tuna-Potato Cakes (page 163)
mixed salad made of shredded lettuce, sliced tomatoes and cucumber with 1 teaspoon (5 ml) mayonnaise
Baked Apple (page 188)
tea or coffee

EVENING MEAL
3-4 oz (90-120 g) grilled chicken
3 oz (90 g) cooked green beans
2 oz (60 g) cooked rice
Cole Slaw Vinaigrette (page 178)
4 oz (120 g) canned peach slices
tea or coffee

SNACKS OR DRINKS AT PLANNED TIMES
15 fl oz (450 ml) skim milk

Serving Information
Men and Teenagers: Add 4 fl oz (120 ml) orange juice, 3 oz (90 g) whole kernel sweet corn, 2 cream crackers with 2 teaspoons (10 ml) low-calorie jam
Teenagers: Add 5 fl oz (150 ml) natural yogurt

DAY 5

MORNING MEAL
2½ fl oz (75 ml) apple juice
Cinnamon-Cheese Toast (page 123)
tea or coffee

MIDDAY MEAL
Curried Beef (page 150)
3 oz (90 g) cooked peas
3 oz (90 g) cooked carrots mashed with 3 oz (90 g) cooked potato
5 fl oz (150 ml) natural yogurt
2 oz (60 g) canned pineapple cubes
tea or coffee

EVENING MEAL
Fillet of Sole Florentine (page 159)
3 oz (90 g) steamed green beans
1½ teaspoons (7.5 ml) margarine
5 oz (150 g) strawberries
4 fl oz (120 ml) wine
tea or coffee

SNACKS OR DRINKS AT PLANNED TIMES
½ pint (300 ml) skim milk

Serving Information
Men and Teenagers: Add 2½ fl oz (75 ml) apple juice, 3 oz (90 g) whole kernel sweet corn, 1 digestive biscuit
Teenagers: Add ½ pint (300 ml) skim milk

DAY 2

MORNING MEAL
4 fl oz (120 ml) grapefruit juice
¾ oz (20 g) porridge oats cooked with water
5 fl oz (150 ml) skim milk
tea or coffee

MIDDAY MEAL
Liver Venetian (page 143)
3 oz (90 g) cooked green beans
salad of sliced red pepper and shredded lettuce with 1½
    teaspoons (7.5 ml) mayonnaise
2 oz (60 g) cooked rice
1 medium apple
tea or coffee

EVENING MEAL
Turkey and Cheese Layer (page 128)
3 oz (90 g) steamed courgettes
green salad with 1 teaspoon (5 ml) mayonnaise
4 oz (120 g) canned fruit salad
tea or coffee

SNACKS OR DRINKS AT PLANNED TIMES
15 fl oz (450 ml) skim milk

Serving Information
Men and Teenagers: Add 1 medium orange, ¾ oz (20 g)
    porridge oats, 2 oz (60 g) cooked rice
Teenagers: Add 5 fl oz (150 ml) natural yogurt

DAY 3

MORNING MEAL
4 oz (120 g) canned fruit salad
1 tablespoon (15 ml) peanut butter
¾ oz (20 g) crispbread
tea or coffee

MIDDAY MEAL
Split Pea Soup (page 164)
2 water biscuits
1 teaspoon (5 ml) margarine
1 medium orange, peeled and sliced
2 oz (60 g) vanilla ice cream
tea or coffee

EVENING MEAL
3-4 oz (90-120 g) grilled lean pork chop with 1 medium apple,
    peeled, cored and sliced in rings, sprinkled with lemon juice
    and grilled until tender
3 oz (90 g) cooked peas
1 medium tomato, halved and grilled
3 oz (90 g) steamed broccoli
tea or coffee

SNACKS OR DRINKS AT PLANNED TIMES
17½ fl oz (525 ml) skim milk

Serving Information
Men and Teenagers: Add 4 oz (120 g) canned pineapple, 2 water
    biscuits, 1 digestive biscuit
Men: Add to soup at Midday Meal 2 oz (60 g) baked beans
Teenagers: Add 5 fl oz (150 ml) natural yogurt

DAY 6

MORNING MEAL
2-inch (5-cm) wedge honeydew melon
1 poached egg
1 slice (1 oz/30 g) bread, toasted
1 teaspoon (5 ml) margarine
tea or coffee

MIDDAY MEAL
3-4 oz (90-120 g) grilled veal
1 medium tomato, halved and grilled
3 oz (90 g) steamed broccoli
3 oz (90 g) steamed carrots dotted with 1 teaspoon (5 ml)
    margarine
1 medium apple
tea or coffee

EVENING MEAL
cheese salad made with shredded lettuce, sliced tomatoes and
    cucumber, spring onion and 2 oz (60 g) grated cheese
3 oz (90 g) boiled beetroot
3 oz (90 g) whole kernel sweet corn
2 teaspoons (10 ml) salad cream
4 oz (120 g) fruit salad
tea or coffee

SNACKS OR DRINKS AT PLANNED TIMES
5 fl oz (150 ml) natural yogurt, ½ pint (300 ml) skim milk

Serving Information
Men and Teenagers: Add 4 oz (120 g) fruit salad, 1½-oz (45-g)
    scone spread with 2 teaspoons (10 ml) low-calorie jam
Teenagers: Add ½ pint (300 ml) skim milk

DAY 7

MORNING MEAL
Honey-Stewed Prunes (page 192)
¾ oz (20 g) wheat flakes
5 fl oz (150 ml) skim milk
tea or coffee

MIDDAY MEAL
3-4 oz (90-120 g) roast lamb
3 oz (90 g) cooked peas
3 oz (90 g) steamed Brussels sprouts
3-oz (90-g) baked jacket potato
2 teaspoons (10 ml) margarine
2-inch (5-cm) wedge honeydew melon
tea or coffee

EVENING MEAL
3-4 oz (90-120 g) grilled plaice dotted with 1 teaspoon (5 ml)
    margarine
3 oz (90 g) steamed broccoli
3 oz (90 g) cooked swede
2 oz (60 g) cooked rice
4 oz (120 g) canned pineapple chunks
tea or coffee

SNACKS OR DRINKS AT PLANNED TIMES
15 fl oz (450 ml) skim milk

Serving Information
Men and Teenagers: Add 2 canned pear halves, 1½-oz (45-g)
    crumpet with 1 teaspoon (5 ml) honey
Teenagers: Add 5 fl oz (150 ml) natural yogurt

WEEK 38

Dried peas, beans, lentils (pulses) are an excellent source of nourishment. They supply protein, iron and other minerals. Usually they need the addition of strong flavouring as their own taste is rather bland and dull. Most pulses require an overnight soak followed by long, gentle cooking, and they keep well in the fridge, after cooking, for about seven days or for several months in the freezer. A great benefit of the pulse group is its low price. It costs considerably less to provide protein for the family with pulses than with conventional meals of meat, fish, etc.

Our suggested dishes combine pulses with a wide variety of flavours, from tomatoes, cheese and herbs in 'Cheese and Lentil Bake' to mushrooms with onion and garlic in 'Greek Style Beans'. We give cooking methods in full detail, so don't be nervous to tackle these recipes, even if the whole subject of pulses is new to you.

DAY 1

MORNING MEAL
½ medium grapefruit
¾ oz (20 g) porridge oats cooked with water, served with 5 fl oz (150 ml) skim milk
tea or coffee

MIDDAY MEAL
3-4 oz (90-120 g) tuna
green salad with lemon juice
3 oz (90 g) cooked beetroot
1 medium tomato
3 oz (90 g) canned whole kernel sweet corn
1 medium apple
tea or coffee

EVENING MEAL
Chick Peas Neopolitan (page 164)
1 medium pear, with 5 fl oz (150 ml) natural yogurt
tea or coffee

SNACKS OR DRINKS AT PLANNED TIMES
5 fl oz (150 ml) skim milk

Serving Information
Men and Teenagers: Add 2 oz (60 g) French bread at Midday Meal; ½ medium grapefruit
Men: Add 2 oz (60 g) cooked red kidney beans at Evening Meal
Teenagers: Add ½ pint (300 ml) skim milk

DAY 4

MORNING MEAL
½ medium grapefruit
1 oz (30 g) smoked salmon
1 slice (1 oz/30 g) wholemeal bread
tea or coffee

MIDDAY MEAL
Mushroom and Lentil Pate (page 165)
green salad with lemon juice
1 oz (30 g) dried apricots chopped, mixed with 5 fl oz (150 ml) natural yogurt
tea or coffee

EVENING MEAL
2-egg omelette cooked in 1 teaspoon (5 ml) vegetable oil
2 medium grilled tomatoes
3 oz (90 g) steamed broccoli
watercress
tea or coffee

SNACKS OR DRINKS AT PLANNED TIMES
½ pint (300 ml) skim milk, 1 medium apple, 1½-oz (45-g) scone with 1½ teaspoons (7.5 ml) raspberry jam

Serving Information
Men and Teenagers: Add 1 digestive biscuit, 1 medium banana
Men: Add ¼ oz (7.5 g) grated Cheddar cheese on 2 water biscuits at Midday Meal
Teenagers: Add ½ pint (300 ml) skim milk

DAY 5

MORNING MEAL
4 oz (120 g) canned sliced peaches
¾ oz (20 g) cornflakes with 5 fl oz (150 ml) skim milk
tea or coffee

MIDDAY MEAL
3-4 oz (90-120 g) peeled prawns
green salad with spring onions and celery
1 teaspoon (5 ml) mayonnaise
1 medium tomato
3 oz (90 g) cooked beetroot
1 slice (1 oz/30 g) wholemeal bread
1 teaspoon (5 ml) low-fat spread
1 medium orange
5 fl oz (150 ml) natural yogurt
tea or coffee

EVENING MEAL
Austrian Beans (page 166)
4 oz (120 g) cooked rice
3 oz (90 g) cooked green beans
5 oz (150 g) orange-flavoured jelly
tea or coffee

SNACKS OR DRINKS AT PLANNED TIMES
5 fl oz (150 ml) skim milk

Serving Information
Men and Teenagers: Add 2 oz (60 g) cooked rice at Evening Meal; 1 medium apple
Men: Add 2 oz (60 g) cooked butter beans at Evening Meal
Teenagers: Add ½ pint (300 ml) skim milk

DAY 2

MORNING MEAL
4 fl oz (120 ml) orange juice
3 oz (90 g) baked beans
1 slice (1 oz/30 g) bread
2 teaspoons (10 ml) low-fat spread
tea or coffee

MIDDAY MEAL
Bean Soup (page 167)
4 oz (120 g) canned peaches
tea or coffee

EVENING MEAL
5-6 oz (130-180 g) uncooked liver, sauteed in 2 teaspoons
   (10 ml) olive oil
3 oz (90 g) steamed cauliflower
3 oz (90 g) steamed potatoes
3 oz (90 g) steamed carrots
1 medium apple
tea or coffee

SNACKS OR DRINKS AT PLANNED TIMES
1 medium portion rhubarb stewed with 5 fl oz (150 ml) natural
   yogurt, ½ pint (300 ml) skim milk

Serving Information
Men and Teenagers: Add 3 oz (90 g) steamed potatoes at
   Evening Meal; 4 fl oz (120 ml) orange juice
Men: Add ½ oz (15 g) grated Cheddar cheese with 2 water
   biscuits at Midday Meal
Teenagers: Add ½ pint (300 ml) skim milk

DAY 3

MORNING MEAL
1 medium banana
¾ oz (20 g) muesli with 5 fl oz (150 ml) skim milk
tea or coffee

MIDDAY MEAL
3-4 oz (90-120 g) lamb chop, grilled
3 oz (90 g) cooked cabbage
3 oz (90 g) cooked potatoes
4 fl oz (120 ml) orange juice
tea or coffee

EVENING MEAL
Greek-Style Beans with Mushrooms (page 164)
2 oz (60 g) French bread
4 fl oz (120 ml) red or white wine
5 fl oz (150 ml) natural yogurt with coffee flavouring and artificial
   sweetener
tea or coffee

SNACKS OR DRINKS AT PLANNED TIMES
5 fl oz (150 ml) skim milk

Serving Information
Men and Teenagers: Add 3 oz (90 g) cooked potatoes at Midday
   Meal, ¾ oz (20 g) muesli at Morning Meal; 2 tablespoons (30
   ml) sultanas
Men: Add 2 oz (60 g) cooked butter beans at Evening Meal
Teenagers: Add ½ pint (300 ml) skim milk

DAY 6

MORNING MEAL
4 oz (120 g) canned pineapple
2½ oz (75 g) cottage cheese
¾ oz (20 g) crispbread
1 teaspoon (5 ml) margarine
tea or coffee

MIDDAY MEAL
3-4 oz (90-120 g) grilled beef sausages
3 oz (90 g) baked beans
1 medium grilled tomato
1 oz (30 g) pitta bread
2 teaspoons (10 ml) margarine
1 medium orange
tea or coffee

EVENING MEAL
3-4 oz (90-120 g) roast chicken
3 oz (90 g) cooked carrots
3 oz (90 g) cooked spring greens
5 oz (150 g) stewed blackcurrants
tea or coffee

SNACKS OR DRINKS AT PLANNED TIMES
5 fl oz (150 ml) skim milk, 5 fl oz (150 ml) natural yogurt

Serving Information
Men and Teenagers: Add 6-oz (180-g) baked jacket potato at
   Evening Meal, 1 medium banana
Teenagers: Add ½ pint (300 ml) skim milk

DAY 7

MORNING MEAL
4 fl oz (120 ml) orange juice
1 poached egg
1 oz (30 g) lean grilled back bacon
1 slice (1 oz/30 g) wholemeal bread
2 teaspoons (10 ml) low-fat spread
tea or coffee

MIDDAY MEAL
3-4 oz (90-120 g) grilled halibut
3 oz (90 g) steamed cauliflower
3 oz (90 g) steamed carrots
3 oz (90 g) canned celery hearts
2 teaspoons (10 ml) margarine
2 canned pear halves with 2½ fl oz (75 ml) natural yogurt and 1
   teaspoon (5 ml) chocolate sauce
tea or coffee

EVENING MEAL
Bean and Cheese Potatoes (page 167)
8 fl oz (240 ml) tomato juice
tea or coffee

SNACKS OR DRINKS AT PLANNED TIMES
7½ fl oz (225 ml) skim milk, 2½ fl oz (75 ml) natural yogurt

Serving Information
Men and Teenagers: Add 6 oz (180 g) steamed potatoes at
   Midday Meal; 1 medium orange
Men: Add ½ oz (15 g) Edam cheese at Evening Meal
Teenagers: Add ½ pint (300 ml) skim milk

WEEK 39

Homemade bread is one of life's simple, delightful pleasures and we include a recipe this week. The whole process of making bread at home is evocative of scents and textures which appeal to the family cook – the warmth of the kitchen, the 'feel' of the dough, the soothing action of kneading, the smell of hot bread as it leaves the tin, they all appeal to some deep, basic home-making instinct. Most of our bread comes now from the supermarket shelf, but more people are seeking out the baker's shop which produces something 'worth getting your teeth into'. The 'staff of life' should be both delicious and satisfying.

Our recipe is for white bread. You may like to try some of the other kinds – wholemeal bread, soda bread, the French flute, even currant bread. All of these can be slotted into your food plan quite properly.

Harvest Festival in our churches at this time of year reminds us of the endless richness of the summer's produce, all for us to savour and enjoy. A large and splendid plait or corn sheaf of bread is often the central feature of the harvest display.

DAY 1

MORNING MEAL
4 fl oz (120 ml) grapefruit juice
1 poached egg
1 slice (1 oz/30 g) **Homemade Bread** (page 174), toasted
1 teaspoon (5 ml) margarine
tea or coffee

MIDDAY MEAL
5 oz (150 g) cottage cheese with mixed salad of shredded lettuce, 1 medium tomato, sliced, 2-inch (5-cm) chunk cucumber, sliced
2 teaspoons (10 ml) salad cream
¾ oz (20 g) crispbread
1 medium apple
tea or coffee

EVENING MEAL
Fresh Mushroom Soup (page 115)
Curried Crab Salad (page 160)
3 oz (90 g) whole kernel sweet corn
2-inch (5-cm) wedge honeydew melon
tea or coffee

SNACKS OR DRINKS AT PLANNED TIMES
5 fl oz (150 ml) natural yogurt, 7½ fl oz (225 ml) skim milk

Serving Information
Men and Teenagers: Add 4 fl oz (120 ml) grapefruit juice, 1 digestive biscuit
Teenagers: Add ½ pint (300 ml) skim milk

DAY 4

MORNING MEAL
4 fl oz (120 ml) orange juice
¾ oz (20 g) porridge oats, cooked with water
5 fl oz (150 ml) skim milk
tea or coffee

MIDDAY MEAL
Vegetable-Cheese Platter (page 118)
¾ oz (20 g) melba toast
2 teaspoons (10 ml) margarine
4 oz (120 g) stewed apple with 3 tablespoons (45 ml) single cream
tea or coffee

EVENING MEAL
3-4 oz (90-120 g) grilled veal chop
3 oz (90 g) cooked peas
3 oz (90 g) steamed green beans
1 teaspoon (5 ml) margarine
4 oz (120 g) cooked rice
1 medium pear
tea or coffee

SNACKS OR DRINKS AT PLANNED TIMES
12½ fl oz (375 ml) skim milk

Serving Information
Men and Teenagers: Add 4 fl oz (120 ml) orange juice, ¾ oz (20 g) porridge oats
Teenagers: Add 5 fl oz (150 ml) natural yogurt

DAY 5

MORNING MEAL
½ medium cantaloupe melon
1 oz (30 g) Cheddar cheese
1 slice (1 oz/30 g) **Homemade Bread** (page 174), toasted
tea or coffee

MIDDAY MEAL
Salmon Salad (page 00)
sliced tomatoes and sliced chicory with 1 teaspoon (5 ml) vegetable oil plus cider vinegar
1 slice (1 oz/30 g) **Homemade Bread** (page 174)
2 medium plums
sparkling mineral water with lemon slice
tea or coffee

EVENING MEAL
3-4 oz (90-120 g) grilled beef sausage
2 oz (60 g) sliced mushrooms sauteed in 1 teaspoon (5 ml) vegetable oil
3 oz (90 g) steamed onion rings
3 oz (90 g) boiled potatoes
5 fl oz (150 ml) natural yogurt with ½ medium banana, sliced
tea or coffee

SNACKS OR DRINKS AT PLANNED TIMES
½ pint (300 ml) skim milk

Serving Information
Men and Teenagers: Add ½ medium banana, 1½-oz (45-g) scone spread with 1 teaspoon (5 ml) honey
Teenagers: Add ½ pint (300 ml) skim milk

DAY 2

MORNING MEAL
4 fl oz (120 ml) grapefruit juice
¾ oz (20 g) cornflakes
5 fl oz (150 ml) skim milk
tea or coffee

MIDDAY MEAL
Baked Cheese Souffle (page 116)
3 oz (90 g) steamed green beans
sliced radishes and cucumber on lettuce with **Dijon-Herb
    Dressing** (page 182)
4 oz (120 g) orange sections
tea or coffee

EVENING MEAL
3-4 oz (90-120 g) grilled steak
Sauteed Mushrooms and Onions (page 171)
green salad with 2 teaspoons (10 ml) low-calorie mayonnaise
3 oz (90 g) cooked potatoes
1 teaspoon (5 ml) margarine
Baked Apple (page 188)
4 fl oz (120 ml) red wine
tea or coffee

SNACKS OR DRINKS AT PLANNED TIMES
15 fl oz (450 ml) skim milk

Serving Information
Men and Teenagers: Add 4 fl oz (120 ml) grapefruit juice, ¾ oz
    (20 g) cornflakes, 3 oz (90 g) cooked potatoes
Teenagers: Add 5 fl oz (150 ml) natural yogurt

DAY 3

MORNING MEAL
1 medium peach, sliced
2½ oz (75 g) cottage cheese
1 slice (1 oz/30 g) **Homemade Bread** (page 174)
tea or coffee

MIDDAY MEAL
3-4 oz (90-120 g) grilled fillet of sole with lemon wedge
3 oz (90 g) cooked cauliflower
3 oz (90 g) steamed carrots dotted with 1 teaspoon (5 ml)
    margarine
4 oz (120 g) canned fruit cocktail
tea or coffee

EVENING MEAL
3-4 oz (90-120 g) grilled chicken livers
3 oz (90 g) steamed onion rings
3 oz (90 g) steamed broccoli
4 oz (120 g) cooked noodles dotted with 2 teaspoons (10 ml)
    margarine
1 medium orange, peeled and diced with **Custard** (page 191)
tea or coffee

SNACKS OR DRINKS AT PLANNED TIMES
15 fl oz (450 ml) skim milk

Serving Information
Men and Teenagers: Add 1 medium apple, 1 slice (1 oz/30 g)
    Homemade bread (page 174)
Teenagers: Add 5 fl oz (150 ml) natural yogurt

DAY 6

MORNING MEAL
½ medium cantaloupe melon
1 boiled egg
1 slice (1 oz/30 g) **Homemade Bread** (page 174)
1 teaspoon (5 ml) margarine □ tea or coffee

MIDDAY MEAL
7-8 oz (210-240 g) baked beans
1-oz (30-g) lean back bacon, grilled
1 medium tomato, halved and grilled
1 slice (1 oz/30 g) **Homemade Bread** (page 174), toasted
1 teaspoon (5 ml) margarine
4 oz (120 g) fruit salad □ tea or coffee

EVENING MEAL
3-4 oz (90-120 g) grilled mackerel with 2 teaspoons (10 ml)
    low-calorie tartare sauce
3 oz (90 g) steamed green beans
3 oz (90 g) boiled carrots and swede, mashed with 1 teaspoon
    (5 ml) margarine
5 oz (150 g) gooseberries, stewed with 1½ teaspoons (7.5 ml)
    honey, with 2½ fl oz (75 ml) natural yogurt
tea or coffee

SNACKS OR DRINKS AT PLANNED TIMES
15 fl oz (450 ml) skim milk

Serving Information
Men and Teenagers: Add 3 oz (90 g) grapes, 1½-oz (45-g)
    muffin, split and toasted, spread with 1 teaspoon (5 ml) low-
    calorie jam
Teenagers: Add 5 fl oz (150 ml) natural yogurt

DAY 7

MORNING MEAL
½ medium banana, sliced
¾ oz (20 g) wheat flakes
5 fl oz (150 ml) skim milk □ tea or coffee

MIDDAY MEAL
3-4 oz (90-120 g) roast chicken
3 oz (90 g) steamed marrow
3 oz (90 g) cooked peas
3-oz (90-g) baked jacket potato with 2 teaspoons (10 ml)
    margarine
4 oz (120 g) canned peach slices with 2½ fl oz (75 ml) natural
    yogurt
tea or coffee

EVENING MEAL
3-4 oz (90-120 g) grilled lean pork chop
3 oz (90 g) steamed leeks
3 oz (90 g) boiled carrots
4 oz (120 g) cooked noodles dotted with 1 teaspoon (5 ml)
    margarine
½ medium cantaloupe melon
tea or coffee

SNACKS OR DRINKS AT PLANNED TIMES
½ pint (300 ml) skim milk

Serving Information
Men and Teenagers: Add ½ medium banana, 3-oz (90-g) baked
    jacket potato
Teenagers: Add 5 fl oz (150 ml) natural yogurt

WEEK 40

Yogurt appears often within this book. It is sometimes used as part of a recipe, sometimes served alone or with fruit as a dessert. The low-fat variety is, of course, the one for slimmers to use. Yogurt is a very ancient milk product, first known in Greece, Turkey and Bulgaria. The British yogurt is pasturised to destroy any harmful bacteria and then homogenised. It is then sold in cartons of varying size and must be kept in a cool temperature (40°F or 4.5°C) until it is eaten. Children usually like yogurt and will often take it as a substitute for milk. It has roughly the same nutritive value as milk. People with digestive problems often find that they can tolerate yogurt without any trouble at all, and as it can be used in sauces and dressings as well as in savoury and sweet dishes, it is a valuable addition to the daily diet.

This week we include it as a part of breakfast, as an accompaniment to pineapple and with a fruit salad – so you can see how versatile it is.

DAY 1

MORNING MEAL
½ medium grapefruit
1 boiled egg
1 slice (1 oz/30 g) wholemeal bread
1 teaspoon (5 ml) margarine
tea or coffee

MIDDAY MEAL
3-4 oz (90-120 g) sliced roast chicken
green salad
2 oz (60 g) cooked rice
2 tablespoons (30 ml) chopped onion and red pepper mixed with
      1½ teaspoons (7.5 ml) mayonnaise
1 medium pear
tea or coffee

EVENING MEAL
Lamb Stew (page 138)
3 oz (90 g) steamed carrots
3 oz (90 g) steamed swede
tea or coffee

SNACKS OR DRINKS AT PLANNED TIMES
½ pint (300 ml) skim milk, 5 fl oz (150 ml) natural yogurt with 2
      tablespoons (30 ml) raisins and rum flavouring

Serving Information
Men and Teenagers: Add 1 medium pear and 3 oz (90 g) grapes;
      add extra 2 oz (60 g) rice at Midday Meal and 3 oz (90 g)
      steamed potatoes at Evening Meal
Teenagers: Add ½ pint (300 ml) skim milk

DAY 4

MORNING MEAL
5 oz (150 g) melon balls
¾ oz (20 g) instant cereal with 5 fl oz (150 ml) hot skim milk
1 slice (1 oz/30 g) wholemeal bread, toasted
1 teaspoon (5 ml) marmalade
tea or coffee

MIDDAY MEAL
2 oz (60 g) Edam cheese
2 sticks celery
1 medium tomato
¾ oz (20 g) crispbread
1 medium pear
tea or coffee

EVENING MEAL
Breadcrumbed Liver (page 146)
green salad
3 oz (90 g) steamed carrots
3 oz (90 g) steamed broccoli
2 teaspoons (10 ml) low-calorie salad dressing
tea or coffee

SNACKS OR DRINKS AT PLANNED TIMES
5 fl oz (150 ml) skim milk, 5 fl oz (150 ml) natural yogurt, mixed
      with 2 teaspoons (10 ml) raspberry jam and 1 oz (30 g) cooked
      dried apricots

Serving Information
Men and Teenagers: Add 4 oz (120 g) cooked noodles at
      Evening Meal; 1 oz (30 g) dried apricots and 1 medium apple
Teenagers: Add ½ pint (300 ml) skim milk

DAY 5

MORNING MEAL
4 fl oz (120 ml) orange juice
1 poached egg
1 slice (1 oz/30 g) bread
1 teaspoon (5 ml) low-fat spread
tea or coffee

MIDDAY MEAL
Stir-Fry Tuna (page 162)
green salad with lemon juice
1 teaspoon (5 ml) low-fat spread
1 slice (1 oz/30 g) wholemeal bread
tea or coffee

EVENING MEAL
3-4 oz (90-120 g) grilled steak
3 oz (90 g) steamed cauliflower
3 oz (90 g) steamed potato
1 medium grilled tomato
2 teaspoons (10 ml) low-fat spread
½ medium apple, chopped and 1 tablespoon (15 ml) raisins with
      5 fl oz (150 ml) natural yogurt
tea or coffee

SNACKS OR DRINKS AT PLANNED TIMES
½ pint (300 ml) skim milk

Serving Information
Men and Teenagers: Add 1 slice (1 oz/30 g) wholemeal bread at
      Midday Meal; 3 oz (90 g) steamed potatoes at Evening Meal;
      1 medium banana
Teenagers: Add ½ pint (300 ml) skim milk

MORNING MEAL
4 fl oz (120 ml) orange juice
¾ oz (20 g) bran flakes
5 fl oz (150 ml) natural yogurt
¾ oz (20 g) crispbread
2 teaspoons (10 ml) low-fat spread
1 teaspoon (5 ml) yeast extract
tea or coffee

MIDDAY MEAL
Cottage Cheese Country Style (page 126)
¾ oz (20 g) melba toast
2 teaspoons (10 ml) low-fat spread
1 medium apple
tea or coffee

EVENING MEAL
3-4 oz (90-120 g) grilled plaice with lemon wedge
3 oz (90 g) cooked green beans
3 oz (90 g) boiled potatoes
1 teaspoon (5 ml) margarine
4 oz (120 g) canned pineapple
tea or coffee

SNACKS OR DRINKS AT PLANNED TIMES
½ pint (300 ml) skim milk

Serving Information
Men and Teenagers: Add ¾-oz (20-g) plain scone; add extra 3 oz
   (90 g) boiled potatoes at Evening Meal, 1 medium banana
Teenagers: Add ½ pint (300 ml) skim milk

MORNING MEAL
8 fl oz (240 ml) tomato juice
1 oz (30 g) Cheddar cheese
1 slice (1 oz/30 g) wholemeal bread
tea or coffee

MIDDAY MEAL
3-4 oz (90-120 g) canned pilchards served on diced cucumber,
   green pepper, onion and tomato salad tossed with 2½ fl oz
   (75 ml) natural yogurt and 1 teaspoon (5 ml) low-calorie
   mayonnaise
3 oz (90 g) cooked beetroot
1 medium apple
tea or coffee

EVENING MEAL
Shredded Chicken with Peanut Sauce (page 134)
4 oz (120 g) boiled rice
3 oz (90 g) steamed broccoli
2 slices canned pineapple with 2½ fl oz (75 ml) natural yogurt
tea or coffee

SNACKS OR DRINKS AT PLANNED TIMES
½ pint (300 ml) skim milk

Serving Information
Men and Teenagers: Add 3 oz (90 g) cooked whole kernel sweet
   corn at Midday Meal and 2 oz (60 g) boiled rice at Evening
   Meal, 4 dried dates
Teenagers: Add ½ pint (300 ml) skim milk

MORNING MEAL
½ medium grapefruit
1 oz (30 g) Cheddar cheese
1 slice (1 oz/30 g) bread □ tea or coffee

MIDDAY MEAL
2 eggs scrambled in 1 teaspoon (5 ml) vegetable oil
1 slice (1 oz/30 g) bread, toasted
1 teaspoon (5 ml) margarine
3 oz (90 g) grilled tomatoes
3 oz (90 g) poached mushrooms
5 fl oz (150 ml) natural yogurt
4 oz (120 g) canned peach slices □ tea or coffee

EVENING MEAL
6 oz (180 g) boil-in-the-bag fish with sauce (any type)
3 oz (90 g) steamed broccoli
3 oz (90 g) steamed carrots
1 teaspoon (5 ml) low-fat spread
green salad
1 teaspoon (5 ml) salad cream
2 small clementines
tea or coffee

SNACKS OR DRINKS AT PLANNED TIMES
½ pint (300 ml) skim milk

Serving Information
Men and Teenagers: Add extra 2 slices (2 oz/60 g) bread at
   Midday Meal; 1 medium fresh fig
Teenagers: Add ½ pint (300 ml) skim milk

MORNING MEAL
½ medium banana
¾ oz (20 g) cornflakes
5 fl oz (150 ml) natural yogurt
¾ oz (20 g) crispbread
2 teaspoons (10 ml) low-fat spread
½ teaspoon (2.5 ml) marmalade □ tea or coffee

MIDDAY MEAL
3-4 oz (90-120 g) roast lamb
3 oz (90 g) spring greens
3 oz (90 g) baked onion
3-oz (90-g) baked jacket potato
1 teaspoon (5 ml) low-fat spread
5 oz (150 g) melon balls
4 fl oz (120 ml) red wine □ tea or coffee

EVENING MEAL
Chicken Hotpot (page 135)
3 oz (90 g) steamed green beans
3 oz (90 g) carrots
2 slices canned pineapple
tea or coffee

SNACKS OR DRINKS AT PLANNED TIMES
½ pint (300 ml) skim milk

Serving Information
Men and Teenagers: Add extra ½ banana; 3-oz (90-g) baked
   jacket potato at Midday Meal; 1 digestive biscuit
Teenagers: Add ½ pint (300 ml) skim milk

WEEK 41

Many of us look forward to the 'sweet conclusion' of a meal and just because we are following a weight-reducing regime we don't have to go without the sweet course altogether. For all pudding-lovers we offer, this week, no less than seven pudding recipes – one for each day! Perhaps you think that Pineapple Cheesecake, Knickerbocker Glory and Rich Fruit Pudding sound just too sinfully indulgent for a book such as this, but rest assured that they are all carefully planned to fit into your weekly limits of intake. The Knickerbocker Glory looks particularly enticing with its layers of ice cream, fruit and biscuit crumbs. The Rich Fruit Pudding has been compared very favourably with a traditional Christmas Pudding and the Rum Sauce that accompanies it makes it taste very special.

One reason why so many dieters fail is because they feel deprived of favourite foods. With this week's menus, no sweet tooth has any excuse at all!

DAY 1

MORNING MEAL
½ medium grapefruit
¾ oz (20 g) muesli
5 fl oz (150 ml) skim milk
tea or coffee

MIDDAY MEAL
toss together 2½ oz (75 g) cottage cheese, 1 tablespoon (15 ml) raisins, 1 small diced satsuma and serve on bed of lettuce
2-oz (60-g) bap with 3 teaspoons (15 ml) low-fat spread
tea or coffee

EVENING MEAL
2-inch (5-cm) wedge honeydew melon
6 oz (180 g) boil-in-the-bag fish in sauce (any type)
3 oz (90 g) cooked peas
3 oz (90 g) cooked carrots
2 oz (60 g) cooked rice
Sweet Pancake with Jam (page 196)
tea or coffee

SNACKS OR DRINKS AT PLANNED TIMES
14 fl oz (420 ml) skim milk

Serving Information
Men and Teenagers: Add 2 oz (60 g) cooked rice at Evening Meal; 1 digestive biscuit, 1 medium apple
Teenagers: Add ½ pint (300 ml) skim milk

DAY 4

MORNING MEAL
1 medium orange
2½ oz (75 g) cottage cheese, lightly grilled on 1 slice (1 oz/30 g) wholemeal bread, toasted
tea or coffee

MIDDAY MEAL
toss together, 3-4 oz (90-120 g) diced cooked chicken, 3 oz (90 g) canned red kidney beans, 1 diced celery stick, 1 grated carrot, 1 grated medium apple sprinkled with lemon juice, 4 teaspoons (120 ml) low-calorie mayonnaise
tea or coffee

EVENING MEAL
3-4 oz (90-120 g) lamb chop, grilled
3 oz (90 g) steamed mushrooms
3 oz (90 g) steamed cauliflower
3 oz (90 g) cooked peas with 2 teaspoons (10 ml) low-fat spread
Knickerbocker Glory (page 197)
tea or coffee

SNACKS OR DRINKS AT PLANNED TIMES
5 fl oz (150 ml) natural yogurt, ½ pint (300 ml) skim milk

Serving Information
Men and Teenagers: Add 1 slice (1 oz/30 g) wholemeal bread, 1 digestive biscuit, 1 medium orange
Teenagers: Add ½ pint (300 ml) skim milk

DAY 5

MORNING MEAL
2 tablespoons (30 ml) raisins mixed with ¾ oz (20 g) porridge oats cooked with water
5 fl oz (150 ml) skim milk
tea or coffee

MIDDAY MEAL
1½-2 oz (45-60 g) sardines
6 oz (180 g) tomato and onion salad dressed with 2 teaspoons (10 ml) mayonnaise and tucked into 2-oz (60-g) pitta bread, split
tea or coffee

EVENING MEAL
4 oz (120 g) canned grapefruit sections
3-4 oz (90-120 g) trout, grilled
3 oz (90 g) braised celery
3 oz (90 g) cooked Brussels sprouts
Bread and Fruit Pudding (page 188)
tea or coffee

SNACKS OR DRINKS AT PLANNED TIMES
½ pint (300 ml) skim milk

Serving Information
Men and Teenagers: Add 3 oz (90 g) boiled potatoes at Evening Meal, 1 digestive biscuit, 1 banana
Teenagers: Add 5 fl oz (150 ml) natural yogurt

DAY 2

MORNING MEAL
2-inch (5-cm) wedge honeydew melon
1 tablespoon (15 ml) peanut butter on 1 slice (1 oz/30 g)
   wholemeal bread, toasted
tea or coffee

MIDDAY MEAL
2 oz (60 g) canned mackerel, mixed with 1 medium tomato,
   skinned and chopped, 2 oz (60 g) cucumber, chopped, 2 oz (60
   g) green pepper, seeded and chopped, 2 oz (60 g) carrot,
   grated, 1 tablespoon (15 ml) onion, chopped, 1 tablespoon (15
   ml) wine vinegar and pinch garlic salt
Pineapple Cheesecake (page 190)
tea or coffee

EVENING MEAL
4 oz (120 g) canned grapefruit sections
3-4 oz (90-120 g) grilled lamb's liver
3 oz (90 g) cooked broad beans
3 oz (90 g) cooked cauliflower
1 medium grilled tomato
1 diced satsuma with 5 fl oz (150 ml) natural yogurt
tea or coffee

SNACKS OR DRINKS AT PLANNED TIMES
5 fl oz (150 ml) skim milk

Serving Information
Men and Teenagers: Add 2 slices (2 oz/60 g) wholemeal bread,
   2 small satsumas
Teenagers: Add ½ pint (300 ml) skim milk

DAY 3

MORNING MEAL
½ medium grapefruit
¾ oz (20 g) cornflakes
5 fl oz (150 ml) skim milk
tea or coffee

MIDDAY MEAL
1 hard-boiled egg, sliced and served with 2 teaspoons (10 ml)
   mayonnaise, sprinkled with pinch red pepper on a bed of
   mixed green salad
1 medium apple
1 digestive biscuit
tea or coffee

EVENING MEAL
3-4 oz (90-120 g) roast chicken
3 oz (90 g) cooked mashed swede with 2 teaspoons (10 ml)
   low-fat spread
3 oz (90 g) steamed sliced carrots
3 oz (90 g) sweet corn
Rice Pudding (page 190)
tea or coffee

SNACKS OR DRINKS AT PLANNED TIMES
11 fl oz (330 ml) skim milk

Serving Information
Men and Teenagers: Add 1 digestive biscuit, 3 oz (90 g) sweet
   corn, 1 medium orange
Teenagers: Add 5 fl oz (150 ml) natural yogurt

DAY 6

MORNING MEAL
4 oz (120 g) canned peaches sliced onto 2½ oz (75 g) quark or
   cottage cheese
¾ oz (20 g) crispbread
2 teaspoons (10 ml) low-fat spread
tea or coffee

MIDDAY MEAL
8 fl oz (240 ml) tomato juice
3-4 oz (90-120 g) grilled beefburger
2-oz (60-g) bap
2 teaspoons (10 ml) low-fat spread
2 teaspoons (10 ml) relish or tomato ketchup
tea or coffee

EVENING MEAL
3-4 oz (90-120 g) plaice, grilled with 1 teaspoon (5 ml) margarine
3 oz (90 g) steamed green beans
3 oz (90 g) steamed courgettes
Strawberry Cream (page 186)
tea or coffee

SNACKS OR DRINKS AT PLANNED TIMES
½ pint (300 ml) skim milk

Serving Information
Men and Teenagers: Add 6 oz (180 g) boiled new potatoes at
   Evening Meal, 1 medium banana
Teenagers: Add ½ pint (300 ml) skim milk

DAY 7

MORNING MEAL
½ medium grapefruit
1 oz (30 g) grated Cheddar cheese, lightly grilled on 1 slice
   (1 oz/30 g) wholemeal bread, toasted
1 grilled medium tomato □ tea or coffee

MIDDAY MEAL
3-4 oz (90-120 g) roast turkey breast
3 oz (90 g) cooked parsnips
3 oz (90 g) steamed spinach
3-oz (90-g) baked jacket potato
1 teaspoon (5 ml) low-fat spread
Rich Fruit Pudding (page 191)
2 oz (60 g) vanilla ice cream
tea or coffee

EVENING MEAL
3-4 oz (90-120 g) tuna
mixed green salad
1 medium tomato, sliced
2 teaspoons (10 ml) mayonnaise
5 oz (150 g) raspberries with 5 fl oz (150 ml) natural yogurt
tea or coffee

SNACKS OR DRINKS AT PLANNED TIMES
9 fl oz (270 ml) skim milk

Serving Information
Men and Teenagers: Add 3 oz (90 g) baked beans at Morning
   Meal; 3-oz (90-g) baked jacket potato at Midday Meal;
   1 medium orange
Teenagers: Add 5 fl oz (150 ml) natural yogurt

WEEK 42

One of the great British traditions is the 'pub lunch'. When you've spent a busy morning in the garden or on other chores, there's something very nice about going down to the pub and relaxing with a beer or some cider while you tackle cheese, crusty bread, some salad and a 'taste' of pickle to spice it up. If the sun shines you can sit on a bench outside; if it's cold, seek the warmth of the 'snug' or the busy bar. It's good to know that your food plan fits so nicely around such a meal.

Cider is one of the oldest alcoholic drinks and has long been a mainstay of the English pub. Many farms grow apples just for cider production and in the West Country you will find 'scrumpy' – a very potent brew, with a deceptively mild taste. Cider can be sparkling or still, sweet or dry, and cider vinegars have an important place in good cooking.

DAY 1

MORNING MEAL
5 oz (150 g) strawberries, sliced
2½ oz (75 g) cottage cheese
1 slice (1 oz/30 g) brown bread, toasted
1 teaspoon (5 ml) margarine
1 teaspoon (5 ml) low-calorie jam
tea or coffee

MIDDAY MEAL
3-4 oz (90-120 g) cooked chicken
chicory and cucumber salad with **Basic Vinaigrette** (page 183)
¾ oz (20 g) crispbread
1 teaspoon (5 ml) margarine
1 medium apple
tea or coffee

EVENING MEAL
3-4 oz (90-120 g) grilled chicken livers
3 oz (90 g) cooked onion rings
3 oz (90 g) cooked green beans
2 medium plums
tea or coffee

SNACKS OR DRINKS AT PLANNED TIMES
5 fl oz (150 ml) natural yogurt, ½ pint (300 ml) skim milk

Serving Information
Men and Teenagers: Add extra 1 slice (1 oz/30 g) brown bread, 1 digestive biscuit, 2 medium plums
Teenagers: Add ½ pint (300 ml) skim milk

DAY 4

MORNING MEAL
2-inch (5-cm) wedge honeydew melon
¾ oz (20 g) porridge oats cooked with water
5 fl oz (150 ml) skim milk
tea or coffee

MIDDAY MEAL
3-4 oz (90-120 g) canned salmon
Apple Slaw (page 180)
1 slice (1 oz/30 g) wholemeal bread
2 teaspoons (10 ml) low-fat spread
1 oz (30 g) dried apricot, cooked with water and 1 teaspoon (5 ml) honey
tea or coffee

EVENING MEAL
chicken and egg salad made with 1½-2 oz (45-60 g) diced cooked chicken, 1 diced hard-boiled egg on green salad with 1 teaspoon (5 ml) vegetable oil and cider vinegar, tomato and cucumber slices
4 oz (120 g) cooked rice
3 oz (90 g) canned fruit cocktail
tea or coffee

SNACKS OR DRINKS AT PLANNED TIMES
15 fl oz (450 ml) skim milk

Serving Information
Men and Teenagers: Add 4 oz (120 g) canned fruit cocktail, 2 oz (60 g) cooked rice, 1 digestive biscuit
Teenagers: Add ½ pint (300 ml) skim milk

DAY 5

MORNING MEAL
4 fl oz (120 ml) orange juice
1 scrambled egg on 1 slice (1 oz/30 g) bread, toasted, spread with 1 teaspoon (5 ml) margarine
tea or coffee

MIDDAY MEAL
3 tablespoons (45 ml) crunchy peanut butter on ¾ oz (20 g) crispbread topped with diced cucumber, radishes and green pepper
3 oz (90 g) green grapes
tea or coffee

EVENING MEAL
Ham and Turkey Casserole (page 138)
3 oz (90 g) cooked Brussels sprouts
3 oz (90 g) cooked broad beans
½ medium banana, sliced on 2 oz (60 g) vanilla ice cream
tea or coffee

SNACKS OR DRINKS AT PLANNED TIMES
15 fl oz (450 ml) skim milk

Serving Information
Men and Teenagers: Add 2½ fl oz (75 ml) apple juice, ½ medium banana, 1½-oz (45-g) crumpet, toasted and spread with 2 teaspoons (10 ml) low-calorie jam
Men: Add extra ½ oz (15 g) ham at Evening Meal
Teenagers: Add ½ pint (300 ml) skim milk

DAY 2

MORNING MEAL
1 medium orange
1 poached egg
1 slice (1 oz/30 g) brown bread, toasted
1 teaspoon (5 ml) margarine
tea or coffee

MIDDAY MEAL
3-4 oz (90-120 g) baked mackerel
3 oz (90 g) steamed courgettes, sliced
3 oz (90 g) cooked carrots, sliced
Lemonade (page 188)
tea or coffee

EVENING MEAL
Turkey Oriental (page 183)
2 oz (60 g) cooked rice dotted with 1 teaspoon (5 ml) margarine
shredded Chinese cabbage topped with grated carrot and
   Gingered Vinaigrette (page 183)
tea or coffee

SNACKS OR DRINKS AT PLANNED TIMES
5 oz (150 g) blackberries with 5 fl oz (150 ml) natural yogurt,
   ½ pint (300 ml) skim milk

Serving Information
Men and Teenagers: Add extra 2 oz (60 g) cooked rice,
   1 digestive biscuit, 1 medium apple
Teenagers: Add ½ pint (300 ml) skim milk

DAY 3

MORNING MEAL
½ medium banana, sliced
¾ oz (20 g) ready-to-eat cereal
5 fl oz (150 ml) skim milk
tea or coffee

MIDDAY MEAL
3-4 oz (90-120 g) grilled beefburger
2-oz (60-g) bap
1 medium tomato
2 small pickled cucumbers
carrot and celery salad with 2 teaspoons (10 ml) mayonnaise,
   and lemon juice
3 oz (90 g) black grapes
tea or coffee

EVENING MEAL
3-4 oz (90-120 g) grilled plaice dotted with 2 teaspoons (10 ml)
   low-fat spread
3 oz (90 g) cooked peas
3 oz (90 g) cooked spinach
5 oz (150 g) stewed blackcurrants
4 fl oz (120 ml) white wine
tea or coffee

SNACKS OR DRINKS AT PLANNED TIMES
15 fl oz (450 ml) skim milk

Serving Information
Men and Teenagers: Add ½ medium banana, 1½-oz (45-g)
   scone spread with 2 teaspoons (10 ml) low-calorie jam
Teenagers: Add ½ pint (300 ml) skim milk

DAY 6

MORNING MEAL
½ medium grapefruit
Cinnamon-Cheese Toast (page 123)
tea or coffee

MIDDAY MEAL
3-4 oz (90-120 g) grilled veal chop
3 oz (90 g) steamed carrots, sliced
1 medium tomato, halved and grilled
green salad with 1 teaspoon (5 ml) vegetable oil and cider
   vinegar
3-oz (90-g) boiled potato
1 medium pear
tea or coffee

EVENING MEAL
3-4 oz (90-120 g) grilled trout
3 oz (90 g) steamed courgettes
mixed salad of lettuce, cucumber and tomato, with 2 teaspoons
   (10 ml) mayonnaise
4 oz (120 g) canned peach slices
tea or coffee

SNACKS OR DRINKS AT PLANNED TIMES
5 fl oz (150 ml) natural yogurt, ½ pint (300 ml) skim milk

Serving Information
Men and Teenagers: Add 2-oz (60-g) Scotch pancake with 2
   teaspoons (10 ml) low-calorie jam, 4 oz (120 g) canned peach
   slices
Teenagers: Add ½ pint (300 ml) skim milk

DAY 7

MORNING MEAL
4 fl oz (120 ml) orange juice
1 boiled egg
1 slice (1 oz/30 g) bread, toasted
1 teaspoon (5 ml) margarine
tea or coffee

MIDDAY MEAL
'Pub Lunch'
2 oz (60 g) Cheddar cheese
2 oz (60 g) French bread
mixed salad of lettuce, tomato, cucumber and spring onion with
   1 teaspoon (5 ml) mayonnaise
2 teaspoons (10 ml) relish
1 medium apple
½ pint (300 ml) beer or cider
tea or coffee

EVENING MEAL
Lemon-Minted Lamb (page 138)
3 oz (90 g) steamed mushrooms
3 oz (90 g) cooked peas
2 stewed plums
tea or coffee

SNACKS OR DRINKS AT PLANNED TIMES
5 fl oz (150 ml) natural yogurt, ½ pint (300 ml) skim milk

Serving Information
Men and Teenagers: Add 4 fl oz (120 ml) orange juice, 2 medium
   plums, 2 oz (60 g) cooked rice at Evening Meal
Teenagers: Add ½ pint (300 ml) skim milk

WEEK 43

Cheese begins as milk, of course. It's soured, added to, thickened, coagulated, settled, drained, ripened, flavoured and moulded. This process can take weeks, even months, and each area of the cheese-producing world adds its own specialities in treatment and additions to produce a characteristic flavour, shape and colour. The most popular British cheese is Cheddar. It's versatile, equally good with savoury and dessert dishes and can be cooked, too.

Cheddar cheese is concentrated protein and fat plus minerals and vitamins – it's protein value is almost double that of meat. It should be stored in a cool place, wrapped in foil, but removed several hours before you serve it. We offer several cheese meals this week, including one hot dish – Cheese and Butter Bean Peppers.

Cheese is one of those foods which can be used to the very last crumb. The odds and ends can be grated and kept to use in cooking. Cheese dishes should be lightly cooked – over-cooking makes it stringy and hard to digest.

DAY 1

MORNING MEAL
½ medium banana, sliced
¾ oz (20 g) muesli
5 fl oz (150 ml) skim milk
tea or coffee

MIDDAY MEAL
3-4 oz (90-120 g) cooked chicken
1 medium tomato
2-3 sticks celery
1 slice (1 oz/30 g) bread
1 teaspoon (5 ml) margarine
1 medium orange
tea or coffee

EVENING MEAL
3-4 oz (90-120 g) grilled salmon
3 oz (90 g) cooked peas
3 oz (90 g) steamed broccoli
2 oz (60 g) cooked rice dotted with 2 teaspoons (10 ml) margarine
1 medium pear
tea or coffee

SNACKS OR DRINKS AT PLANNED TIMES
15 fl oz (450 ml) skim milk

Serving Information
Men and Teenagers: Add ½ medium banana, 2 oz (60 g) cooked rice, 1 digestive biscuit
Teenagers: Add 5 fl oz (150 ml) natural yogurt

DAY 4

MORNING MEAL
2½ fl oz (75 ml) pineapple juice
¾ oz (20 g) cornflakes
5 fl oz (150 ml) skim milk
tea or coffee

MIDDAY MEAL
3-4 oz (90-120 g) cooked chicken
green salad of shredded lettuce, watercress, mustard and cress and sliced cucumber, with **Dill Vinaigrette** (page 183)
3 oz (90 g) whole kernel sweet corn
1 medium orange
tea or coffee

EVENING MEAL
5-6 oz (150-180 g) uncooked lamb's liver cooked in 1 teaspoon (5 ml) oil with 3 oz (90 g) sliced onion
3 oz (90 g) poached mushrooms
4 oz (120 g) cooked rice dotted with 1 teaspoon (5 ml) low-fat spread
4 oz (120 g) fruit salad with 2 oz (60 g) vanilla ice cream
tea or coffee

SNACKS OR DRINKS AT PLANNED TIMES
15 fl oz (450 ml) skim milk

Serving Information
Men and Teenagers: Add 2½ fl oz (75 ml) pineapple juice, 1 digestive biscuit
Teenagers: Add 5 fl oz (150 ml) natural yogurt

DAY 5

MORNING MEAL
4 fl oz (120 ml) orange juice
1 egg, cooked in 1 teaspoon (5 ml) margarine
1 slice (1 oz/30 g) bread, toasted
tea or coffee

MIDDAY MEAL
Cheese and Butter Bean Peppers (page 166)
3 oz (90 g) steamed carrots
green salad with 1 teaspoon (5 ml) vegetable oil and wine vinegar
4 oz (120 g) fruit salad
tea or coffee

EVENING MEAL
3-4 oz (90-120 g) grilled lean lamb chop
3 oz (90 g) cooked peas
3 oz (90 g) steamed cauliflower
6-oz (180-g) baked jacket potato
1 teaspoon (5 ml) margarine
2 medium plums
tea or coffee

SNACKS OR DRINKS AT PLANNED TIMES
5 fl oz (150 ml) natural yogurt, ½ pint (300 ml) skim milk

Serving Information
Men and Teenagers: Add 1 medium apple, 1 digestive biscuit
Men: Add 1 oz (30 g) butter beans at Midday Meal
Teenagers: Add ½ pint (300 ml) skim milk

DAY 2

MORNING MEAL
4 fl oz (120 ml) orange juice
1 boiled egg
1 slice (1 oz/30 g) bread, toasted
1 teaspoon (5 ml) margarine
tea or coffee

MIDDAY MEAL
2 oz (60 g) Cheddar cheese, sliced onto ¾ oz (20 g) crispbread
    with 3-4 celery sticks and 2-inch (5-cm) chunk cucumber
1 tablespoon (15 ml) relish
1 medium orange
tea or coffee

EVENING MEAL
3-4 oz (90-120 g) grilled steak
1 medium tomato, halved and grilled
3 oz (90 g) cooked peas
3 oz (90 g) mushrooms, sauteed in 2 teaspoons (10 ml)
    margarine
4 oz (120 g) fruit salad
tea or coffee

SNACKS OR DRINKS AT PLANNED TIMES
5 fl oz (150 ml) natural yogurt, ½ pint (300 ml) skim milk

Serving Information
Men and Teenagers: Add 4 fl oz (120 ml) orange juice, 3 oz (90 g)
    boiled potatoes, ¾ oz (20 g) crispbread
Teenagers: Add ½ pint (300 ml) skim milk

DAY 3

MORNING MEAL
2½ fl oz (75 ml) pineapple juice
2½ oz (75 g) curd cheese
¾ oz (20 g) melba toast
tea or coffee

MIDDAY MEAL
3-4 oz (90-120 g) canned pilchards with mixed salad of shredded
    lettuce, sliced tomato and cucumber, with 2 teaspoons
    (10 ml) salad cream
1 slice (1 oz/30 g) wholemeal bread
1 teaspoon (5 ml) margarine
1 medium peach
tea or coffee

EVENING MEAL
3-4 oz (90-120 g) grilled haddock dotted with 1 teaspoon (5 ml)
    margarine
Marinated Carrots (page 168)
3 oz (90 g) cooked peas
4 oz (120 g) orange sections
tea or coffee

SNACKS OR DRINKS AT PLANNED TIMES
5 fl oz (150 ml) natural yogurt, ½ pint (300 ml) skim milk

Serving Information
Men and Teenagers: Add 2½ fl oz (75 ml) pineapple juice, 1 slice
    (1 oz/30 g) wholemeal bread, 1 digestive biscuit
Teenagers: Add ½ pint (300 ml) skim milk

DAY 6

MORNING MEAL
4 fl oz (120 ml) orange juice
¾ oz (20 g) porridge oats cooked with water
5 fl oz (150 ml) skim milk
tea or coffee

MIDDAY MEAL
egg and cheese salad made with 1 hard-boiled egg, 2½ oz (75 g)
    cottage cheese, shredded lettuce, 1 medium tomato, sliced,
    2-inch (5-cm) chunk cucumber, sliced, 2 teaspoons (10 ml)
    salad cream
4 oz (120 g) canned peach slices
½ pint (300 ml) beer or cider
tea or coffee

EVENING MEAL
3-4 oz (90-120 g) grilled veal chop
3 oz (90 g) steamed green beans
3 oz (90 g) steamed swede
6-oz (180-g) baked jacket potato
2 teaspoons (10 ml) margarine
4 oz (120 g) canned pineapple
tea or coffee

SNACKS OR DRINKS AT PLANNED TIMES
15 fl oz (450 ml) skim milk

Serving Information
Men and Teenagers: add 4 oz (120 g) canned peach slices,
    1½-oz (45-g) crumpet with 2 teaspoons (10 ml) low-calorie
    jam
Teenagers: Add 5 fl oz (150 ml) natural yogurt

DAY 7

MORNING MEAL
1 medium orange
1 egg, scrambled in 1 teaspoon (5 ml) margarine
1 slice (1 oz/30 g) bread, toasted
tea or coffee

MIDDAY MEAL
3-4 oz (90-120 g) lean roast lamb
3 oz (90 g) cooked carrots
3 oz (90 g) cooked parsnips
2 oz (60 g) cooked rice dotted with 1 teaspoon (5 ml) margarine
1 medium pear
tea or coffee

EVENING MEAL
Sole Italiano (page 158)
3 oz (90 g) cooked broccoli
3 oz (90 g) cooked courgettes
3 oz (90 g) grapes
4 fl oz (120 ml) white wine
tea or coffee

SNACKS OR DRINKS AT PLANNED TIMES
5 fl oz (150 ml) natural yogurt, ½ pint (300 ml) skim milk

Serving Information
Men and Teenagers: Add 3 oz (90 g) grapes, 1½-oz (45-g) scone
    with 2 teaspoons (10 ml) low-calorie jam
Teenagers: Add ½ pint (300 ml) skim milk

WEEK 44

All Hallows E'en conjures up mental pictures of witches and broomsticks and magic spells. In the light of modern science we like to believe that such evil powers have lost their sting, and that the witch had a clever knowledge of herbs and their effects rather than of any magic incantations.

We acknowledge Hallowe'en with a pumpkin recipe – Special Pineapple Pumpkin – on Day 3. The pumpkin belongs to the gourd family and may be cooked as a marrow is cooked. It is much used in America in a sweet and spicy pie and our recipe belongs to this category.

DAY 1

MORNING MEAL
½ medium banana
¾ oz (20 g) muesli
5 fl oz (150 ml) skim milk
tea or coffee

MIDDAY MEAL
3 tablespoons (45 ml) peanut butter
1½ oz (45 g) crispbread
2 teaspoons (10 ml) low-calorie blackcurrant jam
1 medium apple
tea or coffee

EVENING MEAL
3-4 oz (90-120 g) grilled mackerel
3-oz (90-g) baked jacket potato with 2½ fl oz (75 ml) natural yogurt and chopped chives
3 oz (90 g) steamed peas
3 oz (90 g) steamed carrots
mixed green salad with 1 teaspoon (5 ml) olive oil and cider vinegar
tea or coffee

SNACKS OR DRINKS AT PLANNED TIMES
1 medium orange sliced into 2½ fl oz (75 ml) natural yogurt, 5 fl oz (150 ml) skim milk

Serving Information
Men and Teenagers: Add 3-oz (90-g) baked jacket potato, 1 medium orange
Teenagers: Add ½ pint (300 ml) skim milk

DAY 4

MORNING MEAL
2½ fl oz (75 ml) apple juice
2½ oz (75 g) cottage cheese lightly grilled on 1 slice (1 oz/30 g) rye bread, toasted
tea or coffee

MIDDAY MEAL
2 poached eggs on 6 oz (180 g) steamed spinach
mixed green salad with **Basic Vinaigrette** (page 183)
4 oz (120 g) canned pineapple
5 fl oz (150 ml) natural yogurt
tea or coffee

EVENING MEAL
½ medium grapefruit
Salmon Salad (page 162)
1 medium tomato, sliced
3-oz (90-g) baked jacket potato
2 teaspoons (10 ml) low-fat spread
tea or coffee

SNACKS OR DRINKS AT PLANNED TIMES
½ pint (300 ml) skim milk, 1 low-calorie fizzy drink

Serving Information
Men and Teenagers: Add 2-oz (60-g) wholemeal roll at Midday Meal; 1 medium orange
Teenagers: Add 5 fl oz (150 ml) natural yogurt

DAY 5

MORNING MEAL
1 medium orange
¾ oz (20 g) ready-to-eat cereal
5 fl oz (150 ml) skim milk □ tea or coffee

MIDDAY MEAL
Lamb's Liver Creole (page 143)
3 oz (90 g) onion rings, sauteed 3-4 minutes in 1 teaspoon (5 ml) vegetable oil
¾ oz (20 g) crispbread with 2 teaspoons (10 ml) low-fat spread and 2 teaspoons (10 ml) grated Parmesan cheese
2½ fl oz (75 ml) apple juice □ tea or coffee

EVENING MEAL
Tomato Starter (page 114)
3-4 oz (90-120 g) lean roast lamb
3 oz (90 g) cooked carrots
3 oz (90 g) cooked parsnips
6-oz (180-g) baked jacket potato
2 teaspoons (10 ml) low-fat spread
2 oz (60 g) vanilla ice cream
1 medium pear
tea or coffee

SNACKS OR DRINKS AT PLANNED TIMES
5 fl oz (150 ml) natural yogurt, 5 fl oz (150 ml) skim milk

Serving Information
Men and Teenagers: Add 1 digestive biscuit, 1 medium apple
Teenagers: Add ½ pint (300 ml) skim milk

DAY 2

MORNING MEAL
4 fl oz (120 ml) orange juice
1 egg, scrambled in 1 teaspoon (5 ml) margarine on 1 slice
  (1 oz/30 g) bread, toasted
tea or coffee

MIDDAY MEAL
Fruited Cheese Delight (page 124)
watercress salad
1 teaspoon (5 ml) low-calorie mayonnaise
1 slice (1 oz/30 g) rye bread
½ medium banana
tea or coffee

EVENING MEAL
3-4 oz (90-120 g) grilled beefburger with 2 teaspoons (10 ml)
  tomato ketchup or relish
3 oz (90 g) canned whole kernel sweet corn
tomato and onion salad with 1 teaspoon (5 ml) olive oil, wine
  vinegar and pinch oregano
tea or coffee

SNACKS OR DRINKS AT PLANNED TIMES
5 fl oz (150 ml) natural yogurt, ½ pint (300 ml) skim milk

Serving Information
Men and Teenagers: Add 1 slice (1 oz/30 g) rye bread; 3 oz (90 g)
  sweet corn at Evening Meal; 3 oz (90 g) grapes
Teenagers: Add ½ pint (300 ml) skim milk

DAY 3

MORNING MEAL
½ medium grapefruit
¾ oz (20 g) cornflakes
5 fl oz (150 ml) skim milk
tea or coffee

MIDDAY MEAL
2½ oz (75 g) cottage cheese
1 hard-boiled egg, sliced
mixed green salad
3 teaspoons (15 ml) low-calorie mayonnaise
3-oz (90-g) cooked potato, chilled and cubed, tossed with
  chopped onion and 2½ fl oz (75 ml) natural yogurt
tea or coffee

EVENING MEAL
4 fl oz (120 ml) mixed vegetable juice
Rabbit Bourguignon (page 130)
2 oz (60 g) cooked rice
3 oz (90 g) steamed Brussels sprouts
½ pint (300 ml) beer or cider
tea or coffee

SNACKS OR DRINKS AT PLANNED TIMES
Spiced Pineapple Pumpkin (page 187)
½ pint (300 ml) skim milk

Serving Information
Men and Teenagers: Add 3-oz (90-g) cooked potato at Midday
  Meal; 2 oz (60 g) cooked rice at Evening Meal; 3 oz (90 g)
  grapes
Teenagers: Add ½ pint (300 ml) skim milk

DAY 6

MORNING MEAL
½ medium grapefruit
3 oz (90 g) baked beans
1 slice (1 oz/30 g) wholemeal bread
1 teaspoon (5 ml) low-fat spread
tea or coffee

MIDDAY MEAL
3-4 oz (90-120 g) grilled plaice
3 oz (90 g) steamed broccoli
sliced cucumber on lettuce with 1 teaspoon (5 ml) **Savory
  Vinaigrette** (page 183)
1 medium apple
tea or coffee

EVENING MEAL
3-4 oz (90-120 g) grilled steak
3 oz (90 g) braised celery
3 oz (90 g) steamed Brussels sprouts
3 oz (90 g) whole kernel sweet corn
2 teaspoons (10 ml) low-fat spread
Strawberry Cream (page 186)
tea or coffee

SNACKS OR DRINKS AT PLANNED TIMES
¾ oz (20 g) crispbread, 1 teaspoon (5 ml) low-fat spread, 2
  teaspoons (10 ml) low-calorie blackcurrant jam, ½ pint
  (300 ml) skim milk

Serving Information
Men and Teenagers: Add 2 digestive biscuits, 1 medium apple
Teenagers: Add 5 fl oz (150 ml) natural yogurt

DAY 7

MORNING MEAL
1 medium apple
1 oz (30 g) Edam cheese
1-oz (30-g) wholemeal roll
1 teaspoon (5 ml) low-fat spread
tea or coffee

MIDDAY MEAL
3-4 oz (90-120 g) roast chicken
3 oz (90 g) steamed pumpkin with 2 teaspoons (10 ml) low-fat
  spread and black pepper
3 oz (90 g) boiled potatoes mashed with 1 teaspoon (5 ml)
  low-fat spread
1 medium portion rhubarb, stewed with 2 fl oz (60 ml) low-
  calorie orange squash, undiluted
tea or coffee

EVENING MEAL
3-4 oz (90-120 g) sardines
mixed green salad
3 oz (90 g) sliced tomatoes
1 slice (1 oz/30 g) wholemeal bread
1 teaspoon (5 ml) margarine
1 medium pear □ tea or coffee

SNACKS OR DRINKS AT PLANNED TIMES
1 medium orange, 5 fl oz (150 ml) natural yogurt, 7½ fl oz
  (225 ml) skim milk

Serving Information
Men and Teenagers: Add 3-oz (90-g) boiled potato, 1 medium
  banana
Teenagers: Add ½ pint (300 ml) skim milk

WEEK 45

Guy Fawkes Night reminds us of cold nights and black skies and bonfires. What could be better than a hot nourishing soup to warm and cheer us? We provide seven such recipes this week. All the vegetables used will be available, mostly fresh, but some in frozen form. You will find a blender very useful to puree the cooked vegetables before blending them with your stock.

Minestrone is a fine old Italian recipe, a classic soup from the regions of Liguria and Lombardy. It contains a mixture of vegetables, is thickened with pasta and flavoured with garlic and must be served piping hot.

Broccoli Soup is so simple that you can make it in a moment and enjoy it within minutes. Its soft green colour is very pleasing.

DAY 1

MORNING MEAL
½ medium banana, sliced on ¾ oz (20 g) cornflakes
5 fl oz (150 ml) skim milk
1 slice (1 oz/30 g) bread with 1 teaspoon (5 ml) margarine and 1 teaspoon (5 ml) marmalade
tea or coffee

MIDDAY MEAL
Tomato and Marrow Soup (page 111)
2 oz (60 g) Cheddar cheese, grated with green salad and sliced tomatoes
5 fl oz (150 ml) natural yogurt with 2 oz (60 g) canned peach slices
tea or coffee

EVENING MEAL
3-4 oz (90-120 g) trout, grilled with sliced onion rings, bay leaf and lemon juice
3 oz (90 g) cooked green beans
6-oz (180-g) baked jacket potato with 2 teaspoons (10 ml) margarine
1 medium orange
tea or coffee

SNACKS OR DRINKS AT PLANNED TIMES
5 fl oz (150 ml) skim milk

Serving Information
Men and Teenagers: Add 1 slice (1 oz/30 g) wholemeal bread at Midday Meal, 1 digestive biscuit, 4 oz (120 g) canned peach slices, ½ medium banana
Teenagers: Add ½ pint (300 ml) skim milk

DAY 4

MORNING MEAL
3 oz (90 g) grapes
2½ oz (75 g) cottage cheese
1 slice (1 oz/30 g) currant bread
tea or coffee

MIDDAY MEAL
Fresh Mushroom Soup (page 115)
2 eggs, poached
2 slices (1 oz/30 g each) bread, toasted with 4 teaspoons (20 ml) low-fat spread
tea or coffee

EVENING MEAL
2-inch (5-cm) wedge honeydew melon
3-4 oz (90-120 g) grilled lamb's liver
3 oz (90 g) steamed broccoli
3 oz (90 g) steamed carrots
2 teaspoons (10 ml) low-fat spread
5 fl oz (150 ml) natural yogurt with 2 tablespoons (30 ml) raisins
tea or coffee

SNACKS OR DRINKS AT PLANNED TIMES
½ pint (300 ml) skim milk

Serving Information
Men and Teenagers: Add 2 digestive biscuits, 3 oz (90 g) grapes, 2-inch (5-cm) wedge honeydew melon
Teenagers: Add ½ pint (300 ml) skim milk

DAY 5

MORNING MEAL
½ medium grapefruit
1 boiled egg
¾ oz (20 g) crispbread
2 teaspoons (10 ml) low-fat spread
1 teaspoon (5 ml) honey □ tea or coffee

MIDDAY MEAL
5 oz (150 g) cottage cheese mixed with 3 oz (90 g) canned whole kernel sweet corn
2 tablespoons (30 ml) green pepper, chopped
2 tablespoons (30 ml) onion, chopped
2 tablespoons (30 ml) sultanas and 2 teaspoons (10 ml) salad cream
2 cream crackers □ tea or coffee

EVENING MEAL
Broccoli Soup (page 115)
3-4 oz (90-120 g) grilled plaice with 1 teaspoon (5 ml) margarine and lemon juice
3 oz (90 g) steamed cauliflower
3 oz (90 g) cooked broad beans
2 oz (60 g) vanilla ice cream with 5 oz (150 g) stewed blackcurrants □ tea or coffee

SNACKS OR DRINKS AT PLANNED TIMES
5 fl oz (150 ml) natural yogurt, 5 fl oz (150 ml) skim milk

Serving Information
Men and Teenagers: Add 6 oz (180 g) steamed potato at Evening meal, ½ medium grapefruit, 1 medium apple
Teenagers: Add ½ pint (300 ml) skim milk

DAY 2

MORNING MEAL
4 fl oz (120 ml) orange juice
1 oz (30 g) Cheddar cheese toasted on 1 slice (1 oz/30 g) wholemeal bread
tea or coffee

MIDDAY MEAL
3 tablespoons (45 ml) peanut butter
¾ oz (20 g) crispbread
cucumber and tomato slices
5 fl oz (150 ml) natural yogurt with 4 oz (120 g) canned peach slices
tea or coffee

EVENING MEAL
Cauliflower and Courgette Soup (page 110)
3-4 oz (90-120 g) chicken roasted with herbs and lemon juice
3 oz (90 g) cooked peas
2 oz (60 g) cooked noodles
1 teaspoon (5 ml) margarine
1 medium pear
tea or coffee

SNACKS OR DRINKS AT PLANNED TIMES
½ pint (300 ml) skim milk, 1 medium portion stewed rhubarb

Serving Information
Men and Teenagers: Add ¾ oz (20 g) crispbread at Midday Meal; 2 oz (60 g) cooked noodles at Evening Meal; 1 medium apple
Teenagers: Add ½ pint (300 ml) skim milk

DAY 3

MORNING MEAL
½ medium grapefruit
¾ oz (20 g) bran flakes
5 fl oz (150 ml) skim milk
tea or coffee

MIDDAY MEAL
7-8 oz (210-240 g) baked beans
1 slice (1 oz/30 g) bread, toasted
3 oz (90 g) poached mushrooms
1 medium apple
tea or coffee

EVENING MEAL
Minestrone (page 110)
3 oz (90 g) bologna, sliced
tomato and onion salad with 1 teaspoon (5 ml) olive oil and wine vinegar
3 oz (90 g) cooked potato, diced and mixed with 1 tablespoon (15 ml) onion, chopped, and 2 teaspoons (10 ml) mayonnaise
3 oz (90 g) grapes
tea or coffee

SNACKS OR DRINKS AT PLANNED TIMES
5 fl oz (150 ml) skim milk, 5 fl oz (150 ml) natural yogurt

Serving Information
Men and Teenagers: Add extra 3 oz (90 g) potato at Evening Meal; 1 slice (1 oz/30 g) bread at Midday Meal; ½ medium grapefruit
Men: Add extra 1 oz (30 g) bologna at Evening Meal
Teenagers: Add ½ pint (300 ml) skim milk

DAY 6

MORNING MEAL
½ medium banana
¾ oz (20 g) muesli
5 fl oz (150 ml) skim milk
tea or coffee

MIDDAY MEAL
Garden Pea Soup (page 114)
3 oz (90 g) cooked ham
6-oz (180-g) baked jacket potato with 2½ fl oz (75 ml) natural yogurt mixed with chopped chives
3 oz (90 g) cooked asparagus tips with 2 teaspoons (10 ml) margarine
2-inch (5-cm) wedge honeydew melon
tea or coffee

EVENING MEAL
3-4 oz (90-120 g) sardines grilled on 1 slice (1 oz/30 g) wholemeal bread, toasted and spread with 2 teaspoons (10 ml) low-fat spread
2 medium grilled tomatoes
4 oz (120 g) canned pineapple
tea or coffee

SNACKS OR DRINKS AT PLANNED TIMES
5 fl oz (150 ml) skim milk, **Highland 'Fling'** (page 192)

Serving Information
Men and Teenagers: Add ¾ oz (20 g) muesli at Morning Meal; 1 medium apple
Men: Add 1 oz (30 g) cooked ham at Midday Meal
Teenagers: Add ½ pint (300 ml) skim milk

DAY 7

MORNING MEAL
4 fl oz (120 ml) orange juice
1 egg, cooked in 1 teaspoon (5 ml) vegetable oil
1 oz (30 g) grilled lean back bacon
1 medium grilled tomato
1 slice (1 oz/30 g) bread
tea or coffee

MIDDAY MEAL
Cream of Asparagus and Leek Soup (page 112)
3-4 oz (90-120 g) roast beef with fresh horseradish
3 oz (90 g) cooked cabbage
3 oz (90 g) cooked parsnips
3 oz (90 g) cooked potato
4 oz (120 g) fresh fruit salad
tea or coffee

EVENING MEAL
5 oz (150 g) cottage cheese with 4 oz (120 g) canned pineapple
green salad with sliced tomato and 1 teaspoon (5 ml) salad cream
¾ oz (20 g) crispbread with 1 teaspoon (5 ml) low-fat spread
tea or coffee

SNACKS OR DRINKS AT PLANNED TIMES
5 fl oz (150 ml) natural yogurt, 9 fl oz (270 ml) skim milk

Serving Information
Men and Teenagers: Add 3 oz (90 g) cooked potato at Midday Meal, 1 digestive biscuit, 4 dried dates
Teenagers: Add ½ pint (300 ml) skim milk

WEEK 46

Only five weeks to Christmas now, so it's time to start planning. You can take a peep at **Week 52** and prepare your shopping lists in advance. You can probably do some cooking ahead, too, so that you don't feel overwhelmed by all the chores of the festive season. It's important that you enjoy the Christmas break, for if you feel tired and 'martyred' you are likely to turn to unwise eating to comfort yourself.

We suggest some simple meals this week, to give you extra time. The grilled plaice (**Day 3**) is quickly cooked and the sardine and egg salads can be prepared in advance, of course. The Sauteed Shrimps and Corn (**Day 6**) is a little unusual and particularly tasty – do try it.

'Saute' is a cooking method very useful for anyone who wishes to lose weight. It means 'to cook very quickly in a small amount of fat, usually in a shallow, open pan'.

DAY 1

MORNING MEAL
½ medium banana, sliced
¾ oz (20 g) muesli
2½ fl oz (75 ml) natural yogurt
tea or coffee

MIDDAY MEAL
5 oz (150 g) cottage cheese mixed with 2 tablespoons (30 ml) chopped spring onions with lettuce, sliced tomatoes and sliced cucumber
2 teaspoons (10 ml) salad cream
¾ oz (20 g) melba toast
1 teaspoon (5 ml) margarine
1 medium orange
tea or coffee

EVENING MEAL
Split Pea and Mushroom Stew (page 165)
1 slice (1 oz/30 g) wholemeal bread
2 teaspoons (10 ml) low-fat spread
4 oz (120 g) stewed apple with 2½ fl oz (75 ml) natural yogurt

SNACKS OR DRINKS AT PLANNED TIMES
½ pint (300 ml) skim milk

Serving Information
Men and Teenagers: Add ½ medium banana, ¾ oz (20 g) muesli, 1 slice (1 oz/30 g) wholemeal bread
Men: Add 1¼ oz (37.5 g) cottage cheese to salad at Midday Meal
Teenagers: Add 5 fl oz (150 ml) natural yogurt

DAY 4

MORNING MEAL
4 oz (120 g) canned fruit cocktail
¾ oz (20 g) cornflakes
5 fl oz (150 ml) skim milk
tea or coffee

MIDDAY MEAL
Liver with Noodles (page 146)
3 oz (90 g) steamed courgettes
3 oz (90 g) steamed cauliflower
1 slice (1 oz/30 g) wholemeal bread
1 teaspoon (5 ml) margarine
1 medium orange
tea or coffee

EVENING MEAL
3-4 oz (90-120 g) grilled lean pork chop
1 teaspoon (5 ml) horseradish relish
3 oz (90 g) steamed broccoli
3 oz (90 g) steamed carrots dotted with 1 teaspoon (5 ml) low-fat spread
4 oz (120 g) canned pineapple with 2½ fl oz (75 ml) natural yogurt
tea or coffee

SNACKS OR DRINKS AT PLANNED TIMES
½ pint (300 ml) skim milk

Serving Information
Men and Teenagers: Add 4 fl oz (120 ml) orange juice, 1 slice (1 oz/30 g) wholemeal bread, ¾ oz (20 g) cornflakes
Teenagers: Add 5 fl oz (150 ml) natural yogurt

DAY 5

MORNING MEAL
1 medium orange
2½ oz (75 g) cottage cheese
1 slice (1 oz/30 g) wholemeal bread
tea or coffee

MIDDAY MEAL
3-4 oz (90-120 g) canned sardines on mixed salad of shredded lettuce, with 1 medium tomato and sliced cucumber
2 teaspoons (10 ml) low-calorie mayonnaise
1 slice (1 oz/30 g) wholemeal bread
2 teaspoons (10 ml) low-fat spread
1 medium apple
tea or coffee

EVENING MEAL
3-4 oz (90-120 g) grilled herring with 1 tablespoon (15 ml) mustard relish
3 oz (90 g) steamed spinach
3 oz (90 g) steamed carrots dotted with 1 teaspoon (5 ml) margarine
4 oz (120 g) canned mandarin oranges
4 fl oz (120 ml) white wine
tea or coffee

SNACKS OR DRINKS AT PLANNED TIMES
5 fl oz (150 ml) natural yogurt, ½ pint (300 ml) skim milk

Serving Information
Men and Teenagers: Add 1 medium pear, 1 slice (1 oz/30 g) wholemeal bread, 1 digestive biscuit
Teenagers: Add ½ pint (300 ml) skim milk

DAY 2

MORNING MEAL
½ medium grapefruit
1 poached egg
1 slice (1 oz/30 g) wholemeal bread
1 teaspoon (5 ml) low-fat spread
tea or coffee

MIDDAY MEAL
3-4 oz (90-120 g) canned salmon with 2 oz (60 g) sliced celery,
   1 oz (30 g) diced onion and 2 teaspoons (10 ml) low-calorie
   mayonnaise
3 oz (90 g) baked beans
2 small satsumas
½ pint (300 ml) beer or cider
tea or coffee

EVENING MEAL
3-4 oz (90-120 g) roast beef
1 tablespoon (15 ml) horseradish relish
3 oz (90 g) cooked peas
3-oz (90-g) baked jacket potato
3 teaspoons (15 ml) low-fat spread
4 oz (120 g) canned fruit salad
tea or coffee

SNACKS OR DRINKS AT PLANNED TIMES
5 fl oz (150 ml) natural yogurt, ½ pint (300 ml) skim milk

Serving Information
Men and Teenagers: Add 3 oz (90 g) grapes and 1 digestive
   biscuit
Teenagers: Add ½ pint (300 ml) skim milk

DAY 3

MORNING MEAL
1 medium apple
1 oz (30 g) Cheddar cheese
1 slice (1 oz/30 g) wholemeal bread
tea or coffee

MIDDAY MEAL
2 hard-boiled eggs, sliced onto shredded lettuce with 1 medium
   tomato sliced, and 2-3 spring onions and 2 teaspoons (10 ml)
   mayonnaise
3 oz (90 g) whole kernel sweet corn
Baked Apple (page 188)
Custard (page 191)
tea or coffee

EVENING MEAL
3-4 oz (90-120 g) grilled plaice with lemon juice
3 oz (90 g) cooked Brussels sprouts
3 oz (90 g) steamed green beans dotted with 1 teaspoon (5 ml)
   margarine
1 medium orange, peeled and diced into 5 fl oz (150 ml) natural
   yogurt
tea or coffee

SNACKS OR DRINKS AT PLANNED TIMES
5 fl oz (150 ml) skim milk

Serving Information
Men and Teenagers: Add 1 medium pear; 6 oz (180 g) cooked
   potatoes at Evening Meal
Teenagers: Add 5 fl oz (150 ml) natural yogurt

DAY 6

MORNING MEAL
2½ fl oz (75 ml) apple juice
1 oz (30 g) Cheshire cheese grilled on 1 slice (1 oz/30 g) bread,
   toasted
tea or coffee

MIDDAY MEAL
open sandwich made with 3-4 oz (90-120 g) sliced chicken,
   shredded lettuce, sliced tomatoes on 1 slice (1 oz/30 g)
   wholemeal bread, spread with 1 teaspoon (5 ml) margarine
   and topped with 2 teaspoons (10 ml) low-calorie mayonnaise
4 oz (120 g) orange sections
tea or coffee

EVENING MEAL
Sauteed Prawns and Corn (page 160)
3 oz (90 g) steamed broccoli
3 oz (90 g) cooked peas
2 medium plums, stoned and diced, mixed with 2½ fl oz (75 ml)
   natural yogurt
tea or coffee

SNACKS OR DRINKS AT PLANNED TIMES
15 fl oz (450 ml) skim milk

Serving Information
Men and Teenagers: Add 2 medium plums, 1 slice (1 oz/30 g)
   wholemeal bread, 3 oz (90 g) boiled potatoes
Teenagers: Add 5 fl oz (150 ml) natural yogurt

DAY 7

MORNING MEAL
4 fl oz (120 ml) orange juice
¾ oz (20 g) porridge oats cooked with water
5 fl oz (150 ml) skim milk
tea or coffee

MIDDAY MEAL
Cheese Omelette (page 120)
green salad with 1 teaspoon (5 ml) oil with wine vinegar
1 slice (1 oz/30 g) rye bread
1 teaspoon (5 ml) low-fat spread
4 oz (120 g) canned pineapple
2 oz (60 g) vanilla ice cream
tea or coffee

EVENING MEAL
3-4 oz (90-120 g) grilled steak
1 medium tomato, halved and grilled
3 oz (90 g) steamed green beans
3 oz (90 g) boiled potatoes
1 teaspoon (5 ml) low-fat spread
½ medium banana, sliced into **Custard** (page 191)
tea or coffee

SNACKS OR DRINKS AT PLANNED TIMES
½ pint (300 ml) skim milk

Serving Information
Men and Teenagers: Add ½ medium banana, ¾ oz (20 g)
   porridge oats, 3 oz (90 g) boiled potatoes
Teenagers: Add 5 fl oz (150 ml) natural yogurt

WEEK 47

Chinese Cookery is now very popular. It has a lightness and delicacy of flavour which makes it especially delicious. It is often quickly cooked and is usually accompanied by spicy sauces. The utensil associated with Chinese cooking is, of course, the wok. This is simply a round-bottomed frying pan with a dome-shaped cover, and it is used in China for stir-frying, braising and steaming. We can buy woks in hardware departments here and you will find them useful for the quick cooking of vegetables and small pieces of meat or fish or chicken.

Dill is used, also, this week. It is a member of the parsley family, has a piquant flavour and is often used in pickling cucumbers. We combine it with olive oil, wine vinegar and garlic to produce a lovely salad dressing (Day 3).

DAY 1

MORNING MEAL
Honey-Stewed Prunes (page 192)
¾ oz (20 g) porridge oats, cooked in water
5 fl oz (150 ml) skim milk
tea or coffee

MIDDAY MEAL
Soused Herring (page 158)
1 small onion, sliced
1 medium tomato, sliced and 2 oz (60 g) cooked rice mixed with
    1 teaspoon (5 ml) oil with 2 teaspoons (10 ml) wine vinegar
2½ fl oz (75 ml) pineapple juice
tea or coffee

EVENING MEAL
Chinese Salad (page 180)
1-oz (30-g) pitta bread
2 teaspoons (10 ml) low-fat spread
2 small tangerines
tea or coffee

SNACKS OR DRINKS AT PLANNED TIMES
5 fl oz (150 ml) natural yogurt, 5 fl oz (150 ml) skim milk, 1
    digestive biscuit

Serving Information
Men and Teenagers: Add 4 fl oz (120 ml) orange juice; 2-oz
    (60-g) pitta bread at Evening Meal
Teenagers: Add ½ pint (300 ml) skim milk

DAY 4

MORNING MEAL
4 oz (120 g) grapefruit sections
1 oz (30 g) Cheddar cheese
1 slice (1 oz/30 g) bread
tea or coffee

MIDDAY MEAL
3-4 oz (90-120 g) steamed lemon sole
3 oz (90 g) steamed courgettes
3 oz (90 g) steamed cauliflower
2 oz (60 g) cooked noodles
1 teaspoon (5 ml) margarine
4 oz (120 g) canned pineapple with 2 oz (60 g) vanilla ice cream
tea or coffee

EVENING MEAL
Marinated Mushrooms (page 110)
3-4 oz (90-120 g) grilled pork chop
3 oz (90 g) steamed broccoli
3 oz (90 g) steamed carrots dotted with 1 teaspoon (5 ml)
    margarine
4 oz (120 g) canned peach slices
tea or coffee

SNACKS OR DRINKS AT PLANNED TIMES
5 fl oz (150 ml) natural yogurt with 1 teaspoon (5 ml) honey,
    ½ pint (300 ml) skim milk

Serving Information
Men and Teenagers: Add 4 oz (120 g) grapefruit sections, 2 oz
    (60 g) cooked noodles at Midday Meal, 1 digestive biscuit
Teenagers: Add ½ pint (300 ml) skim milk

DAY 5

MORNING MEAL
4 fl oz (120 ml) grapefruit juice
¾ oz (20 g) puffed rice
5 fl oz (150 ml) skim milk
tea or coffee

MIDDAY MEAL
Chinese-Style Pancakes (page 118)
3 oz (90 g) cooked bean sprouts
3 oz (90 g) steamed mushrooms
1 medium pear
tea or coffee

EVENING MEAL
3-4 oz (90-120 g) roast veal
6 oz (180 g) Chinese leaves, shredded and sauteed for 2 minutes
    in 1 teaspoon (5 ml) margarine
3 oz (90 g) celery hearts
2-inch (5-cm) wedge honeydew melon with pinch ground ginger
tea or coffee

SNACKS OR DRINKS AT PLANNED TIMES
5 fl oz (150 ml) natural yogurt, 5 fl oz (150 ml) skim milk,
    2 digestive biscuits with 2 teaspoons (10 ml) low-fat spread
    and 2 teaspoons (10 ml) low-calorie raspberry jam

Serving Information
Men and Teenagers: Add 4 fl oz (120 ml) grapefruit juice, 2 oz
    (60 g) cooked noodles at Evening Meal
Teenagers: Add ½ pint (300 ml) skim milk

DAY 2

MORNING MEAL
2-inch (5-cm) wedge honeydew melon
1 boiled egg
1 slice (1 oz/30 g) granary bread
1 teaspoon (5 ml) margarine
tea or coffee

MIDDAY MEAL
4 fl oz (120 ml) tomato juice
3-4 oz (90-120 g) peeled prawns
green salad with sliced tomatoes, cucumber and spring onions
    with 1 teaspoon (5 ml) mayonnaise
4 oz (120 g) canned pineapple
tea or coffee

EVENING MEAL
Oriental Beef (page 150)
bean sprouts and mushroom salad with lemon juice
2 oz (60 g) cooked rice
tea or coffee

SNACKS OR DRINKS AT PLANNED TIMES
Pineapple-Coconut Biscuits (page 186)
½ pint (300 ml) skim milk

Serving Information
Men and Teenagers: Add 2 oz (60 g) cooked rice at Evening
    Meal; ¾-oz (20-g) crumpet spread with 2 teaspoons (10 ml)
    low-calorie jam, 4 oz (120 g) canned pineapple
Teenagers: Add 5 fl oz (150 ml) natural yogurt

DAY 3

MORNING MEAL
½ medium banana, sliced over ¾ oz (20 g) muesli with 5 fl oz
    (150 ml) skim milk
tea or coffee

MIDDAY MEAL
3-4 oz (90-120 g) grilled chicken
3 oz (90 g) cucumber, sliced
chopped spring onions and celery strips on shredded lettuce
    with **Dill Vinaigrette** (page 183)
1 slice (1 oz/30 g) granary bread
1 teaspoon (5 ml) margarine
tea or coffee

EVENING MEAL
8 fl oz (240 ml) tomato juice
3-4 oz (90-120 g) grilled calf's liver
2 oz (60 g) cooked noodles
3 oz (90 g) cooked peas
green salad with ½ teaspoon (2.5 ml) oil with wine vinegar
8 fresh lychees
tea or coffee

SNACKS OR DRINKS AT PLANNED TIMES
5 fl oz (150 ml) natural yogurt with 2 teaspoons (10 ml) low-
    calorie jam, 5 fl oz (150 ml) skim milk

Serving Information
Men and Teenagers: Add ½ medium banana, sliced, on 1 slice
    (1 oz/30 g) currant bread, toasted, 1 digestive biscuit
Teenagers: Add ½ pint (300 ml) skim milk

DAY 6

MORNING MEAL
5 oz (150 g) cantaloupe melon cubes
2½ oz (75 g) cottage cheese
2 cream crackers
tea or coffee

MIDDAY MEAL
3-4 oz (90-120 g) grilled plaice dotted with 1 teaspoon (5 ml)
    margarine
3 oz (90 g) steamed carrots
3 oz (90 g) steamed potatoes
green salad with **Savory Vinaigrette** (page 183)
8 fresh lychees
tea or coffee

EVENING MEAL
Sweet and Sour Pork Fillet (page 140)
2 oz (60 g) cooked rice
tea or coffee

SNACKS OR DRINKS AT PLANNED TIMES
5 fl oz (150 ml) natural yogurt with 1 teaspoon (5 ml) honey,
    ½ pint (300 ml) skim milk

Serving Information
Men and Teenagers: Add 2 oz (60 g) cooked rice at Evening Meal
    and 4 oz (120 g) canned pineapple chunks
Teenagers: Add ½ pint (300 ml) skim milk

DAY 7

MORNING MEAL
2½ fl oz (75 ml) pineapple juice
1 egg, scrambled in 1 teaspoon (5 ml) margarine with 1 slice
    (1 oz/30 g) bread, toasted
1 teaspoon (5 ml) margarine
tea or coffee

MIDDAY MEAL
Chicken with Fresh Mushrooms (page 132)
3 oz (90 g) cooked peas
2 oz (60 g) cooked rice
green salad with lemon juice
1 medium orange
4 fl oz (120 ml) white wine
tea or coffee

EVENING MEAL
2½ oz (75 g) cottage cheese
1½-2 oz (45-60 g) peeled prawns
1 teaspoon (5 ml) mayonnaise
finely sliced radish, celery and pepper salad with lemon juice and
    ½ teaspoon (2.5 ml) honey
4 oz (120 g) canned peach slices
tea or coffee

SNACKS OR DRINKS AT PLANNED TIMES
5 fl oz (150 ml) natural yogurt, ½ pint (300 ml) skim milk

Serving Information
Men and Teenagers: Add 2½ fl oz (75 ml) pineapple juice and
    4 oz (120 g) cooked rice at Midday Meal
Teenagers: Add ½ pint (300 ml) skim milk

WEEK 48

Meat is always considered to be one of the more expensive forms of protein, so we have set out, this week, to show you some cheaper cuts and categories which can help your housekeeping budget.

Tripe doesn't deserve its poor reputation. It's one of the most easily digested protein foods and it combines with stronger flavours very well. We have used a curry sauce for the dish on Day 1.

Liver and kidneys are not expensive and they are first class in nutrition value, high in B vitamins and iron. We serve chicken livers with green noodles – an unusual combination. Kidneys are made even more exotic by the inclusion of red wine during cooking. The amount is small, so won't push your budget 'over the top'.

DAY 1

MORNING MEAL
½ medium banana
¾ oz (20 g) muesli with 5 fl oz (150 ml) natural yogurt
tea or coffee

MIDDAY MEAL
3-4 oz (90-120 g) tuna
green salad
1 medium tomato
3 oz (90 g) beetroot
2 teaspoons (10 ml) low-calorie mayonnaise
2 cream crackers
1 medium orange
tea or coffee

EVENING MEAL
Curried Tripe (page 144)
2 small clementines
tea or coffee

SNACKS OR DRINKS AT PLANNED TIMES
½ pint (300 ml) skim milk

Serving Information
Men and Teenagers: Add 1 slice (1 oz/30 g) wholemeal bread and 1 teaspoon (5 ml) honey at Morning Meal; ½ medium banana; 2 cream crackers at Midday Meal
Teenagers: Add ½ pint (300 ml) skim milk

DAY 4

MORNING MEAL
½ medium grapefruit
¾ oz (20 g) cornflakes
5 fl oz (150 ml) skim milk
tea or coffee

MIDDAY MEAL
Meatball and Vegetable Stir-Fry (page 140)
¼ small pineapple
tea or coffee

EVENING MEAL
7-8 oz (210-240 g) baked beans on 1 slice (1 oz/30 g) bread, toasted
2 teaspoons (10 ml) low-fat spread
3 oz (90 g) poached mushrooms
1 medium grilled tomato
3 oz (90 g) grapes
tea or coffee

SNACKS OR DRINKS AT PLANNED TIMES
5 fl oz (150 ml) natural yogurt with 1 medium portion stewed rhubarb, 5 fl oz (150 ml) skim milk

Serving Information
Men and Teenagers: Add 2 slices (1 oz/30 g each) currant bread and 2 teaspoons (10 ml) low-calorie raspberry jam, 1 medium banana
Teenagers: Add ½ pint (300 ml) skim milk

DAY 5

MORNING MEAL
4 fl oz (120 ml) orange juice
1 boiled egg .
1 slice (1 oz/30 g) wholemeal bread
2 teaspoons (10 ml) low-fat spread
tea or coffee

MIDDAY MEAL
3 tablespoons (45 ml) peanut butter
¾ oz (20 g) crispbread
tomato and cucumber salad with wine vinegar and garlic salt
3 oz (90 g) grapes
tea or coffee

EVENING MEAL
6 oz (180 g) boil-in-the-bag fish in sauce (any type)
3 oz (90 g) boiled potatoes
3 oz (90 g) steamed leeks
3 oz (90 g) cooked peas
2 small clementines
tea or coffee

SNACKS OR DRINKS AT PLANNED TIMES
5 fl oz (150 ml) natural yogurt, ½ pint (300 ml) skim milk

Serving Information
Men and Teenagers: Add 2 digestive biscuits, 3 oz (90 g) grapes
Teenagers: Add ½ pint (300 ml) skim milk

DAY 2

MORNING MEAL
4 fl oz (120 ml) orange juice
1 oz (30 g) Cheddar cheese, grilled on 1 slice (1 oz/30 g) bread
1 medium grilled tomato
tea or coffee

MIDDAY MEAL
1 hard-boiled egg, chopped
2½ oz (75 g) cottage cheese mixed with 2 tablespoons (30 ml) sultanas and sprinkling of curry powder
celery, cucumber and green pepper salad, mixed with 2 teaspoons (10 ml) mayonnaise
¾ oz (20 g) crispbread with 1 teaspoon (5 ml) low-fat spread
tea or coffee

EVENING MEAL
3-4 oz (90-120 g) roast chicken
3 oz (90 g) cooked Brussels sprouts
3 oz (90 g) cooked swede
3 oz (90 g) boiled potatoes with 1 teaspoon (5 ml) low-fat spread
5 oz (150 g) raspberry jelly with 5 oz (150 g) raspberries
tea or coffee

SNACKS OR DRINKS AT PLANNED TIMES
5 fl oz (150 ml) natural yogurt, ½ pint (300 ml) skim milk

Serving Information
Men and Teenagers: Add 3 oz (90 g) boiled potatoes at Evening Meal; 8 fl oz (240 ml) tomato juice
Teenagers: Add ½ pint (300 ml) skim milk

DAY 3

MORNING MEAL
¾ oz (20 g) porridge oats cooked with water
5 fl oz (150 ml) skim milk
2 tablespoons (30 ml) raisins
tea or coffee

MIDDAY MEAL
3-4 oz (90-120 g) grilled plaice
3 oz (90 g) steamed green beans
3 oz (90 g) steamed carrots
5 fl oz (150 ml) natural yogurt with 1 oz (30 g) dried apricots, chopped
tea or coffee

EVENING MEAL
Chicken Livers and Green Noodles (page 140)
3 oz (90 g) cooked peas
4 fl oz (120 ml) red wine
1 medium orange
tea or coffee

SNACKS OR DRINKS AT PLANNED TIMES
5 fl oz (150 ml) skim milk, 1 digestive biscuit

Serving Information
Men and Teenagers: Add 1½-oz (45-g) muffin at Morning Meal with 2 teaspoons (10 ml) low-calorie marmalade, 6 oz (180 g) grapes
Teenagers: Add ½ pint (300 ml) skim milk

DAY 6

MORNING MEAL
1 medium orange
¾ oz (20 g) puffed wheat
5 fl oz (150 ml) skim milk
tea or coffee

MIDDAY MEAL
2 oz (60 g) Cheddar cheese
1 slice (1 oz/30 g) French bread
2 teaspoons (10 ml) low-fat spread
2 pickled onions
1 medium tomato
watercress
5 fl oz (150 ml) natural yogurt with ½ medium banana, sliced
tea or coffee

EVENING MEAL
Kidneys in Red Wine (page 151)
¼ small pineapple
tea or coffee

SNACKS OR DRINKS AT PLANNED TIMES
5 fl oz (150 ml) skim milk

Serving Information
Men and Teenagers: Add ¾ oz (20 g) puffed wheat at Morning Meal; ½ medium banana
Teenagers: Add ½ pint (300 ml) skim milk

DAY 7

MORNING MEAL
2½ oz (75 g) cottage cheese with 4 oz (120 g) sliced canned peaches
1 slice (1 oz/30 g) wholemeal bread
2 teaspoons (10 ml) low-fat spread
½ teaspoon (2.5 ml) marmalade □ tea or coffee

MIDDAY MEAL
3-4 oz (90-120 g) roast lamb
3 oz (90 g) steamed cabbage
3 oz (90 g) cooked carrots
3 oz (90 g) cooked potato
2 teaspoons (10 ml) low-fat spread
4 oz (120 g) fresh fruit salad
5 fl oz (150 ml) natural yogurt
4 fl oz (120 ml) red wine □ tea or coffee

EVENING MEAL
2-egg omelette with pinch mixed herbs
green salad with 1 medium tomato
1-oz (30-g) Scotch pancake with 1 teaspoon (5 ml) margarine and 1 teaspoon (5 ml) raspberry jam
1 medium orange □ tea or coffee

SNACKS OR DRINKS AT PLANNED TIMES
½ pint (300 ml) skim milk

Serving Information
Men and Teenagers: Add 3 oz (90 g) cooked potato at Midday Meal; 1-oz (30-g) Scotch pancake at Evening Meal; 4 oz (120 g) fresh fruit salad
Teenagers: Add ½ pint (300 ml) skim milk

WEEK 49

You will be very busy with Christmas preparations this week, so we've planned a set of menus which allow you to get out of the kitchen. But don't imagine that this means that your meals will be any less delicious or nutritious. The beauty of the Weight Watchers Food Plan is that it can adapt to so many varied lifestyles. You can be a devoted and painstaking cook if you wish, or you can spend a minimum of time at the cooker and sink. It's just up to you.

You'll enjoy some of this week's home-produced fast food. There are salads, of course, but we suggest hot meals, too, for these cold days. There's 'boil-in-the-bag' fish, grilled plaice, sauteed liver, omelettes, grilled chops and stir-fry chicken. Who could be bored with such a varied menu plan as this? So make your list, stock your larder and get on with the Christmas shopping!

DAY 1

MORNING MEAL
4 fl oz (120 ml) orange juice
¾ oz (20 g) porridge oats, cooked with water and served with 5 fl oz (150 ml) skim milk □ tea or coffee

MIDDAY MEAL
3-4 oz (90-120 g) corned beef with 2 teaspoons (10 ml) relish
mixed green salad with 1 medium tomato, sliced, and 2-inch (5-cm) chunk cucumber, sliced, with 2 teaspoons (10 ml) salad cream
1½ oz (45 g) crispbread
2 teaspoons (10 ml) low-fat spread
2 teaspoons (10 ml) low-calorie raspberry jam
1 medium apple □ tea or coffee

EVENING MEAL
6 oz (180 g) boil-in-the-bag fish in sauce (any type)
3 oz (90 g) steamed carrots
3 oz (90 g) steamed courgettes
3 oz (90 g) boiled potatoes, mashed with 2 teaspoons (10 ml) low-fat spread
2 small tangerines with 5 fl oz (150 ml) natural yogurt
tea or coffee

SNACKS OR DRINKS AT PLANNED TIMES
5 fl oz (150 ml) skim milk

Serving Information
Men and Teenagers: Add 3 oz (90 g) boiled potatoes, 4 fl oz (120 ml) orange juice
Teenagers: Add ½ pint (300 ml) skim milk

DAY 4

MORNING MEAL
½ medium grapefruit
¾ oz (20 g) cornflakes with 5 fl oz (150 ml) skim milk
tea or coffee

MIDDAY MEAL
2-egg omelette or 2 hard-boiled eggs with green salad, with 2 teaspoons (10 ml) salad cream
1 medium tomato, sliced
1 slice (1 oz/30 g) bread
3 oz (90 g) grapes
tea or coffee

EVENING MEAL
3-4 oz (90-120 g) grilled haddock
3 oz (90 g) cooked peas
3 oz (90 g) cooked swede, mashed with 3 oz (90 g) boiled potato
2 teaspoons (10 ml) margarine
½ medium banana
tea or coffee

SNACKS OR DRINKS AT PLANNED TIMES
15 fl oz (450 ml) skim milk

Serving Information
Men and Teenagers: Add 1½-oz (45-g) scone, ½ medium banana
Teenagers: Add 5 fl oz (150 ml) natural yogurt

DAY 5

MORNING MEAL
4 fl oz (120 ml) grapefruit juice
2½ oz (75 g) cottage cheese
1 slice (1 oz/30 g) currant bread
2 teaspoons (10 ml) low-calorie strawberry jam
1 teaspoon (5 ml) margarine
tea or coffee

MIDDAY MEAL
3-4 oz (90-120 g) canned sardines
cucumber, onion and lettuce salad with 1 teaspoon (5 ml) mayonnaise
1 medium tomato, sliced
1 slice (1 oz/30 g) bread
1 teaspoon (5 ml) margarine
1 medium apple
tea or coffee

EVENING MEAL
3-4 oz (90-120 g) grilled lamb chop
3 oz (90 g) steamed spinach
3 oz (90 g) cooked parsnips
1 medium pear
tea or coffee

SNACKS OR DRINKS AT PLANNED TIMES
½ pint (300 ml) skim milk, 5 fl oz (150 ml) natural yogurt

Serving Information
Men and Teenagers: Add 1 digestive biscuit, 1 slice (1 oz/30 g) currant bread, 4 fl oz (120 ml) grapefruit juice, 1 medium apple
Teenagers: Add ½ pint (300 ml) skim milk

DAY 2

MORNING MEAL
4 fl oz (120 ml) orange juice
1 boiled egg
1-oz (30-g) bread roll
1 teaspoon (5 ml) low-fat spread
tea or coffee

MIDDAY MEAL
salad made with lettuce, cucumber and tomato, topped with
  2½ oz (75 g) cottage cheese, mixed with 1 teaspoon (5 ml)
  salad cream and pinch curry powder
Pancakes with Orange Sauce (page 116)
tea or coffee

EVENING MEAL
3-4 oz (90-120 g) grilled fillet of plaice
3 oz (90 g) steamed carrots
3 oz (90 g) cooked peas
3 oz (90 g) canned sweet corn
4 oz (120 g) canned pineapple chunks
tea or coffee

SNACKS OR DRINKS AT PLANNED TIMES
9 fl oz (270 ml) skim milk, 5 fl oz (150 ml) natural yogurt

Serving Information
Men and Teenagers: Add 1-oz (30-g) bread roll, 4 oz (120 g)
  canned pineapple chunks
Teenagers: Add ½ pint (300 ml) skim milk

DAY 3

MORNING MEAL
½ medium grapefruit
1 oz (30 g) Cheddar cheese
1 slice (1 oz/30 g) bread
tea or coffee

MIDDAY MEAL
3-4 oz (90-120 g) canned tuna
mixed salad of lettuce, sliced tomato and cucumber with lemon
  juice
1 slice (1 oz/30 g) bread
1 teaspoon (5 ml) margarine
½ medium banana with 5 fl oz (150 ml) natural yogurt
tea or coffee

EVENING MEAL
5-6 oz (150-180 g) uncooked lamb's liver, sauteed in
  2 teaspoons (10 ml) vegetable oil
3 oz (90 g) cooked cauliflower
3 oz (90 g) steamed leeks
1 medium pear
tea or coffee

SNACKS OR DRINKS AT PLANNED TIMES
½ pint (300 ml) skim milk

Serving Information
Men and Teenagers: Add 4 oz (120 g) cooked noodles at
  Evening Meal; 1 medium apple
Teenagers: Add ½ pint (300 ml) skim milk

DAY 6

MORNING MEAL
4 fl oz (120 ml) grapefruit juice
1 oz (30 g) Edam cheese
1 slice (1 oz/30 g) bread, toasted
1 teaspoon (5 ml) margarine
tea or coffee

MIDDAY MEAL
7-8 oz (210-240 g) baked beans served on 1 slice (1 oz/30 g)
  bread, toasted, spread with 1 teaspoon (5 ml) margarine
1 medium grilled tomato
3 oz (90 g) poached mushrooms
4 oz (120 g) canned fruit salad
tea or coffee

EVENING MEAL
3-oz (90-g) grilled kipper
3 oz (90 g) cooked beetroot
tomato, lettuce and onion salad with wine vinegar
1 slice (1 oz/30 g) bread, spread with 1 teaspoon (5 ml)
  margarine
1 medium orange
tea or coffee

SNACKS OR DRINKS AT PLANNED TIMES
½ pint (300 ml) skim milk, 5 fl oz (150 ml) natural yogurt

Serving Information
Men and Teenagers: Add 1 digestive biscuit, 4 oz (120 g) canned
  fruit salad
Men: Add 1-oz (30-g) grilled kipper at Evening Meal
Teenagers: Add ½ pint (300 ml) skim milk

DAY 7

MORNING MEAL
4 fl oz (120 ml) grapefruit juice
¾ oz (20 g) puffed rice with 5 fl oz (150 ml) skim milk
tea or coffee

MIDDAY MEAL
3-4 oz (90-120 g) roast lamb
3-oz (90-g) baked jacket potato with 2 teaspoons (10 ml) low-fat
  spread
3 oz (90 g) boiled leeks
3 oz (90 g) steamed carrots
Spiced Peaches (page 195)
tea or coffee

EVENING MEAL
Chicken Stir-Fry (page 130)
4 oz (120 g) cooked noodles
spring onion, celery, cucumber and lettuce salad with lemon
  juice
1 medium apple
tea or coffee

SNACKS OR DRINKS AT PLANNED TIMES
15 fl oz (450 ml) skim milk

Serving Information
Men and Teenagers: Add extra 3-oz (90-g) baked jacket potato,
  4 fl oz (120 ml) grapefruit juice
Teenagers: Add 5 fl oz (150 ml) natural yogurt

WEEK 50

What about putting a new kitchen aid on your list for Father Christmas? You will be delighted to find how you can be inspired to new heights of invention and achievement by a good blender or food processor.

Many of us have used a blender or mixer for years, but the food processor adds a whole new dimension to kitchen help. It will grind, mince, blend, mix, slice, grate, extract juice, shred. In fact the only food it won't deal with is egg whites, for it can't incorporate air as it works.

Processors work at a fast, strong speed and you have to time them carefully. You can reduce food to a pulp within seconds. For instance, you can process cooked vegetables plus stock into a marvellous soup – and without thickening agents. Pates and mousses can be produced so easily and salad jobs – such as slicing hard cabbage for cole slaw – are done in a trice.

Buy the best processor you can afford and you will have a versatile 'servant' who will be with you for years.

DAY 1

MORNING MEAL
2½ fl oz (75 ml) apple juice
1 slice (1 oz/30 g) wholemeal bread, toasted
2½ oz (75 g) curd cheese topped with 2 teaspoons (10 ml) low-calorie jam
tea or coffee

MIDDAY MEAL
5-6 oz (150-180 g) uncooked chicken livers and 2 oz (60 g) onion sliced, sauteed with 2 teaspoons (10 ml) vegetable oil
3 oz (90 g) steamed green beans
mixed green salad with lemon juice and 1 teaspoon (5 ml) imitation bacon bits
tea or coffee

EVENING MEAL
8 fl oz (240 ml) tomato juice
Fillet of Sole Florentine (page 159)
3 oz (90 g) steamed savoy cabbage
3-oz (90-g) baked jacket potato
tea or coffee

SNACKS OR DRINKS AT PLANNED TIMES
1 medium apple sliced with 5 fl oz (150 ml) natural yogurt, ½ pint (300 ml) skim milk

Serving Information
Men and Teenagers: Add 1 slice (1 oz/30 g) wholemeal bread, 3 oz (90 g) cooked sweet corn, 2 medium oranges
Teenagers: Add ½ pint (300 ml) skim milk

DAY 4

MORNING MEAL
4 oz (120 g) canned peaches
¾ oz (20 g) porridge oats cooked with water
5 fl oz (150 ml) skim milk
tea or coffee

MIDDAY MEAL
Cheese Souffle (page 116)
3 oz (90 g) cooked peas
1 medium grilled tomato
4 oz (120 g) canned mandarin oranges
tea or coffee

EVENING MEAL
2-inch (5-cm) wedge melon
Chicken and Pork Meatballs (page 142)
3 oz (90 g) steamed cabbage
3 oz (90 g) steamed cauliflower
4 fl oz (120 ml) white wine
tea or coffee

SNACKS OR DRINKS AT PLANNED TIMES
1½-oz (45-g) toasted crumpet with 2 teaspoons (10 ml) low-fat spread, ½ pint (300 ml) skim milk

Serving Information
Men and Teenagers: Add 6 oz (180 g) cooked potatoes at Evening Meal, 1 medium banana
Teenagers: Add 5 fl oz (150 ml) natural yogurt

DAY 5

MORNING MEAL
2-inch (5-cm) wedge melon
1 boiled egg
1 slice (1 oz/30 g) wholemeal bread
2 teaspoons (10 ml) low-fat spread ☐ tea or coffee

MIDDAY MEAL
2½ oz (75 g) cottage cheese creamed together with 1½-2 oz (45-60 g) tuna fish, drained and flaked with lemon juice
mixed green salad
2 water biscuits
2 teaspoons (10 ml) low-fat spread ☐ tea or coffee

EVENING MEAL
½ medium grapefruit
3-4 oz (90-120 g) grilled chicken with herbs and lemon juice
Fennel with Parmesan Cheese (page 172)
3 oz (90 g) cooked carrots
3 oz (90 g) boiled mashed swede
2 teaspoons (10 ml) low-fat spread ☐ tea or coffee

SNACKS OR DRINKS AT PLANNED TIMES
½ medium banana, with 5 fl oz (150 ml) natural yogurt, ½ pint (300 ml) skim milk

Serving Information
Men and Teenagers: Add 2 digestive biscuits, ½ medium banana
Teenagers: Add ½ pint (300 ml) skim milk

DAY 2

MORNING MEAL
4 fl oz (120 ml) grapefruit juice
¾ oz (20 g) cornflakes
5 fl oz (150 ml) skim milk □ tea or coffee

MIDDAY MEAL
1 teaspoon (5 ml) concentrated yeast extract dissolved with hot
    water to taste
Tomato Stuffed with Herb Cheese (page 126)
2-oz (60-g) slice French bread
2 teaspoons (10 ml) margarine □ tea or coffee

EVENING MEAL
3 oz (90 g) boiled ham
3 oz (90 g) braised celery
3 oz (90 g) steamed carrots, sliced
2 oz (60 g) cooked noodles
2 teaspoons (10 ml) low-fat spread
1 medium apple, baked
2 oz (60 g) vanilla ice cream □ tea or coffee

SNACKS OR DRINKS AT PLANNED TIMES
1 medium orange, 5 fl oz (150 ml) skim milk, 5 fl oz (150 ml)
    natural yogurt

Serving Information
Men and Teenagers: Add 2 cream crackers sprinkled with
    1 teaspoon (5 ml) Parmesan cheese, 4 fl oz (120 ml) grapefruit
    juice
Men: Add 1 oz (30 g) ham at Evening Meal
Teenagers: Add ½ pint (300 ml) skim milk

DAY 3

MORNING MEAL
2½ fl oz (75 ml) apple juice
1 oz (30 g) Cheddar cheese, grated
¾-oz (20-g) toasted muffin
tea or coffee

MIDDAY MEAL
3-4 oz (90-120 g) baked cod
1 medium grilled tomato
3 oz (90 g) cooked Brussels sprouts
tossed salad with **Tarragon Vinaigrette** (page 183)
1 slice (1 oz/30 g) rye bread, toasted
1 teaspoon (5 ml) low-fat spread
tea or coffee

EVENING MEAL
1 medium cooked corn-on-the-cob
1 teaspoon (5 ml) low-fat spread
Veal Stew (page 127)
bean sprouts and green pepper rings on lettuce with
    2 teaspoons (10 ml) low-calorie mayonnaise
1 medium portion stewed rhubarb
5 fl oz (150 ml) natural yogurt
tea or coffee

SNACKS OR DRINKS AT PLANNED TIMES
2 small satsumas, 1 medium apple, ½ pint (300 ml) skim milk

Serving Information
Men and Teenagers: Add 2 water biscuits, 1 medium orange
Teenagers: Add ½ pint (300 ml) skim milk

DAY 6

MORNING MEAL
½ medium banana
¾ oz (20 g) muesli
5 fl oz (150 ml) natural yogurt
tea or coffee

MIDDAY MEAL
5 oz (150 g) cottage cheese mixed with 2 tablespoons (30 ml)
    raisins and pinch curry powder
tomato, cucumber and celery, sliced on lettuce with
    2 teaspoons (10 ml) low-calorie mayonnaise
¾ oz (20 g) melba toast
tea or coffee

EVENING MEAL
½ medium grapefruit
3 oz (90 g) steamed smoked haddock
2 teaspoons (10 ml) low-fat spread
2 oz (60 g) steamed mushrooms
3 oz (90 g) cooked spinach
1-oz (30-g) wholemeal roll
2 teaspoons (10 ml) low-fat spread
tea or coffee

SNACKS OR DRINKS AT PLANNED TIMES
1 digestive biscuit, ½ pint (300 ml) skim milk

Serving Information
Men and Teenagers: Add 1-oz (30-g) wholemeal roll, ½ medium
    banana
Men: Add 1 oz (30 g) smoked haddock at Evening Meal
Teenagers: Add 5 fl oz (150 ml) natural yogurt

DAY 7

MORNING MEAL
1 medium orange, peeled and sliced
1 tablespoon (15 ml) peanut butter
¾ oz (20 g) crispbread
tea or coffee

MIDDAY MEAL
3-4 oz (90-120 g) roast beef
3-oz (90-g) potato roast in 1 teaspoon (5 ml) vegetable oil
3 oz (90 g) steamed parsnips
3 oz (90 g) carrots, sliced
1 medium baked onion
1 medium baked apple topped with 5 oz (150 g) stewed
    blackberries and 3 tablespoons (45 ml) single cream
tea or coffee

EVENING MEAL
Mushroom Omelette (page 120)
tomato and chicory salad with lemon juice
tea or coffee

SNACKS OR DRINKS AT PLANNED TIMES
5 fl oz (150 ml) natural yogurt, 1 teaspoon (5 ml) honey, ½ pint
    (300 ml) skim milk

Serving Information
Men and Teenagers: Add 2 digestive biscuits, 1 medium orange
Teenagers: Add ½ pint (300 ml) skim milk

WEEK 51

The most bland and innocuous dish can be enlivened by a good dressing. You take a basic assembly of ingredients and add flavours to fit a dozen different tastes. This week we give you recipes for several vinaigrettes, all of which can be made in advance and stored in the fridge and produced later to 'spike' green salads which accompany other dishes.

The principle of enhancing food with dressings is an excellent one. It means that one's tastebuds are pleased and a feeling of pleasure and satisfaction achieved. It is essential that anyone following a weight-loss regime should enjoy the food allowed, for a sense of deprivation and misery leads only to the abandoning of the diet. Pleasure in food is not sinful – it's a simple necessity. The dressing recipes that we offer help with this, and it's interesting to note that their success depends not on fats or cream, but on good vinegar plus herbs and flavourings.

DAY 1

MORNING MEAL
½ medium banana
¾ oz (20 g) porridge oats cooked with water
5 fl oz (150 ml) skim milk
tea or coffee

MIDDAY MEAL
Cream of Cauliflower Soup (page 115)
2 oz (60 g) Brie cheese
1 slice (1 oz/30 g) wholemeal bread, toasted
1 teaspoon (5 ml) margarine
1 glass mineral water with twist of lemon
1 medium orange
tea or coffee

EVENING MEAL
3-oz (90-g) frankfurter sausage
3 oz (90 g) canned sauerkraut
3 oz (90 g) boiled potato, mashed with 2 teaspoons (10 ml)
    low-fat spread and pinch mace
green salad with **Oregano Vinaigrette** (page 183)
tea or coffee

SNACKS OR DRINKS AT PLANNED TIMES
2 small satsumas, 12½ fl oz (375 ml) skim milk

Serving Information
Men and Teenagers: Add 2 slices (2 oz/60 g) wholemeal bread,
    3 oz (90 g) mashed potato at Evening Meal, 6 oz (180 g)
    grapes
Men: Add 1-oz (30-g) frankfurter sausage at Evening Meal
Teenagers: Add 5 fl oz (150 ml) natural yogurt

DAY 4

MORNING MEAL
2 tablespoons (30 ml) raisins
¾ oz (20 g) muesli
5 fl oz (150 ml) natural yogurt
tea or coffee

MIDDAY MEAL
7-8 oz (210-240 g) baked beans
1 slice (1 oz/30 g) wholemeal bread, toasted
1 teaspoon (5 ml) margarine
mixed green salad with **Basic Vinaigrette** (page 183)
tea or coffee

EVENING MEAL
3-4 oz (90-120 g) lamb chop, grilled
3 oz (90 g) steamed Brussels sprouts
3 oz (90 g) steamed cabbage
6 oz (180 g) boiled potato pureed with 2 teaspoons (10 ml)
    low-fat spread
1 medium baked apple with **Custard** (page 191)
tea or coffee

SNACKS OR DRINKS AT PLANNED TIMES
5 fl oz (150 ml) skim milk, 1 medium orange

Serving Information
Men and Teenagers: Add 1 digestive biscuit, 1 medium orange
Teenagers: Add ½ pint (300 ml) skim milk

DAY 5

MORNING MEAL
2½ fl oz (75 ml) pineapple juice
1 egg scrambled, with 1 teaspoon (5 ml) low-fat spread
1 slice (1 oz/30 g) wholemeal bread, toasted
1 teaspoon (5 ml) low-fat spread
tea or coffee

MIDDAY MEAL
3 tablespoons (45 ml) peanut butter
¾ oz (20 g) crispbread with sliced cucumber
1 medium orange
tea or coffee

EVENING MEAL
4 breadcrumbed fish fingers, grilled
3 oz (90 g) steamed mushrooms
3 oz (90 g) cooked peas
2 teaspoons (10 ml) tomato ketchup
2 canned pear halves
tea or coffee

SNACKS OR DRINKS AT PLANNED TIMES
½ pint (300 ml) skim milk, 5 fl oz (150 ml) natural yogurt

Serving Information
Men and Teenagers: Add 6 oz (180 g) baked beans at Evening
    Meal, 2 small satsumas
Teenagers: Add 5 fl oz (150 ml) natural yogurt

DAY 2

MORNING MEAL
½ medium banana
1 boiled egg
1 slice (1 oz/30 g) wholemeal bread, toasted
1 teaspoon (5 ml) low-fat spread
tea or coffee

MIDDAY MEAL
3-4 oz (90-120 g) grilled haddock
3 oz (90 g) cooked green beans
grated carrot and white cabbage, tossed with 3 teaspoons
  (15 ml) low-calorie mayonnaise
tea or coffee

EVENING MEAL
Creamed Cabbage and Ham (page 148)
3 oz (90 g) cooked parsnips
2 oz (60 g) cooked pasta shells
5 fl oz (150 ml) natural yogurt
6 canned apricot halves
tea or coffee

SNACKS OR DRINKS AT PLANNED TIMES
8 fl oz (240 ml) skim milk, 1 medium orange

Serving Information
Men and Teenagers: Add 2 digestive biscuits, 1 medium banana
Men: Add 1 oz (30 g) ham at Evening Meal
Teenagers: Add ½ pint (300 ml) skim milk

DAY 3

MORNING MEAL
½ medium grapefruit
2½ oz (75 g) curd cheese
2 teaspoons (10 ml) low-calorie blackcurrant jam
1 slice (1 oz/30 g) wholemeal bread, toasted
tea or coffee

MIDDAY MEAL
2 poached eggs on 6 oz (180 g) steamed spinach
1 teaspoon (5 ml) margarine
1 grilled medium tomato
tea or coffee

EVENING MEAL
2½ fl oz (75 ml) pineapple juice
Far East Scallops (page 152)
4 oz (120 g) cooked rice
mixed green salad with **Gingered Vinaigrette** (page 183)
tea or coffee

SNACKS OR DRINKS AT PLANNED TIMES
2 dried dates chopped into 5 fl oz (150 ml) natural yogurt, ½ pint
  (300 ml) skim milk

Serving Information
Men and Teenagers: Add 1-oz (30-g) brown roll at Midday Meal;
  2 dried dates
Teenagers: Add 5 fl oz (150 ml) natural yogurt

DAY 6

MORNING MEAL
1 medium apple
2½ oz (75 g) cottage cheese
¾ oz (20 g) crispbread
2 teaspoons (10 ml) low-fat spread
1 teaspoon (5 ml) yeast extract
tea or coffee

MIDDAY MEAL
5-6 oz (150-180 g) uncooked chicken livers, sauteed in 1
  teaspoon (5 ml) margarine
1 oz (30 g) grilled lean back bacon
1 medium grilled tomato
3 oz (90 g) cooked peas
2 oz (60 g) cooked rice
tea or coffee

EVENING MEAL
Sauteed Curried Veal and Aubergine (page 131)
3 oz (90 g) steamed courgettes
2 oz (60 g) cooked pasta shells
2 canned peach halves with 5 fl oz (150 ml) natural yogurt
tea or coffee

SNACKS OR DRINKS AT PLANNED TIMES
8 fl oz (240 ml) tomato juice with dash Worcestershire sauce,
  ½ pint (300 ml) skim milk

Serving Information
Men and Teenagers: Add 1 digestive biscuit, 1 medium banana
Teenagers: Add 5 fl oz (150 ml) natural yogurt

DAY 7

MORNING MEAL
1 oz (30 g) dried apricots, chopped
¾ oz (20 g) wheat flakes
5 fl oz (150 ml) skim milk
¾-oz (20-g) toasted muffin with 1 teaspoon (5 ml) margarine
1 teaspoon (5 ml) low-calorie marmalade
tea or coffee

MIDDAY MEAL
3-4 oz (90-120 g) roast chicken
3 oz (90 g) steamed cauliflower
3 oz (90 g) boiled, mashed swede
3 oz (90 g) cooked sweet corn
2 teaspoons (10 ml) low-fat spread
¼ fresh pineapple
5 fl oz (150 ml) natural yogurt
4 fl oz (120 ml) white wine □ tea or coffee

EVENING MEAL
½ medium grapefruit
2 oz (60 g) grated Cheddar cheese grilled on 1 slice (1 oz/30 g)
  wholemeal bread, toasted
sliced tomato and onion rings with **Basic Vinaigrette** (page
  183) □ tea or coffee

SNACKS OR DRINKS AT PLANNED TIMES
5 fl oz (150 ml) skim milk

Serving Information
Men and Teenagers: Add 6-oz (180-g) baked jacket potato at
  Midday Meal; 1 medium orange
Teenagers: Add ½ pint (300 ml) skim milk

WEEK 52

Of course we all associate Christmas with parties and warmth and fun and families and good food and drink. We've certainly provided the last two items in this week's menus. The important thing is that the food and drink does not have to mean the abandoning of your weight-loss regime and the acquisition of feelings of guilt plus several unwelcome pounds. You'll find most of the traditional dishes here plus lots of good ideas to keep you feeling 'spoiled'. Some of them may be different from what you've had in past years – strawberries for breakfast and crab for supper for instance – but the point is that you are different too. You're slimmer, more health-conscious, happier than you used to be. You've learned to eat well while losing weight. You know that you can stay slim if you wish. You enjoy Christmas for the right reasons now – for the fun and warmth and people and gifts. Food has taken its rightful place for you. It's a pleasure still, but not the all-important factor it all too often used to be.

DAY 1

MORNING MEAL
4 fl oz (120 ml) grapefruit juice
2½ oz (75 g) curd cheese
1 slice (1 oz/30 g) wholemeal bread, toasted
1 teaspoon (5 ml) margarine
1 teaspoon (5 ml) low-calorie blackcurrant jam
tea or coffee

MIDDAY MEAL
3-4 oz (90-120 g) sliced cooked chicken
mixed green salad with 3 oz (90 g) sliced baby beetroot
1 water biscuit
Basic Vinaigrette (page 183) □ tea or coffee

Christmas Eve Cocktail Party
Hot Mushroom Turnovers (page 112)
cucumber, celery, green pepper, raw carrot cut in thin slivers
    with **Curry Dip** (page 184)
8 fl oz (240 ml) tomato juice with twist of lemon

EVENING MEAL
6 oz (180 g) boil-in-the-bag fish in sauce (any type)
3 oz (90 g) steamed spinach
3 oz (90 g) steamed sliced carrots
5 fl oz (150 ml) natural yogurt with 1 dried fig, diced
tea or coffee

SNACKS OR DRINKS AT PLANNED TIMES
7 fl oz (210 ml) skim milk

Serving Information
Men and Teenagers: Add 4 water biscuits, 1 medium banana
Teenagers: Add 5 fl oz (150 ml) natural yogurt

DAY 4

MORNING MEAL
8 fl oz (240 ml) tomato juice
1 poached egg
¾-oz (20-g) toasted muffin
1 teaspoon (5 ml) margarine □ tea or coffee

MIDDAY MEAL
3-4 oz (90-120 g) liver sausage
mixed salad
3 oz (90 g) diced beetroot
¾ oz (20 g) crispbread
2 teaspoons (10 ml) low-fat spread
4 oz (120 g) canned fruit cocktail
5 fl oz (150 ml) natural yogurt □ tea or coffee

EVENING MEAL
Cream of Cauliflower Soup (page 115)
3-4 oz (90-120 g) sliced turkey
3 oz (90 g) steamed courgettes
3 oz (90 g) boiled mashed swede
¼ small fresh pineapple
tea or coffee

SNACKS OR DRINKS AT PLANNED TIMES
¾-oz (20-g) toasted muffin, 1 teaspoon (5 ml) margarine,
    7½ fl oz (225 ml) skim milk

Serving Information
Men and Teenagers: Add ¾ oz (20 g) crispbread at Midday
    Meal; 1 medium orange
Teenagers: Add ½ pint (300 ml) skim milk

DAY 5

MORNING MEAL
½ medium grapefruit
¾ oz (20 g) instant cereal
5 fl oz (150 ml) hot skim milk
tea or coffee

MIDDAY MEAL
toss together 3-4 oz (90-120 g) mackerel fillets, flaked, 3 oz
    (90 g) shredded white cabbage, 1 grated carrot and onion
    rings, with **Creamy Yogurt Dressing** (page 184)
1 medium orange
tea or coffee

EVENING MEAL
2-egg omelette cooked in 1 teaspoon (5 ml) vegetable oil
3 oz (90 g) steamed mushrooms
3 oz (90 g) steamed broccoli
6-oz (180-g) baked jacket potato
2 teaspoons (10 ml) low-fat spread
2 canned pear halves
tea or coffee

SNACKS OR DRINKS AT PLANNED TIMES
1 digestive biscuit, ½ pint (300 ml) skim milk

Serving Information
Men and Teenagers: Add 2 digestive biscuits, 1 medium orange
Teenagers: Add 5 fl oz (150 ml) natural yogurt

DAY 2

MORNING MEAL
4 fl oz (120 ml) grapefruit juice
1 oz (30 g) grated Cheddar cheese grilled on 1 slice (1 oz/30 g)
  wholemeal bread, toasted □ tea or coffee

MIDDAY MEAL
Tomato Starter (page 114)
3-4 oz (90-120 g) roast turkey with **Spicy Plum Sauce** (page 184)
3-oz (90-g) **Roast Potato** (page 175)
3 oz (90 g) cooked parsnips
3 oz (90 g) cooked carrots
3 oz (90 g) steamed Brussels sprouts
Rich Fruit Pudding (page 191)
2½ fl oz (75 ml) natural yogurt
4 fl oz (120 ml) white wine □ tea or coffee

EVENING MEAL
3-4 oz (90-120 g) canned crabmeat
1 wedge iceberg lettuce, shredded
3 oz (90 g) sliced cucumber
2 teaspoons (10 ml) low-calorie mayonnaise
2 small clementines
tea or coffee

SNACKS OR DRINKS AT PLANNED TIMES
14 fl oz (420 ml) skim milk

Serving Information
Men and Teenagers: Add 1 slice (1 oz/30 g) wholemeal bread,
  3 oz (90 g) sweet corn, 4 small clementines
Teenagers: Add ½ pint (300 ml) skim milk

DAY 3

MORNING MEAL
5 oz (150 g) canned strawberries
¾ oz (20 g) cornflakes
5 fl oz (150 ml) skim milk □ tea or coffee

MIDDAY MEAL
3-4 oz (90-120 g) roast loin of pork with 2 oz (60 g) pureed cooked
  apple
3 oz (90 g) boiled, mashed swede
3 oz (90 g) steamed courgettes
6-oz (180-g) baked jacket potato
1 teaspoon (5 ml) low-fat spread
4 fl oz (120 ml) white wine
Pineapple-Orange 'Cream' (page 188)
tea or coffee

EVENING MEAL
1 medium corn-on-the-cob
1 teaspoon (5 ml) low-fat spread
Salmon Mousse (page 152)
1 medium sliced tomato
lettuce and onion rings
1 small clementine □ tea or coffee

SNACKS OR DRINKS AT PLANNED TIMES
1 slice (1 oz/30 g) currant bread with 1 teaspoon (5 ml) low-fat
  spread, 5 fl oz (150 ml) skim milk

Serving Information
Men and Teenagers: Add 1 digestive biscuit, 1 dried fig
Teenagers: Add 5 fl oz (150 ml) natural yogurt

DAY 6

MORNING MEAL
1 medium orange
1 tablespoon (15 ml) peanut butter
¾ oz (20 g) crispbread □ tea or coffee

MIDDAY MEAL
1 oz (30 g) Cheddar cheese grilled on 1 slice (1 oz/30 g)
  wholemeal bread, toasted, topped with 1 poached egg
1 medium grilled tomato
2 small clementines
tea or coffee

EVENING MEAL
2-inch (5-cm) wedge honeydew melon
5-6 oz (150-180 g) uncooked lamb's liver sauteed in 2 teaspoons
  (10 ml) vegetable oil and onion rings
3 oz (90 g) cooked French beans
3 oz (90 g) cooked peas
2 oz (60 g) cooked noodles tossed in 2 teaspoons (10 ml)
  Parmesan cheese
tea or coffee

SNACKS OR DRINKS AT PLANNED TIMES
5 fl oz (150 ml) natural yogurt, ½ pint (300 ml) skim milk

Serving Information
Men and Teenagers: Add 1 slice (1 oz/30 g) wholemeal bread,
  1 medium orange
Teenagers: Add ½ pint (300 ml) skim milk

DAY 7

MORNING MEAL
2-inch (5-cm) wedge melon
¾ oz (20 g) cornflakes
5 fl oz (150 ml) skim milk
tea or coffee

MIDDAY MEAL
3-4 oz (90-120 g) roast veal
3 oz (90 g) cooked sliced carrots
3 oz (90 g) cooked sliced turnips
Sweet and Sour Cabbage (page 172)
3 oz (90 g) boiled potato
3 medium dessert plums
tea or coffee

EVENING MEAL
3-4 oz (90-120 g) trout, grilled
3 oz (90 g) steamed spinach
3 oz (90 g) cooked potato, diced and chilled, tossed with
  4 teaspoons (20 ml) low-calorie mayonnaise
5 fl oz (150 ml) natural yogurt
2 teaspoons (10 ml) low-calorie jam
tea or coffee

SNACKS OR DRINKS AT PLANNED TIMES
2 cream crackers, 2 teaspoons (10 ml) grated Parmesan cheese,
  5 fl oz (150 ml) skim milk

Serving Information
Men and Teenagers: Add 1 digestive biscuit, 1 medium banana
Teenagers: Add 5 fl oz (150 ml) natural yogurt

STARTERS

The 'starter' of a meal should be the foretaste of the delights to come. Whether you select Stuffed Mushroom Starter or Cock-A-Leekie, or any of the other starter recipes, your meal will begin on a high note that makes adherence to your weight-loss programme easy. And the delicious inspirations in this section can be music to your palate.

Cauliflower and Courgette Soup

See Menu Plans for Weeks 1, 25 and 45.

1 medium cauliflower, about 1½ lbs (720 g)

1¼ pints (750 ml) water

4 oz (120 g) carrots, sliced

4 oz (120 g) celery, sliced

1 bay leaf

6 oz (180 g) small courgettes, cut into ½-inch (1-cm) slices

2 teaspoons (10 ml) lemon juice

¾ teaspoon (3.75 ml) salt

¼ teaspoon (1.25 ml) thyme

pinch each ground allspice and ground nutmeg

Chop two thirds of the cauliflower; break remainder into small florets and reserve. In medium saucepan combine chopped cauliflower, water, carrots, celery and bay leaf. Bring to the boil; cover and simmer for 30 minutes. Discard bay leaf. Transfer mixture to blender container and puree until smooth; return to saucepan. Add reserved florets and remaining ingredients; simmer uncovered, stirring occasionally, 20-25 minutes or until florets and courgettes are tender-crisp.
Makes 4 servings.
Per serving: 40 calories.

Minestrone

See Menu Plan for Week 45.

1 pint (600 ml) beef stock made with 1 stock cube

1 tablespoon (15 ml) tomato puree

4 oz (120 g) onion, chopped

3 oz (90 g) carrots, sliced

3 oz (90 g) courgettes, sliced

1 sachet dried bouquet garni

salt and pepper to taste

garlic powder to taste

3 teaspoons (15 ml) cornflour

4 oz (120 g) cooked pasta rings

chopped fresh parsley to garnish

Place stock, tomato puree, onion, carrots, courgettes and bouquet garni in large saucepan. Season with salt, pepper and garlic powder. Bring to the boil, cover and simmer for 15-20 minutes, or until vegetables are soft. Mix cornflour with 1 tablespoon (15 ml) cold water, add to soup and bring to the boil, stirring constantly. Add pasta rings and allow to simmer for a further 5 minutes. Serve piping hot sprinkled with parsley.
Makes 2 servings.
Per serving: 141 calories.

Marinated Mushrooms

See Menu Plan for Week 47.

6 oz (180 g) small mushroom caps

2 tablespoons (30 ml) lemon juice

1 tablespoon (15 ml) finely chopped shallots

2 teaspoons (10 ml) vegetable oil

1 clove garlic, chopped

2 fl oz (60 ml) tarragon vinegar

½ teaspoon (2.5 ml) salt

pinch pepper

artificial sweetener to equal 1 teaspoon (5 ml) sugar

2 parsley sprigs, chopped

2 large, crisp lettuce leaves, formed into cups

Place mushrooms in small bowl; sprinkle with lemon juice. Combine shallots, oil and garlic in saucepan and heat. Add vinegar, salt and pepper. Simmer 5 minutes. Remove from heat. Add mushrooms, sweetener and parsley. Toss to combine. Cover and marinate in refrigerator overnight. Serve in lettuce leaf cups.
Makes 2 servings.
Per serving: 56 calories.

Cock-a-Leekie

See Menu Plan for Week 4.

8 fl oz (240 ml) chicken stock, made with ½ stock cube

3 oz (90 g) leek, shredded

2 oz (60 g) onion, chopped

¾ oz (20 g) rice

pinch salt

pinch pepper

1 teaspoon (5 ml) fresh chopped parsley

Place all ingredients together in a saucepan and simmer gently for half an hour.
Makes 1 serving.
Per serving: 150 calories.

Tomato Soup

See Menu Plan for Week 37.

2 x 14 oz (420 g) cans whole tomatoes, chopped

4 medium celery sticks, thinly sliced

3 oz (90 g) onion, finely chopped

½ small clove garlic, chopped

½ teaspoon (2.5 ml) honey

¼ teaspoon (1.25 ml) salt

pinch white pepper

Pour tomatoes and juice into large saucepan; add celery and garlic; cover and bring to the boil. Reduce heat to low and simmer for 45 minutes. Puree in blender container. Reheat. Stir in honey, salt, and pepper to taste.
Makes 2 servings.
Per serving: 82 calories.

Tomato and Marrow Soup

See Menu Plan for Week 45.

1½ chicken stock cubes

4 fl oz (120 ml) boiling water

12 fl oz (360 ml) tomato juice

2 teaspoons (10 ml) dried onion flakes

12 oz (360 g) marrow, peeled, cored and diced

1 teaspoon (5 ml) basil

salt and pepper to taste

artificial sweetener to taste

Dissolve stock cubes in boiling water. Place in large saucepan, add tomato juice, onion flakes, marrow and basil. Bring to the boil, cover and simmer gently for about 10 minutes or until marrow is very tender. Pour soup into blender container and puree until smooth. Return soup to pan and reheat. Taste and adjust seasoning. Serve piping hot.
Makes 3 servings.
Per serving: 62 calories.

Vegetable Medley Soup

See Menu Plan for Week 7.

4 teaspoons (20 ml) vegetable oil

8 oz (240 g) courgettes, diced

4 oz (120 g) mushrooms, quartered

6 oz (180 g) green beans, cut into 2-inch (5-cm) lengths

4 oz (120 g) carrots, sliced

4 oz (120 g) onions, chopped

2 oz (60 g) celery, diced

3 oz (90 g) green pepper, seeded and diced

1 pint (600 ml) chicken stock made with 2 stock cubes

4 tablespoons (60 ml) tomato puree

1-2 teaspoons (5-10 ml) Worcestershire sauce

½ teaspoon (2.5 ml) thyme

dash chili sauce (optional)

10 fl oz (300 ml) skim milk

1 tablespoon (15 ml) chopped fresh parsley

Heat oil in large pan; add next 7 ingredients and saute, stirring occasionally, for 10 minutes. Add remaining ingredients except milk and parsley; bring to the boil, cover and simmer 30-40 minutes, stirring occasionally. Stir in milk; heat but do not boil. Garnish with parsley.
Makes 4 servings.
Per serving: 125 calories.

Stuffed Mushroom Starter

See Menu Plan for Week 8.

12 large mushrooms, approximately 12 oz (360 g)

2 tablespoons (30 ml) lemon juice

2 oz (60 g) green pepper, finely chopped

2 oz (60 g) celery, finely chopped

2 oz (60 g) spring onions, finely chopped

1 clove garlic, crushed

pinch each salt and pepper

6 fl oz (180 ml) chicken stock made with 1 stock cube

1 tablespoon (15 ml) grated Parmesan cheese

2 teaspoons (10 ml) chopped fresh parsley

parsley sprigs to garnish

Wash mushrooms and sprinkle with lemon juice. Remove and finely chop stems. Combine stems, peppers, celery, spring onions and garlic in non-stick pan. Cook over low heat, stirring occasionally, until tender; add salt and pepper. Fill each mushroom cap with an equal amount of stuffing; place in shallow casserole. Add stock to casserole and sprinkle mushrooms with Parmesan cheese. Cover and bake at 400°F, 200°C, Gas Mark 6 for 20-25 minutes. Garnish with chopped parsley and parsley sprigs and serve immediately.
Makes 4 servings.
Per serving: 30 calories.

Hot Mushroom Turnovers

See Menu Plan for Week 52.

3 oz (90 g) flour

¼ teaspoon (1.25 ml) salt

8 teaspoons (40 ml) margarine

2 fl oz (60 ml) natural yogurt

4 oz (120 g) mushrooms, finely chopped

1 tablespoon (15 ml) dried onion flakes

1 tablespoon (15 ml) chopped fresh parsley

¼ teaspoon (1.25 ml) Worcestershire sauce

1 clove garlic, crushed

pinch each thyme, salt and pepper

Mix flour and salt in a bowl. Rub in margarine until mixture resembles fine breadcrumbs. Add yogurt and mix thoroughly; form into a ball and chill about 1 hour. Combine remaining ingredients in non-stick pan; cook until mushrooms are soft and all the moisture has evaporated. Remove from heat. Preheat oven to 375°F, 190°C, Gas Mark 5. Roll out dough to about ⅛-inch (0.3-cm) thickness. With a pastry wheel, cut lengthwise strips 2½ inches (6.5 cm) apart; then cut crosswise, making 2½ inch (6.5 cm) squares. Re-roll scraps of dough and continue cutting until all dough is used. Place an equal amount of mushroom mixture on each square (about 1 teaspoon (5 ml) and fold in half to enclose filling and form a triangle; seal well by pressing edges together with prongs of a fork. Bake on non-stick baking sheet about 15 minutes or until lightly browned.
Makes 8 servings, about 3 turnovers each.
Per serving: 83 calories.

Cream of Asparagus and Leek Soup

See Menu Plans for Weeks 9 and 45.

6 medium canned asparagus spears

2 tablespoons (30 ml) margarine

6 oz (180 g) leeks, chopped, white portion only

1 tablespoon (15 ml) flour

1 pint (600 ml) chicken stock, made with 2 stock cubes

6 fl oz (180 ml) skim milk

pinch each salt, white pepper, and ground nutmeg

Cut off stems of asparagus, reserving tips. Puree stems in blender container or bowl of food processor. Melt margarine in saucepan; add leeks and saute until soft. Stir in flour, cook for 1-2 minutes. Gradually stir in stock and pureed asparagus. Bring to the boil, stirring; cover and simmer for 10 minutes. Add asparagus tips, milk, and seasonings. Heat but do not allow to boil.
Makes 6 servings.
Per serving: 71 calories.

Cream of Asparagus and Leek Soup
Hot Mushroom Turnovers

Green Bean and Red Cabbage Starter

See Menu Plan for Week 32.

2 teaspoons (10 ml) olive oil
3 oz (90 g) green beans, sliced, parboiled
½ clove garlic, chopped with ½ teaspoon (2.5 ml) salt
½ teaspoon (2.5 ml) fresh ginger root, chopped
6 oz (180 g) thinly sliced red cabbage
¼ teaspoon (1.25 ml) salt
pinch celery seeds
pinch marjoram
½ teaspoon (2.5 ml) lemon juice

Heat oil in medium non-stick frying pan. Add green beans, garlic and ginger. Saute over medium heat until beans are just tender-crisp, about 2-3 minutes. Do not overcook. Remove beans from pan and keep warm. Add cabbage, salt, celery seeds, and marjoram to pan. Cook, stirring occasionally, until cabbage is tender. Stir in lemon juice. Return beans to pan and stir to combine with cabbage.
Makes 2 servings.
Per serving: 71 calories.

Tomato Starter

See Menu Plans for Weeks 44 and 52.

12 oz (360 g) tomatoes, skinned
3 oz (90 g) onion, thinly sliced
1 teaspoon (5 ml) fresh basil
2 teaspoons (10 ml) lemon juice
salt and pepper

Thinly slice tomatoes and divide equally with onion between 4 small dishes. Sprinkle each with a little of the basil, lemon juice, salt and pepper. Chill before serving.
Makes 4 servings.
Per serving: 18 calories.

Beef Stock

This can be prepared and then frozen for use when needed. Freeze in 6-fl oz (180-ml) portions and defrost only the amount that is required for a recipe. This can be done in ice cube trays; once frozen, store the cubes in a plastic bag.

4 lbs (1 kg 920 g) beef bones
3 oz (90 g) celery, sliced
3 oz (90 g) carrots, sliced
3 oz (90 g) onion, studded with 4 whole cloves
6 pints (3 litres 600 ml) water
5 parsley sprigs
5 peppercorns
¼ teaspoon (1.25 ml) thyme
1 small bay leaf

Place bones on rack in roasting pan. Roast at 400°F, 200°C, Gas Mark 6 for 1 hour. While bones are roasting, cook celery, carrots, and clove-studded onion in separate baking pan in oven for 30 minutes. Transfer bones and vegetables to a large saucepan; add remaining ingredients. Bring to the boil; reduce heat and remove scum from surface, partially cover and simmer 3 hours or until reduced by half. Strain liquid to remove solids. Refrigerate stock until fat congeals on surface. Remove and discard fat.
Makes about 3 pints (1 litre 800 ml).
Per 6 fl oz (180 ml) serving: 12 calories

Chicken Stock

See Beef Stock recipe for storage ideas.

2-lb (960-g) chicken carcase or bones
4 pints (2 litres 400 ml) water
6 oz (180 g) onion
3 oz (90 g) carrots, sliced
3 oz (90 g) celery, sliced
5 parsley sprigs
3 peppercorns
pinch thyme

Combine all ingredients in large saucepan. Bring to the boil; reduce heat, remove scum from surface, partially cover, and simmer 2½ hours or until reduced by about one third. Strain liquid to remove solids. Refrigerate stock until fat congeals on surface. Remove and discard fat.
Makes about 3 pints (1 litre 800 ml).
Per 6 fl oz (180 ml) serving: 12 calories

Garden Pea Soup

See Menu Plan for Week 45.

6 oz (180 g) peas, fresh or frozen
1 pint (600 ml) water
1 chicken stock cube
2-3 sprigs mint
salt and pepper to taste

Combine peas, water, stock cube, mint, salt and pepper in a saucepan. Bring to the boil, cover and simmer until peas are soft. Transfer to blender container and puree until smooth. Reheat, adjust seasoning.
Makes 2 servings.
Per serving: 45 calories.

Cream of Cauliflower Soup

See Menu Plans for Weeks 5, 17, 22, 51 and 52.

1 lb (480 g) cauliflower florets
1½ pints (900 ml) water
2 chicken stock cubes
2 teaspoons (10 ml) arrowroot
10 fl oz (300 ml) skim milk
2 tablespoons (30 ml) chopped fresh parsley
pinch white pepper

Place cauliflower in saucepan. Add water and stock cubes, bring to the boil. Cover and simmer for 15-20 minutes or until cauliflower is soft. Transfer mixture in 3 batches to blender container and puree. Return puree to saucepan and heat. Combine arrowroot with milk and pour into cauliflower mixture; cook, stirring constantly, until thickened. Stir in parsley and pepper and serve.
Makes 4 servings.
Per serving: 54 calories.

Gazpacho

See Menu Plan for Week 33.

16 fl oz (480 ml) tomato juice
3 oz (90 g) cucumber, peeled, seeded and finely diced
2 oz (60 g) celery, finely diced
2 oz (60 g) green pepper, finely diced
2 tablespoons (30 ml) spring onion, sliced
2 tablespoons (30 ml) olive oil
1 teaspoon (5 ml) Worcestershire sauce
1 teaspoon (5 ml) chopped fresh parsley
½ teaspoon (2.5 ml) salt
pinch freshly ground pepper
1 clove garlic, finely chopped
sprig of celery to garnish

Combine all ingredients in medium bowl. Cover and chill overnight. Stir just before serving, and garnish with celery.
Makes 4 servings.
Per serving: 97 calories.

Broccoli Soup

See Menu Plan for Week 45.

6 oz (180 g) fresh or frozen broccoli
1 pint (600 ml) chicken stock made with 1 cube
1 oz (30 g) low-fat dry milk
salt and pepper to taste

Wash broccoli and cook in chicken stock until tender. Transfer to blender and puree until smooth. Add dry milk, puree for a further few seconds. Season and reheat before serving, but do not allow to boil.
Makes 2 servings.
Per serving: 75 calories.

Fresh Mushroom Soup

See Menu Plans for Weeks 39 and 45.

6 oz (180 g) mushrooms, sliced
2 oz (60 g) onion, finely chopped
4 teaspoons (20 ml) flour
16 fl oz (480 ml) water
1 chicken stock cube, crumbled
pinch thyme
pinch each salt and pepper
2 teaspoons (10 ml) chopped fresh parsley

Heat non-stick frying pan to low heat. Add mushrooms and onion; cook over low heat, stirring, about 2 minutes or until softened. Stir in flour and cook until mixture is lightly browned. Gradually stir in water, stock cube and thyme. Bring mixture to the boil, stirring; reduce heat and simmer 10 minutes or until slightly thickened. Season with salt and pepper. Just before serving, sprinkle with parsley.
Makes 2 servings.
Per serving: 49 calories.

EGGS AND CHEESE

Eggs and cheese may be two of the most versatile foods around. Each can stand on its own as the basis for a meal or do a delicious disappearing act in conjunction with other ingredients. Cold cheese dishes such as Cheese-Salad Sandwich and Tomato Stuffed with Herb Cheese will help you beat the heat on a hot day. Used together, cheese and eggs are a winning combination in omelettes and quiches, while fluffy beaten egg whites help your souffles rise to new heights.

Pancakes with Orange Sauce

See Menu Plan for Week 49.

Pancake

1 egg

2 tablespoons (30 ml) skim milk

¾ oz (20 g) flour

2 teaspoons (10 ml) oil

Sauce

4 fl oz (120 ml) orange juice

2 teaspoons (10 ml) arrowroot

½ teaspoon (2.5 ml) honey

Beat egg and milk together. Gradually beat into flour to make a smooth batter. Heat 1 teaspoon (5 ml) of oil in non-stick frying pan. Pour half the pancake mixture in and cook, turning once, until both sides are golden brown. Place on plate and keep warm. Repeat the process with the rest of the mixture.

Mix orange juice and arrowroot together thoroughly in a small saucepan and slowly bring to the boil. Cook for one minute, add honey and mix thoroughly. Pour some over each pancake; roll up and serve.
Makes 1 serving.
Per serving: 345 calories.

Cheese Souffle

See Menu Plan for Week 50.

1 tablespoon (15 ml) margarine

1 tablespoon (15 ml) finely chopped onion

2 tablespoons (30 ml) flour

8 fl oz (240 ml) buttermilk

2 oz (60 g) strong Cheddar cheese, coarsely grated

¼ teaspoon (1.25 ml) each powdered mustard and salt

2 eggs, separated

pinch ground red pepper

2 teaspoons (10 ml) chopped chives

Preheat oven to 375°F, 190°C, Gas Mark 5. Melt margarine in saucepan; add onion and saute until softened. Stir in flour and cook over low heat for 2 minutes. Remove pan from heat and gradually stir in buttermilk. Return to heat and bring to the boil, stirring. Remove from heat; add cheese, mustard and salt; stir until cheese is melted. Beat in egg yolks, one at a time; add red pepper. Whisk egg whites until stiff peaks form. Gently fold whites and chives into yolk mixture. Turn souffle into a 2-pint (1.2-litre) souffle dish. Bake 25 minutes. Serve immediately.
Makes 2 servings.
Per serving: 379 calories.

Baked Cheese Souffle

See Menu Plans for Weeks 7, 23 and 39.

4 slices (1 oz/30 g each) white bread, toasted

4 oz (120 g) Cheddar cheese, sliced

4 eggs, size 4 to 5, separated

1 teaspoon (5 ml) French mustard

2 teaspoons (10 ml) grated Parmesan cheese

pinch each salt and pepper

Preheat oven to 350°F, 180°C, Gas Mark 4. Arrange toast on non-stick baking tin; top with cheese. Using an electric mixer, beat egg yolks for 3-4 minutes or until thick and pale. Beat in mustard, Parmesan cheese, salt and pepper. Using clean beaters, whisk egg whites until stiff but not dry. Carefully fold into the yolk mixture. Gently spoon egg mixture over. Bake for 20 minutes.
Makes 4 servings.
Per serving: 275 calories.

Baked Cheese Souffle

Chinese-Style Pancakes

See Menu Plans for Weeks 21 and 47.

4 oz (120 g) white cabbage, shredded
4 oz (120 g) cooked brown rice
2 oz (60 g) carrot, grated
2 oz (60 g) spring onion, sliced
1 teaspoon (5 ml) sesame seeds, toasted
1 clove garlic, finely chopped
½ teaspoon (2.5 ml) finely chopped fresh ginger root
pinch pepper
4 eggs, beaten
4 teaspoons (20 ml) soy sauce
2 teaspoons (10 ml) vegetable oil
6 fl oz (180 ml) chicken stock made with ½ stock cube
2 teaspoons (10 ml) cornflour, blended with 1 tablespoon (15 ml) water

Combine cabbage, rice, carrot, 1 oz (30 g) spring onion, sesame seeds, garlic, ginger and pepper. In separate bowl beat eggs with 3 teaspoons (15 ml) soy sauce; stir into vegetable mixture. Heat ½ teaspoon (2.5 ml) oil in non-stick pan. Pour in quarter of mixture; cook, turning once, until pancakes are brown on each side and vegetables are tender. Remove from pan and keep warm. Repeat until all batter is used. In small saucepan combine stock, remaining teaspoon soy sauce, and 1 oz (30 g) spring onion. Bring to the boil; stir in blended cornflour and cook, stirring constantly, until thickened. Serve sauce over pancakes.
Makes 2 servings.
Per serving: 345 calories.

Vegetable-Cheese Platter

See Menu Plans for Weeks 16 and 39.

5 oz (150 g) curd cheese
2½ fl oz (75 ml) natural yogurt
½ teaspoon (2.5 ml) prepared mustard
¼ teaspoon (1.25 ml) salt
½ clove garlic, crushed
pinch white pepper
2 tablespoons (30 ml) grated carrot
2 tablespoons (30 ml) chopped green pepper
2 tablespoons (30 ml) chopped celery
6 oz (180 g) cucumber, peeled and cut lengthwise into quarters
2 eggs, hard-boiled and cut lengthwise into quarters
8 small celery sticks
2 medium tomatoes, cut into 8 wedges
chopped fresh parsley to garnish

Combine cheese with yogurt, mustard, salt, garlic, and pepper. Add carrot, green pepper and chopped celery; mix well and chill for 1 hour. Spoon cheese mixture on to centre of serving plate. Cut each cucumber quarter in half crosswise. Arrange cucumber spears, eggs, celery sticks and tomato wedges alternately around edge of plate. Garnish with parsley.
Makes 2 servings.
Per serving: 255 calories.

Matzo Brei

See Menu Plan for Week 16.

2 eggs
2 fl oz (60 ml) water
¼ teaspoon (1.25 ml) ground cinnamon
¼ teaspoon (1.25 ml) salt
1-oz (30-g) matzo board, broken into pieces
2 teaspoons (10 ml) margarine

In a medium bowl beat eggs lightly. Stir in water, cinnamon and salt; add matzo and let stand 15 minutes. Melt margarine in a non-stick pan; add matzo mixture, cover and cook over medium heat until browned on bottom. With a spatula, loosen sides of matzo mixture, slide on to a dish and invert into pan to brown other side.
Makes 2 servings.
Per serving: 150 calories.

Welsh Rarebit

See Menu Plan for Week 9.

1 oz (30 g) Caerphilly cheese, finely grated
1 teaspoon (5 ml) margarine
½ teaspoon (2.5 ml) prepared mustard
dash Worcestershire sauce
1 slice (1 oz/30 g) bread, toasted

Preheat grill. Combine cheese, margarine, mustard and Worcestershire sauce and stir until smooth. Spread mixture on to hot toast and place under grill until cheese has melted. Serve at once.
Makes 1 serving.
Per serving: 230 calories.

Chili-Cheese Rarebit

See Menu Plans for Weeks 5 and 35.

2 teaspoons (10 ml) margarine

1 tablespoon (15 ml) chopped onion

2 tablespoons (30 ml) diced green pepper

8 oz (240 g) canned tomatoes, chopped

¾ teaspoon (3.75 ml) chili powder, or to taste

4 oz (120 g) strong Cheddar cheese, grated

1 teaspoon (5 ml) cornflour, blended with 1 tablespoon (15 ml) water

2 slices (1 oz/30 g each) rye bread, toasted

Melt margarine in saucepan; add onion and saute until softened. Add green pepper and saute about 3 minutes longer. Add tomatoes and chili powder and simmer mixture 10 minutes or until some of the liquid has evaporated. Add cheese and stir until it is melted. Stir in blended cornflour and simmer, stirring constantly until thickened. Remove from heat, serve over toast.
Makes 2 servings.
Per serving: 361 calories.

Layered Aubergine-Cheese Bake

See Menu Plan for Week 6.

1 small aubergine, about 10 oz (300 g)

1 teaspoon (5 ml) salt

2 oz (60 g) Emmenthal cheese, grated

2 oz (60 g) Mozzarella cheese, grated

½ teaspoon (2.5 ml) oregano

½ teaspoon (2.5 ml) chopped fresh parsley

pinch white pepper

With vegetable peeler, peel skin of aubergine lengthwise at 1-inch (2.5-cm) intervals to produce a striped effect. Cut aubergine crosswise into 8 slices, about ¼-inch (0.5-cm) each. Sprinkle with salt on both sides. Place slices on a rack over a pan. Let stand 30 minutes. Pat slices dry with paper towels. Combine the cheeses, oregano, parsley and pepper. Place 2 slices of aubergine in bottom of an ovenproof dish; top with quarter of the cheese mixture. Repeat procedure three more times, ending with cheese on top. Insert cocktail sticks into each stack. Cover and bake at 350°F, 180°C, Gas Mark 4 for 25 minutes. Remove cocktail sticks before serving.
Makes 2 servings.
Per serving: 195 calories.

Pancakes with Lemon Juice

See Menu Plan for Week 10.

1½ oz (45 g) flour

pinch salt

1 egg white

5 fl oz (150 ml) skim milk

4 tablespoons (60 ml) water

grated rind of ½ lemon

yellow food colouring (optional)

1 teaspoon (5 ml) vegetable oil

2 teaspoons (10 ml) sugar

juice of ½ lemon

Sift flour and salt into a bowl.

Beat in egg white, milk, water, lemon rind and colouring if used. Heat ¼ teaspoon (1.25 ml) oil in a small non-stick frying pan. Pour in quarter of mixture and cook over moderate heat until golden underneath. Turn and cook second side. Repeat procedure three more times. Serve sprinkled with sugar and lemon juice.
Makes 2 servings.
Per serving: 151 calories.

Cheese Salad Sandwich

See Menu Plan for Week 7.

1 tablespoon (15 ml) vegetable oil

1 tablespoon (15 ml) wine vinegar

1 tablespoon (15 ml) water

pinch dill

pinch oregano

pinch pepper

4 oz (120 g) Edam cheese, cut into strips

1 inch (2.5 cm) cucumber, sliced

4 radishes, sliced

1 tablespoon (15 ml) chopped spring onion

2 pitta breads, 1 oz (30 g) each

Combine first 6 ingredients in bowl. Add remaining ingredients except pitta breads; stir to coat cheese and vegetables. Cover and marinate in refrigerator for at least 1 hour. Cut each pitta bread halfway around edge and open to form a pocket. Spoon half of salad mixture into each pitta pocket.
Makes 2 servings.
Per serving: 312 calories.

Broccoli Quiche

See Menu Plan for Week 21.

3 oz (90 g) flour

¾ teaspoon (3.75 ml) salt

8 teaspoons (40 ml) margarine

2 fl oz (60 ml) natural yogurt

5 oz (150 g) cooked broccoli, well drained and chopped

1 oz (30 g) spring onion, finely chopped

4 teaspoons (20 ml) imitation bacon bits

8 oz (240 g) Emmenthal cheese, grated

4 eggs, lightly beaten

2 oz (60 g) low-fat dry milk

8 fl oz (240 ml) water

pinch pepper

Mix flour and ¼ teaspoon (1.25 ml) salt in mixing bowl. Rub margarine in until mixture resembles fine breadcrumbs. Add yogurt and mix thoroughly; form into a ball. Roll dough out to approximately ⅛-inch (0.3-cm) thickness. Fit into a 9-inch (23-cm) pie plate; flute edges and put aside. Combine vegetables and bacon bits. Cover bottom of pastry shell with 4 oz (120 g) cheese; add entire vegetable mixture. Combine eggs, dry milk and water, ½ teaspoon (2.5 ml) salt and pepper. Pour egg mixture over vegetables; top evenly with remaining cheese. Bake at 325°F, 160°C, Gas Mark 3, for 50-60 minutes or until knife, when inserted in centre, comes out clean. Remove from oven and let stand 10 minutes before serving.
Makes 8 servings.
Per serving: 283 calories.

Mushroom Omelette

See Menu Plans for Weeks 1, 4, 26 and various other weeks.

6 oz (180 g) mushrooms, sliced

1 stick celery, chopped

½ teaspoon (2.5 ml) salt

2 eggs

pinch freshly ground pepper

1 teaspoon (5 ml) margarine

Heat non-stick pan over medium heat; add mushrooms, celery and salt. Cover and cook until mushrooms are tender. Set aside and keep warm. Beat together eggs and pepper. Melt margarine in 7-inch (18-cm) non-stick frying pan; when pan is hot pour in eggs and cook over medium heat. As eggs begin to set, using a fork carefully lift cooked edges of omelette and tilt pan so that uncooked portion flows underneath. When bottom of omelette is lightly browned and top surface is still moist, spread mushroom mixture over half the omelette. Fold other half over mushroom mixture. Invert omelette on to plate.
Makes 1 serving.
Per serving: 238 calories.

Cheese Omelette

See Menu Plan for Week 46.

1 teaspoon (5 ml) margarine

1 egg

1 tablespoon (15 ml) water

pinch salt

1 oz (30 g) Cheddar cheese, grated

Melt margarine until hot in a 6½-inch (16.5-cm) non-stick frying or omelette pan. Mix egg, water and salt and beat with wire whisk. Pour egg mixture into pan and cook until bottom is lightly browned and firm. Sprinkle grated cheese over egg. Place under grill as close to heat source as possible; grill until top puffs and turns light brown. Remove from grill and fold omelette in half. Slide out of pan onto heated plate.
Makes 1 serving.
Per serving: 245 calories.

French Omelette

See Menu Plans for Weeks 2 and 36.

2 eggs

4 teaspoons (20 ml) water

¼ teaspoon (1.25 ml) salt

pinch pepper

1 teaspoon (5 ml) margarine

Using a wire whisk or fork combine all ingredients except margarine. Melt margarine in a 7-inch (18-cm) non-stick frying pan. When pan is hot, pour in egg mixture and cook over medium heat. As mixture begins to set, using a fork, carefully lift cooked edges of egg mixture and tilt pan so that uncooked portion flows underneath. When bottom of omelette is lightly browned and top surface is still moist, fold omelette in half; invert onto a warm plate and serve.
Makes 1 serving.
Per serving: 220 calories.

Broccoli Quiche

Gypsy Cheese Salad

See Menu Plans for Weeks 8 and 17.

10 oz (300 g) cottage cheese

2 tablespoons (30 ml) diced red pepper

2 tablespoons (30 ml) grated carrot

1 medium apple, cored, diced and sprinkled with lemon juice

2 tablespoons (30 ml) chopped fresh parsley

4 drops chili sauce

1 teaspoon (5 ml) Worcestershire sauce

4 large lettuce leaves

1 medium tomato, about 3 oz (90 g), cut into wedges

8 oz (240 g) cucumber, sliced

Combine all ingredients except lettuce, tomatoes and cucumber. Serve on lettuce leaves, surrounded by tomato wedges and cucumber slices.
Makes 2 servings.
Per serving: 187 calories.

Open Grilled Cheese Sandwich

See Menu Plans for Weeks 3 and 6.

4 oz (120 g) Cheddar cheese, sliced

2 slices (1 oz/30 g each) white or wholemeal bread, toasted

1 medium tomato, sliced (optional)

Preheat grill. Place 2 oz (60 g) of cheese on each slice of bread. Top each with half of the tomato slices, if desired. Grill for 3-4 minutes or until cheese melts.
Makes 2 servings.
Per serving: 301 calories.

Stuffed French Toast

See Menu Plan for Week 12.

2½ oz (75 g) cottage cheese

1 tablespoon (15 ml) raisins

¼ teaspoon (1.25 ml) vanilla flavouring

¼ teaspoon (1.25 ml) brown sugar

2 slices (1 oz/30 g each) wholemeal bread

1 egg

1 tablespoon (15 ml) water

1 teaspoon (5 ml) low-fat spread

2 teaspoons (10 ml) low-calorie strawberry jam

Combine first 4 ingredients; spread on one slice of bread and top with remaining bread to form a sandwich. In small bowl, beat egg with water; transfer to small shallow pan and soak sandwich, turning occasionally, for 10 minutes or until all egg is absorbed. Melt spread in small frying pan; add sandwich. Cook until bottom is golden brown; turn and brown other side. Top with strawberry jam and serve.
Makes 1 serving.
Per serving: 385 calories.

Baked 'Cheesy' Pitta Bread

See Menu Plan for Week 13.

2 teaspoons (10 ml) margarine

6 oz (180 g) mushrooms, sliced

5 oz (150 g) curd cheese

2 oz (60 g) Mozzarella cheese, cut into ¼-inch (0.5-cm) cubes

pinch each salt and pepper

2 pitta breads, 1 oz (30 g) each

Melt margarine in frying pan; add mushrooms and saute until tender. Drain on paper towels. Combine mushrooms with curd and Mozzarella cheeses. Season with salt and pepper. Divide mixture into 2 portions. Cut opening at edge of each pitta to form pocket. Spoon one portion cheese mixture into each pitta pocket. Wrap each stuffed pitta in foil and bake at 350°F, 180°C, Gas Mark 4 for 15 minutes.
Makes 2 servings.
Per serving: 267 calories.

Macaroni-Cheese Salad

See Menu Plan for Week 20.

4 oz (120 g) hot cooked short-cut macaroni

4 oz (120 g) strong Cheddar cheese, coarsely grated

2½ fl oz (75 ml) natural yogurt

4 teaspoons (20 ml) low-calorie mayonnaise

1 teaspoon (5 ml) French-style mustard

2 tablespoons (30 ml) celery, diced

2 tablespoons (30 ml) red pepper, diced

2 tablespoons (30 ml) green pepper, diced

salt and pepper

4 green pepper strips

Combine macaroni with half of the cheese; toss until cheese is melted. Combine remaining cheese with yogurt, mayonnaise and mustard; add to macaroni mixture and stir well. Add celery and diced peppers. Toss well and season to taste. Serve at once garnished with pepper strips.
Makes 2 servings.
Per serving: 338 calories.

Egg Salad

See Menu Plans for Weeks 3 and 32.

2 eggs, hard-boiled and chopped

4 teaspoons (20 ml) low-calorie mayonnaise

¼ teaspoon (1.25 ml) prepared French mustard

2 tablespoons (30 ml) chopped celery

2 tablespoons (30 ml) diced green or red pepper

pinch each salt and white pepper

Combine eggs with mayonnaise and mustard. Add celery, diced pepper, salt and pepper, and combine.
Makes 1 serving.
Per serving: 213 calories.

Mushroom-Stuffed Eggs

See Menu Plan for Week 5.

2 teaspoons (10 ml) margarine

1 tablespoon (15 ml) chopped spring onion

4 oz (120 g) mushrooms, finely chopped

pinch each salt, pepper and thyme

4 eggs, hard-boiled

4 teaspoons (20 ml) low-calorie mayonnaise

1½ teaspoons (7.5 ml) lemon juice

8 parsley sprigs

Melt margarine in non-stick pan; add spring onion and saute for 2 minutes. Add mushrooms, salt, pepper and thyme and cook 3-5 minutes or until all liquid has evaporated; cool. Cut each egg in half lengthwise; remove yolks and reserve whites. Rub yolks through a sieve into a bowl. Add mushroom mixture, mayonnaise and lemon juice; stir to combine. Fill each egg white with an equal amount of mixture and garnish with a parsley sprig.
Makes 2 servings.
Per serving: 239 calories.

Cinnamon-Cheese Toast

See Menu Plans for Weeks 5, 20, 32 and various other weeks.

2½ oz (75 g) cottage cheese

artificial sweetener to equal 1 teaspoon (5 ml) sugar

pinch ground cinnamon

1 slice (1 oz/30 g) brown bread, toasted

1 teaspoon (5 ml) desiccated coconut

Mix cottage cheese with sweetener and cinnamon. Spread on toast. Sprinkle with coconut; grill for 2-3 minutes or until bubbly.
Makes 1 serving.
Per serving: 161 calories.

Swiss Cheese Bake

See Menu Plan for Week 24.

3 oz (90 g) leeks

1 teaspoon (5 ml) margarine

2 teaspoons (10 ml) flour

¼ teaspoon (1.25 ml) ground nutmeg

1½ oz (45 g) boiled ham, thinly sliced

3 oz (90 g) potato, baked or boiled in skin, sliced

1 oz (30 g) Emmenthal Cheese, grated

Wash leeks thoroughly, cut into 4-5-inch (10-12.5-cm) lengths. Boil in salted water for about 5 minutes, or until tender. Drain and reserve liquid. Melt margarine in pan; stir in flour, cook 1 minute. Remove from heat and gradually stir in 6 fl oz (180 ml) cooking liquid from the leeks and cook until thickened, stirring occasionally. Add nutmeg. Wrap ham round leeks and place in ovenproof dish. Cover with potatoes, then with sauce and sprinkle with grated cheese. Bake at 350°F, 180°C, Gas Mark 4 for 15-20 minutes.
Makes 1 serving.
Per serving: 357 calories.

Cheese and Vegetable Risotto

See Menu Plan for Week 24.

1½ oz (45 g) carrots, diced

1½ oz (45 g) peas

1½ oz (45 g) turnips, diced

1½ oz (45 g) swede, diced

1 oz (30 g) onion, diced

¾ oz (20 g) long grain rice

8 fl oz (240 ml) mixed vegetable juice

1 stock cube

2 oz (60 g) Cheddar cheese, grated

Put carrots, peas, turnips, swede and onion in a saucepan; add rice, mixed vegetable juice and stock cube. Bring to the boil; stir, reduce heat, cover pan and simmer gently for about 20 minutes until vegetables are tender and liquid absorbed. Place on warmed plate, sprinkle with grated cheese and serve at once.
Makes 1 serving.
Per serving: 395 calories.

Crepes Divan

See Menu Plans for Weeks 31 and 37.

Crepes

2 eggs

1½ oz (45 g) flour

4 tablespoons (60 ml) water

pinch salt

Filling

4 oz (120 g) skinned and boned cooked chicken, cut into cubes

3 oz (90 g) cooked broccoli, chopped

3 oz (90 g) cooked mushrooms, sliced

½ teaspoon (2.5 ml) onion powder

pinch pepper

Sauce

2 teaspoons (10 ml) margarine

4 teaspoons (20 ml) flour

6 fl oz (180 ml) hot chicken stock made with ½ stock cube

5 fl oz (150 ml) skim milk, heated

pinch each salt, pepper and ground nutmeg

Garnish

parsley sprigs

To Prepare Crepes: Combine first 4 ingredients in blender container; puree until smooth. Let stand 10 minutes. Heat non-stick frying pan. Pour quarter of batter (about 3 tablespoons (45 ml) into pan; quickly tilt pan to spread batter evenly over surface. Cook until underside is dry; turn crepe and cook a few seconds longer. Repeat process three more times to make four crepes.

To Prepare Filling: Place chicken, broccoli and mushrooms in bowl; add onion powder and pepper and toss to combine.

To Prepare Sauce: Melt margarine in small saucepan; stir in flour. Remove from heat; gradually stir in stock and milk; return to heat and cook gently, stirring, until thickened. Season with salt, pepper and nutmeg.

To Serve: Spoon quarter of filling onto centre of each crepe; roll crepe to enclose filling. Place seam-side down in ovenproof dish; top with sauce. Bake at 400°F, 200°C, Gas Mark 6 about 20 minutes or until heated through. Garnish with parsley.
Makes 2 servings.
Per serving: 353 calories.

Fruited Cheese Delight

See Menu Plan for Week 44.

10 oz (300 g) cottage cheese

1 teaspoon (5 ml) each honey and lemon juice

artificial sweetener to equal 1 teaspoon (5 ml) sugar

drop vanilla flavouring

pinch salt

3 oz (90 g) grapes, cut into halves and deseeded

1½ oz (45 g) diced carrot, ¼-inch (0.5-cm) cubes

¾ teaspoon (3.75 ml) unflavoured gelatine

2½ fl oz (75 ml) apple juice

Combine cheese, honey, lemon juice, sweetener, vanilla and salt in blender container; puree until very smooth. Transfer to bowl; stir in grapes and carrots. Sprinkle gelatine over apple juice in small bowl and let stand to soften. Place bowl over pan of heated water and stir juice until gelatine is dissolved; cool slightly. Add dissolved gelatine to cheese mixture; stir to combine. Spoon into 2 individual dishes; cover and refrigerate until firm, about 3-4 hours.
Makes 2 servings.
Per serving: 190 calories.

Spaghetti Cheese with Herbs

See Menu Plan for Week 32.

2 teaspoons (10 ml) margarine

½ clove garlic, chopped with ¼ teaspoon (1.25 ml) salt

4 oz (120 g) cooked spaghetti

½ teaspoon (2.5 ml) chopped fresh parsley

¼ teaspoon (1.25 ml) oregano

pinch thyme

2 oz (60 g) Danish blue cheese, grated

5 oz (150 g) curd cheese

Melt margarine in medium saucepan. Add garlic and saute 1 minute. Add spaghetti, parsley, oregano and thyme; saute over low heat, stirring occasionally, about 5 minutes or until spaghetti is heated through. Spoon pasta on to serving plate. Sprinkle Danish blue cheese over centre of pasta. Spoon curd cheese over blue cheese. Serve at once.
Makes 2 servings.
Per serving: 310 calories.

Crepes Divan

Cottage Cheese Country Style

See Menu Plan for Week 40.

5 oz (150 g) cottage cheese
1½ oz (45 g) carrot, diced
¾ oz (20 g) each diced celery and radishes
3 oz (90 g) peas, fresh or frozen, blanched
½ teaspoon (2.5 ml) each celery salt and pepper

Combine ingredients and cover with plastic wrap. Refrigerate at least 1 hour to allow flavours to blend. Serve chilled.
Makes 1 serving.
Per serving: 181 calories.

Spinach Frittata

See Menu Plan for Week 20.

4 eggs, well beaten
6 oz (180 g) cooked, well-drained spinach, chopped
2 tablespoons (30 ml) chopped fresh parsley
¼ teaspoon (1.25 ml) salt
¼ clove garlic, finely chopped
pinch each pepper and grated nutmeg
1 tablespoon (15 ml) margarine
2 tablespoons (30 ml) spring onion, chopped
1 teaspoon (5 ml) sesame seeds, lightly toasted

Combine eggs, spinach, parsley, salt, garlic, pepper and nutmeg. Mix well. Melt margarine in 12-inch (30.5-cm) non-stick frying pan with flameproof handle. Add spring onion and saute 2 minutes. Pour in egg-spinach mixture. Cook over moderately high heat, briskly shaking pan back and forth to prevent sticking. When underside is lightly browned, grill for a few minutes until frittata is set. Sprinkle with sesame seeds.
Makes 2 servings.
Per serving: 275 calories.

Peach and Cottage Cheese Mould

See Menu Plan for Week 31.

3 teaspoons (15 ml) unflavoured gelatine
4 tablespoons (60 ml) cold water
8 oz (240 g) canned sliced peaches
10 oz (300 g) cottage cheese
2½ fl oz (75 ml) natural yogurt
2 teaspoons (10 ml) honey
1 teaspoon (5 ml) lemon juice
artificial sweetener to equal 1 teaspoon (5 ml) sugar
pinch ground cinnamon
lettuce leaves to garnish

Dissolve gelatine in water in basin over pan of hot water. Drain juice from sliced peaches into dissolved gelatine; stir to combine. Cut peaches into ¼-inch (0.5-cm) pieces and place in bowl. Add cottage cheese, yogurt, honey, lemon juice, sweetener and cinnamon; stir to combine. Stir in gelatine mixture. Spoon into 1½-pint (900-ml) souffle dish. Cover and chill at least 6 hours. Dip dish into hot water for a few seconds to loosen mould, then turn out onto serving plate. Garnish with lettuce leaves.
Makes 2 servings.
Per serving: 248 calories.

Tomato Stuffed with Herb Cheese

See Menu Plans for Weeks 2, 26 and 50.

10 oz (300 g) cottage cheese
1 oz (30 g) spring onion, finely chopped
1 tablespoon (15 ml) chopped fresh parsley
1 tablespoon (15 ml) chopped fresh dill (optional)
1 small clove garlic, finely chopped
pinch each salt and white pepper
6 oz (180 g) tomatoes
2 parsley sprigs

Combine cottage cheese with spring onion, parsley, dill, garlic, salt and pepper. With pointed knife, remove stem end of each tomato. Make 4 vertical intersecting cuts through top of each tomato, almost to the base, dividing tomatoes into eighths; spread tomatoes open. Fill centre of each tomato with half the herb cheese; garnish each with one parsley sprig.
Makes 2 servings.
Per serving: 151 calories.

POULTRY, VEAL AND RABBIT

The delicate flavours of chicken and veal lend themselves to a variety of sauces, seasonings and accompaniments. We have created some delicious recipes with an international flair. Chicken Cavalfiore, Chicken Greek Style, Turkey and Cheese Layer and Rabbit Bourguignon are some of the marvellous recipes you will find in this section.

Veal Stew

See Menu Plan for Week 50.

12 oz (360 g) boneless lean veal, cut into 1-inch (2.5-cm) cubes

1 pint (600 ml) beef stock made with 2 stock cubes

2 tablespoons (30 ml) tomato puree

6 oz (180 g) courgettes

2 tablespoons (30 ml) onion, finely chopped

¼ teaspoon (1.25 ml) salt

generous pinch each thyme and pepper

6 oz (180 g) sliced celery, cut into ¼-inch (0.5-cm) thick slices

Heat non-stick frying pan over high heat. Cook veal until browned on all sides. Remove veal from pan and place in medium saucepan, with stock and tomato puree. Bring to the boil; reduce heat, cover and simmer until veal is tender, about 20 minutes. Meanwhile, cut courgettes into ¼-inch (0.5-cm) thick slices and cut each slice into quarters. Add courgettes, onion, salt, thyme and pepper to frying pan in which veal was browned. Cover and cook gently, stirring occasionally, until courgettes are tender-crisp. Add to veal with celery and cook for further 10 minutes.
Makes 2 servings.
Per serving: 235 calories.

Italian Veal and Peppers

See Menu Plan for Week 25.

2 tablespoons (30 ml) vegetable oil

1½ lbs (720 g) lean stewing veal, cut into 1-inch (2.5-cm) cubes

4 tablespoons (60 ml) tomato puree

10 fl oz (300 ml) chicken stock, made with 2 stock cubes

8 oz (240 g) onions, sliced

2 cloves garlic, crushed

1 teaspoon (5 ml) basil

1 teaspoon (5 ml) oregano

freshly ground pepper to taste

1 lb (480 g) green peppers, seeded and cut into ½-inch (1-cm) strips

Heat oil in thick-based or non-stick frying pan, add veal and saute 3-4 minutes. Add all remaining ingredients except green peppers. Cover and cook over low heat for 45 minutes. Add peppers and continue cooking for 10 minutes longer or until veal and peppers are tender.
Makes 4 servings.
Per serving: 298 calories.

Braised Chicken with Vegetables

See Menu Plan for Week 14.

2 teaspoons (10 ml) vegetable oil

1½ lb (720 g) chicken pieces, skinned

¼ teaspoon (1.25 ml) salt

pinch pepper

3 oz (90 g) onion, chopped

1 clove garlic, crushed

1 medium green pepper, seeded and coarsely chopped

1 medium tomato, skinned and chopped

2 oz (60 g) mushrooms, sliced

5 fl oz (150 ml) water

1 tablespoon (15 ml) chopped fresh parsley

Heat vegetable oil in a medium saucepan. Saute chicken, turning as necessary, until lightly browned. Sprinkle with salt and pepper. Using a slotted spoon remove chicken from pan. Saute onion and garlic in oil remaining in pan until onion is lightly browned. Add green pepper and saute 2 minutes longer. Add chicken, tomato, mushrooms, water and parsley; bring to the boil. Reduce heat, cover and simmer 35 minutes. Remove cover and simmer 5 minutes longer or until chicken is tender.
Makes 2 servings.
Per serving: 355 calories.

Turkey and Cheese Layer

See Menu Plan for Week 37.

12 oz (360 g) skinned and boned turkey breast, cut into 3 equal slices
12 oz (360 g) mushrooms, sliced
2 oz (60 g) green pepper, diced
salt
½ teaspoon (2.5 ml) grated orange peel
pinch pepper
4 oz (120 g) Mozzarella cheese, grated
12 oz (360 g) potatoes, cut into ⅛-inch (0.3-cm) thick slices

Place turkey between sheets of wax or greaseproof paper and beat until very thin, about $1/16$-inch (0.2-cm) thick. Set aside. Heat non-stick pan, add mushrooms, green pepper and pinch of salt. Cook over medium heat, stirring occasionally, until mushrooms are tender and moisture has evaporated. Set aside.

Place one slice of turkey in bottom of non-stick baking tin. In a small cup, combine a large pinch of salt, orange peel and pepper; sprinkle one third of mixture over turkey. Top with one third of the cheese, then one third of the potatoes, then one third of the mushroom mixture. Repeat turkey, cheese and potato layers, seasoning turkey as before. Top potatoes with remaining turkey and sprinkle with remaining seasonings. Stand remaining potato slices upright along sides of baking dish. Spread remaining mushroom mixture over turkey and top evenly with remaining cheese. Cover with aluminium foil; punch hole in centre of foil to allow steam to escape and bake at 350°F, 180°C, Gas Mark 4 for 40 minutes. Remove foil and bake until cheese browns, about 10 minutes longer.
Makes 4 servings.
Per serving: 226 calories.

Turkey Oriental

See Menu Plan for Week 42.

8 oz (240 g) can pineapple chunks, drained and juice reserved
2 tablespoons (30 ml) tomato puree
1 tablespoon (15 m) cornflour blended with 3 fl oz (90 ml) water
1 tablespoon (15 ml) soy sauce
8 oz (240 g) skinned and boned cooked turkey, cut into 2-inch (5-cm) strips
6 oz (180 g) small tomatoes, halved
1 medium green pepper, seeded, cut into 1-inch (2.5-cm) pieces
3 oz (90 g) drained canned water chestnuts, thinly sliced
3 oz (90 g) peas

In large pan combine pineapple juice, tomato puree, cornflour, water and soy sauce. Cook over low heat, stirring constantly with wire whisk, until mixture thickens. Add pineapple chunks, turkey and vegetables; cover and cook until heated (green pepper should be tender-crisp).
Makes 2 servings.
Per serving: 285 calories.

Chicken Kebabs

See Menu Plans for Weeks 6 and 35.

2 oz (60 g) onion, sliced
2 fl oz (60 ml) cider vinegar
1 teaspoon (5 ml) soy sauce
5 peppercorns, crushed
1 clove garlic, split
1 bay leaf
2 fl oz (60 ml) water
12 oz (360 g) skinned and boned chicken breasts, cut into pieces
1 x 4 oz (120 g) onion, cut into 8 wedges
1 x 4 oz (120 g) green pepper, seeded and cut into 8 pieces
8 small tomatoes
¼ teaspoon (1.25 ml) salt
pinch coarsely ground pepper
lettuce and cucumber to garnish

Combine first 6 ingredients in bowl; add water and stir to combine. Add the chicken, cover and refrigerate overnight. Remove chicken and discard marinade. Thread each of four 9-inch (27-cm) skewers with 3 oz (180 g) chicken pieces, 2 onion wedges, 2 green pepper pieces, and 2 small tomatoes, alternating chicken with vegetables. Sprinkle with salt and pepper. Place on rack in grill pan and grill about 8 minutes; turn and grill 5-8 minutes longer or until chicken is tender. Serve kebabs with lettuce and cucumber.
Makes 2 servings.
Per serving: 254 calories.

Chicken Kebabs

Ginger-Grilled Chicken

See Menu Plans for Weeks 11, 23 and 33.

2 teaspoons (10 ml) soy sauce

1 teaspoon (5 ml) grated fresh ginger root

1 clove garlic, crushed

2 chicken breasts, 8 oz (240 g) each

Combine soy sauce, ginger and garlic. Lift skin and brush chicken with soy mixture; turn and brush underside. Cover and let stand at room temperature 1 hour. Grill chicken on rack, skin-side down, 10 minutes. Turn and grill 8-10 minutes longer or until chicken is tender. Remove and discard skin before serving.
Makes 2 servings.
Per serving: 265 calories.

Rabbit Bourguignon

See Menu Plan for Week 44.

1 tablespoon (15 ml) vegetable oil

1 lb (480 g) rabbit, cut into pieces

2 oz (60 g) onion, sliced

2 cloves garlic, crushed

4 oz (120 g) mushrooms, sliced

4 oz (120 g) carrots, sliced

15 oz (450 g) canned crushed tomatoes

4 teaspoons (20 ml) red Burgundy wine

½ teaspoon (2.5 ml) salt

pinch freshly ground pepper

chopped fresh parsley to garnish

Heat oil in large frying pan; add rabbit and brown evenly on all sides. Remove rabbit from pan and set aside. In same pan com-bine onion and garlic and saute until soft. Stir in mushrooms and carrots and continue to saute until vegetables are tender-crisp. Stir in tomatoes and bring to the boil. Reduce heat and simmer several minutes. Add rabbit, wine, salt and pepper; cover and cook for 45 minutes. If mixture becomes too dry, adjust con-sistency by adding water. Gar-nish with parsley.
Makes 2 servings.
Per serving: 331 calories.

Chicken Stir-Fry

See Menu Plan for Week 49.

2 teaspoons (10 ml) vegetable oil

6 oz (180 g) skinned and boned chicken breast

1½ oz (45 g) onion, sliced

1½ oz (45 g) mushrooms, sliced

3 oz (90 g) bean sprouts

2 teaspoons (10 ml) soy sauce

1 teaspoon (5 ml) arrowroot or cornflour

4 fl oz (120 ml) chicken stock made with ¼ stock cube

Heat oil in wok or deep frying pan. Cut chicken into fine strips. Add to oil and saute for 3 minutes. Add onions and mush-rooms and saute for 2-3 minutes. Add bean sprouts and saute for a further minute; sprinkle on soy sauce. Mix arrowroot or corn-flour with the stock. Pour this over chicken and stir well. Cover and simmer for a further 10 minutes. Serve at once.
Makes 1 serving.
Per serving: 328 calories.

Chicken Donna

See Menu Plan for Week 9.

2 teaspoons (10 ml) margarine

1½ lbs (720 g) skinned chicken portions, preferably leg, thigh and breast*

2 oz (60 g) small white onions, cut into quarters

2 cloves garlic, finely chopped

8 oz (240 g) sliced courgettes, ½-inch (1-cm) thick slices

6 oz (180 g) quartered mushrooms

2 tablespoons (30 ml) lemon juice

2 teaspoons (10 ml) flour

6 fl oz (180 ml) chicken stock made with 1 stock cube

pinch each salt and pepper

2 teaspoons (10 ml) white wine, optional

chopped fresh parsley to garnish

Melt margarine in frying pan; add chicken portions and saute gently, turning occasionally, until browned. Remove and keep warm. In same pan saute onions and garlic for 2-3 minutes without burning. Add courgettes and mushrooms and sprinkle with lemon juice; cook, stirring occasionally, until just tender. In small bowl gradually blend flour with stock until combined; add to vegetable mixture and cook, stirring constantly, until thick-ened. Add chicken, salt and pepper. Cover and simmer for 15 minutes. Add white wine and parsley and serve immediately.
Makes 2 servings.
Per serving: 382 calories.

*1½ lbs (720 g) chicken portions will yield about 8 oz (240 g) skinned and boned cooked meat.

Sweet and Sour Chicken Stir-Fry

See Menu Plan for Week 32.

2 teaspoons (10 ml) vegetable oil

8 oz (240 g) cooked chicken, cut into thin strips

salt and pepper

4 oz (120 g) canned crushed pineapple

1 teaspoon (5 ml) honey

1 teaspoon (5 ml) lemon juice

Heat oil in medium non-stick frying pan. Add chicken, half teaspoon salt and pinch pepper. Saute over high heat, stirring occasionally, until chicken begins to brown. Combine pineapple and honey; add to chicken and saute 3 minutes more. Remove pan from heat and stir in lemon juice; serve at once.
Makes 2 servings.
Per serving: 243 calories.

Sauteed Curried Veal and Aubergine

See Menu Plan for Week 51.

8 oz (240 g) aubergine, peeled and diced, cut into ½-inch (1-cm) cubes

1 teaspoon (5 ml) salt

12 oz (360 g) minced veal

2 oz (60 g) onion, sliced

2 teaspoons (10 ml) olive oil

1 teaspoon (5 ml) curry powder

pinch chili powder

In colander, combine aubergine with quarter teaspoon salt; toss and let stand 30 minutes. Pat dry with paper towels. Cook veal in non-stick pan over high heat, breaking meat apart into pieces,

until slightly browned but not cooked through. Reduce heat to medium; add onion and oil and saute 3-5 minutes. Add aubergine and continue sauteeing, stirring occasionally, until aubergine starts to brown. Stir in remaining salt and curry and chili powders; continue cooking until mixture is well browned and moisture has evaporated.
Makes 2 servings.
Per serving: 255 calories.

Sesame Chicken with Green Beans

See Menu Plans for Weeks 1, 26 and 32.

2 teaspoons (10 ml) olive oil

½ teaspoon (2.5 ml) sesame seeds

8 oz (240 g) skinned and boned cooked chicken, cut into ¼-inch (0.5-cm) strips

2 teaspoons (10 ml) desiccated coconut, toasted

½ teaspoon (2.5 ml) salt

pinch pepper

12 oz (360 g) cooked whole green beans

Heat non-stick pan. Add olive oil and sesame seeds; cook over medium heat, stirring frequently, until seeds turn light brown. Add chicken and saute until pieces are heated. Stir in coconut, salt and pepper. Serve over hot green beans.
Makes 2 servings.
Per serving: 278 calories.

Chicken and Bean Casserole

See Menu Plan for Week 11.

4 x 6-oz (180-g) chicken breasts

2 tablespoons (30 ml) onion, chopped

1 clove garlic, finely chopped

4 teaspoons (20 ml) olive oil

2 sticks celery, diced

2 tablespoons (30 ml) tomato puree

8 oz (240 g) canned tomatoes, chopped, reserve juice

¼ teaspoon (1.25 ml) each oregano and salt

pinch pepper

12 oz (360 g) drained canned kidney or butter beans

2 teaspoons (10 ml) chopped fresh parsley

Grill chicken on rack under hot grill for 10 minutes, turning once. In deep non-stick saucepan, saute onion and garlic in oil until softened; add celery. Stir in tomato puree; add tomatoes with reserved juice, oregano, salt and pepper. Bring mixture to the boil; reduce heat and simmer 5 minutes. Add chicken and beans; stir to combine. Cover and cook gently for 15 minutes. Remove cover and cook 5 minutes longer or until some of the liquid has evaporated and chicken is tender. Sprinkle with parsley.
Makes 4 servings.
Per serving: 290 calories.

Chicken Teriyaki

See Menu Plan for Week 12.

2½ fl oz (75 ml) apple juice

2 tablespoons (30 ml) soy sauce

1 tablespoon (15 ml) cider vinegar

1 teaspoon (5 ml) honey

½ teaspoon (2.5 ml) grated orange rind

¼ teaspoon (1.25 ml) fresh ginger root, finely chopped

12 oz (360 g) skinned and boned chicken breasts, cut into ½-inch (1-cm) cubes

1 teaspoon (5 ml) vegetable oil

Combine first 6 ingredients, add chicken. Cover and refrigerate overnight or at least 6 hours, stirring occasionally. Heat oil in medium frying pan; remove chicken from marinade and saute in heated oil 8 minutes, stirring often. Add marinade; cook 2 minutes longer.
Makes 2 servings.
Per serving: 243 calories.

Chicken Greek Style

See Menu Plan for Weeks 4 and 27.

6 fl oz (180 ml) chicken stock made with 1 stock cube

2 tablespoons (30 ml) lemon juice

2 x 8-oz (240-g) chicken breasts, skinned

2 teaspoons (10 ml) olive oil

½ teaspoon (2.5 ml) salt

½ teaspoon (2.5 ml) oregano

pinch each garlic powder and white pepper

Pour stock and lemon juice into small ovenproof casserole. Rub each chicken breast with 1 tea-spoon (5 ml) oil and place in casserole. Sprinkle with seasonings; cover and bake at 350°F, 180°C, Gas Mark 4 for 40 minutes or until tender.
Makes 2 servings.
Per serving: 314 calories.

Chicken with Fresh Mushrooms

See Menu Plan for Week 47.

12 oz (360 g) chicken meat, sliced into thin strips

8 oz (240 g) fresh mushrooms, thinly sliced

2 teaspoons (10 ml) white wine

1 tablespoon (15 ml) soy sauce

1 teaspoon (5 ml) cornflour

1 fl oz (30 ml) water

6 fl oz (180 ml) chicken stock made with ½ stock cube

2 teaspoons (10 ml) spring onions, chopped

Marinate the chicken strips and sliced mushrooms in the wine and soy sauce for 30 minutes. Mix cornflour and 1 fl oz (30 ml) water and set aside. In a large non-stick frying pan, bring the 6 fl oz (180 ml) chicken stock to the boil and add the marinated chicken and mushroom slices. Cover and cook for 3 minutes. Add cornflour mixture; bring to the boil, stirring, and cook until chicken and mushrooms are well glazed. Sprinkle with chopped spring onions.
Makes 2 servings.
Per serving: 220 calories.

Chicken Provencale

See Menu Plans for Weeks 8 and 25.

2 teaspoons (10 ml) olive oil

1½ lbs (720 g) skinned chicken portions, preferably breast, leg, and thigh*

6 oz (180 g) mushrooms, sliced

6 oz (180 g) tomatoes, skinned, seeded and chopped

6 oz (180 g) green or red peppers, sliced

4 oz (120 g) onion, sliced

1 clove garlic, crushed

1 teaspoon (5 ml) oregano

pinch salt and pepper

4 teaspoons (20 ml) white wine

4 black olives, stoned and sliced

1 tablespoon (15 ml) chopped fresh parsley

Heat oil in non-stick frying pan, add chicken portions and saute gently until lightly browned. Remove chicken and set aside. In same pan saute all vegetables with garlic until tender. Add oregano, salt and pepper. Arrange chicken and vegetables in small casserole; add wine. Cover and bake at 375°F, 190°C, Gas Mark 5, for 45 minutes. Garnish with black olives and parsley.
Makes 2 servings.
Per serving: 382 calories.

*1½ lbs (720 g) chicken portions will yield about 8 oz (240 g) skinned and boned chicken meat.

Chicken Provencale

Shredded Chicken with Peanut Sauce

See Menu Plan for Week 40.

1½ teaspoons (7.5 ml) vegetable oil

3 oz (90 g) skinned and boned chicken breast, cut into thin strips

1 oz (30 g) onion, finely diced

1 clove garlic, crushed

1½ tablespoons (22.5 ml) crunchy-style peanut butter

1 tablespoon (15 ml) each lemon juice and soy sauce

artificial sweetener to taste

dash chili sauce

Heat vegetable oil in wok or non-stick frying pan until hot. Stir-fry strips of chicken for about 3 minutes or until firm to the touch. With a slotted spoon remove chicken and reserve. Add onion to wok or non-stick pan and stir-fry 2 minutes or until onion becomes translucent. Add garlic and continue to stir-fry until garlic becomes golden. Remove wok or non-stick pan from heat, stir in remaining ingredients, including chicken, and cook until heated through.
Makes 1 serving.
Per serving: 318 calories.

Cold Chicken Platter

See Menu Plan for Week 2.

8 oz (240 g) skinned, boned and cooked chicken breast

5 fl oz (150 ml) natural yogurt

4 teaspoons (20 ml) tomato ketchup

1 tablespoon (15 ml) mayonnaise

1 oz (30 g) pickled cucumber, finely chopped

1 oz (30 g) green pepper, diced

½ oz (15 g) spring onion, chopped

1 tablespoon (15 ml) chopped capers

dash artificial sweetener

pinch each salt and pepper

2 oz (60 g) lettuce, shredded

2 oz (60 g) mushrooms, sliced and tossed with lemon juice

1 oz (30 g) red pepper, cut into strips

Thinly slice chicken breast and set aside. Combine yogurt, ketchup and mayonnaise. Add pickled cucumber, green pepper, spring onion, capers, sweetener, salt and pepper. Arrange lettuce on small platter; top with chicken slices and spread with dressing. Arrange sliced mushrooms on lettuce. Garnish chicken with red pepper strips.
Makes 2 servings.
Per serving: 240 calories.

Chicken Capri with Potatoes

See Menu Plan for Week 16.

2 teaspoons (10 ml) margarine

3 oz (90 g) red pepper, seeded and cut into 1-inch (2.5-cm) pieces

6 oz (180 g) cooked potatoes, cut into large cubes

8 oz (240 g) skinned, cooked chicken, cut into ½-inch (1-cm) cubes

½ small clove garlic

¼ teaspoon (1.25 ml) salt

8 oz (240 g) canned tomatoes, pureed

½ teaspoon (2.5 ml) oregano

¼ teaspoon (1.25 ml) basil

pinch thyme

Melt margarine in small pan. Add red pepper; cover and cook over low heat about 5 minutes – pepper should still be crisp. Combine pepper, potatoes and chicken in deep 3-pint (1.75-litre) casserole. Chop garlic with salt. Using flat side of knife, mash garlic and salt together to form a paste. Combine garlic paste with pureed tomatoes, oregano, basil and thyme. Add to casserole and stir to combine. Cover and bake 25-30 minutes at 350°F, 180°C, Gas Mark 4, or until heated through.
Makes 2 servings.
Per serving: 293 calories.

Chicken Breasts with Tarragon

See Menu Plan for Week 15.

1 teaspoon (5 ml) vegetable oil

1 x 6-oz (180-g) skinned chicken breast, halved

pinch tarragon

1 oz (30 g) onion, chopped

1 oz (30 g) carrot, chopped

2 tablespoons (30 ml) dry white wine with 2 tablespoons (30 ml) water

1 tablespoon (15 ml) chopped fresh parsley

Heat oil in non-stick frying pan, add chicken breast and saute until browned on both sides, ending with bone side down. Sprinkle chicken evenly with tarragon, then onion and carrot. Pour wine and water over and around the chicken; cover and reduce heat. Simmer 25-30 minutes or until chicken is tender. Remove chicken to serving dish and keep warm. Add half the parsley to pan and cook, stirring, until liquid is slightly reduced. Pour liquid over chicken, top with remaining parsley.
Makes 1 serving.
Per serving: 280 calories.

Curried Chicken Salad

See Menu Plan for Week 3.

2 oz (60 g) canned pineapple chunks

4 teaspoons (20 ml) low-calorie mayonnaise

1 teaspoon (5 ml) lemon juice

¼ teaspoon (1.25 ml) curry powder

pinch each salt and white pepper

8 oz (240 g) skinned and boned cooked chicken, cut into 1-inch (2.5-cm) pieces

4 oz (120 g) cucumber, peeled and diced

½ medium apple, cored and diced

2 x 3-oz (90-g) green peppers, cut into halves lengthwise and seeded

lettuce leaves

Combine first 5 ingredients. Add chicken, cucumber and apple; toss to combine. Divide mixture into 4 equal portions and place 1 portion in each pepper half. Serve each person 2 stuffed pepper halves on lettuce leaves.
Makes 2 servings.
Per serving: 228 calories.

Chicken Hotpot

See Menu Plan for Week 40.

1½ teaspoons (7.5 ml) margarine

8-oz (240-g) chicken portion, skinned

¼ chicken stock cube dissolved in 6 fl oz (180 ml) boiling water

3 oz (90 g) tomato, seeded and diced

1½ oz (45 g) onion, thinly sliced

1 teaspoon (5 ml) dry white wine

1 clove garlic, crushed

½ teaspoon (2.5 ml) sugar

3 oz (90 g) sweetcorn

Melt margarine in a thick-based or non-stick saucepan, add chicken portion and brown on all sides. Add remaining ingredients except corn; cover and cook gently for about 35 minutes or until chicken is tender. Add corn and cook for about 8-10 minutes more or until heated through,

adding a little more water if contents of pan become too dry.
Makes 1 serving.
Per serving: 388 calories.

Chicken Salad Oriental

See Menu Plan for Week 7.

1 tablespoon (15 ml) wine vinegar

1 teaspoon (5 ml) sesame or vegetable oil

1 teaspoon (5 ml) soy sauce

1 teaspoon (5 ml) water

1 teaspoon (5 ml) lemon juice

4 oz (120 g) skinned and boned cooked chicken, cut into 1-inch (2.5-cm) pieces

2 oz (60 g) blanched and chilled mange tout peas

1 oz (30 g) canned water chestnuts, drained and diced

2 tablespoons (30 ml) carrot, grated

1 tablespoon (15 ml) green pepper, chopped

Combine first 5 ingredients. Add remaining ingredients and toss to combine.
Makes 1 serving.
Per serving: 255 calories.

MEATS

Looking for something more interesting than plain old beefburgers? Recipes like Lemon Minted Lamb, Ham with Rice and Water Chestnuts, Kidneys in Red Wine, Liver with Noodles suggest the variety of meats and the range of cooking techniques that are at your fingertips.

Mediterranean Stew

See Menu Plan for Week 3.

1½ lbs (720 g) chuck steak, cut into 1-inch (2.5-cm) cubes

3 tablespoons (45 ml) low-fat spread

4 oz (120 g) onions, sliced

16 fl oz (480 ml) water

4 tablespoons (60 ml) tomato puree

2 tablespoons (30 ml) raisins

2 tablespoons (30 ml) wine vinegar

2 teaspoons (10 ml) red wine (optional)

1 teaspoon (5 ml) honey

1 clove garlic, crushed

1 bay leaf

1 cinnamon stick or pinch ground cinnamon

¼ teaspoon (1.25 ml) each ground cloves and ground cumin

Grill beef on rack about 20 minutes or until rare, turning once. Melt low-fat spread in medium saucepan. Add onions and steak; cook 5 minutes, stirring occasionally. Add remaining ingredients and stir to combine. Cover and simmer over very low heat for 2-2½ hours, stirring occasionally. Remove bay leaf and cinnamon stick before serving.
Makes 4 servings.
Per serving: 375 calories.

Lamb Kebabs

See Menu Plan for Week 27.

1½ lbs (720 g) boneless lamb, cut into cubes

10 fl oz (300 ml) natural yogurt

juice of 1 lemon

12 oz (360 g) small tomatoes, halved

8 oz (240 g) large button mushrooms

6 oz (180 g) green pepper, cut into 8 pieces, and blanched

2 sticks celery, each stick cut into 4, and blanched

6 oz (180 g) small whole onions, peeled and blanched

garlic salt to taste

Marinate cubed lamb in yogurt and lemon juice for 6-8 hours, or overnight. Thread 4 kebab skewers with alternating pieces of meat and vegetables, reserving the remaining marinade. Season completed kebabs with garlic salt. Arrange skewers on a rack in a baking tin and cook in the oven at 375°F, 190°C, Gas Mark 5 for about 30 minutes. Heat reserved marinade gently in small pan, but do not boil. Use as a sauce to accompany the kebabs. Serve with green salad.
Makes 4 servings.
Per serving: 353 calories.

Pork Goulash

See Menu Plan for Week 5.

1½ lbs (720 g) pork fillet, cut into 1½-inch (4-cm) cubes

8 oz (240 g) onions, sliced

1 tablespoon (15 ml) paprika

3 tablespoons (45 ml) tomato puree

4 fl oz (120 ml) water (optional)

1 lb (480 g) canned sauerkraut, rinsed and drained

½ teaspoon (2.5 ml) salt

pinch ground red pepper (optional)

5 fl oz (150 ml) natural yogurt

1 teaspoon (5 ml) flour

sprig of parsley to garnish

Grill pork on rack in grill pan for 6 minutes, turning to brown evenly. Cook onions in non-stick saucepan until lightly browned. Stir in paprika. Add tomato puree, pork and water; cover and simmer for 10 minutes, stirring occasionally. Place sauerkraut in separate saucepan with water to cover; bring to the boil. Boil 5 minutes; drain and add to pork mixture with salt and red pepper if desired. Stir well and heat through. Mix yogurt with flour, stir into pork mixture and cook, stirring constantly, until just thickened. Garnish with parsley.
Makes 4 servings.
Per serving: 380 calories.

Pork Goulash

Lemon-Minted Lamb

See Menu Plans for Weeks 35 and 42.

2 teaspoons (10 ml) olive oil

2 small cloves garlic, chopped

4 fl oz (120 ml) water

1 tablespoon (15 ml) lemon juice

½ teaspoon (2.5 ml) salt

pinch freshly ground pepper

2 tablespoons (30 ml) fresh mint leaves, chopped

2 x 8-oz (240-g) lamb chops

Heat oil in small pan; add garlic and saute. Remove from heat and cool a moment. Stir in water, lemon juice, salt and pepper; sprinkle mint over mixture and simmer about 10 minutes. Place chops on rack in grill pan, under medium heat. Grill 4 minutes on each side or until done to taste. Transfer chops to serving dish and pour lemon-mint sauce over meat.
Makes 2 servings.
Per serving: 325 calories.

Red Pepper Steak

See Menu Plan for Week 13.

12 oz (360 g) lean rump steak

1 tablespoon (15 ml) vegetable oil

1 medium red pepper, seeded and cut into thin strips

6 fl oz (180 ml) beef stock, made with ½ stock cube

1 teaspoon (5 ml) soy sauce

2 teaspoons (10 ml) cornflour, blended with 1 tablespoon (15 ml) water

pinch pepper

Grill steak on a rack until rare; cut into thin strips. Heat oil in pan; add red pepper strips and saute until tender. Add steak, stock and soy sauce and cook for 3 minutes. Gradually stir in blended cornflour and cook until sauce thickens. Season with pepper.
Makes 2 servings.
Per serving: 379 calories.

Lamb Burgers

See Menu Plan for Week 21.

12 oz (360 g) lean minced lamb

1 tablespoon (15 ml) chopped fresh parsley

½ clove garlic, finely chopped

½ teaspoon (2.5 ml) salt

pinch oregano

2 teaspoons (10 ml) olive oil

2 oz (60 g) onion, sliced

1 medium red pepper, peeled, seeded and cut into strips

1 medium tomato, skinned, seeded and chopped

2 pitta breads, 1 oz (30 g) each, warmed

English mustard to taste

Combine lamb, parsley, garlic, salt and oregano. Moisten hands in warm water and roll mixture into 'sausages' each approximately 2 inches (5 cm) long. Put on rack in grill pan; grill on all sides until evenly browned. Keep warm. Heat oil in non-stick pan; saute onion and pepper until soft. Add tomato; saute 1 minute longer. Slice each pitta one-third of the way around edge to form a pocket. Stuff each pocket with half of the 'sausages' and top meat with half of the vegetable mixture. Serve with mustard.
Makes 2 servings.
Per serving: 181 calories.

Lamb Stew

See Menu Plan for Week 40.

6 oz (180 g) fillet of lamb, cubed

½ teaspoon (2.5 ml) olive oil

1 oz (30 g) onion, chopped

½ teaspoon (2.5 ml) flour

3 fl oz (90 ml) chicken stock made with ¼ stock cube

1 oz (30 g) carrots, sliced

1 oz (30 g) celery, sliced

1 clove garlic, finely chopped

½ bay leaf, crumbled

pinch thyme

2 oz (60 g) cooked pearl barley

1 tablespoon (15 ml) chopped fresh parsley

Grill lamb cubes on a rack in a grill pan, 4 inches (10 cm) from source of heat until cooked through. Heat oil in a non-stick saucepan and add onion, stir and cook until golden. Sprinkle with flour and continue to cook, stirring, until onions are browned. Add lamb cubes and remaining ingredients except chopped parsley. Stir, cover and simmer about 25 minutes, or until lamb is tender. Garnish with chopped parsley.
Makes 1 serving.
Per serving: 394 calories.

Ham and Turkey Casserole

See Menu Plan for Week 42.

4 oz (120 g) skinned and boned cooked turkey, diced

3 oz (90 g) cooked ham, diced

4 oz (120 g) cooked tagliatelle

3 oz (90 g) green pepper, diced, blanched

1 oz (30 g) low-fat dry milk, mixed with 4 fl oz (120 ml) water

1 tablespoon (15 ml) chopped fresh parsley

2 teaspoons (10 ml) grated Parmesan cheese

pinch pepper

Combine all ingredients; mix thoroughly. Spoon into medium casserole; cover with foil. Bake at 400°F, 200°C, Gas Mark 6 until thoroughly heated, about 25-30 minutes.
Makes 2 servings.
Per serving: 290 calories.

Orange Lamb with Rosemary

See Menu Plan for Week 15.

6 oz (180 g) boneless lamb, cubed

1½ oz (45 g) spring onion, chopped

1 teaspoon (5 ml) vegetable oil

6 fl oz (180 ml) chicken stock, made with ½ stock cube

2 oz (60 g) cooked pearl barley

1 medium orange, peeled and thinly sliced

1 tablespoon (15 ml) lemon juice

½ teaspoon (2.5 ml) crushed rosemary leaves

pinch each salt and pepper

On a rack in a grill pan, cook lamb until rare, about 10 minutes; in a non-stick pan saute spring onion in oil until lightly browned. Add lamb and all remaining ingredients; stir to combine. Cover and cook over gentle heat for 45-50 minutes or until lamb is tender. Adjust seasoning.
Makes 1 serving.
Per serving: 485 calories.

Savoury Mince with Noodles

See Menu Plan for Week 28.

1 teaspoon (5 ml) sage

1 clove garlic, crushed

artificial sweetener to taste

½ teaspoon (2.5 ml) curry powder

1 teaspoon (5 ml) Worcestershire sauce

2 tablespoons (30 ml) tomato puree

10 fl oz (300 ml) water

½ beef stock cube

4 oz (120 g) onion, chopped

4 oz (120 g) cooked minced beef

2 oz (60 g) hot cooked noodles

1 teaspoon (5 ml) vegetable oil

Place first 9 ingredients in a saucepan and bring to the boil. Simmer until sauce is thick, add mince, mix well and simmer for a further 10 minutes. Toss noodles in oil, arrange on serving dish and serve with sauce.
Makes 1 serving.
Per serving: 430 calories.

Grilled Ham Steak with Pineapple

See Menu Plans for Weeks 2 and 17.

2 slices canned pineapple, with 2 tablespoons (30 ml) juice

½-1 teaspoon (2.5-5 ml) prepared English mustard

1 teaspoon (5 ml) honey

6-oz (180-g) cooked boned ham steak

Mix pineapple juice with mustard and honey. Place ham steak on rack in grill pan and spread with half the mustard mixture. Grill 3-4 minutes. Turn steak, top with pineapple slices and spoon remaining mustard mixture over pineapple. Grill 3-4 minutes longer or until pineapple is lightly browned and steak is hot.
Makes 2 servings.
Per serving: 170 calories.

Steak Pizzaiola with Spanish Sauce

See Menu Plan for Week 31.

2 teaspoons (10 ml) olive oil

2 tablespoons (30 ml) finely chopped onion

2 small cloves garlic, chopped

6 oz (180 g) tomatoes, skinned and chopped

¼ teaspoon (1.25 ml) oregano

salt and pepper

2 teaspoons (10 ml) chopped fresh parsley

4 black olives, stoned and sliced

2 x 6-oz (180-g) pieces lean sirloin steak

Heat oil in saucepan; add onion and garlic and saute until onion is tender. Add tomatoes, oregano, salt and pinch pepper and simmer 10 minutes, stirring occasionally. Stir in parsley and half the sliced olives; keep warm. Sprinkle steaks with pinch pepper and place on rack in grill pan. Grill 2-3 minutes on each side or until done to taste. Transfer steaks to serving plate. Spoon tomato sauce over meat and garnish with remaining olives.
Makes 2 servings.
Per serving: 353 calories.

Sweet and Sour Pork Fillet

See Menu Plan for Week 47.

12 oz (360 g) lean pork fillet

juice of 1 lemon

2 teaspoons (10 ml) corn oil

1 clove garlic, crushed

8 oz (240 g) beansprouts

4 oz (120 g) mushrooms, thinly sliced

3 oz (90 g) red pepper, thinly sliced

8 oz (240 g) canned pineapple chunks with 4 tablespoons (60 ml) juice

2 tablespoons (30 ml) soy sauce

1 tablespoon (15 ml) wine vinegar

1 teaspoon (5 ml) brown sugar

2 spring onions, chopped

Grill pork fillet under medium heat for 12-15 minutes, or until cooked, turning once. Moisten during cooking time with lemon juice if fillet seems dry. Slice cooked pork thinly, cover with foil and set aside in a warm place. In a large non-stick frying pan or wok, heat oil and saute garlic over a high heat. Add vegetables and saute for 30 seconds. Add the pineapple and juice, soy sauce, wine vinegar, brown sugar and remaining lemon juice. Cover and cook for 3 minutes. Arrange sliced pork fillet on top of vegetables in a serving dish and sprinkle with chopped spring onions.
Makes 2 servings.
Per serving: 388 calories.

Meatball and Vegetable Stir-Fry

See Menu Plan for Week 48.

1½ lbs (720 g) lean minced beef

8 teaspoons (40 ml) vegetable oil

1 slice fresh ginger root, finely chopped

1 clove garlic, finely chopped

8 oz (240 g) broccoli, broken into sprigs

8 oz (240 g) cauliflower, broken into sprigs

8 oz (240 g) green beans, sliced

8 oz (240 g) courgettes, thinly sliced

1 teaspoon (5 ml) sugar

½ teaspoon (2.5 ml) salt

1 tablespoon (15 ml) soy sauce

8 teaspoons (40 ml) red wine

5 fl oz (150 ml) water

2 teaspoons (10 ml) cornflour blended with 2 teaspoons (10 ml) water

1 lb (480 g) cooked rice

Form mince into small balls and cook on a rack under medium grill for approximately 6-8 minutes turning to brown all sides; remove from grill and set aside. Heat oil in large non-stick pan; add ginger root and garlic; saute over low heat without colouring. Add broccoli, cauliflower, beans and courgettes. Cook, stirring, 2-3 minutes. Add sugar, salt, soy sauce, wine, water and meatballs. Cover and simmer for approximately 5 minutes; add cornflour paste; adjust seasonings. Cook, stirring until thickened. Serve at once with rice.
Makes 4 servings.
Per serving: 636 calories.

Chicken Livers and Green Noodles

See Menu Plan for Week 48.

1 clove garlic, finely chopped

2 medium onions, chopped

4 tablespoons (60 ml) olive oil

4 oz (120 g) canned tomatoes, pureed and sieved

1 teaspoon (5 ml) fresh basil, chopped

1 sprig rosemary

½ teaspoon (2.5 ml) marjoram

pinch cinnamon

salt and cayenne pepper to taste

8 teaspoons (40 ml) red wine

1½ lbs (720 g) chicken livers, quartered

2 teaspoons (10 ml) flour, seasoned

1 lb (480 g) cooked green tagliatelle (green noodles)

4 teaspoons (20 ml) Parmesan cheese

Saute garlic and onions in 2 tablespoons (30 ml) olive oil in a medium pan. Add pureed tomatoes, herbs, seasonings and wine and simmer for about 20 minutes, stirring occasionally until smooth and slightly thickened. Dust chicken livers with seasoned flour and saute in remaining 2 tablespoons (30 ml) oil. Add to sauce and cook for 10 minutes. Remove rosemary sprig. Pour chicken liver sauce over noodles. Sprinkle with Parmesan cheese.
Makes 4 servings.
Per serving: 550 calories.

Chicken Livers and Green Noodles

Chicken and Pork Meatballs

See Menu Plan for Week 50.

6 oz (180 g) lean boned pork, cut into pieces

6 oz (180 g) skinned and boned chicken, cut into pieces

¾ teaspoon (3.75 ml) salt

½ clove garlic, finely chopped

¼ teaspoon (1.25 ml) tarragon

pinch pepper

3 oz (90 g) cooked potatoes, diced

1 teaspoon (5 ml) margarine

Either finely mince pork and chicken or process in bowl of food processor; add salt, garlic, tarragon and pepper, and mix well. Using a spoon, mash potatoes into meat mixture. Shape mixture into 6 or 8 equal balls; transfer to rack on baking sheet and bake at 350°F, 180°C, Gas Mark 4 for 35 minutes or until cooked through. Melt margarine in frying pan; add meatballs and brown, turning frequently.
Makes 2 servings.
Per serving: 295 calories.

Pork Chili Burgers

See Menu Plan for Week 34.

12 oz (360 g) minced lean pork

3 oz (90 g) onion, finely chopped, blanched

3 oz (90 g) green pepper, finely chopped, blanched

4 teaspoons (20 ml) tomato ketchup

1 teaspoon (5 ml) chili powder

1 clove garlic, finely chopped

½ teaspoon (2.5 ml) salt

pinch pepper

5 fl oz (150 ml) natural yogurt

parsley sprigs to garnish

Combine pork with next 7 ingredients; mix well. Shape mixture into 4 patties. Grill on rack, about 8 minutes on each side or until cooked through. Top each burger with yogurt and garnish with parsley.
Makes 2 servings.
Per serving: 372 calories.

Pork Chops with Orange Slices

See Menu Plan for Week 29.

8 x 4-oz (120-g) pork chops, trimmed

salt and pepper to taste

8 oz (240 g) onion, thinly sliced

4 tablespoons (60 ml) tomato puree mixed with 8 fl oz (240 ml) water

4 teaspoons (20 ml) grated lemon rind

4 medium oranges, sliced in rings

1 teaspoon (5 ml) marjoram

parsley to garnish

Season chops and grill on rack 4 inches (10 cm) from source of heat for 4-5 minutes on each side until brown. Turn off grill and place chops in small baking dish. Add onions, tomato puree, water and lemon rind. Arrange orange rings on top, sprinkle with marjoram and bake, covered, at 400°F, 200°C, Gas Mark 6 for 20-30 minutes or until meat is cooked through and onions are tender. Serve piping hot garnished with parsley.
Makes 4 servings.
Per serving: 292 calories.

Mexican Beef Patties

See Menu Plan for Week 26.

3 oz (90 g) button mushrooms, sliced

1 teaspoon (5 ml) chopped chives

2 teaspoons (10 ml) finely chopped celery

2 teaspoons (10 ml) finely chopped red pepper

6 oz (180 g) minced beef

2 oz (60 g) Cheddar cheese, grated

2 tablespoons (30 ml) chopped fresh parsley

2 teaspoons (10 ml) Worcestershire sauce

1 teaspoon (5 ml) salt

pinch pepper

In small non-stick frying pan, cook mushrooms, chives, celery and red pepper until vegetables are soft and accumulated liquid evaporated. Mix with remaining ingredients. Form into 2 patties; grill on rack in grill pan, turning once, until done to taste.
Makes 2 servings.
Per serving: 310 calories.

Pork with Fennel Seeds

See Menu Plan for Week 7.

12 oz (360 g) lean pork fillet, cut into ¾-inch (2-cm) thick slices

1 tablespoon (15 ml) fennel seeds, ground in blender

4 teaspoons (20 ml) low-fat spread

1 clove garlic, crushed

1 tablespoon (15 ml) plain flour

6 fl oz (180 ml) beef stock made with 1 stock cube

pinch pepper

Roll pork slices in ground fennel seeds. Place on rack and grill 10 minutes, turning once. Heat low-fat spread with garlic in small saucepan; stir in flour. Gradually add beef stock, stirring constantly, until sauce is smooth and thickened; add pepper. Transfer pork slices to small non-stick frying pan; top with sauce, cover, and simmer 15-20 minutes.
Makes 2 servings.
Per serving: 370 calories.

Barbecued Pork Chops

See Menu Plan for Week 35.

2 lbs (960 g) lean pork spare rib chops

8 oz (240g) canned tomatoes, pureed

2 tablespoons (30 ml) plus 2 teaspoons (10 ml) chili sauce

4 teaspoons (20 ml) Worcestershire sauce

4 teaspoons (20 ml) lemon juice

2 teaspoons (10 ml) prepared mustard

½ teaspoon (2.5 ml) paprika

pinch each pepper, ground cumin and salt

Arrange pork chops in baking pan. Combine remaining ingredients, mixing well. Pour over chops; cover and refrigerate overnight. Remove chops from pan and scrape off sauce. Transfer remaining sauce to small saucepan and set aside. Place chops on rack in baking pan; bake at 325°F, 160°C, Gas Mark 3 for 1¼ hours. While chops are baking, bring sauce to the boil; reduce heat and simmer 15

minutes. Transfer chops to serving dish and top with sauce.
Makes 4 servings.
Per serving: 320 calories.

Tarragon Chicken Livers

See Menu Plan for Week 19.

4 teaspoons (20 ml) low-fat spread

3 oz (90 g) onion, chopped

12 oz (360 g) chicken livers

1 tablespoon (15 ml) sliced spring onion

2 teaspoons (10 ml) red wine

½ teaspoon (2.5 ml) tarragon

2 slices (1 oz/30 g each) white bread, toasted and cut into triangles

1 tablespoon (15 ml) chopped fresh parsley

Melt low-fat spread in medium pan; add onion and saute until tender. Add chicken livers and saute until firm, about 5-7 minutes. Add spring onion, red wine and tarragon; cook 2 minutes longer. Place toast triangles on plate; top with liver mixture. Garnish with parsley.
Makes 2 servings.
Per serving: 352 calories.

Lamb's Liver Creole

See Menu Plans for Weeks 2, 17 and 44.

3 oz (90 g) onions, diced

1½ oz (45 g) green pepper, chopped

12 oz (360 g) canned tomatoes

¼ teaspoon (1.25 ml) salt

pinch ground cumin

12 oz (360 g) lamb's liver, sliced

Combine first 5 ingredients in saucepan; bring to the boil; cover and simmer until onion is cooked. Meanwhile grill liver about 2 minutes or until top is browned. Turn and grill for 2 minutes more. Add liver to tomato mixture. Heat 2 minutes and serve.
Makes 2 servings.
Per serving: 341 calories.

Liver Venetian

See Menu Plans for Weeks 4 and 37.

1 teaspoon (5 ml) olive oil

2 oz (60 g) onion, thinly sliced

1 clove garlic, crushed

4 oz (120 g) mushrooms, sliced

12 oz (360 g) calf's liver, cut into bite-size pieces

2 teaspoons (10 ml) white wine

pinch each salt and pepper

1 tablespoon (15 ml) chopped fresh parsley

Heat oil in small non-stick frying pan. Add onion and garlic and saute until onion is translucent. Add mushrooms and cook briefly. Add liver and saute just until pink disappears. Add white wine, salt, and pepper. Sprinkle with parsley and serve.
Makes 2 servings.
Per serving: 299 calories.

Curried Tripe

See Menu Plan for Week 48.

1½ lbs (720 g) tripe
8 teaspoons (40 ml) vegetable oil
2 cloves garlic, finely chopped
1 slice fresh ginger root, finely chopped
1 medium onion, sliced
16 oz (480 g) canned tomatoes, pureed and sieved
10 fl oz (300 ml) chicken stock made with 1 stock cube
2 tablespoons (30 ml) curry powder
1 teaspoon (5 ml) salt
good pinch white pepper
6 oz (180 g) carrots, sliced
1 green pepper, roughly chopped
fresh coriander leaves or parsley for garnish
1 lb (480 g) cooked rice

Wash tripe well; rub with salt and rinse thoroughly. Parboil in salted water (1 tablespoon (15 ml) salt to 1½ pints (900 ml) water) for 15 minutes. Drain, discarding water. Cut into 1-inch (2.5-cm) cubes. Heat oil in pan; add garlic, ginger and onions and saute. Add tripe and saute until lightly browned. Add pureed tomatoes, stock, curry powder, salt and pepper. Bring to the boil; cover and simmer 1 hour. Add carrots and continue to cook 25 minutes. Add green pepper and cook 10 minutes longer. Garnish with coriander or parsley and serve with steamed rice.
Makes 4 servings.
Per serving: 381 calories.

Chicken Livers Sauteed in Wine

See Menu Plans for Weeks 12 and 36.

2 teaspoons (10 ml) margarine
2 oz (60 g) onion, sliced
1 clove garlic, crushed
12 oz (360 g) chicken livers
1 tablespoon (15 ml) red wine
pinch each salt and pepper

Melt margarine in medium frying pan; add onion and garlic and saute until tender. Add chicken livers and saute, stirring occasionally, for 5-7 minutes or until livers are cooked. Add remaining ingredients. Heat and serve.
Makes 2 servings.
Per serving: 323 calories.

Liver and Noodle Casserole

See Menu Plan for Week 22.

6 oz (180 g) calf or ox liver, cut into ½-inch (1-cm) cubes
2 oz (60 g) onion, sliced
1½ oz (45 g) green pepper, diced
2 tablespoons (30 ml) tomato puree
4 fl oz (120 ml) water
pinch thyme
3-4 drops gravy browning
salt and pepper to taste
2 oz (60 g) cooked noodles
1½ oz (45 g) cooked carrots, sliced

Brown liver, onion and green pepper in a preheated non-stick frying pan over moderately high heat. Mix tomato puree with water; add to liver with thyme, gravy browning, salt and pepper. Cook over gentle heat until liver is tender. Stir in noodles and carrots and heat thoroughly.
Makes 1 serving.
Per serving: 389 calories.

Irish Stew

See Menu Plan for Week 11.

1½ lbs (720 g) lean fillet of lamb
1 pint (480 ml) chicken stock made with 1 stock cube
1½ lbs (720 g) potatoes, sliced
8 oz (240 g) onions, sliced
2 tablespoons (30 ml) chopped fresh parsley and thyme, mixed
1 teaspoon (5 ml) salt
pinch pepper

Trim all visible fat from meat and cut into bite-sized pieces. Put meat on a rack in grill pan and cook, turning once, until all juices stop running. Meanwhile, put remaining ingredients in saucepan; add meat, cover and cook approximately 30-40 minutes or until meat and vegetables are tender.
Makes 4 servings.
Per serving: 450 calories.

Irish Stew

Liver Pate

See Menu Plan for Week 25.

1½ lbs (720 g) chicken livers

juice of 2 lemons

4 teaspoons (20 ml) Worcestershire sauce

1 teaspoon (5 ml) each salt and nutmeg

½ teaspoon (2.5 ml) garlic powder

4 slices (1 oz/30 g each) white bread, made into crumbs

lettuce leaves

4 medium apples, cored and sliced

1 tablespoon (15 ml) lemon juice

Combine first 5 ingredients in saucepan. Cover and simmer for 10 minutes. Stir in breadcrumbs. Transfer to blender container and puree until smooth. Turn into 1-lb (480-g) loaf tin lined with greaseproof or non-stick paper; smooth top; chill for 2-3 hours. Turn out on to serving plate; slice. Arrange lettuce leaves and apple slices tossed in lemon juice around pate.
Makes 4 servings.
Per serving: 345 calories.

Chicken Liver Pilaf

See Menu Plan for Week 7.

1 tablespoon (15 ml) vegetable oil

12 oz (360 g) chicken livers

4 oz (120 g) onions, chopped

6 oz (180 g) mushrooms, sliced

4 oz (120 g) celery, sliced

4 oz (120 g) cooked brown rice

1 teaspoon (5 ml) each salt and basil

pinch ground nutmeg

Heat oil in non-stick frying pan.

Add livers and cook until firm. Using a slotted spoon, remove livers from pan. Add onions to pan and saute until softened but not browned; add mushrooms and celery and saute for 5-8 minutes or until tender. Add liver to vegetable mixture with rice, seasoning and herbs and cook, stirring often, until heated.
Makes 2 servings.
Per serving: 393 calories.

Breadcrumbed Liver

See Menu Plan for Week 40.

6 oz (180 g) calf's liver, cut into ¼-inch (0.5-cm) slices

juice of ½ lemon

¾ oz (20 g) dried breadcrumbs

¼ teaspoon (1.25 ml) fennel seeds (optional)

pinch each salt and pepper

1 tablespoon (15 ml) vegetable oil

lemon slices to garnish

Marinate liver slices in lemon juice for ½ hour. Put breadcrumbs, fennel seeds, salt and pepper in blender and puree until the seeds are crushed. Spread crumb mixture in a shallow plate; press liver slices into crumbs to coat; turn and repeat until all crumbs are used. In a non-stick pan saute breaded liver slices in oil until golden on each side. Garnish with lemon slices.
Makes 1 serving.
Per serving: 445 calories.

Liver with Noodles

See Menu Plan for Week 46.

1 tablespoon (15 ml) olive oil

1½ oz (45 g) onion, diced

1 clove garlic, finely chopped

12 oz (360 g) sliced ox liver, cut into 1-inch (2.5-cm) strips

8 oz (240 g) canned tomatoes, pureed

¼ teaspoon (1.25 ml) oregano

pinch each salt and pepper

4 oz (120 g) cooked bow-tie noodles

2 teaspoons (10 ml) grated Parmesan cheese

Heat oil in pan; add onion and garlic and saute until onion is softened. Add liver and saute over high heat for 2-4 minutes until firm and tender. Stir in pureed tomatoes, oregano, salt and pepper; reduce heat to moderate and cook, stirring occasionally, for 2 minutes. Add noodles and cook for a further 2 minutes. Transfer to flameproof dish, sprinkle with cheese and brown under grill.
Makes 2 servings.
Per serving: 453 calories.

Beef Pie

See Menu Plans for Weeks 9 and 25.

12 oz (360 g) cubed shin of beef

12 fl oz (360 ml) beef stock made with 1 stock cube

pinch mixed herbs

4 oz (120 g) carrots, sliced

3 oz (90 g) mushrooms, sliced

4 oz (120 g) celery, diced

4 oz (120 g) onions, diced

12 oz (360 g) potatoes

4 teaspoons (20 ml) flour

4 teaspoons (20 ml) margarine

4 oz (120 g) Cheddar cheese, grated

1 tablespoon (15 ml) chopped chives

Place beef cubes on rack in grill pan; grill until browned on all sides. Transfer beef to medium saucepan; add 10 fl oz (300 ml) stock and herbs. Cover and simmer for approximately 1½ hours. Add carrots, mushrooms, celery and onions. Simmer for further ½ hour until vegetables and meat are just tender. Meanwhile put potatoes in pan, cover with cold water, bring to the boil; cover and cook until tender; drain. In small bowl gradually add remaining stock to flour, stirring constantly to form a smooth paste; add to beef and vegetables. Bring to the boil, stirring. Cook for 2 minutes. Spoon equal amounts of mixture into 4 individual casseroles. Mash potatoes with margarine; stir in cheese and chives. Pipe or spoon potato mixture over meat in casseroles. Bake at 375°F, 190°C, Gas Mark 5 for 20 minutes, or cook under hot grill until potatoes are lightly browned.
Makes 4 servings.
Per serving: 370 calories.

Casseroled Liver

See Menu Plan for Week 29.

4 slices (1 oz/30 g each) white bread, made into crumbs

4 teaspoons (20 ml) onion flakes

2 tablespoons (30 ml) chopped fresh parsley

rind of 2 lemons, grated

8 teaspoons (40 ml) low-fat spread

juice of 2 lemons

1½ lbs (720 g) lamb's liver, cut into thin slices

1 pint (600 ml) beef stock, made with 2 stock cubes

2 tablespoons (30 ml) cornflour blended with 2 tablespoons (30 ml) water

Combine breadcrumbs, onion flakes, parsley and lemon rind. Melt low-fat spread in cup over hot water, add lemon juice, pour into breadcrumb mixture and mix well. Leave to cool. Lay slices of liver flat, divide stuffing evenly between each piece, roll up and secure with a cocktail stick. If using thick slices of liver, slit down centre to make pocket and fill with stuffing. Place in ovenproof casserole, pour stock over liver and bake at 425°F, 220°C, Gas Mark 7 for 30 minutes. Remove liver from stock; keep warm. Put blended cornflour into a small pan; pour in stock; bring to the boil, stirring. Adjust seasoning. Serve sauce with liver.
Makes 4 servings.
Per serving: 443 calories.

Sweet and Sour Liver

See Menu Plan for Week 10.

2½ fl oz (75 ml) pineapple juice

2 teaspoons (10 ml) wine vinegar

1½ teaspoons (7.5 ml) soy sauce

pinch each ground ginger and ground allspice

1 teaspoon (5 ml) cornflour, blended with 2 teaspoons (10 ml) water

1 teaspoon (5 ml) vegetable oil

2 tablespoons (30 ml) finely chopped onion

12 oz (360 g) lamb's liver, cut into ¼-inch (0.5-cm) thick slices

2 teaspoons (10 ml) chopped fresh parsley

salt and pepper

In small saucepan combine pineapple juice, vinegar, soy sauce, ginger and allspice. Heat. Stir in blended cornflour. Cook over medium heat, stirring constantly, until sauce comes just to the boil and begins to thicken. Keep warm. Grease frying pan with vegetable oil. Sprinkle onion over bottom of frying pan. Place liver slices over onion and sprinkle with parsley and pinch each salt and pepper. Cook about 2 minutes, then turn slices over. Sprinkle with pinch each salt and pepper and cook about 1-2 minutes longer or until liver is slightly pink inside when cut with a knife. Transfer slices to serving plate and spoon sauce over liver.
Makes 2 servings.
Per serving: 253 calories.

Pork and Vegetable Medley

See Menu Plan for Week 14.

12 oz (360 g) lean pork fillet
1 tablespoon (15 ml) vegetable oil
1½ oz (45 g) onion, diced
1 clove garlic, crushed
1 tablespoon (15 ml) soy sauce
3 oz (90 g) broccoli florets
2 oz (60 g) celery, diagonally sliced
3 oz (90 g) frozen peas
1½ oz (45 g) drained canned water chestnuts, cut into thin strips
6 fl oz (180 ml) chicken stock made with 1 stock cube

Cut away all visible fat from fillet; cut into ¼-inch (0.5-cm) thick slices and cook on a rack under a hot grill for 5 minutes each side or until cooked through. Keep warm. Heat oil in frying pan. Add onion and garlic; saute until softened. Sprinkle with soy sauce. Add broccoli, celery, peas and water chestnuts; toss to combine. Add stock, cover and simmer 5 minutes. Add pork and continue to cook for a further 6-8 minutes or until vegetables are tender-crisp.
Makes 2 servings.
Per serving: 329 calories.

Creamed Cabbage and Ham

See Menu Plan for Week 51.

2 teaspoons (10 ml) margarine
4 oz (120 g) onion, sliced
1 clove garlic, crushed
4 oz (120 g) carrots, cut into matchstick strips
9 oz (270 g) white cabbage, thinly sliced
6 oz (180 g) cooked ham, sliced and cut into thin strips
4 teaspoons (20 ml) flour
6 fl oz (180 ml) cold chicken stock, made with 1 stock cube
4 fl oz (120 ml) skim milk
pinch ground nutmeg
pinch freshly ground pepper

Melt margarine in medium pan. Add onion and garlic and saute until translucent. Add carrots and stir-fry 3 minutes. Add cabbage; cover and cook gently until wilted, about 10 minutes; stir in ham. Place flour in bowl and gradually add stock, stirring until smooth; stir into ham mixture. Add milk, nutmeg and pepper. Cook, stirring constantly, about 3 minutes or until thickened.
Makes 2 servings.
Per serving: 304 calories.

Oven-Baked Burgers

See Menu Plan for Week 32.

12 oz (360 g) minced beef
3 oz (90 g) onion, finely chopped
3 oz (90 g) green pepper, finely chopped
¾ teaspoon (3.75 ml) salt
2 teaspoons (10 ml) prepared English mustard
pinch basil
pinch pepper

Combine all ingredients in large bowl; mix well. Form mixture into 4 equal patties. Place patties on a rack in baking tin and bake at 350°F, 180°C, Gas Mark 4 for 25 minutes.
Makes 2 servings.
Per serving: 375 calories.

Beef and Corn Casserole

See Menu Plan for Week 1.

8 oz (240 g) cooked beef, minced
6 oz (180 g) drained canned sweet corn
3 oz (90 g) red pepper, seeded and cut into thin strips, blanched
4 fl oz (120 ml) beef stock made with ½ stock cube
pinch pepper

In a medium casserole combine beef, corn, red pepper strips, stock and pepper; toss well. Cover and bake for 30 minutes at 350°F, 180°C, Gas Mark 4.
Makes 2 servings.
Per serving: 380 calories.

Beef and Corn Casserole

Oriental Beef

See Menu Plan for Week 47.

12 oz (360 g) lean rump steak

2 teaspoons (10 ml) corn oil

1 clove garlic, finely chopped

3 oz (90 g) onion, thinly sliced

3 oz (90 g) green pepper, thinly sliced

6 oz (180 g) canned water chestnuts, thinly sliced

2 tablespoons (30 ml) soy sauce

2 teaspoons (10 ml) chopped spring onions

Grill steak under high heat for 4-5 minutes or until rare, turning once. Slice thinly and set aside in a warm place. In a large non-stick frying pan or wok, heat corn oil and saute garlic over low heat. Add the vegetables, increase heat and stir-fry in the hot oil for 10 seconds. Turn vegetables with a spatula and add the soy sauce. Cover with lid and cook for 5-6 minutes. Stir meat into vegetable mixture. Serve sprinkled with chopped spring onions.
Makes 2 servings.
Per serving: 339 calories.

Savoury Tripe

See Menu Plan for Week 8

12 oz (360 g) tripe, washed well

2 teaspoons (10 ml) olive oil

4 oz (120 g) onion, sliced

1 clove garlic, crushed

8 oz (240 g) canned tomatoes, pureed

2 oz (60 g) celery, sliced

½ teaspoon (2.5 ml) fennel seeds

15 fl oz (450 ml) chicken stock, made with 2 stock cubes

4 oz (120 g) carrots, sliced

1 tablespoon (15 ml) chopped fresh parsley

pinch each salt and red pepper

4 teaspoons (20 ml) red wine

Cut tripe into bite-size pieces. Place in saucepan with water to cover and bring to the boil. Reduce heat, cover and simmer for approximately ½ hour. Drain and set aside. Heat oil in medium saucepan; add onion and garlic and saute until translucent. Add pureed tomatoes, celery and fennel seeds; simmer for a few minutes. Add stock and tripe. Cover and simmer for approximately 2½ hours. Add carrots, parsley, salt and pepper; cook ½ hour longer. Stir in wine.
Makes 2 servings.
Per serving: 200 calories.

Marinated Rump Steak

See Menu Plans for Weeks 14 and 35.

2 teaspoons (10 ml) soy sauce

1 teaspoon (5 ml) honey

4 teaspoons (20 ml) red wine

pinch ground ginger

12 oz (360 g) lean rump steak

1 teaspoon (5 ml) finely chopped spring onion

Combine soy sauce, honey, wine and ginger. Place steak in shallow casserole; pour marinade over steak and marinate in refrigerator for 30 minutes, turning once. Transfer steak to rack in grill pan; discard marinade. Grill 5 minutes on each side or until cooked to taste.

Place steak on serving dish; garnish with spring onions.
Makes 2 servings.
Per serving: 338 calories.

Curried Beef

See Menu Plan for Week 37.

12 oz (360 g) minced beef

1 teaspoon (5 ml) vegetable oil

2 oz (60 g) onion, diced

½ medium cooking apple, peeled, cored and chopped

1 tablespoon (15 ml) raisins

2-3 teaspoons (10-15 ml) lemon juice

1 teaspoon (5 ml) curry powder

pinch salt

7 fl oz (210 ml) water

1 teaspoon (5 ml) arrowroot

Form mince into several small flat cakes and put on rack in grill pan. Grill, turning occasionally, 5 minutes or until thoroughly browned; transfer to a bowl and mash with fork until crumbly. Heat oil in saucepan; add onion and saute until softened. Stir in grilled meat, apple, raisins, 2 teaspoons (10 ml) lemon juice, curry powder and salt. Add 6 fl oz (180 ml) water and mix well. Simmer partially covered, stirring occasionally, for 45 minutes or until meat is tender. Mix arrowroot with remaining water; stir into meat mixture and cook, stirring constantly, until thickened. Add additional lemon juice to taste.
Makes 2 servings.
Per serving: 465 calories.

Ham with Rice and Water Chestnuts

See Menu Plan for Week 16.

2 teaspoons (10 ml) vegetable oil
6 oz (180 g) cooked ham, sliced and cut into thin strips
3 oz (90 g) drained canned water chestnuts, cut into slivers
2 pinches salt
pinch white pepper
4 oz (120 g) cooked brown rice
1 teaspoon (5 ml) chopped fresh parsley
pinch thyme

Heat oil in large non-stick pan. Add ham, water chestnuts, pinch salt and pepper. Cook over medium heat, stirring occasionally, until ham is browned and slightly crisp, about 3-5 minutes. In a small bowl combine rice, parsley, remaining pinch salt and thyme. Add to ham mixture. Continue cooking until rice is heated through.
Makes 2 servings.
Per serving: 267 calories.

Sausages in Tomato Sauce with Rice

See Menu Plan for Week 28.

8 oz (240 g) onion, chopped
1½ lbs (720 g) canned tomatoes
2 cloves garlic, crushed
oregano to taste
salt and pepper to taste
1½ lbs (720 g) beef sausages
8 oz (240 g) hot cooked rice

In non-stick pan, cook onions over gentle heat until transparent. Add tomatoes with juice, garlic and oregano. Bring to the boil and simmer for 15-20 minutes until reduced to a thick sauce. Adjust seasoning to taste. Meanwhile, grill sausages until cooked through and brown on all sides. To serve, place sausages on bed of rice and pour tomato sauce over.
Makes 4 servings.
Per serving: 446 calories.

Kidneys in Red Wine

See Menu Plan for Week 48.

1½ lbs (720 g) lamb's kidneys
8 teaspoons (40 ml) margarine
2 medium onions, chopped
8 oz (240 g) mushrooms, sliced
1 teaspoon (5 ml) tarragon
2 tablespoons (30 ml) fresh chopped parsley
8 tablespoons (120 ml) red wine
pepper to taste
1 lb (480 g) cooked rice

Remove outer membranes from kidneys; split in half lengthwise and snip out cores with scissors. Wash well. Drain. Melt margarine in non-stick frying pan and saute kidneys over high heat 3-5 minutes. Remove and keep warm. Add onions to pan, saute 5 minutes; add mushrooms and herbs; saute for further 5 minutes until onion is translucent. Add wine to pan and bring to the boil. Return kidneys to pan, season with pepper; cover and cook for 10 minutes until very hot. Serve with rice.
Makes 4 servings.
Per serving: 416 calories.

Frankfurter Stir-Fry

See Menu Plan for Week 33.

1 teaspoon (5 ml) vegetable oil
2 oz (60 g) onion, sliced
6 oz (180 g) frankfurters, cut diagonally into 1-inch (2.5-cm) pieces
3 oz (90 g) peas, blanched
3 oz (90 g) carrot, in matchsticks, blanched
1½ oz (45 g) celery, sliced diagonally, blanched
8 oz (240 g) canned pineapple chunks
1 teaspoon (5 ml) soy sauce
1 teaspoon (5 ml) cornflour mixed with 3 tablespoons (45 ml) water

Heat oil in non-stick pan; add onion and saute until tender. Add frankfurters, peas, carrot and celery, and cook, stirring constantly, for 5 minutes. Add pineapple chunks and soy sauce; cook 2 minutes longer, stirring constantly. Add cornflour paste and cook until sauce thickens.
Makes 2 servings.
Per serving: 345 calories.

FISH

Fish dishes range from the delicate to the hardy. You can be as creative as your imagination allows. Use fish in casseroles, salads and soups, or as kebabs. Fish can be poached, grilled, baked or sauteed. Serve any of our taste-tempting suggestions and you won't have to 'fish' for compliments.

Trout with Mushroom Stuffing

See Menu Plan for Week 34.

1 teaspoon (5 ml) margarine

1 tablespoon (15 ml) spring onion, finely chopped

3 oz (90 g) mushrooms, chopped

2 tablespoons (30 ml) celery, finely chopped

1 tablespoon (15 ml) chopped red pepper

1 teaspoon (5 ml) lemon juice

¼ teaspoon (1.25 ml) salt

1 tablespoon (15 ml) chopped fresh parsley

2 teaspoons (10 ml) low-calorie mayonnaise

1 teaspoon (5 ml) French mustard

2 x 8-oz (240-g) trout, filleted

Melt margarine in small non-stick pan; add spring onion and saute briefly, being careful not to burn. Add mushrooms, celery, red pepper, lemon juice and salt; saute until tender. Remove from heat and stir in parsley, mayonnaise and mustard. Arrange fish fillets in baking dish. Spread vegetable mixture over fillets; cover and bake at 400°F, 200°C, Gas Mark 6 for about 20 minutes or until fish flakes easily when tested with a fork.
Makes 2 servings.
Per serving: 241 calories.

Salmon Mousse

See Menu Plans for Weeks 3 and 52.

2 teaspoons (10 ml) unflavoured gelatine

4 tablespoons (60 ml) water

2 tablespoons (30 ml) lemon juice

1 tablespoon (15 ml) finely chopped onion

8 oz (240 g) drained, skinned and boned canned salmon

5 fl oz (150 ml) skim milk

2½ tablespoons (37.5 ml) natural yogurt

2 tablespoons (30 ml) low-calorie mayonnaise

2 teaspoons (10 ml) chopped fresh dill, or ½ teaspoon (2.5 ml) dried dill weed (optional)

½ teaspoon (2.5 ml) each white pepper and salt

Dissolve gelatine in water in bowl over pan of hot water. Place lemon juice with onion in blender container; puree 30 seconds. Add remaining ingredients except gelatine. Puree until smooth. Finally add gelatine. Pour mixture into a 2-pint (1.2-litre) mould that has been rinsed in cold water. Chill for at least 4 hours. Unmould before serving.
Makes 2 servings.
Per serving: 255 calories.

Far East Scallops

See Menu Plan for Week 51.

2 teaspoons (10 ml) vegetable oil

2 oz (60 g) onion, sliced

½ clove garlic, chopped

4 oz (120 g) mushrooms, sliced

4 oz (120 g) broccoli in small florets, blanched

3 oz (90 g) drained canned sliced bamboo shoots

2 teaspoons (10 ml) soy sauce

dash sherry flavouring

12 oz (360 g) scallops cut into ¼-inch (0.5-cm) slices

6 fl oz (180 ml) chicken stock, made with 1 stock cube

2 teaspoons (10 ml) cornflour

1 tablespoon (15 ml) water

Heat oil in wok or frying pan. Add onion and garlic and saute about 1 minute. Add mushrooms, broccoli and bamboo shoots; stir-fry over high heat about 3 minutes. Stir in soy sauce and flavouring. Add scallops and stir-fry 4 minutes. Pour in stock. Blend cornflour with water and stir into pan. Bring to boil, stirring constantly, cook about 3 minutes or until thickened.
Makes 2 servings.
Per serving: 268 calories.

Far East Scallops

Poached Cod with French Beans and Tomatoes

See Menu Plan for Week 16.

1 small carrot, chopped

1 celery stick, chopped

3 tablespoons (45 ml) lemon juice

4 parsley sprigs

4 peppercorns, crushed

12 oz (360 g) cod fillets

2 teaspoons (10 ml) olive oil

2 oz (60 g) onion, sliced

pinch mixed herbs

6 oz (180 g) whole French beans, blanched and cut into 1½-inch (4-cm) slices

salt and pepper

4 small tomatoes, quartered

In medium pan combine carrot, celery, 2 tablespoons (30 ml) lemon juice, parsley sprigs and peppercorns; add fish and enough water to barely cover fillets. Cover with sheet of foil, bring to a slow simmer. Do not boil. Simmer fish until *almost* completely cooked through – about 3-5 minutes. Transfer fish to serving dish and set aside. Discard poaching liquid and wipe pan dry.

Heat oil in pan and add onion and herbs. Cover and cook over low heat until onion slices are soft. Add French beans and continue cooking until tender.

Cut fish into large chunks and sprinkle with pinch each salt and pepper. Add fish and tomatoes to pan; cook until fish is cooked through; about 3-5 minutes, occasionally stirring gently. *Do not overcook.* Sprinkle with rest of lemon juice and pinch each salt and pepper just before serving.
Makes 2 servings.
Per serving: 215 calories.

Cod with Lemon

See Menu Plan for Week 11.

2 cod fillets, 6 oz (180 g) each

1 teaspoon (5 ml) vegetable oil

pinch salt

pinch each white pepper and paprika

4 lemon slices

1 tablespoon (15 ml) small capers

2 teaspoons (10 ml) low-fat spread

2 teaspoons (10 ml) chopped fresh parsley

Place fish, skin-side up in flame-proof dish; brush with half the oil. Grill under medium grill until starting to brown. Turn carefully ; brush with remaining oil and sprinkle with salt and pepper. Grill for further 3-5 minutes until nearly cooked. Add lemon slices and capers and cook for 2-3 minutes to lightly brown lemon. Top each serving with 1 teaspoon (5 ml) low-fat spread; allow to melt. Sprinkle each with 1 teaspoon (5 ml) chopped parsley.
Makes 2 servings.
Per serving: 182 calories.

Cod-Vegetable Bake

See Menu Plans for Weeks 6 and 36.

8 oz (240 g) courgettes, sliced into ¼-inch (0.5-cm) thick slices

4 tablespoons (60 ml) tomato puree, mixed with 5 fl oz (150 ml) water

1 small clove garlic, finely chopped with pinch salt

pinch each summer savory, thyme and pepper

12 oz (360 g) cod fillets

6 oz (180 g) broccoli florets, blanched (optional)

1 teaspoon (5 ml) lemon juice

pinch salt

Blanch courgettes for 2 minutes in boiling salted water until tender-crisp. Drain; rinse with cold water and set aside. In small saucepan combine tomato puree, water, garlic, herbs and pepper. Bring to the boil; reduce heat and simmer 5 minutes. Set aside. Preheat oven to 350°F, 180°C, Gas Mark 4. Place fillets in bottom of ovenproof dish (not aluminium). If desired, place broccoli florets alongside fillets. Sprinkle fillets with lemon juice and salt. Arrange courgette slices over fish in an overlapping pattern. Be sure fish is completely covered. Spoon tomato mixture around edge of fish and vegetables. Cover with foil and bake for 20-25 minutes or until fish flakes easily. When serving, spoon tomato sauce over vegetables.
Makes 2 servings.
Per serving: 196 calories.

Baked Prawns Thermidor

See Menu Plan for Week 25.

4 tablespoons (60 ml) margarine
3 oz (90 g) mushrooms, sliced
4 tablespoons (60 ml) flour
½ teaspoon (2.5 ml) dry mustard
10 fl oz (300 ml) skim milk
8 oz (240 g) cooked peeled prawns
salt and pinch ground red pepper
2 slices (1 oz/30 g each) white bread, made into crumbs
2 oz (60 g) Parmesan cheese, grated
2 oz (60 g) Cheddar cheese, grated
½ teaspoon (2.5 ml) paprika
parsley sprigs to garnish

Melt margarine in non-stick saucepan; add mushrooms. Cook for 5 minutes. Blend in flour and mustard. Cook gently for 1 minute. Remove pan from heat; stir in milk. Return to heat; bring to the boil, stirring constantly. Add prawns; stir to combine. Season with salt and pepper to taste. Transfer mixture to 3-pint (1.75-litre) casserole. Combine breadcrumbs, Parmesan cheese, Cheddar cheese and paprika. Sprinkle over prawn mixture. Bake at 400°F, 200°C, Gas Mark 6 for 20 minutes or until top is brown and bubbly. Garnish with parsley sprigs.
Makes 4 servings.
Per serving: 408 calories.

Fish and Rice Salad

See Menu Plan for Week 32.

6 oz (180 g) cooked smoked haddock
4 oz (120 g) cooked short-grain brown rice
2 tablespoons (30 ml) red pepper, diced
2 teaspoons (10 ml) olive oil
1 teaspoon (5 ml) lemon juice
½ teaspoon (2.5 ml) salt
pinch thyme
pinch pepper

Place fish, rice and red pepper in medium bowl. Do not combine. Combine oil, lemon juice, salt, thyme and pepper. Pour over fish, rice and red pepper. Toss gently to combine, breaking fish into large chunks. Serve at once.
Makes 2 servings.
Per serving: 200 calories.

Baked Haddock

See Menu Plan for Week 34.

12 oz (360 g) haddock fillets
2 teaspoons (10 ml) mayonnaise
1 teaspoon (5 ml) German mustard
1 teaspoon (5 ml) lemon juice
1 teaspoon (5 ml) each chopped chives and chopped fresh parsley
pinch each salt and freshly ground pepper
2 teaspoons (10 ml) grated Parmesan cheese

Arrange fillets in shallow 1½-pint (900-ml) baking dish. Combine remaining ingredients, except cheese; stir well. Spread mixture over fish and sprinkle with cheese. Bake at 400°F, 200°C, Gas Mark 6, for 20 minutes or until fish flakes easily and top is golden.
Makes 2 servings.
Per serving: 156 calories.

Calamari with Spaghetti

The word 'calamari' is derived from the Latin calamus, which means pen. Calamari are squid with pen-shaped skeletal structures.
See Menu Plan for Week 21.

2 teaspoons (10 ml) olive oil
2 oz (60 g) onion, sliced
3 garlic cloves, finely chopped
12 oz (360 g) calamari, cleaned and sliced
8 oz (240 g) canned crushed plum tomatoes
1 teaspoon (5 ml) salt
pinch pepper
4 oz (120 g) hot cooked spaghetti
1 tablespoon (15 ml) chopped fresh parsley

Heat oil in small to medium saucepan. Add onion and garlic; saute until translucent. Add calamari; cook, stirring occasionally, until moisture evaporates. Add tomatoes, salt and pepper. Cover and simmer until calamari is tender, approximately 45 minutes to 1 hour. Pour liquid and sauce over spaghetti and sprinkle with parsley.
Makes 2 servings.
Per serving: 245 calories.

Skate with Lemon Sauce

See Menu Plan for Week 30.

½ teaspoon (2.5 ml) salt

10 fl oz (300 ml) water

3 tablespoons (45 ml) plus 1 teaspoon (5 ml) wine vinegar

1 sachet bouquet garni

6 peppercorns

2 x 8-oz (240-g) wings of skate

4 oz (120 g) onion, sliced

1 teaspoon (5 ml) vegetable oil

juice and rind of 1 lemon

salt and black pepper to taste

1 teaspoon (5 ml) freshly chopped parsley

1 teaspoon (5 ml) thyme

2 teaspoons (10 ml) cornflour blended with 1 tablespoon (15 ml) water

watercress to garnish

Prepare a court bouillon by dissolving the salt in 8 fl oz (240 ml) water in a saucepan. Add 3 tablespoons (45 ml) vinegar, bouquet garni and peppercorns. Bring to the boil and boil for 5 minutes. Leave to cool. Cut the skate into 4 pieces and place it in a large saucepan. Strain the court bouillon onto the fish. Bring slowly to boiling point, cover the pan and simmer for about 10 minutes. Meanwhile prepare sauce. Saute the sliced onion gently in oil in a non-stick pan until soft. Add 2 fl oz (60 ml) water, lemon juice, 1 teaspoon (5 ml) vinegar, seasoning and herbs to the cooked onion. Bring to the boil, add lemon peel and simmer gently. Stir in cornflour mixture. Stir until thickened. Arrange the cooked skate in a heated serving dish. Pour the prepared sauce over the fish and garnish with sprigs of watercress.
Makes 2 servings.
Per serving: 234 calories.

Sardine Salad

See Menu Plans for Weeks 2 and 21.

4 oz (120 g) drained canned sardines

1 oz (30 g) spring onion, chopped

1 tablespoon (15 ml) low-calorie mayonnaise

½ teaspoon (2.5 ml) prepared mustard

1 teaspoon (5 ml) lemon juice

lettuce leaves

Mash sardines. Add spring onion, mayonnaise, mustard and lemon juice. Serve on a plate lined with lettuce leaves.
Makes 1 serving.
Per serving: 236 calories.

Baked Hake Steaks

See Menu Plan for Week 28.

2 tablespoons (30 ml) lemon juice

½ teaspoon (2.5 ml) salt

½ teaspoon (2.5 ml) paprika

4 x 6-oz (180-g) hake steaks

4 oz (120 g) onion, chopped

6 oz (180 g) green pepper, cut into strips

8 teaspoons (40 ml) low-fat spread

1 lemon, cut in wedges

Combine lemon juice, salt and paprika. Pour into a shallow ovenproof dish. Add fish and leave to marinate for 1 hour, turning once. Cook onions in a non-stick pan with a little water until soft. Drain. Arrange strips of green pepper over hake steaks, sprinkle onions over fish and dot with low-fat spread. Bake uncovered at 425°F, 220°C, Gas Mark 7 for 15 minutes or until fish flakes. Serve with lemon wedges.
Makes 4 servings.
Per serving: 181 calories.

Kipper Pate

See Menu Plan for Week 30.

6 oz (180 g) canned kipper fillets, drained

1 oz (30 g) low-fat dry milk

2 tablespoons (30 ml) water

4 teaspoons (20 ml) margarine

cayenne pepper to taste

1 tablespoon (15 ml) lemon juice

¼ teaspoon (1.25 ml) powdered mace (optional)

lemon and cucumber slices to garnish

Place all ingredients except lemon and cucumber slices in a bowl and mash or pound well until they form a paste. Transfer to a small dish, garnish with lemon and cucumber. Chill well before serving.
Makes 2 servings.
Per serving: 330 calories.

Skate with Lemon Sauce

Piquant Lemon Sole

See Menu Plan for Week 15.

1 teaspoon (5 ml) margarine, softened

1 teaspoon (5 ml) flour

1 teaspoon (5 ml) relish, any type

1 teaspoon (5 ml) lemon juice

¼ teaspoon (1.25 ml) Worcestershire sauce

1 x 6-oz (180-g) fillet lemon sole

Combine first 5 ingredients into a chunky paste and spread on lemon sole fillet. Place fish in ovenproof dish; cover and bake at 450°F, 230°C, Gas Mark 8 for 12-16 minutes or until fish is opaque and flakes easily when tested with a fork. Serve with juices in dish.
Makes 1 serving.
Per serving: 201 calories.

Sole Veronique

See Menu Plans for Weeks 7 and 34.

1 teaspoon (5 ml) lemon juice

salt

½ bay leaf

3 peppercorns

5 fl oz (150 ml) water

12 oz (360 g) sole fillets

1 tablespoon (15 ml) margarine

1 tablespoon (15 ml) flour

5 fl oz (150 ml) skim milk

4 teaspoons (20 ml) white wine

6 oz (180 g) small white grapes, cut into halves, deseeded

pinch white pepper

Combine lemon juice, pinch salt, bay leaf and peppercorns in medium frying pan; add water

and bring to the boil. Add fillets; reduce heat, cover and simmer 5 minutes until cooked. Using a slotted spoon, remove fillets and keep warm in serving dish. Strain liquid and reserve 2 fl oz (60 ml). Melt margarine in saucepan over medium heat. Stir in flour and cook, stirring constantly, for 2 minutes. Remove pan from heat; gradually stir in milk and reserved liquid. Return to the boil, stirring constantly, and cook until smooth and thick. Stir in wine, then 5 oz (150 g) grapes and pinch each salt and white pepper. Pour sauce over fish and serve decorated with remaining grapes.
Makes 2 servings.
Per serving: 304 calories.

Sole Italiano

See Menu Plan for Week 43.

4 oz (120 g) canned tomatoes, crushed

2 tablespoons (30 ml) onion, finely chopped

2 fl oz (60 ml) water

¼ teaspoon (1.25 ml) oregano

¼ teaspoon (1.25 ml) salt

pinch pepper

4 teaspoons (20 ml) low-fat spread

12 oz (360 g) sole fillets

2 tablespoons (30 ml) flour

parsley sprigs to garnish

In large non-stick frying pan, combine tomatoes, onion, water, oregano, salt and pepper; cook over medium heat until vegetables are tender. Remove vegetables from pan and keep warm. Using same pan, melt low-fat spread. Coat fish with

flour; place in pan and brown over medium heat about 5 minutes on each side or until fish flakes easily. Transfer fish to serving plate and top with vegetables. Garnish with parsley sprigs.
Makes 2 servings.
Per serving: 239 calories.

Soused Herring

See Menu Plans for Weeks 30 and 47.

6 x 8-oz (240-g) herrings, boned

salt and pepper

1 tablespoon (15 ml) dried onion flakes

8 fl oz (240 ml) white wine vinegar

2 tablespoons (30 ml) water

1 clove garlic, crushed (optional)

1 blade mace

green salad for serving

Clean herrings, cut off heads and tails. Season well with salt and pepper and roll fish up; secure with wooden cocktail sticks. Arrange rolled herrings in shallow ovenproof dish, sprinkle with onion flakes and add vinegar, water, garlic and mace. Cover dish with foil and cook in slow oven, 300°F, 150°C, Gas Mark 2 for 1-1½ hours, or until tender. Cool; remove cocktail sticks before serving. Arrange a salad on serving plate and place fish on top.
Makes 6 servings.
Per serving: 312 calories.

Fillet of Sole Florentine

See Menu Plans for Weeks 4, 23, 37 and 50.

2 teaspoons (10 ml) margarine

1 tablespoon (15 ml) lemon juice

½ teaspoon (2.5 ml) salt

½ teaspoon (2.5 ml) cornflour, blended with 2 tablespoons (30 ml) water

3 oz (90 g) cooked spinach, well drained and chopped

2 oz (60 g) cooked mushrooms, sliced

12 oz (360 g) fillet of sole

pinch each white pepper, garlic powder and paprika

thin lemon slices and chopped fresh parsley to garnish

Melt margarine in small saucepan, add lemon juice, ¼ teaspoon (1.25 ml) salt and blended cornflour. Cook, stirring constantly, until thickened. Spread spinach over bottom of shallow, oval-shaped casserole. Sprinkle with ¼ teaspoon (1.25 ml) salt. Spread mushrooms over spinach; place fish over vegetables and pour lemon sauce over fish. Sprinkle with seasonings; cover and bake at 400°F, 200°C, Gas Mark 6 for 20-30 minutes or until fish flakes when touched with a fork. Then grill for 1 minute. Garnish with slices of lemon and chopped parsley.
Makes 2 servings.
Per serving: 199 calories.

Rock Fish Kebabs

See Menu Plan for Week 20.

1 tablespoon (15 ml) lemon juice

1 teaspoon (5 ml) brown sauce

½ clove garlic, finely chopped

pinch chervil

12 oz (360 g) boned rock fish, cut into 1¼-inch (3-cm) cubes

2 medium green peppers, cut into 1¼-inch (3-cm) squares

6 small tomatoes

Combine lemon juice, brown sauce, garlic and chervil. Add rock fish cubes; toss to coat. Cover and marinate in refrigerator for 1 hour, turning pieces once or twice. Divide fish, peppers and tomatoes into 2 equal portions; thread each portion on to 2 skewers, alternating ingredients. Put skewers on rack in grill pan; grill for 5 minutes, brushing occasionally with remaining marinade. Turn and cook 3-4 minutes longer or until fish is done.
Makes 2 servings.
Per serving: 176 calories.

Tuna Boats

See Menu Plan for Week 4.

8 oz (240 g) canned tuna, finely flaked

4 teaspoons (20 ml) mayonnaise

2 tablespoons (30 ml) canned pimiento, diced

4 stoned green olives, finely sliced

2 teaspoons (10 ml) lemon juice

1 teaspoon (5 ml) relish, any type

4 large celery sticks

Combine tuna and mayonnaise; add pimiento, olives, lemon juice and relish. Stuff each celery stick with quarter of the mixture. Wrap in plastic wrap and chill until ready to use.
Makes 2 servings.
Per serving: 255 calories.

Fish Greek Style

See Menu Plan for Week 9.

1 lb (480 g) monk or rock fish fillets

2 teaspoons (10 ml) olive oil

4 oz (120 g) onions, sliced

1 clove garlic, crushed

4 oz (120 g) mushrooms, sliced

1 medium tomato, skinned, seeded, and chopped

6 fl oz (180 ml) chicken stock made with 1 stock cube

pinch each oregano, salt and white pepper

1 tablespoon (15 ml) white wine

1 tablespoon (15 ml) chopped fresh parsley

4 black olives, stoned and sliced lengthwise

Wipe and bone fish; set aside. Heat oil in small pan; add onions and garlic and saute until translucent; add mushrooms and tomato and cook, stirring constantly, until mushrooms are just tender. Add stock, oregano, salt and pepper. Simmer for a few minutes; add wine. Arrange fish in a shallow ovenproof dish; pour vegetable mixture over fish. Cover and bake at 400°F, 200°C, Gas Mark 6 for approximately 30 minutes or until fish flakes easily. Remove from oven; garnish with parsley and olives. Serve immediately.
Makes 2 servings.
Per serving: 255 calories.

Curried Crab Salad

See Menu Plan for Week 39.

8 oz (240 g) drained canned crab meat, flaked, set aside 3 or 4 pieces of crab meat for garnish

1½ oz (45 g) mushrooms, thinly sliced

2 tablespoons (30 ml) chopped green pepper

1 tablespoon (15 ml) lemon juice

pinch each salt and white pepper

2½ fl oz (75 ml) natural yogurt

2 teaspoons (10 ml) mayonnaise

½-¾ teaspoon (2.5-3.75 ml) curry powder

1 tablespoon (15 ml) chopped fresh parsley

1 teaspoon (5 ml) chopped chives

1 medium tomato, cut into thin wedges

4 oz (120 g) chunk cucumber, cut into 8 slices

parsley sprigs to garnish

Combine remaining crab meat, mushrooms, green pepper, 2 teaspoons (10 ml) lemon juice, salt and pepper. In small bowl mix yogurt with mayonnaise, curry powder, 2 teaspoons (10 ml) chopped parsley, chives and remaining teaspoon of lemon juice. Pour over crab meat mixture and toss carefully. Cover and chill 1 hour. Spoon crab meat salad on to centre of serving dish. Surround with tomato wedges and cucumber slices. Sprinkle with remaining chopped parsley and garnish with reserved crab meat and parsley sprigs.
Makes 2 servings.
Per serving: 136 calories.

Crab Meat Mould

See Menu Plan for Week 4.

1 tablespoon (15 ml) unflavoured gelatine

6 fl oz (180 ml) water

8 oz (240 g) cooked fresh or drained canned white crab meat, flaked

5 fl oz (150 ml) natural yogurt

2 tablespoons (30 ml) finely chopped onion

2 tablespoons (30 ml) thinly sliced celery

2 tablespoons (30 ml) minced green or red pepper

2 tablespoons (30 ml) lemon juice

4 teaspoons (20 ml) mayonnaise

1 teaspoon (5 ml) prepared mustard

dash each Worcestershire sauce and chili sauce

1 large tomato, sliced

2 teaspoons (10 ml) chopped fresh parsley

Dissolve gelatine in water in bowl over pan of hot water. Combine remaining ingredients except tomato and parsley in separate bowl; stir in gelatine mixture. Pour into 1-pint (600-ml) mould that has been rinsed in cold water. Chill until firm; at least 3 hours. Unmould on to serving plate. Garnish with tomato slices and sprinkle with parsley.
Makes 2 servings.
Per serving: 181 calories.

Sauteed Prawns and Corn

See Menu Plan for Week 46.

1 teaspoon (5 ml) margarine

1 teaspoon (5 ml) vegetable oil

4 oz (120 g) spring onions, sliced

1 clove garlic, finely chopped

6 oz (180 g) drained canned sweet corn

1 teaspoon (5 ml) each brown sugar and salt

pinch freshly ground pepper

8 oz (240 g) peeled cooked prawns

1 teaspoon (5 ml) cornflour blended with 2 fl oz (60 ml) water

chopped fresh parsley to garnish

Heat margarine and oil in medium pan. Add spring onions and garlic and saute briefly. Stir in sweet corn, sugar, salt and pepper; cook about 3 minutes. Add prawns and saute 1 minute longer. Add blended cornflour and cook, stirring constantly, until thickened. Serve garnished with chopped parsley.
Makes 2 servings.
Per serving: 318 calories.

Sauteed Prawns and Corn

Baked Fish Casserole

See Menu Plan for Week 1.

12 oz (360 g) shredded white cabbage, lightly boiled

4 oz (120 g) sliced cooked onions

2 oz (60 g) cooked thinly-sliced carrot

12 oz (360 g) boned cooked halibut, in chunks

pinch garlic salt

2 tablespoons (30 ml) margarine

2 tablespoons (30 ml) flour

10 fl oz (300 ml) skim milk

2 oz (60 g) mature Cheddar cheese

½ teaspoon (2.5 ml) salt

pinch each white pepper and ground allspice

1 teaspoon (5 ml) chopped fresh parsley

Put vegetables in a large casserole. Add fish and garlic salt and stir gently to combine. Melt margarine in small saucepan; add flour and cook over low heat 2-3 minutes, stirring constantly. Add milk gradually, stirring briskly with wire whisk; continue to stir briskly until sauce is a smooth consistency. Add Cheddar cheese, salt, pepper and allspice. Continue to cook, stirring constantly until sauce has thickened and cheese is melted. Combine sauce with vegetables and fish in casserole; sprinkle with parsley. Cover and bake at 350°F, 180°C, Gas Mark 4 for 30 minutes.
Makes 4 servings.
Per serving: 289 calories.

Lunch Box Fish and Cheese

See Menu Plan for Week 17.

2 pitta breads (1 oz/30 g each)

shredded lettuce

4 oz (120 g) canned tuna, flaked

2 oz (60 g) Cheddar cheese, grated

1 teaspoon (5 ml) lemon juice

1 teaspoon (5 ml) chopped fresh parsley

¼ teaspoon (1.25 ml) salt

Cut each pitta bread one third of the way around edge to create pocket. Set aside. Combine all remaining ingredients; toss well. Fill each pocket with half of fish mixture.
Makes 2 servings.
Per serving: 294 calories.

Salmon Salad

See Menu Plans for Weeks 5, 27, 31, 39 and 44.

1 oz (30 g) onion, finely chopped

½ teaspoon (2.5 ml) lemon juice

8 oz (240 g) drained, skinned, boned and flaked canned salmon

1 oz (30 g) celery, diced

1 oz (30 g) cucumber, peeled and diced

1 oz (30 g) carrot, grated

4 teaspoons (20 ml) low-calorie mayonnaise

¼ teaspoon (1.25 ml) salt

pinch white pepper

Combine all ingredients. Mix well. Chill and serve.
Makes 2 servings.
Per serving: 199 calories.

Stir-Fry Tuna

See Menu Plan for Week 40.

1 teaspoon (5 ml) vegetable oil

½ medium red apple, peeled, cored and diced

1 oz (30 g) onion, thinly sliced and separated into rings

4 oz (120 g) canned tuna, broken into chunks

1 teaspoon (5 ml) curry powder

pinch dry mustard

1½ oz (45 g) frozen peas

1 tablespoon (15 ml) raisins

2 tablespoons (30 ml) dry white wine

Put oil in thick-based, non-stick frying pan. Add apple and onion and saute for about 1 minute. Add remaining ingredients and cook for about 5 minutes or until mixture is hot and well blended.
Makes 1 serving.
Per serving: 412 calories.

Poached Halibut Parmesan

See Menu Plan for Week 19.

4 teaspoons (20 ml) lemon juice

pinch each salt and pepper

6 fl oz (180 ml) water

6-oz (180-g) boneless halibut steak

1 tablespoon (15 ml) low-fat spread

½ teaspoon (2.5 ml) chopped fresh parsley

½ clove garlic, crushed

1 teaspoon (5 ml) grated Parmesan cheese

In saucepan combine lemon juice, salt and pepper; add water and bring to the boil. Add fish to liquid and poach for 8-10 minutes or until fish flakes easily with a fork. Meanwhile, melt low-fat spread in small saucepan; add parsley and garlic and saute until garlic is tender. Place fish on plate and top with parsley and garlic mixture. Sprinkle with Parmesan cheese.

Makes 1 serving.
Per serving: 270 calories.

Prawns with Crispy Topping

See Menu Plan for Week 1.

4 teaspoons (20 ml) margarine

1 oz (30 g) red pepper, diced

1 small clove garlic, finely chopped with ½ teaspoon (2.5 ml) salt

1 lb (480 g) cooked peeled prawns

2 slices (1 oz/30 g each) bread, made into crumbs

1 teaspoon (5 ml) chopped fresh parsley

Melt margarine in large non-stick frying pan; add pepper and garlic and saute over medium heat for 1 minute. Add prawns and saute, turning occasionally, until prawns are heated through; about 2-4 minutes. Using a slotted spoon, remove prawns; keep warm. Stir breadcrumbs into margarine mixture in pan; cook, stirring occasionally until breadcrumbs are golden. Stir in parsley. Divide prawns onto 4 plates. Top each portion of prawns with an equal amount of breadcrumb mixture.

Makes 4 servings.
Per serving: 196 calories.

Tuna-Potato Cakes

See Menu Plan for Week 37.

6 oz (180 g) potatoes, finely grated and squeezed to remove excess moisture

2 tablespoons (30 ml) onion

2 teaspoons (10 ml) flour

1 teaspoon (5 ml) lemon juice

4 oz (120 g) drained canned tuna, roughly flaked

2 eggs, beaten

¼ teaspoon (1.25 ml) salt

¼ teaspoon (1.25 ml) allspice

pinch pepper

In medium bowl combine potatoes, onion, flour and lemon juice; stir in tuna, eggs, salt, allspice and pepper. Do not over mix (tuna should remain in small chunks). Heat medium non-stick pan over medium heat. Spoon half of potato batter into pan in two equal portions. Form each portion into round cake and brown on both sides. Repeat with remaining batter.

Makes 2 servings.
Per serving: 295 calories.

Cod Baked in Foil

See Menu Plan for Week 29.

12 oz (360 g) tomatoes, skinned

8 oz (240 g) button mushrooms, left whole and washed

8 oz (240 g) onion, chopped

1 teaspoon (5 ml) salt

freshly ground black pepper to taste

4 x 8-oz (240-g) cod steaks

8 teaspoons (40 ml) low-fat spread

chopped fresh parsley

Chop tomatoes and mix with mushrooms, onion and seasoning. Stand fish steaks in a large ovenproof dish. Pile tomato mixture on top, dot with low-fat spread, and cover casserole with lid or aluminium foil. Cook at 400°F, 200°C, Gas Mark 6 for about 30 minutes. Just before serving, sprinkle with chopped parsley.

Makes 4 servings.
Per serving: 244 calories.

Mackerel Patties

See Menu Plan for Week 26.

1 tablespoon (15 ml) margarine

2 tablespoons (30 ml) onion, diced

2 tablespoons (30 ml) celery, diced

8 oz (240 g) cooked mackerel fillets, flaked

3 oz (90 g) cooked potatoes, mashed

1 teaspoon (5 ml) chopped fresh parsley

pinch each salt and pepper

1 slice (1 oz/30 g) white bread, lightly toasted and made into crumbs

Melt margarine in pan; add onion and saute for 2 minutes. Add celery and cook until softened. In a bowl combine flaked mackerel, mashed potatoes, onion and celery mixture, parsley, salt and pepper. Form into 4 patties and coat with breadcrumbs. Place patties on non-stick baking sheet; bake at 350°F, 180°C, Gas Mark 4 for 8 minutes or until crumbs are golden. Turn and bake patties for 8-10 minutes more.

Makes 2 servings.
Per serving: 387 calories.

DRIED PEAS/BEANS AND PEANUT BUTTER

Dried peas and beans are food plants whose pods open along two seams when the seeds within are ripe. The seeds are usually the edible part of the pod. Peas, chick peas (garbanzos), lima beans and soybeans are the best known. High in nutrition, easy to prepare and very economical, they are also delicious. That is probably why they have been cultivated and consumed for over 8,000 years.

N.B. 1 oz (30 g) dried peas/beans yields approximately 3 oz (90 g) cooked.

Split Pea Soup

See Menu Plan for Week 37.

4 oz (120 g) dried green split peas, soaked overnight and drained

24 fl oz (720 ml) water

½ medium onion, finely chopped

4 oz (120 g) carrots, diced

2 sticks celery, diced

pinch thyme

pinch chervil

pinch white pepper

2 teaspoons (10 ml) margarine

2 teaspoons (10 ml) flour

5 fl oz (150 ml) skim milk

½ teaspoon (2.5 ml) salt

In medium saucepan combine peas, water and onion. Bring to the boil, cover. Reduce heat and simmer until peas are soft, about 1½-2 hours, or until peas are just cooked. Add carrots, celery, thyme, chervil and pepper to saucepan; simmer until all vegetables are tender, about 20 minutes. Puree in blender container and return to pan. Meanwhile, in small saucepan, melt margarine. Stir in flour and cook 2 minutes. Remove from heat; gradually stir in milk. Bring to the boil, stirring; cook 2 minutes. Briskly stir into blended vegetables. Add salt and heat through – about 5 minutes. Serve at once.
Makes 2 servings.
Per serving: 273 calories.

Chick Peas Neopolitan

See Menu Plan for Week 38.

3 oz (90 g) onion, chopped

2 tablespoons (30 ml) olive oil

1 clove garlic, crushed

14 oz (420 g) canned crushed tomatoes

1 bay leaf

pinch salt

pinch pepper

pinch chili powder

1 teaspoon (5 ml) brown sugar

12 oz (360 g) cooked chick peas, drained

8 oz (240 g) cooked pasta

2 teaspoons (10 ml) grated Parmesan cheese

Saute onion gently in oil in medium saucepan for 5 minutes, until transparent. Stir in garlic and saute for further 5 minutes. Add tomatoes and bay leaf and let mixture cook over medium heat for 10 minutes or until most of liquid has evaporated, leaving a thick sauce. Season with salt, pepper and chili powder and finally sugar. Mix in chick peas and cook for a further few minutes to heat through; remove bay leaf. Check seasoning before serving equally over two portions of cooked pasta. Sprinkle each portion with 1 teaspoon (5 ml) grated Parmesan cheese.
Makes 2 servings.
Per serving: 478 calories.

Greek-Style Beans with Mushrooms

See Menu Plan for Week 38.

12 oz (360 g) button mushrooms, wiped

2 teaspoons (10 ml) lemon juice

3 oz (90 g) onion, finely chopped

1 clove garlic, cut in half

5 fl oz (150 ml) wine vinegar

5 fl oz (150 ml) water

bouquet garni

pinch each of salt and pepper

6 teaspoons (30 ml) corn oil

3 tablespoons (45 ml) tomato puree

1 teaspoon (5 ml) soft brown sugar

12 oz (360 g) cooked butter beans, drained

chopped fresh parsley

Cook mushrooms for 5 minutes only, in boiling, salted water with lemon juice added. Drain well. Put onion, garlic, vinegar, water, bouquet garni, salt and pepper in a small pan. Bring to the boil and simmer for 5 minutes. Remove garlic and leave liquid to cool. When cold mix with oil and tomato puree. Add sugar. Pour over mushrooms and beans in deep bowl. Leave for 3-4 hours in cool place, turning occasionally. Remove bouquet garni and sprinkle with parsley before serving.

Makes 2 servings.
Per serving: 357 calories.

Chick Pea Croquettes

See Menu Plans for Weeks 9 and 31.

12 oz (360 g) drained canned chick peas (garbanzos)

1½ oz (45 g) dried breadcrumbs

½ clove garlic, finely chopped with ½ teaspoon (2.5 ml) salt

¼ teaspoon (1.25 ml) each basil, marjoram and thyme

¼ teaspoon (1.25 ml) hot pepper sauce

pinch paprika pepper

chopped fresh parsley

10 fl oz (300 ml) natural yogurt

In blender container or bowl of food processor, puree chick peas until finely chopped. Transfer to basin. Add remaining ingredients except yogurt; mix well, making sure seasonings are well distributed. Shape mixture into 10 flat cakes. Place on non-stick baking sheet and bake at 350°F, 180°C, Gas Mark 4 for 15 minutes. Garnish with parsley and serve with yogurt.

Makes 2 servings.
Per serving: 350 calories.

Split Pea and Mushroom Stew

See Menu Plan for Week 46.

12 fl oz (360 ml) beef stock made with 1 stock cube

4 oz (120 g) dried green split peas, soaked overnight

4 fl oz (120 ml) water

2 oz (60 g) green beans cut in 1-inch (2.5-cm) lengths

4 tablespoons (60 ml) tomato puree

6 oz (180 g) mushrooms, sliced

pinch each salt and pepper

¼ teaspoon (1.25 ml) lemon juice

¼ teaspoon (1.25 ml) chili powder

pinch ground cumin

few drops Worcestershire sauce

4 oz (120 g) cooked macaroni shells

Combine stock and peas in medium saucepan. Cover and bring to the boil. Reduce heat and simmer until peas are tender, about 30 minutes. Add water, green beans and tomato puree; continue simmering for 5 minutes longer. In medium frying pan combine mushrooms, salt and pepper. Cook over medium heat, stirring occasionally, until mushrooms are tender. Add mushrooms (plus any pan liquid), lemon juice, chili powder, cumin and Worcestershire sauce to peas. Simmer 10 minutes longer. Stir in macaroni shells and cook until heated.

Makes 2 servings.
Per serving: 288 calories.

Mushroom and Lentil Pate

See Menu Plan for Week 38.

2 eggs

2 oz (60 g) lentils, any type, finely ground

4 fl oz (120 ml) water

2 tablespoons (30 ml) grated onion

6 oz (180 g) mushrooms, finely chopped

4 teaspoons (20 ml) margarine

1 large clove garlic

pinch each salt and pepper

juice and grated rind of ½ lemon

1 tablespoon (15 ml) fresh chopped parsley

Hard-boil eggs. Mix ground lentils with half the water in small, heavy-based saucepan. Cook, stirring constantly over low heat for 10 minutes, adding more water as necessary, until lentils cook to a thick paste. Turn out into basin to cool, and mix in grated onion. Cook mushrooms in 2 teaspoons (10 ml) margarine in frying pan over fairly high heat, stirring constantly until beginning to soften. Cool. Shell and chop eggs; mix mushrooms and eggs with lentil mixture and remaining margarine, melted. Rub serving dish well with cut clove of garlic. Season pate with salt, pepper, lemon juice and parsley. Add lemon rind to mixture and mix thoroughly. Spoon into serving dish; cover and refrigerate until needed.

Makes 2 servings.
Per serving: 188 calories.

Savoury Butter Bean Salad

See Menu Plan for Week 14.

2 teaspoons (10 ml) vegetable oil

3 oz (90 g) onion, chopped

1 clove garlic, crushed

8 oz (240 g) canned tomatoes

1 tablespoon (15 ml) tomato puree

½ teaspoon (2.5 ml) each ground cumin and ground coriander

¼ teaspoon (1.25 ml) salt

pinch ground turmeric

4 fl oz (120 ml) water

12 oz (360 g) cooked butter beans, drained

Heat oil in saucepan; add onion and garlic and saute until softened. Add tomatoes, tomato puree, cumin, coriander, salt and turmeric; stir. Add water and bring to the boil; reduce heat and simmer 10 minutes. Add beans, cover and simmer 5 minutes. Remove cover and simmer 5 minutes longer.
Makes 2 servings.
Per serving: 240 calories.

Savoury Beans

See Menu Plan for Week 15.

1 teaspoon (5 ml) vegetable oil

2 oz (60 g) onion, diced

½ teaspoon (2.5 ml) sage

3 oz (90 g) tomatoes, skinned and diced

7-8 oz (210-240 g) canned baked beans

1 slice (1 oz/30 g) bread, toasted

Heat oil in small non-stick saucepan, add onion and saute until browned and soft. Add sage

and tomatoes; saute for 2 minutes, add beans and cook until heated through. Serve on slice of toast.
Makes 1 serving.
Per serving: 263 calories.

Sauteed Chick Peas Italian Style

See Menu Plan for Week 23.

1 tablespoon (15 ml) olive oil

2 cloves garlic, crushed

12 oz (360 g) canned chick peas, drained

4 tablespoons (60 ml) tomato puree

6 fl oz (180 ml) water

½ teaspoon (2.5 ml) oregano

pinch each salt and pepper

2 teaspoons (10 ml) fresh chopped parsley

2 teaspoons (10 ml) grated Parmesan cheese

Heat oil in medium saucepan; add garlic and saute 2 minutes. Add remaining ingredients except parsley and cheese and cook 20 minutes, stirring frequently. Sprinkle evenly with parsley and Parmesan cheese.
Makes 2 servings.
Per serving: 228 calories.

Cheese and Butter Bean Peppers

See Menu Plan for Week 43.

4 x 6-oz (180-g approx) green peppers

4 oz (120 g) celery, diced

3 oz (90 g) onion, diced

12 oz (360 g) drained canned butter beans, mashed

8 oz (240 g) canned tomatoes, drained and chopped

1 tablespoon (15 ml) basil

4 oz (120 g) Cheddar cheese, grated

pinch each salt and pepper

Cut tops from peppers and remove seeds. Reserve tops. Parboil peppers and tops 2 minutes; drain and set aside. Combine celery and onion in non-stick pan and cook until tender. Transfer to a bowl; add remaining ingredients and mix thoroughly. Spoon quarter of mixture into each pepper. Replace tops. Place stuffed peppers in baking dish with 4 tablespoons (60 ml) water; cover and bake at 375°F, 190°C, Gas Mark 5 for 40-50 minutes.
Makes 4 servings.
Per serving: 230 calories.

Austrian Beans

See Menu Plan for Week 38.

1 medium onion, thinly sliced

1 clove garlic, crushed

1 tablespoon (15 ml) vegetable oil

1 tablespoon (15 ml) cider vinegar

2 teaspoons (10 ml) soft brown sugar

1 medium dessert apple, peeled

2 tablespoons (30 ml) raisins

12 oz (360 g) cooked drained butter beans

pinch salt

2 teaspoons (10 ml) chopped fresh parsley

Saute onion and garlic together in oil over moderate heat until soft. Add vinegar and sugar and mix well. Remove from heat; grate apple directly into pan; add

raisins. Return pan to cooker, add beans and stir all together over low heat until beans are heated through. Season with salt. Turn into heated serving dish and sprinkle with chopped parsley.
Makes 2 servings.
Per serving: 357 calories.

Bean and Cheese Potatoes

See Menu Plan for Week 38.

2 x 6-oz (180-g) potatoes for baking

6 oz (180 g) cooked haricot beans, drained

2 oz (60 g) Leicester cheese, grated

2½ fl oz (75 ml) natural yogurt

2 teaspoons (10 ml) chopped fresh rosemary

2 teaspoons (10 ml) chopped fresh parsley

1 teaspoon (5 ml) grated lemon rind

pinch salt and pepper

Scrub potatoes well, score with a sharp knife to prevent bursting and bake in moderate oven, 350°F, 180°C, Gas Mark 4 until cooked; approximately 1 hour. When potatoes are soft, cut in half and scoop centres out carefully into a bowl, reserving the skins. Mash potato in a bowl; add haricot beans, cheese and yogurt and season with herbs, lemon rind, salt and pepper. Pack into potato skins, mounding the filling; place on baking tin; cover with foil and heat in oven for about 10 minutes.
Makes 2 servings.
Per serving: 359 calories.

'Re-fried' Beans

See Menu Plan for Week 19.

2 teaspoons (10 ml) vegetable oil

3 oz (90 g) onion, chopped

1 clove garlic, chopped

6 oz (180 g) drained canned kidney beans

2 tablespoons (30 ml) tomato puree

2 teaspoons (10 ml) chili powder

pinch ground cumin

pinch salt

2 oz (60 g) grated Cheddar cheese

Heat oil in small pan; add onion and garlic and saute until tender. Add kidney beans, tomato puree, chili powder, cumin and salt. Cook, stirring often, for 5 minutes. Turn into non-stick casserole. Top with cheese and bake at 350°F, 180°C, Gas Mark 4, for 10-15 minutes or until cheese is melted.
Makes 2 servings.
Per serving: 272 calories.

Bean Soup

See Menu Plan for Week 38.

6 oz (180 g) potato, diced

6 oz (180 g) onion, chopped

1 pint (600 ml) water

12 oz (360 g) cooked, drained red kidney beans

2 stock cubes

2 teaspoons (10 ml) lemon juice

pinch salt and pepper

fresh chopped parsley

Cook potato and onion in water until soft. Add beans, stock cubes and lemon juice. Puree soup in blender container, return

to pan, reheat and season to taste. Serve piping hot sprinkled with parsley.
Makes 2 servings.
Per serving: 267 calories.

Curried Kidney Beans

See Menu Plan for Week 13.

1 tablespoon (15 ml) vegetable oil

3 oz (90 g) onion, chopped

1 medium apple, cored and diced

1 clove garlic, crushed

1 tablespoon (15 ml) flour

2 teaspoons (10 ml) curry powder

7½ fl oz (225 ml) chicken stock made with ½ stock cube

12 oz (360 g) canned kidney beans, drained

pinch each salt and pepper

2 tablespoons (30 ml) sliced spring onion

Heat oil in saucepan; add onion, apple and garlic and saute until tender. Stir in flour and curry powder and cook over low heat, stirring constantly, for 2 minutes. Stirring with a wire whisk, gradually add stock; cook, stirring constantly, until sauce thickens. Add kidney beans and cook until heated. Add salt and pepper and garnish with spring onion.
Makes 2 servings.
Per serving: 256 calories.

VEGETABLES

Vegetables are about the most versatile of all of nature's gifts. Pureed, steamed or spiced, baked, grilled or diced – there are almost as many ways to serve vegetables as there are vegetable varieties. Discover new taste treats by adding unusual vegetables to your standard repertoire. From crunchy crudites to substantial casseroles, depend on vegetable dishes for colour, texture and nutrition.

Herbed Vegetables

See Menu Plan for Week 10.

3 oz (90 g) mushrooms, cut into ¼-inch (0.5-cm) thick slices

pinch salt

2 teaspoons (10 ml) margarine

pinch each thyme, chervil and rosemary

6 oz (180 g) courgettes, cut into ¼-inch (0.5-cm) thick slices, blanched

6 oz (180 g) broccoli florets, blanched

2 oz (60 g) red pepper, cut into ¼-inch (0.5-cm) wide strips

1 teaspoon (5 ml) lemon juice

Heat large non-stick frying pan; add mushrooms and salt. Cook over medium heat about 3 minutes to evaporate moisture in mushrooms. They should be tender but not limp. Drain on paper towels. Wipe frying pan dry with a paper towel. Melt margarine in frying pan; add thyme, chervil and rosemary and saute 30 seconds. Stir in courgettes, broccoli, mushrooms and red pepper. Cover and cook, stirring occasionally, about 2-3 minutes. Stir in lemon juice and serve.
Makes 2 servings.
Per serving: 77 calories.

Marinated Carrots

See Menu Plan for Week 43.

4 fl oz (120 ml) white wine vinegar

2 fl oz (60 ml) water

½ teaspoon (2.5 ml) pickling spice, tied in muslin

pinch salt

1 clove garlic

1 lb (480 g) carrots, cut into ¼-inch (0.5-cm) thick sticks

dash artificial sweetener

1 teaspoon (5 ml) chopped fresh dill weed or pinch dried dill weed

1 teaspoon (5 ml) chopped fresh parsley

pinch pepper

In small saucepan combine vinegar, water, pickling spice, salt and garlic; simmer 5 minutes. In another saucepan cook carrots in boiling water for 3 minutes. Drain and transfer to a shallow dish just large enough to hold carrots in one layer. Remove and discard pickling spice and garlic clove from vinegar mixture. Add sweetener to spiced vinegar and pour over hot carrots; toss. Sprinkle with dill, parsley and pepper. Cover tightly and chill at least 3 hours, turning every half hour.
Makes 8 servings.
Per serving: 9 calories.

Green Beans and Tomatoes Hungarian Style

See Menu Plans for Weeks 5 and 22.

8 oz (240 g) green beans, cut into 1-inch (2.5-cm) lengths

2 teaspoons (10 ml) margarine

2 oz (60 g) onion, chopped

8 oz (240 g) canned tomatoes, with juice, roughly chopped

¼ teaspoon (1.25 ml) paprika

pinch salt

Place green beans in saucepan with boiling, salted water to cover and blanch 5 minutes. Drain in colander and refresh under cold running water; set aside. Melt margarine in saucepan; add onion and saute until softened. Stir in tomatoes and paprika and simmer 5-8 minutes. Add beans and simmer, stirring occasionally, 5 minutes or until beans are tender-crisp; season and serve.
Makes 2 servings.
Per serving: 81 calories.

Roast Potatoes (Grains, Pasta and Potatoes)
Green Beans and Tomatoes Hungarian Style

Courgette Basil

See Menu Plan for Week 35.

4 teaspoons (20 ml) low-fat spread

2 medium courgettes, about 5 oz (150 g) each, cut into thin strips

1 tablespoon (15 ml) chopped fresh basil, or 1 teaspoon (5 ml) dried basil

pinch freshly ground pepper

Melt low-fat spread in medium pan; add courgettes and saute, tossing constantly for 5 minutes. Season with basil and pepper.
Makes 2 servings.
Per serving: 65 calories.

Curried Vegetables

See Menu Plan for Week 24.

1½ teaspoons (7.5 ml) coriander

1 teaspoon (5 ml) turmeric

½ teaspoon (2.5 ml) cumin

½ teaspoon (2.5 ml) ground ginger

½ teaspoon (2.5 ml) chili powder

8 fl oz (240 ml) boiling water

2 tablespoons (30 ml) onion flakes

1 lb (480 g) tomatoes, skinned and roughly chopped

1 lb (480 g) carrots, diced

12 oz (360 g) broad beans, fresh or frozen

12 oz (360 g) potato, diced

1 medium cauliflower, cut into florets

2 tablespoons (30 ml) lemon juice

salt and pepper to taste

1 tablespoon (15 ml) chopped fresh parsley

Make a paste with coriander, turmeric, cumin, ginger and chili powder and 1 tablespoon (15 ml) cold water. Gradually add boiling water, stirring all the time. Soak onion flakes, drain and dry-fry in non-stick pan until brown. Stir in tomatoes and curry spices; bring to the boil. Add carrots, broad beans, potatoes, cauliflower, lemon juice, salt and pepper with just enough water to cover the vegetables. Stir well and bring to the boil. Cover pan, simmer until vegetables are tender but still crisp, shaking occasionally to prevent sticking. Garnish with chopped parsley. Divide into 4 equal portions and serve as a starter or as an accompaniment to meat or poultry.
Makes 4 servings.
Per serving: 167 calories.

Courgettes Italian Style

See Menu Plans for Weeks 4 and 17.

2 x 5 oz (150 g) courgettes, cut into 1-inch (2.5-cm) slices

3 oz (90 g) tomato, seeded and chopped

1 clove garlic, crushed

½ teaspoon (2.5 ml) basil

½ teaspoon (2.5 ml) salt

pinch freshly ground pepper

Combine tomato, garlic and basil in small saucepan; cook gently 5 minutes. Add courgettes, salt and pepper. Cover and cook over low heat until courgettes are just tender, about 10 minutes. Serve immediately or refrigerate and serve chilled.
Makes 2 servings.
Per serving: 29 calories.

Orange Broccoli

See Menu Plan for Week 3.

4 fl oz (120 ml) orange juice

2 teaspoons (10 ml) grated orange rind

2 teaspoons (10 ml) lemon juice

2 teaspoons (10 ml) vegetable oil

1 teaspoon (5 ml) soy sauce

pinch each salt and pepper

9 oz (270 g) broccoli florets, blanched

Combine orange juice, orange rind, lemon juice, vegetable oil, soy sauce, salt and pepper; stir well. Add broccoli; toss. Chill for at least 1 hour. Toss again just before serving.
Makes 2 servings.
Per serving: 85 calories.

Minted Carrots

See Menu Plan for Week 21.

8 oz (240 g) carrots, cut in matchsticks

8 fl oz (240 ml) orange juice

½ teaspoon (2.5 ml) finely chopped fresh ginger root

pinch each salt and pepper

1 tablespoon (15 ml) chopped fresh mint

Combine all ingredients except mint in small saucepan. Cover and bring to the boil; reduce heat and simmer about 7-8 minutes or until carrots are fork-tender. Transfer carrots and liquid to bowl. Cover and chill overnight. Garnish with mint just before serving.
Makes 4 servings.
Per serving: 30 calories.

Sauteed Mushrooms and Onions

See Menu Plan for Week 39.

1 teaspoon (5 ml) vegetable oil
2 oz (60 g) onion, sliced
3 oz (90 g) mushrooms, sliced
pinch each salt and pepper

Heat oil in frying pan; add onion and saute over medium heat until onion slices are translucent. Add mushrooms, salt and pepper and saute until mushrooms are cooked.
Makes 2 servings.
Per serving: 32 calories.

Green Vegetable Salad

See Menu Plan for Week 24.

12 oz (360 g) cooked and sliced fresh or frozen runner beans
6 oz (180 g) celery, diced
2 tablespoons (30 ml) finely chopped onion
6 oz (180 g) green pepper, chopped
6 oz (180 g) pickled cucumbers, chopped
6 oz (180 g) cucumber, sliced
3 tablespoons (45 ml) tarragon vinegar
3 tablespoons (45 ml) white wine vinegar
artificial sweetener to taste
freshly ground black pepper to taste

Mix all ingredients in a large bowl, season well. Cover and chill overnight in refrigerator.
Makes 4 servings.
Per serving: 39 calories.

Savoury Cabbage

See Menu Plan for Week 24.

1 lb (480 g) white cabbage, shredded
4 oz (120 g) onion, chopped
1 clove garlic, crushed
4 tablespoons (60 ml) chicken stock made with ½ stock cube
1 tablespoon (15 ml) wine vinegar
2 teaspoons (10 ml) lemon juice
½ teaspoon (2.5 ml) caraway seeds
1 bay leaf
salt and pepper to taste
2 tablespoons (30 ml) margarine, melted

Place cabbage, onion, garlic, stock, vinegar, lemon juice, caraway seeds, bay leaf and seasoning in saucepan. Bring to the boil; cover and simmer gently for about 10 minutes or until soft but still crisp. Drain. Pour margarine over cabbage and transfer to hot serving dish.
Makes 4 servings.
Per serving: 93 calories.

Chinese Cabbage and Tomato Medley

See Menu Plans for Weeks 9, 27 and 35.

2 teaspoons (10 ml) olive oil
1 garlic clove, crushed
8 oz (240 g) Chinese cabbage, chopped
2 medium tomatoes, skinned, seeded and chopped
pinch each salt and pepper

Heat oil in medium saucepan; add garlic and saute, being careful not to brown. Add cabbage, tomato, salt and pepper. Cover and simmer for approximately 15 minutes or until cabbage is just tender.
Makes 2 servings.
Per serving: 77 calories.

Cauliflower with Mushroom Sauce

See Menu Plan for Week 17.

8 oz (240 g) cauliflower florets, cooked
2 teaspoons (10 ml) margarine
1½ oz (45 g) mushrooms, sliced
1 tablespoon (15 ml) chopped spring onion
2 teaspoons (10 ml) flour
⅛ teaspoon (0.6 ml) salt
pinch white pepper
4 fl oz (120 ml) skim milk
2 teaspoons (10 ml) grated Parmesan cheese

Arrange cauliflower in small non-stick baking tin; set aside. Melt margarine in small saucepan; add mushrooms and spring onion and saute for 1 minute. Stir in flour, salt and pepper; cook, stirring constantly, until flour is absorbed. Stirring continuously, pour in milk and cook until slightly thickened. Pour sauce over cauliflower and sprinkle evenly with cheese. Bake at 450°F, 230°C, Gas Mark 8 approximately 10-15 minutes or until top is lightly browned.
Makes 2 servings.
Per serving: 115 calories.

Sweet and Sour Cabbage

See Menu Plan for Week 52.

2-3 tablespoons (30-45 ml) white wine vinegar

artificial sweetener to equal 6 teaspoons (30 ml) sugar

1 teaspoon (5 ml) salt

4 whole cloves

4 peppercorns

2 bay leaves

pinch each ground coriander and freshly ground pepper

12 oz (360 g) red cabbage, thinly sliced

4 teaspoons (20 ml) margarine

6 oz (180 g) onions, chopped

2 medium green apples, peeled, cored and sliced

Combine first 7 ingredients; add cabbage and toss well. Set aside and allow to marinate for 1 hour. Melt margarine in medium pan. Add onions and saute until translucent. Add cabbage and marinade to pan. Cover and cook gently for about 30 minutes. Stir in apples and simmer 10 minutes longer.
Makes 4 servings.
Per serving: 86 calories.

Slow-Cooked Vegetable Medley

See Menu Plan for Week 1.

2 teaspoons (10 ml) olive oil

9 oz (270 g) white cabbage, thinly sliced

3 oz (90 g) leeks, halved and thinly sliced

4 oz (120 g) carrots, cut into matchstick lengths

1 teaspoon (5 ml) chopped fresh parsley

¼ teaspoon (1.25 ml) celery seed

1 small clove garlic, finely chopped with 1 teaspoon (5 ml) salt

Heat oil in large non-stick pan. Add cabbage, leeks and carrots. Toss to coat with oil. Cover and cook over low heat, tossing occasionally, about 45 minutes or until cabbage is soft and carrots are tender. During last 15 minutes of cooking, stir in parsley, celery seed and chopped garlic and salt.
Makes 2 servings.
Per serving: 93 calories.

Savoury Grilled Tomatoes

See Menu Plans for Weeks 5 and 31.

2 medium tomatoes, halved

dash soy sauce

pinch each white pepper, garlic powder, thyme and basil

Place tomato halves in grill pan, cut-side up. Sprinkle with soy sauce, seasonings and herbs. Grill under medium heat for about 6-8 minutes until cooked.
Makes 2 servings.
Per serving: 12 calories.

Fennel with Parmesan Cheese

See Menu Plans for Weeks 8, 27 and 50.

8 oz (240 g) fennel bulb, sliced

6 fl oz (180 ml) chicken stock made with 1 stock cube

2 teaspoons (10 ml) grated Parmesan cheese

1 small clove garlic, finely chopped

1 teaspoon (5 ml) chopped fresh parsley

In saucepan combine fennel and stock; bring to the boil. Reduce heat, cover and simmer approximately 15 minutes. Drain and transfer fennel to shallow casserole. Keeping fennel slices intact if possible, sprinkle with cheese and garlic. Grill under a medium grill to melt cheese. Sprinkle with parsley and serve immediately.
Makes 2 servings.
Per serving: 24 calories.

Red Salad

See Menu Plan for Week 24.

2 x 3-oz (90-g) tomatoes, skinned

1 tablespoon (15 ml) mayonnaise

2½ fl oz (75 ml) natural yogurt

2 teaspoons (10 ml) chopped fresh parsley

parsley sprigs to garnish

Cut tomatoes in half. Mix together mayonnaise and yogurt and add chopped parsley. Spoon yogurt mixture over tomatoes and chill well. Garnish with sprigs of parsley before serving.
Makes 1 serving.
Per serving: 83 calories.

Fennel with Parmesan Cheese

GRAINS, PASTA AND POTATOES

It's true that 'man does not live by bread alone', but bread is still said to be the staff of life. Now you can enliven meals with some exciting new recipes featuring grains, pasta and potatoes. Homemade White Bread, Bacon-Flavoured Potato Salad and Kedgeree and Mushroom Grill give old favourites a new twist – sense appeal. Aroma, appearance, taste and texture are important aspects of your menu plan.

Homemade Bread

See Menu Plan for Week 39.

1 lb (480 g) strong white flour
2 teaspoons (10 ml) salt
½ oz (15 g) margarine
½ oz (15 g) fresh yeast
½ pint (300 ml) warm water

For Brushing

skim milk

Sift flour and salt into a bowl; rub in margarine. Mix yeast to smooth and creamy liquid with a little of the warm water. Blend in rest of water. Add all at once to dry ingredients. Mix to a firm dough, adding more flour if needed, until dough leaves sides of bowl clean. Turn out on to lightly floured board. Knead thoroughly for 10 minutes. Cover and leave to rise until dough doubles in size. Turn out on to lightly floured board and knead until firm. Shape to fit 1-lb (480-g) loaf tin. Brush tin with melted margarine and put in dough. Cover and leave to rise until dough doubles in size and reaches top of tin. Brush with skim milk. Bake in centre of hot oven, 450°F, 230°C, Gas Mark 8, for 30-40 minutes or until loaf shrinks slightly from sides of tin and crust is golden brown. Cool on wire rack.
Makes 1 loaf.

Mock Kishka

See Menu Plan for Week 16.

3 oz (90 g) carrot, finely chopped
2 oz (60 g) celery, finely chopped
1½ oz (45 g) onion, finely chopped
2 oz (60 g) matzo boards, crumbled
4 teaspoons (20 ml) margarine, melted
¼ teaspoon (1.25 ml) salt
pinch pepper
parsley sprigs to garnish

Combine carrot, celery, onion, matzo, margarine, salt and pepper, and mix together until the mixture holds together. Form into a small loaf about 5 inches (13 cm) long and 1½ inches (4 cm) wide. Place on non-stick baking sheet; bake at 400°F, 200°C, Gas Mark 6 for 30-40 minutes or until well browned. Let stand 10 minutes. Using a spatula, transfer to serving dish and allow to cool completely. Garnish with parsley. Cut into 8 equal slices.
Makes 4 servings (2 slices each).
Per serving: 82 calories.

Layered Sandwich

See Menu Plan for Week 22.

2 teaspoons (10 ml) low-fat spread
3 slices (1 oz/30 g each) bread
1 hard-boiled egg, sliced
sliced tomatoes
cucumber
lettuce
1¼ oz (37.5 g) cottage cheese
1 oz (30 g) canned sardines, mashed and mixed with 2 teaspoons (10 ml) low-calorie tomato ketchup

Spread low-fat spread on to both sides of 1 slice of bread and on one side of each of the other 2 slices. Using one of the single side low-fat spread pieces of bread, arrange slices of egg on it and top with slices of tomato, cucumber and lettuce. Put the double low-fat spread slice of bread on top of this and spread cottage cheese and sardine mixture on to it. Place slices of tomato, cucumber and lettuce on to mixture. Place last slice of bread on top and carefully cut sandwich into desired shape.
Makes 1 serving.
Per serving: 434 calories.

Bacon-Flavoured Potato Salad

See Menu Plan for Week 14.

6 oz (180 g) small potatoes, unpeeled

2 teaspoons (10 ml) vegetable oil

1½ oz (45 g) onion, diced

2 teaspoons (10 ml) imitation bacon bits

2 teaspoons (10 ml) red wine vinegar

pinch salt

pinch pepper

Boil potatoes in water until just tender, but not soft; about 10 minutes. Drain and allow to cool. Heat oil in small frying pan; add diced onion and saute until tender. Add bacon bits and cook 2 minutes longer. Peel potatoes and cut into cubes. Gently toss potatoes with vinegar. Add onion mixture and seasonings; toss gently to combine.
Makes 2 servings.
Per serving: 135 calories.

Roast Potatoes

See Menu Plan for Week 52.

12 oz (360 g) potatoes

2 tablespoons (30 ml) vegetable oil

salt and pepper to taste

Cut potatoes into pieces. Place in saucepan with water to cover and bring to the boil; cook for 2 minutes; drain. Put potatoes in baking tin, brush with oil, sprinkle with salt and pepper. Cook at 400°F, 200°C, Gas Mark 6 for 30-40 minutes, or until crisp on the outside and soft inside.
Makes 4 servings.
Per serving: 234 calories.

Parsley Soup

See Menu Plan for Week 31.

1 pint (600 ml) chicken stock made with 2 stock cubes

1 head lettuce, chopped

8 fl oz (240 ml) water

6 oz (180 g) potatoes, diced

2 tablespoons (30 ml) chopped fresh parsley

pinch white pepper

In saucepan combine stock, lettuce, water, potatoes and parsley. Bring to the boil; reduce heat, cover and simmer 20 minutes. Add white pepper. In several batches, puree mixture in blender container. Return soup to saucepan. Heat and serve.
Makes 4 servings.
Per serving: 57 calories.

Fruited Matzo Kugel

See Menu Plan for Week 16.

6 oz (180 g) cooking apple, peeled, cored and coarsely grated

1 teaspoon (5 ml) lemon juice

4 eggs

8 teaspoons (40 ml) margarine

2 teaspoons (10 ml) sugar

1 teaspoon (5 ml) cinnamon

3 oz (90 g) matzo meal

3 tablespoons (45 ml) raisins

4 teaspoons (20 ml) potato flour

2 teaspoons (10 ml) honey

1 oz (30 g) dried apricot halves, each cut into 3 strips

pinch salt

In small bowl toss grated apple with lemon juice and set aside. Separate 2 of the eggs, combine yolks with 2 whole eggs; reserve 2 whites. Cream 6 teaspoons (30 ml) margarine with sugar and cinnamon. Gradually beat in eggs until mixture is light and fluffy. Add matzo meal, raisins, potato flour and grated apple mixture; stir to combine. Let stand 30 minutes. Coat sides and bottom of 1-lb (480-g) loaf tin with 2 teaspoons (10 ml) margarine. Spread honey on bottom of pan. Arrange apricot strips decoratively over honey. Preheat oven to 325°F, 160°C, Gas Mark 3. In separate bowl beat egg whites with salt until stiff peaks form. Fold whites into matzo mixture. Carefully spoon batter into tin over fruit. Bake for 1 hour. Remove from oven and allow to cool in tin 5 minutes. Using a small spatula, loosen edges and invert on to rack to cool.
Makes 4 servings.
Per serving: 326 calories.

Garlic Bread

See Menu Plan for Week 3.

4 teaspoons (20 ml) margarine

2 teaspoons (10 ml) chopped fresh parsley

1 clove garlic, crushed

8 slices (½ oz/15 g each) French bread

Preheat grill. In a small bowl cream margarine with parsley and garlic. Spread each slice of French bread with an equal amount of margarine mixture. Place in grill pan; grill for 1 minute.
Makes 4 servings.
Per serving: 106 calories.

Apple and Oatmeal Breakfast

See Menu Plan for Week 6.

10 fl oz (300 ml) skim milk

6 fl oz (180 ml) water

1½ oz (45 g) porridge oats

4 oz (120 g) peeled, cored cooking apple, chopped

artificial sweetener to equal 4 teaspoons (20 ml) sugar

few drops vanilla flavouring

pinch ground cloves

Heat milk and water in heavy-based non-stick milk pan. Stir in oats. Bring to the boil, reduce heat and cook, uncovered, for about 3 minutes, until cereal begins to thicken, stirring occasionally. Add apple, sweetener, vanilla and cloves. Cook, stirring occasionally, for about 3 minutes until cereal is desired consistency.
Makes 2 servings.
Per serving: 155 calories.

Kedgeree and Mushroom Grill

See Menu Plan for Week 22.

1 x 3-oz (90-g) large flat mushroom

½ teaspoon (2.5 ml) vegetable oil

2 oz (60 g) cooked rice

*1 oz (30 g) cooked smoked haddock, flaked

chopped chives

1 tablespoon (15 ml) grated cheese

Brush top sides of mushroom with vegetable oil and grill for 2-3 minutes. Meanwhile, combine rice, haddock and chives. Turn mushroom over and grill for a further 1 minute. Remove mushroom from grill, top with rice mixture, sprinkle with cheese and return to grill and cook until cheese is golden brown.
Makes 1 servings.
Per serving: 186 calories.

*Any cooked or canned fish can be substituted for smoked haddock.

Oatmeal with Spiced Fruit Ambrosia

See Menu Plans for Weeks 9, 21 and 31.

10 fl oz (300 ml) skim milk

6 fl oz (180 ml) water

1½ oz (45 g) fine oatmeal

8 oz (240 g) canned fruit cocktail, drained, with 2 tablespoons (30 ml) juice, reserved

artificial sweetener to equal 2 teaspoons (10 ml) sugar

pinch ground ginger and ground cinnamon

2 teaspoons (10 ml) desiccated coconut, toasted

Heat milk and water in heavy-based non-stick milk pan. Slowly stir in oatmeal. Bring to the boil, reduce heat and cook 10 minutes or until oatmeal is thickened, stirring occasionally. Remove from heat. Stir reserved juice into oatmeal; add sweetener, ginger and cinnamon. Stir to combine. Place half of fruit in bottom of each of 2 cereal bowls; spoon half the oatmeal over each. Decorate each with 1 teaspoon (5 ml) coconut.
Makes 2 servings.
Per serving: 216 calories.

Macaroni with Cheese and Peanut Sauce

See Menu Plan for Week 22.

2 oz (60 g) cooked macaroni

3 oz (90 g) cooked cauliflower florets

3 oz (90 g) cooked carrots, sliced

Sauce

2 teaspoons (10 ml) low-fat spread

3 oz (90 g) button mushrooms, sliced

1½ tablespoons (22.5 ml) crunchy peanut butter

2½ oz (75 g) curd cheese

2 fl oz (60 ml) skim milk

salt and pepper to taste

sprig of parsley to garnish

Cook macaroni, cauliflower and carrots and keep warm. Melt low-fat spread in pan and saute mushrooms until tender. Blend peanut butter and curd cheese together then mix in milk. Stir this mixture into mushrooms. Bring to the boil, stirring; season to taste and simmer for further 2-3 minutes. Thin down if necessary with extra milk. Pour over macaroni and cauliflower; stir quickly with a fork. Garnish with parsley. Serve at once with a mixed salad.
Makes 1 serving.
Per serving: 403 calories.

Macaroni with Cheese and Peanut Sauce

SALADS

Fresh crisp greens, bright flavourful vegetables, aromatic herbs and spices – that's what salads are made of. But don't stop there! Try some of our salad specialties and your meal is sure to be a delight. Braised Leek Salad, Chicory and Beetroot Salad and Curried Cole Slaw are fresh and unusual combinations of seasonal produce. Make salads a year-round part of your menu plan.

Braised Leek Salad

See Menu Plan for Week 23.

6 fl oz (180 ml) chicken stock made with ½ stock cube

4 fl oz (120 ml) water

6 oz (180 g) leeks, white part only, cut into 2-inch (5-cm) pieces

4 teaspoons (20 ml) olive oil

1 tablespoon (15 ml) red wine vinegar

1 teaspoon (5 ml) chopped fresh parsley

½ teaspoon (2.5 ml) drained capers, chopped

pinch each salt and freshly ground pepper

2 large lettuce leaves

1 medium tomato, sliced

In small saucepan combine stock and water; bring to the boil. Add leeks; reduce heat, cover and simmer for 25 minutes. Remove from heat and cool leeks in stock. When cooled, remove leeks, using a slotted spoon, and discard stock. In small bowl combine olive oil, vinegar, parsley, capers, salt and pepper. Line each of 2 small plates with a lettuce leaf. Spoon an equal amount of leeks on to each plate and garnish each portion with half of the tomato slices. Pour half of dressing over each serving.
Makes 2 servings.
Per serving: 128 calories.

Curried Cole Slaw

See Menu Plans for Weeks 2, 7, 16 and various other weeks.

6 oz (180 g) white cabbage, shredded

2 tablespoons (30 ml) green pepper, chopped

2 tablespoons (30 ml) carrot, grated

¼ teaspoon (1.25 ml) salt

pinch celery seed

pinch pepper

4 tablespoons (60 ml) water

4 tablespoons (60 ml) cider vinegar

2 teaspoons (10 ml) dried onion flakes

1 teaspoon (5 ml) lemon juice

pinch curry powder

Combine cabbage, green pepper, carrot, salt, celery seed and pepper; set aside. Combine remaining ingredients and let stand 5 minutes; add to cabbage mixture. Toss and refrigerate at least 2 hours. Toss again just before serving.
Makes 2 servings.
Per serving: 50 calories.

Cole Slaw Vinaigrette

See Menu Plans for Weeks 4 and 37.

4 tablespoons (60 ml) cider vinegar

2 tablespoons (30 ml) plus 2 teaspoons (10 ml) vegetable oil

1 teaspoon (5 ml) celery seed

¼ teaspoon (1.25 ml) dry mustard

pinch garlic powder

9 oz (270 g) white cabbage, shredded

1½ oz (45 g) carrot, grated

2 tablespoons (30 ml) green pepper, diced

Using a wire whisk, combine vinegar, oil, celery seed, mustard and garlic powder. Add remaining ingredients; toss. Chill at least 1 hour.
Makes 4 servings.
Per serving: 96 calories.

Chicory and Beetroot Salad

See Menu Plan for Week 9.

½ teaspoon (2.5 ml) Dijon mustard

2 teaspoons (10 ml) olive oil

½ small clove garlic, crushed

2 teaspoons (10 ml) tarragon vinegar

pinch each salt and freshly ground pepper

6 oz (180 g) chicory, sliced into ½-inch (1-cm) pieces

6 oz (180 g) whole beetroots, cooked, skinned and diced

Whisk mustard with oil and garlic. When mixture begins to thicken add vinegar, salt and pepper. Just before serving, combine chicory and beetroots in salad bowl; add dressing and toss.
Makes 2 servings.
Per serving: 92 calories.

Broccoli Salad

See Menu Plan for Week 7.

1 lb (480 g) broccoli florets, blanched

4 oz (120 g) small tomatoes, quartered

4 black olives, stoned and sliced

3 tablespoons (45 ml) spring onions, sliced

2 tablespoons (30 ml) plus 2 teaspoons (10 ml) olive oil

2 tablespoons (30 ml) plus 2 teaspoons (10 ml) red wine vinegar

1 tablespoon (15 ml) water

1 teaspoon (5 ml) prepared mustard

1 clove garlic, crushed

pinch each salt and freshly ground pepper

Combine broccoli, tomatoes, olives and spring onions. Add remaining ingredients to blender container; puree for 30 seconds. Pour over broccoli salad and toss to combine.
Makes 4 servings.
Per serving: 121 calories.

Mixed Vegetable Salad

See Menu Plan for Week 2.

12 oz (360 g) green beans, sliced and blanched

6 oz (180 g) frozen peas, blanched and chilled

3 oz (90 g) carrot, grated

1 oz (30 g) celery leaves, chopped, from heart

2 tablespoons (30 ml) lemon juice

2 teaspoons (10 ml) chopped fresh chives

½ teaspoon (2.5 ml) salt

½ teaspoon (2.5 ml) chopped fresh parsley

pinch pepper

Combine beans, peas, carrot and celery leaves. Add lemon juice, chives, salt, parsley and pepper. Toss well and chill 1 hour.
Makes 2 servings.
Per serving: 75 calories.

Cucumber and Tomato Salad

See Menu Plans for Weeks 1 and 26.

1 lettuce leaf

3 oz (90 g) tomato, sliced

3 oz (90 g) cucumber, sliced

1 tablespoon (15 ml) wine vinegar

1½ teaspoons (7.5 ml) olive oil

1 teaspoon (5 ml) imitation bacon bits

Line small plate with lettuce leaf. Arrange tomato and cucumber slices on lettuce. Combine remaining ingredients. When ready to serve, pour dressing over salad.
Makes 1 serving.
Per serving: 95 calories.

Bean Salad

See Menu Plans for Weeks 4 and 21.

2½ teaspoons (12.5 ml) lemon juice

½ teaspoon (2.5 ml) chopped fresh mint

2 teaspoons (10 ml) olive oil

½ teaspoon (2.5 ml) dill weed (optional)

10 oz (300 g) green beans, blanched and cut into 2-inch (5-cm) lengths

4 oz (120 g) celery, sliced

pinch each salt and pepper

2 teaspoons (10 ml) coarsely chopped fresh parsley

3 oz (90 g) tomatoes, skinned and quartered

Combine lemon juice and mint in medium-size bowl. Set aside. In non-stick frying pan, heat oil; add dill weed if used and saute 20 seconds. Stir in beans, celery, salt, and pepper. Saute about 2 minutes. Remove from heat; add to lemon juice mixture with parsley. Toss and refrigerate. Before serving toss salad and add tomatoes.
Makes 2 servings.
Per serving: 83 calories.

Chinese Salad

See Menu Plan for Week 47.

8 oz (240 g) skinned and boned cooked chicken meat

6 oz (180 g) Chinese leaves

3 oz (90 g) canned water chestnuts

3 oz (90 g) cucumber

3 oz (90 g) red pepper

3 oz (90 g) onion

2 tablespoons (30 ml) wine vinegar

2 teaspoons (10 ml) soy sauce

2 teaspoons (10 ml) olive oil

½ teaspoon (2.5 ml) ginger root, finely grated

½ garlic clove, crushed

pinch salt

pinch pepper

Slice first 6 ingredients into thin strips. Mix last 7 ingredients. Place the sliced chicken and vegetables together in a deep bowl, pour dressing over and toss well to combine.
Makes 2 servings.
Per serving: 274 calories.

Radish Salad

See Menu Plan for Week 5.

6 oz (180 g) radishes, sliced

1 tablespoon (15 ml) spring onion, chopped

2 teaspoons (10 ml) chopped fresh parsley

4 tablespoons (60 ml) wine vinegar

1 teaspoon (5 ml) vegetable oil

¼ teaspoon (1.25 ml) salt

dash artificial sweetener (optional)

Combine radishes with spring onion and parsley. Combine vinegar, oil, salt, and sweetener if desired. Toss with radish mixture.
Makes 2 servings.
Per serving: 38 calories.

Apple Slaw

See Menu Plans for Weeks 35 and 42.

1 lb (480 g) shredded white cabbage

2½ fl oz (75 ml) apple juice

3 oz (90 g) carrots, grated

2 tablespoons (30 ml) diced green pepper

2 tablespoons (30 ml) diced celery

2 tablespoons (30 ml) chopped onion

4 teaspoons (20 ml) mayonnaise

¼ teaspoon (1.25 ml) salt

pinch white pepper

parsley sprigs to garnish

Combine cabbage and apple juice, mixing well. Put in refrigerator for ½ hour.

In another bowl combine remaining ingredients except parsley; add to cabbage mixture. Put in refrigerator for ½ hour longer. Just before serving, toss well and garnish with parsley.
Makes 4 servings.
Per serving: 43 calories.

Fruit Slaw

See Menu Plans for Weeks 12 and 35.

12 oz (360 g) shredded white cabbage

1 medium apple, cored and cut into small pieces

1 tablespoon (15 ml) raisins

1 tablespoon (15 ml) sesame seeds, toasted

5 fl oz (150 ml) natural yogurt

2 oz (60 g) canned crushed pineapple

2 tablespoons (30 ml) low-calorie mayonnaise

1 tablespoon (15 ml) lemon juice

In large bowl combine cabbage, apple, raisins and 2 teaspoons (10 ml) sesame seeds. In small bowl combine remaining ingredients except sesame seeds. Add to cabbage mixture; toss to combine. Cover and chill overnight. Sprinkle with 1 teaspoon (5 ml) sesame seeds just before serving.
Makes 4 servings.
Per serving: 85 calories.

Fruit Slaw

SAUCES, SALAD DRESSINGS AND DIPS

You mix and match parts of your wardrobe, adding different accessories for different occasions. You can do the same thing with the foods you eat, using sauces, dressings and dips as flavour accents. Sweet or sour, spicy or bland, dress up your meals with the perfect accompaniments.

Dijon-Herb Dressing

See Menu Plans for Weeks 4, 6, 9 and various other weeks.

2 teaspoons (10 ml) red wine vinegar

½ teaspoon (2.5 ml) Dijon mustard

1 tablespoon (15 ml) water

1 teaspoon (5 ml) olive oil

½ teaspoon (2.5 ml) chopped fresh parsley

pinch freshly ground pepper

Combine red wine vinegar and mustard; add water. Stirring with a small wire whisk, gradually add olive oil. Stir in remaining ingredients.
Makes 2 servings.
Per serving: 24 calories.

Gravy

See Menu Plan for Week 20.

6 fl oz (180 ml) water

½ stock cube

1 teaspoon (5 ml) cornflour

ground black pepper

pinch mixed herbs

gravy browning

Combine all ingredients except gravy browning in small saucepan. Slowly bring to the boil, stirring. Add gravy browning; cook for 1-2 minutes.
Makes 1 serving.
Per serving: 20 calories.

Thousand Island Dressing

See Menu Plans for Weeks 2 and 6.

10 fl oz (300 ml) natural yogurt

2 tablespoons (30 ml) low-calorie tomato ketchup

1 tablespoon (15 ml) diced pickled cucumber

4 teaspoons (20 ml) mayonnaise

½ teaspoon (2.5 ml) horseradish sauce

¼ teaspoon (1.25 ml) prepared mustard

dash each salt and soy sauce

Combine all ingredients in bowl; mix well. Chill.
Makes 4 servings.
Per serving: 49 calories.

Yogurt Dip or Dressing

See Menu Plans for Weeks 6, 9 and 35.

5 fl oz (150 ml) natural yogurt

2 teaspoons (10 ml) prepared mustard

1 teaspoon (5 ml) chopped fresh parsley

1 clove garlic, crushed

Combine all ingredients; mix well. Chill.
Makes 2 or 4 servings.
Per ¼ recipe: 24 calories.

Lemon Salad Dressing

See Menu Plans for Weeks 2, 9, 17 and 35.

2 tablespoons (30 ml) lemon juice

2 tablespoons (30 ml) water

2 teaspoons (10 ml) olive oil

½ teaspoon (2.5 ml) prepared mustard

¼ teaspoon (1.25 ml) crushed garlic

dash each Worcestershire sauce, artificial sweetener, salt, freshly ground pepper and crushed thyme (optional)

Combine all ingredients in small jar with lid. Mix well. Shake well before serving.
Makes 4 servings.
Per serving: 23 calories.

Mint Sauce

See Menu Plans for Weeks 24 and 34.

2 tablespoons (30 ml) finely chopped mint

1 tablespoon (15 ml) cider vinegar

1 tablespoon (15 ml) water

artificial sweetener to equal 4 teaspoons (20 ml) sugar

Combine all ingredients in small jar with lid and shake vigorously.
Makes 1-2 servings.
Per serving: 3 calories.

Basic Vinaigrette

See Menu Plans for Weeks 1, 3, 4 and various other weeks.

4 teaspoons (20 ml) olive oil or vegetable oil

1 tablespoon (15 ml) white wine vinegar

pinch salt

¼ teaspoon (1.25 ml) prepared mustard

Combine all ingredients; mix well.
Makes 4 servings.
Per serving: 45 calories.

Cider Vinaigrette

See Menu Plans for Weeks 14, 23, 26 and 33.

Substitute cider vinegar for wine vinegar in Basic Vinaigrette.
Makes 4 servings.
Per serving: 45 calories.

Garlic Vinaigrette

See Menu Plans for Weeks 2, 5, 7 and 16.

Prepare Basic Vinaigrette, omitting salt. With flat side of knife, mash small garlic clove with pinch salt to form a paste. Add paste to dressing.
Makes 4 servings.
Per serving: 45 calories.

Dill Vinaigrette

See Menu Plans for Weeks 6, 12, 43 and 47.

1 clove garlic

pinch salt

1 tablespoon (15 ml) red wine vinegar

1 tablespoon (15 ml) water

1 tablespoon (15 ml) olive oil

½ teaspoon (2.5 ml) chopped fresh dill

freshly ground pepper to taste

Mash garlic with salt. Combine mashed garlic, vinegar and water. Stirring with a small wire whisk, gradually add olive oil. Stir in dill and season with pepper.
Makes 2 servings.
Per serving: 68 calories.

Tarragon Vinaigrette

See Menu Plans for Weeks 1, 5, 7 and 50.

Substitute tarragon vinegar for wine vinegar in Basic Vinaigrette.
Makes 4 servings.
Per serving: 45 calories.

Gingered Vinaigrette

See Menu Plans for Weeks 3, 42, 51 and various other weeks.

Add quarter teaspoon very finely chopped fresh ginger root to Basic Vinaigrette.
Makes 4 servings.
Per serving: 45 calories.

Oregano Vinaigrette

See Menu Plans for Weeks 8, 13, 17 and 51.
*Substitute oregano vinegar for wine vinegar in Basic Vinaigrette.
Makes 4 servings.
Per serving: 45 calories.

*To make your own Oregano Vinegar, add 1 or 2 fresh sprigs of oregano to a small bottle of wine vinegar and leave it to infuse for a few days before using.

Savory Vinaigrette

See Menu Plans for Weeks 9, 16, 44 and various other weeks.

Add pinch each thyme and summer savory to Basic Vinaigrette.
Makes 4 servings.
Per serving: 45 calories.

Herb Dressing

See Menu Plans for Weeks 2 and 5.

3 tablespoons (45 ml) vegetable oil

2 tablespoons (30 ml) water

1 tablespoon (15 ml) wine vinegar

1 teaspoon (5 ml) basil

½ teaspoon (2.5 ml) chopped fresh parsley

pinch garlic powder

pinch oregano

Combine all ingredients in jar with lid. Shake well until combined. Use immediately or store and shake before serving.
Makes 6 servings.
Per serving: 68 calories.

Lemon 'Butter' Sauce

See Menu Plan for Week 2.

2 tablespoons (30 ml) low-fat spread, melted

2½ fl oz (75 ml) water

2 tablespoons (30 ml) white wine

2 teaspoons (10 ml) cornflour

2 tablespoons (30 ml) lemon juice

2 tablespoons (30 ml) finely chopped fresh parsley.

In saucepan melt low-fat spread. Add water and white wine and bring to the boil. Combine cornflour with lemon juice and add to wine mixture. Cook, stirring constantly, until thickened. Stir in parsley.
Makes 6 servings.
Per serving: 30 calories.

Curry Dip

See Menu Plan for Week 52.

5 fl oz (150 ml) natural yogurt

¼ teaspoon (1.25 ml) curry powder

¼ teaspoon (1.25 ml) lemon juice

pinch each ground cumin, salt and white pepper

Combine all ingredients in small bowl; mix well and chill.
Makes 4 servings.
Per serving: 19 calories.

Spicy Plum Sauce

See Menu Plans for Weeks 25 and 52.

8 medium plums

pinch mixed spice

artificial sweetener to taste

2 teaspoons (10 ml) arrowroot or cornflour

Stone plums and cut into dice. Place in small saucepan with just enough water to cover; add spice, bring to the boil and cook until soft; add sweetener to taste. Mix arrowroot or cornflour with a little water to a thin paste; add this to plums and cook until thickened.
Makes 4 servings.
Per serving: 34 calories.

Vinaigrette Parmesan

See Menu Plan for Week 4.

Substitute 2 teaspoons (10 ml) grated Parmesan cheese for mustard in Basic Vinaigrette.
Makes 4 servings.
Per serving: 55 calories.

Creamy Yogurt Dressing

See Menu Plan for Week 52.

10 fl oz (300 ml) natural yogurt

4 teaspoons (20 ml) chopped fresh parsley

4 teaspoons (20 ml) chopped chives

4 teaspoons (20 ml) mayonnaise

1-2 teaspoons (5-10 ml) prepared mustard, to taste

2 teaspoons (10 ml) soy sauce

pinch ground ginger

Combine all ingredients; mix well. Chill.
Makes 4 servings.
Per serving: 46 calories.

Russian Dressing

See Menu Plans for Weeks 3, 4 and various other weeks.

2 teaspoons (10 ml) low-calorie mayonnaise

½ teaspoon (2.5 ml) chili sauce

2 teaspoons (10 ml) relish, any type

Combine all ingredients; stir well.
Makes 1 serving.
Per serving: 31 calories.

Russian Dressing
Spicy Plum Sauce
Curry Dip

DESSERTS, SNACKS AND DRINKS

Desserts and snacks should be as nourishing as everything else you eat. But that doesn't mean they have to be boring. Blend good nutrition with creativity and stir up special treats like Frozen Apple Banana Dessert, Coconut Honey Shake and Hot Mocha Milk. They all make sensible eating, fun. A glass of wine or beer now and then makes special occasions even more festive.

Strawberry Cream

See Menu Plans for Weeks 41 and 44.

2 tablespoons (30 ml) unflavoured gelatine

4 fl oz (120 ml) water

1¼ lbs (600 g) fresh or frozen strawberries

1 pint (600 ml) natural yogurt

artificial sweetener to equal 2 teaspoons (10 ml) sugar

Dissolve gelatine in water in small bowl over pan of hot water. Reserve 12 strawberries for decoration. Put rest in blender container with yogurt and sweetener and puree until smooth. Add dissolved gelatine and puree. Pour into 4 individual dishes and chill in refrigerator for 1 hour. Decorate with remaining strawberries and serve at once.
Makes 4 servings.
Per serving: 138 calories.

Pineapple-Coconut Biscuits

See Menu Plan for Week 47.

1½ oz (45 g) flour

artificial sweetener to equal 2 teaspoons (10 ml) sugar

¼ teaspoon (1.25 ml) baking powder

2 oz (60 g) low-fat dry milk

4 oz (120 g) canned, drained, crushed pineapple, plus 2 tablespoons (30 ml) juice

1 tablespoon (15 ml) water

¼ teaspoon (1.25 ml) vanilla flavouring

2 teaspoons (10 ml) desiccated coconut

Sift together first 3 ingredients; add remaining ingredients except coconut and mix well. Drop teaspoonsful of mixture on to non-stick baking sheet, allowing room for biscuits to spread. Sprinkle biscuits with coconut. Bake at 350°F, 180°C, Gas Mark 4 for 15 minutes or until lightly browned. Remove from sheet; cool on rack.
Makes 2 servings.
Per serving: 225 calories.

Swedish Apple Bake

See Menu Plans for Weeks 16 and 17.

1½ oz (45 g) flour

artificial sweetener to equal 4 teaspoons (20 ml) sugar

¾ teaspoon (3.75 ml) baking powder

¾ teaspoon (3.75 ml) ground cinnamon

pinch each ground allspice, ground nutmeg and salt

8 oz (240 g) peeled and cored cooking apple, diced

2 eggs, beaten with 3 tablespoons (45 ml) water

½ teaspoon (2.5 ml) honey

¼ teaspoon (1.25 ml) lemon juice

¼ teaspoon (1.25 ml) vanilla flavouring

ground cinnamon for topping

Combine flour, artificial sweetener, baking powder, spices and salt; sift into a medium bowl. Add apple and stir to coat with dry ingredients. Add remaining ingredients and stir to combine. Line 2-lb (960-g) loaf tin with non-stick paper. Spoon apple mixture into tin. Cover with foil and bake at 350°F, 180°C, Gas Mark 4 for 40 minutes. Let stand for 10 minutes. Sprinkle top of cake with cinnamon. Cut into slices and serve warm.
Makes 2 servings.
Per serving: 248 calories.

Strawberry-Apple Frost

See Menu Plan for Week 14.

10 fl oz (300 ml) natural yogurt

5 oz (150 g) fresh or frozen strawberries, reserve 2 whole berries

2½ fl oz (75 ml) apple juice

2½ teaspoons (12.5 ml) sugar

1 teaspoon (5 ml) vanilla flavouring

4 ice cubes

Combine all ingredients except reserved berries in blender container; puree until frothy. Divide into 2 stemmed glasses; garnish each serving with a strawberry.
Makes 2 servings.
Per serving: 135 calories.

Spiced Orange Ambrosia

See Menu Plan for Week 9.

2 medium oranges, cut into wedges

¼ teaspoon (1.25 ml) ground cinnamon

1 teaspoon (5 ml) honey, warmed

2 teaspoons (10 ml) desiccated coconut

Sprinkle orange wedges with cinnamon. Dip into warmed honey and then into desiccated coconut. Grill on rack until coconut is lightly toasted. Serve warm.
Makes 2 servings.
Per serving: 75 calories.

Spiced Pineapple Pumpkin

See Menu Plan for Week 44.

¾ teaspoon (3.75 ml) unflavoured gelatine

2½ fl oz (75 ml) apple juice

8 oz (240 g) canned or cooked pumpkin

1½ teaspoons (7.5 ml) honey

pinch each ground cinnamon and ground allspice

8 oz (240 g) canned crushed pineapple

Sprinkle gelatine over apple juice in a small bowl. Place bowl over pan of hot water and leave to dissolve; remove bowl from water. In a larger bowl combine pumpkin, honey, cinnamon and allspice. Mix well, stir in gelatine mixture. Spread quarter of mixture over bottom of each of 2 individual dishes; top each with 2 oz (60 g) pineapple. Repeat layers and chill at least 1 hour.
Makes 2 servings.
Per serving: 97 calories.

Cherry Tarts

See Menu Plans for Weeks 8 and 27.

Crust

2 digestive biscuits, crushed

¼ teaspoon (1.25 ml) ground cinnamon

4 teaspoons (20 ml) low-fat spread, melted

Filling

8 oz (240 g) frozen dark sweet cherries, thawed and drained

4 teaspoons (20 ml) lemon juice

pinch ground cloves and cinnamon

2 teaspoons (10 ml) arrowroot, blended with 4 teaspoons (20 ml) water

To Prepare Crust: Combine digestive biscuit crumbs and cinnamon; add low-fat spread and mix thoroughly. Divide mixture into two 4-inch (10-cm) foil-lined Yorkshire pudding tins or aluminium foil dishes, pressing mixture firmly with back of spoon on to bottom and up sides to form crust. Chill in refrigerator.
To Prepare Filling: In a small saucepan combine cherries, lemon juice, cloves and cinnamon and cook until heated. Add blended arrowroot to saucepan, bring to the boil stirring gently so as not to crush cherries. Remove from heat, cool 10 minutes, and pour into prepared crusts. Chill.
Makes 2 servings.
Per serving: 174 calories.

Pineapple-Orange 'Cream'

See Menu Plans for Weeks 9 and 52.

6 teaspoons (30 ml) unflavoured gelatine

8 fl oz (240 ml) water

8 fl oz (240 ml) orange juice

8 oz (240 g) canned crushed pineapple

artificial sweetener to equal 6 teaspoons (30 ml) sugar

2 tablespoons (30 ml) lemon juice

10 fl oz (300 ml) natural yogurt

Dissolve gelatine in 4 fl oz (120 ml) water in bowl over pan of hot water. In bowl combine orange juice, pineapple and juice, remaining water, sweetener and lemon juice; stir in gelatine mixture. Chill until almost set. Whip in yogurt. Pour into dessert dishes and chill until set.
Makes 4 servings.
Per serving: 99 calories.

Lemonade

See Menu Plans for Weeks 31 and 42.

4 fl oz (120 ml) fresh lemon juice

artificial sweetener to equal 6 teaspoons (30 ml) sugar

16 fl oz (480 ml) water

2-3 ice cubes

Combine lemon juice and sweetener in blender container; pour in water. Puree, adding ice cubes one at a time.
Makes 2 servings.
Per serving: 4 calories.

Bread and Fruit Pudding

See Menu Plan for Week 41.

4 teaspoons (20 ml) margarine

4 slices (1 oz/30 g each) white bread

8 tablespoons (120 ml) raisins

1 pint (600 ml) skim milk

4 eggs, beaten

6 teaspoons (30 ml) caster sugar

gound nutmeg to garnish

Spread 1 teaspoon (5 ml) margarine on each bread slice and cut slices into small squares. Layer bread squares and raisins in an ovenproof dish, finishing with bread. Warm the milk with the caster sugar and add to beaten eggs; strain mixture over raisins and bread. Sprinkle with nutmeg and bake at 375°F, 190°C, Gas Mark 5, for 30-40 minutes or until pudding is set and top is golden brown.
Makes 4 servings.
Per serving: 410 calories.

Baked Spiced Pears

See Menu Plan for Week 25.

4 medium pears

32 cloves

10 fl oz (300 ml) water

3 teaspoons (15 ml) brown sugar

Peel the pears. Press 8 cloves into each pear. Put the pears in a baking dish, add the water and brown sugar. Cover and bake at 375°F, 190°C, Gas Mark 5, for 1 hour or until tender. Serve hot or cold.
Makes 4 servings.
Per serving: 63 calories.

Baked Apples

See Menu Plans for Weeks 3, 4, **8 and various other weeks.**

2 medium apples

artificial sweetener to equal 2 teaspoons (10 ml) sugar

pinch each ground cinnamon and ground nutmeg

2 fl oz (60 ml) water

1 teaspoon (5 ml) lemon juice

Core apples; place in ovenproof dish. Sprinkle sweetener, cinnamon and nutmeg over the apples. Add water and lemon juice and bake at 450°F, 230°C, Gas Mark 8 for 25 minutes or until tender.
Makes 2 servings.
Per serving: 45 calories.

Baked Spiced Pears

Stuffed Baked Apple

See Menu Plan for Week 12.

1 medium apple, cored
1 tablespoon (15 ml) raisins
1 teaspoon (5 ml) lemon juice
½ teaspoon (2.5 ml) desiccated coconut
½ teaspoon (2.5 ml) honey
pinch ground cinnamon
1 teaspoon (5 ml) water

Peel apple one third of the way down. Combine remaining ingredients except water. Stuff into cored apple. Place water in bottom of a small ovenproof dish, just large enough to hold apple. Add filled apple, cover with foil and bake at 350°F, 180°C, Gas Mark 4 for 35-45 minutes.
Makes 1 serving.
Per serving: 140 calories.

Pineapple Sorbet

See Menu Plans for Weeks 7 and 35.

1 pint (600 ml) natural yogurt
1 lb (480 g) canned crushed pineapple
artificial sweetener to equal 6 teaspoons (30 ml) sugar
1 tablespoon (15 ml) lemon juice

Combine all ingredients in blender container; puree until smooth. Transfer to a shallow dish; place in freezer. Stir every hour to break up ice crystals until frozen, at least 3-4 hours. Thaw for 10 minutes before serving.
Makes 4 servings.
Per serving: 115 calories.

Rice Pudding

See Menu Plans for Weeks 27 and 41.

8 oz (240 g) cooked brown rice, hot
16 fl oz (480 ml) skim milk
4 eggs
8 tablespoons (120 ml) sultanas
2 tablespoons (30 ml) brown sugar
4-5 drops vanilla flavouring
¼ teaspoon (1.25 ml) ground cinnamon
¼ teaspoon (1.25 ml) ground nutmeg
ground cinnamon to garnish

Combine all ingredients in a mixing bowl. Pour into a baking dish, cover tightly with aluminium foil and bake at 350°F, 180°C, Gas Mark 4 for 40 minutes or until set. Sprinkle with cinnamon and serve.
Makes 4 servings.
Per serving: 371 calories.

Minted Passion Cooler

See Menu Plan for Week 19.

3 medium passion fruits
5 fl oz (150 ml) natural yogurt
5 fl oz (150 ml) skim milk
3 teaspoons (15 ml) caster sugar
3 sprigs mint

Scoop out the contents of the passion fruit with a teaspoon and beat them together with the yogurt, milk and caster sugar in a bowl. Pour into chilled glasses and top each with a sprig of mint.
Makes 3 servings.
Per serving: 77 calories.

Pineapple Cheesecake

See Menu Plans for Weeks 27 and 41.

5 tablespoons (75 ml) plus 1 teaspoon (5 ml) low-fat spread
8 digestive biscuits, crumbled
6 teaspoons (30 ml) unflavoured gelatine
2 fl oz (60 ml) water
juice and grated rind of 1 lemon
10 oz (300 g) curd cheese
10 fl oz (300 ml) natural yogurt
8 oz (240 g) canned crushed pineapple, drained
artificial sweetener to equal 8 teaspoons (40 ml) sugar
2-4 drops vanilla flavouring
lemon twists to garnish

Line base of 7-8-inch (18-20.5-cm) loose-based cake tin with non-stick paper.
To Prepare Base: melt low-fat spread in basin over hot water, add crumbled biscuits and press on to base of tin. Chill.
To Prepare Filling: dissolve gelatine in water in small bowl over pan of hot water; add lemon juice and rind. Blend cheese with yogurt, pineapple, sweetener and vanilla flavouring. Puree thoroughly in blender until all contents are smooth, add dissolved gelatine mixture and puree to mix. Pour on to biscuit base and chill until set. Carefully remove from tin. Decorate with lemon twists.
Makes 4 servings.
Per serving: 419 calories.

Rich Fruit Pudding

See Menu Plans for Weeks 41 and 52.

2 slices (1 oz/30 g each) brown bread, made into crumbs

1½ oz (45 g) self-raising flour

6 tablespoons (90 ml) natural bran

4 tablespoons (60 ml) raisins

2 tablespoons (30 ml) currants

2 tablespoons (30 ml) sultanas

grated rind ½ lemon

grated rind ½ orange

1-2 teaspoons (5-10 ml) mixed spice

4 fl oz (120 ml) skim milk

4 teaspoons (20 ml) low-fat spread

1 teaspoon (5 ml) rum flavouring

½ teaspoon (2.5 ml) gravy browning (use more for darker pudding)

2 oz (60 g) cooked carrots, mashed

2 teaspoons (10 ml) sugar

Combine first 9 ingredients in a large basin. Mix thoroughly. Put milk, 3 teaspoons (15 ml) low-fat spread, rum flavouring and gravy browning into a saucepan. Gradually heat mixture and stir until low-fat spread melts. Remove from heat, allow to cool slightly; pour into blender container, add carrots and sugar. Puree until contents are smooth. Pour this mixture on to the dry ingredients and beat thoroughly. Grease a 2-pint (1.2-litre) pudding basin, with clip-on lid, with remaining low-fat spread. Pour mixture into the greased basin, fasten lid, and then cover tightly with foil – or use greaseproof paper and then foil. Put pudding into the top of a double steamer and cook for 4½-5 hours. Allow pudding to stand for at least 5 minutes before turning out.
Makes 4 servings.
Per serving: 255 calories.

Custard

See Menu Plan for Week 12 and various other weeks.

10 fl oz (300 ml) skim milk

2 tablespoons (30 ml) custard powder

artificial sweetener to equal 1 tablespoon (15 ml) sugar

Heat 9 fl oz (270 ml) milk in saucepan. Mix custard powder to a cream with 1 fl oz (30 ml) skim milk. Add creamed mixture to hot milk, stirring continuously until sauce thickens. Remove from heat and add artificial sweetener.
Makes 2 servings.
Per serving: 101 calories.

Frozen Apple-Banana Dessert

See Menu Plans for Weeks 1 and 6.

10 fl oz (300 ml) skim milk

1 medium apple, peeled, cored and cut into pieces

½ medium banana, sliced

1 oz (30 g) low-fat dry milk

artificial sweetener to equal 4 teaspoons (20 ml) sugar

2 drops almond flavouring

Combine all ingredients in blender container; puree until smooth. Pour into plastic container and freeze. Remove from freezer and thaw slightly. Return to blender container. Puree until smooth. Pour into 2 dessert dishes and freeze. Leave in refrigerator to soften a little – for about 30 minutes – before serving.
Makes 2 servings.
Per serving: 143 calories.

Hot Cocoa

See Menu Plan for Week 2.

2 oz (60 g) low-fat dry milk

2 teaspoons (10 ml) cocoa

12 fl oz (360 ml) water

2 teaspoons (10 ml) soft brown sugar

Combine dry milk and cocoa in saucepan; gradually stir in water, blending thoroughly. Bring to the boil, stirring constantly; boil 2 minutes. Remove from heat, add soft brown sugar and serve.
Makes 2 servings.
Per serving: 121 calories.

Coconut-Honey Shake

See Menu Plan for Week 3.

8 fl oz (240 ml) sparkling mineral water

5 fl oz (150 ml) natural yogurt

artificial sweetener to equal 2 teaspoons (10 ml) sugar (optional)

2 teaspoons (10 ml) desiccated coconut

1 teaspoon (5 ml) each honey and vanilla flavouring

pinch ground cinnamon

3-4 ice cubes

Combine all ingredients except ice cubes in blender container. Puree until smooth, adding ice cubes one at a time. Serve immediately.
Makes 2 servings.
Per serving: 78 calories.

Honey-Stewed Prunes

See Menu Plans for Weeks 2, 6, 7 and various other weeks.

4 oz (120 g) dried prunes

1 teaspoon (5 ml) honey

pinch ground cinnamon

pinch ground allspice

Place prunes in small saucepan and add water to cover. Bring to the boil; reduce heat and stir in honey, cinnamon and allspice. Cover and simmer 20-30 minutes. Serve warm.
Makes 4 servings.
Per serving: 44 calories.

Hot Mocha Milk

See Menu Plans for Weeks 1 and 14.

1 pint (600 ml) skim milk

4 teaspoons (20 ml) cocoa

2 teaspoon (10 ml) instant coffee

artificial sweetener to equal 4 teaspoons (20 ml) sugar

½ teaspoon (2.5 ml) vanilla flavouring

In small saucepan combine milk, cocoa and coffee; bring to the boil. Remove from heat. Stir in sweetener and vanilla flavouring and serve.
Makes 2 x 10-fl oz (300-ml) servings or 4 x 5-fl oz (150-ml) servings.
Per 5-fl oz (150-ml) serving: 64 calories.

Highland 'Fling'

See Menu Plan for Week 45.

10 fl oz (300 ml) skim milk

5 fl oz (150 ml) natural yogurt

5 fl oz (150 ml) very strong black coffee

6 fl oz (180 ml) Scotch whisky

4 teaspoons (20 ml) caster sugar

Place all ingredients in a blender and puree until smooth. Serve in chilled glasses.
Makes 4 servings.
Per serving: 157 calories.

Coconut-Coffee Mounds

See Menu Plans for Weeks, 2, 8 and 35.

2 oz (60 g) low-fat dry milk

artificial sweetener to equal 6 teaspoons (30 ml) sugar

4 teaspoons (20 ml) instant coffee

2 tablespoons (30 ml) water

½ teaspoon (2.5 ml) vanilla flavouring

2 teaspoons (10 ml) desiccated coconut

Combine first 3 ingredients. Sprinkle with water and vanilla. Stir until mixture forms dry paste that holds together. Wet hands and shape mixture into small balls, ½-inch (1-cm) in diameter. Roll balls in coconut to coat. Chill in freezer for at least 40 minutes. Serve or keep in refrigerator until ready to use. Makes about 16 balls.
Makes 4 servings.
Per serving: 69 calories.

Hot Mocha Milk
Coconut-Honey Shake
Coconut-Coffee Mounds

Profiteroles and Chocolate Sauce

See Menu Plan for Week 17.

8 teaspoons (40 ml) low-fat spread

2 fl oz (60 ml) water

1½ oz (45 g) self-raising flour

2 small eggs

4 teaspoons (20 ml) chocolate spread

Filling

12 tablespoons (180 ml) single cream

3 teaspoons (15 ml) cornflour

2 tablespoons (30 ml) water

½ teaspoon (2.5 ml) vanilla flavouring

Preheat oven to 400°F, 200°C, Gas Mark 6. Melt low-fat spread in medium saucepan. Add water and bring to the boil. Add flour, all at once, and stir vigorously until mixture leaves the sides of the saucepan. Cool slightly and then add eggs, one at a time, beating thoroughly after each addition until mixture is smooth. Line a baking sheet with silicone paper. Spoon mixture into 8 portions on to tray. Bake for 15 minutes and then reduce oven temperature to 350°F, 180°C, Gas Mark 4; bake for a further 15 minutes. Remove buns from oven and turn off heat. Pierce buns to release steam; return to oven for 10 minutes leaving oven door ajar. Transfer to cooling tray. Make filling by bringing cream to the boil in a saucepan. Mix cornflour with the water and add to the cream with vanilla flavouring. Bring to the boil, stirring constantly, and cook for 1 minute. Pour into basin and leave until cold. Fill buns with the cream and top with the chocolate spread.
Makes 4 servings. Two profiteroles equal 1 serving.
Per serving: 212 calories.

Turkish Chilled Tomato Soup

See Menu Plan for Week 27.

10 fl oz (300 ml) natural yogurt

1 teaspoon (5 ml) olive oil

juice of ½ lemon

1 teaspoon (5 ml) curry powder

pinch dried thyme

16 fl oz (480 ml) tomato juice

pinch salt

1 tablespoon (15 ml) chopped fresh chives

In a large bowl beat together yogurt, olive oil, lemon juice, curry powder and thyme until well mixed. Gradually stir in the tomato juice until thoroughly blended. Season with salt. Cover and chill. Serve in individual soup bowls sprinkled with chopped chives.
Makes 2 servings.
Per serving: 170 calories.

Curried Bananas

See Menu Plan for Week 5.

2 teaspoons (10 ml) vegetable oil

½ teaspoon (2.5 ml) curry powder

pinch ground turmeric

2 medium bananas, peeled

pinch salt

10 fl oz (300 ml) natural yogurt

4 teaspoons (20 ml) desiccated coconut

2 lemon wedges

Heat oil gently in non-stick frying pan; add curry powder and turmeric and cook for 1 minute, stirring. Cut bananas in half lengthwise; add to pan, sprinkle with salt and cook bananas, turning once until soft. Spoon yogurt over and continue to cook gently until thoroughly heated, stirring occasionally. Sprinkle with coconut and serve at once with lemon wedges.
Makes 2 servings.
Per serving: 230 calories.

Tropical Shake

See Menu Plan for Week 23.

10 fl oz (300 ml) natural yogurt

4 ice cubes, crushed

½ banana, peeled and thickly sliced

4 oz (120 g) pineapple, crushed

Place all ingredients in blender and puree until smooth. Serve in chilled glasses.
Makes 2 servings.
Per serving: 150 calories.

Mushroom Dip

See Menu Plan for Week 6.

4 oz (120 g) mushrooms, finely chopped

4 spring onions, finely chopped

1 teaspoon (5 ml) vegetable oil

5 fl oz (150 ml) natural yogurt

1 small clove garlic, crushed

pinch salt

2 sticks celery, cut into 2-inch (5-cm) lengths

2 tablespoons (30 ml) finely chopped fresh dill (optional)

In non-stick frying pan saute mushrooms and spring onions in oil over a moderate heat until golden brown, stirring frequently. Remove from the heat and allow to cool for 10-15 minutes. In a bowl, blend yogurt and garlic until smooth. Add the sauteed mushrooms and spring onions and sprinkle with the salt. Mix well. Cover and chill. Sprinkle with chopped dill if desired. Serve with celery sticks.
Makes 1 serving.
Per serving: 178 calories.

Apricot Frappe

See Menu Plan for Week 16.

12 oz (360 g) canned apricots

5 fl oz (150 ml) skim milk

5 fl oz (150 ml) natural yogurt

juice of ½ lemon

½ teaspoon (2.5 ml) finely grated lemon rind

3 teaspoons (15 ml) caster sugar

½ teaspoon (2.5 ml) vanilla flavouring

9 ice cubes, finely crushed

3 thin lemon slices to garnish

Place the apricots, milk, yogurt, lemon juice, lemon rind, sugar, vanilla flavouring and crushed ice into a blender and puree until smooth. Pour into chilled glasses and serve at once garnished with lemon slices.
Makes 3 servings.
Per serving: 84 calories.

Pear Frozen Yogurt

See Menu Plans for Weeks 3, 23 and 25.

4 canned pear halves with 4 tablespoons (60 ml) juice

10 fl oz (300 ml) natural yogurt

artificial sweetener to equal 8 teaspoons (40 ml) sugar

2 tablespoons (30 ml) lemon juice

Combine all ingredients in blender container; pureè until smooth. Transfer to shallow dish; place in freezer. Stir every hour to break up ice crystals until frozen, about 3 hours. Thaw for 10 minutes before serving.
Makes 2 servings.
Per serving: 136 calories.

Apple Meringue

See Menu Plan for Week 28.

4 medium cooking apples

1 teaspoon (5 ml) ground cinnamon

rind of ½ lemon

1 teaspoon (5 ml) honey

2 egg whites

3 teaspoons (15 ml) caster sugar

Preheat oven to 300°F, 150°C, Gas Mark 2. Peel, core and slice apples and place in a saucepan with 1 tablespoon (15 ml) water. Cook until tender. Stir in cinnamon, lemon rind and honey. Transfer to ovenproof dish. Whisk egg whites until stiff and then fold in caster sugar. Spoon over apple mixture. Cook in oven for about 20-30 minutes or until puffed up and pale golden.
Makes 4 servings.
Per serving: 76 calories.

Spiced Peaches

See Menu Plan for Week 49.

4 oz (120 g) canned sliced peaches

¼ teaspoon (1.25 ml) allspice

1 tablespoon (15 ml) dry white wine

Drain canned peaches and reserve juice. Arrange peaches on a heatproof dish, sprinkle with allspice, put under hot grill and cook until heated through. Gently warm juice and wine. Place peaches in serving dish and pour over warmed wine and juice and serve at once.
Makes 1 serving.
Per serving: 62 calories.

Lady Fingers

See Menu Plan for Week 10.

1 very ripe, medium banana

2 eggs, separated

½ teaspoon (2.5 ml) vanilla flavouring

1½ oz (45 g) flour

pinch salt

1 tablespoon (15 ml) sugar

Preheat oven to 375°F, 190°C, Gas Mark 5. Slice banana into bowl of food processor or blender. Add egg yolks and vanilla; puree until smooth. Sift flour and salt together. In separate bowl whisk egg whites with sugar until stiff. Gently fold banana mixture into egg whites, then gradually fold in sifted flour. Line baking tray with nonstick paper. Spoon mixture into piping bag that has been fitted with a plain nozzle. Pipe 4-inch (10-cm) fingers of mixture on to baking tray, leaving a space of 2 inches (5 cm) between each. Bake about 12 minutes or until lightly browned. Transfer to wire rack and allow to cool slightly. Serve warm.
Makes 2 servings.
Per serving: 235 calories.

Sweet Pancake with Jam

See Menu Plan for Week 41.

4 eggs, beaten

4 fl oz (120 ml) skim milk

4 tablespoons (60 ml) low-fat spread, melted

4 tablespoons (60 ml) flour

½ teaspoon (2.5 ml) vanilla flavouring

2 tablespoons (30 ml) lemon juice (optional)

3 tablespoons (45 ml) low-calorie jam

Combine all ingredients except lemon juice and jam in small bowl. Beat until smooth. Pour into a preheated non-stick frying pan with flameproof handle and cook until underside is brown and top is set. Place under grill to brown top. Sprinkle with lemon juice, if desired. Serve with jam.
Makes 4 servings.
Per serving: 224 calories.

Fruit Sundae

See Menu Plans for Weeks, 2, 6, 7 and various other weeks.

16 oz (480 g) canned apricot halves

2 medium bananas, peeled and sliced

8 oz (240 g) vanilla ice cream, divided into 4

4 teaspoons (20 ml) chocolate sauce

Divide first three ingredients equally between four dessert dishes – top each serving with 1 teaspoon (5 ml) of chocolate sauce. Serve at once.
Makes 4 servings.
Per serving: 212 calories.

Knickerbocker Glory

See Menu Plan for Week 41.

4 digestive biscuits, crumbled

8 oz (240 g) canned sliced peaches

10 oz (300 g) strawberries, reserve 4 for garnish

8 oz (240 g) vanilla ice cream

In 4 tall sundae glasses, layer biscuit crumbs, peaches, strawberries and ice cream. Repeat layers finishing with ice cream and decorate with reserved strawberries.
Makes 4 servings.
Per serving: 210 calories.

Knickerbocker Glory

INDEX

A

Ambrosia
oatmeal with spiced fruit, 176
spiced orange, 187
Apple
baked, 188
baked stuffed, 190
and banana dessert, frozen, 191
meringue, 195
and oatmeal breakfast, 176
slaw, 180
–strawberry frost, 187
Swedish bake, 186
Apricot frappe, 195
Asparagus and leek soup, 112
Aubergine
–cheese bake, 119
and sauteed curried veal, 131
Austrian beans, 166-7

B

Bacon-flavoured potato salad, 175
Baked apples, 188
stuffed, 190
Baked cheese souffle, 116
Baked fish casserole, 162
Baked haddock, 155
Baked hake steaks, 156
Baked prawns thermidor, 155
Baked spiced pears, 188
Banana
and apple frozen dessert, 191
curried, 194
lady fingers, 196
Barbecued pork chops, 143
Basic vinaigrette, 183
Beans
Austrian, 166-7
and cheese peppers, 166
and cheese potatoes, 167
and chicken casserole, 131
curried, 167
French, with poached cod and tomatoes, 154
Greek-style, with mushroom, 164
green, with red cabbage, 114
green, with sesame chicken, 131
green, with tomatoes Hungarian-style, 168
're-fried' beans, 167
salad, 179
savoury salad, 166
soup, 167
Beef
and corn casserole, 148
Mediterranean stew, 136
Mexican patties, 142
pie, 147
savoury mince with noodles, 139
stock, 114
Beetroot and chicory salad, 178-9
Braised leek salad, 178
Bread
and fruit pudding, 188
garlic, 175
homemade, 175
Breadcrumbed liver, 146
Broccoli
quiche, 120
salad, 179
soup, 115

Burgers
lamb, 138
oven-baked, 148
pork chili, 142
Butter beans
Austrian, 166-7
and cheese peppers, 166
Greek-style, with mushrooms, 164
savoury salad, 166

C

Cabbage
Chinese, and tomato medley, 171
creamed, and ham, 148
savoury, 171
sweet and sour, 172
Calamari with spaghetti, 155
Carrots
marinated, 168
minted, 170
Casseroles
baked fish, 162
beef and corn, 148
chicken and bean, 131
chicken hotpot, 139
ham and turkey, 138-9
liver, 147
liver and noodle, 144
See also Stew
Cauliflower
and courgette soup, 110
cream soup, 115
with mushroom sauce, 171
Cheese
aubergine cheese bake, 119
baked cheesy pitta bread, 122
and bean potatoes, 167
broccoli quiche, 120
and butter bean peppers, 166
chili-cheese rarebit, 119
cinnamon toast, 123
cottage cheese country-style, 126
fennel with parmesan 172
fruited cheese delight, 124
gypsy salad, 122
and lunch box fish, 162
macaroni cheese salad, 122
open grilled sandwich, 122
and peanut sauce, with macaroni, 176
poached halibut parmesan, 162-3
and salad sandwich, 119
souffle, 116
with spaghetti and herbs, 124
stuffed French toast, 122
Swiss cheese bake, 123
tomato and herb cheese, 126
and turkey layer, 128
and vegetable platter, 118
and vegetable risotto, 123
Welsh rarebit, 118
Cheesecake, pineapple, 190
Cherry tart, 187
Chicken
and bean casserole, 131
braised, with vegetables, 127
breasts, with tarragon, 135
Capri, with potatoes, 134
cold platter, 134
donna, 130
ginger-grilled, 130
Greek-style, 132
kebabs, 128
livers and green noodles, 140

liver pilaf, 146
with mushrooms, 132
and pork meatballs, 142
provencale, 132
sesame, with green beans, 131
shredded, with peanut sauce, 134
stir-fry, 130
stock, 114
sweet and sour, 131
teriyaki, 132
Chick peas
croquettes, 165
neapolitan, 164
sauteed, Italian-style, 166
Chicory and beetroot salad, 178-9
Chili
–cheese rarebit, 119
pork burgers, 142
're-fried' beans, 167
Chinese cabbage and tomato medley, 171
Chinese salad, 180
Chinese-style pancakes, 117
Chocolate sauce, 194
Cider vinaigrette, 183
Cinnamon-cheese toast, 123
Cock-a-leekie, 111
Cocoa, 191
Coconut
–coffee mounds, 192
–honey shake, 192
and pineapple biscuits, 186
Cod
baked in foil, 163
with lemon, 154
poached, with French beans and tomatoes, 154
–vegetable bake, 154
Coffee and coconut mounds, 192
Cold chicken platter, 134
Cole slaw
curried, 178
vinaigrette, 178
Corn
and beef casserole, 148
with sauteed prawns, 160
Cottage cheese
cinnamon-cheese toast, 123
country-style, 126
fruited cheese delight, 124
gypsy salad, 122
peach mould, 126
stuffed French toast, 122
tomato stuffed with herb cheese, 126
Courgette
basil, 170
and cauliflower soup, 110
Italian-style, 170
Crab
curried, 160
meat mould, 160
Creamy yogurt dressing, 184
Cream of asparagus and leek soup, 112
Cream of cauliflower soup, 115
Creamed cabbage and ham, 148
Crepes divan, 124
Croquettes, split pea, 165
Cucumber and tomato salad, 179
Curd cheese platter, with vegetables, 118

Curry (and curried dishes)
banana, 194
beef, 150
chicken salad, 139
cole slaw, 178
crab salad, 160
dip, 184
kidney beans, 167
tripe, 144
veal and aubergine, 131
vegetable, 170
Custard, 191

D

Dijon-herb dressing, 182
Dill vinaigrette, 183
Dips
curry, 184
mushroom, 195
yogurt, 182

E

Eggs (and egg dishes)
brocoli quiche, 120
Chinese-style pancakes, 117
crepes divan, 124
matzo brei, 118
mushroom omelette, 120
mushroom-stuffed, 123
pancakes with lemon juice, 119
pancakes with orange sauce, 116
salad, 123
sweet pancakes, with jam, 196

F

Falafel, 165
Far East scallops, 152
Fennel
with parmesan cheese, 172
seeds with pork, 142-3
Fillet of sole florentine, 159
Fish
casserole, 162
cod, baked in foil, 163
cod, with lemon, 154
cod, poached with French beans and tomatoes, 154
cod-vegetable bake, 154
haddock, baked, 155
hake steaks, baked, 156
halibut, parmesan, 162
herring, soused, 158
kedgeree and mushroom grill, 176
kipper pate, 156
lemon sole, piquant, 158
mackerel patties, 163
rock fish kebabs, 159
salmon mousse, 152
salmon salad, 162
skate with lemon sauce, 156
smoked haddock and rice salad, 155
sole fillet, Florentine, 159
sole Italiano, 158
sole veronique, 158
stir-fry tuna, 162
trout with mushroom stuffing, 152
tuna boats, 159
tuna lunch box, 162
tuna-potato cakes, 163
See also Seafood
Frankfurter stir-fry, 151
French beans, with poached cod and tomatoes, 154

INDEX

French omelette, 120
Frozen apple-banana dessert, 191
Fruit
  ambrosia, spiced, and oatmeal, 176
  apple and banana frozen dessert, 191
  apple meringue, 195
  apple and oatmeal breakfast, 176
  apricot frappe, 195
  baked apples, 188
  baked spiced pears, 190
  baked stuffed apples, 190
  banana and apple frozen dessert, 191
  bananas, curried, 194
  cherry tart, 187
  coconut-coffee mounds, 192
  coconut-honey shake, 192
  coconut and pineapple biscuits, 186
  lady fingers, 196
  orange and pineapple cream, 188
  orange spiced ambrosia, 187
  peaches, spiced, 195
  pears, baked spiced, 188
  pear frozen yogurt, 195
  pineapple cheesecake, 190
  pineapple and orange 'cream', 188
  pineapple and pumpkin, spiced, 187
  pineapple sorbet, 190
  plum sauce, 184
  prunes, honey-stewed, 192
  slaw, 180
  strawberry-apple frost, 187
  strawberry cream, 186
  stuffed baked apples, 190
  Swedish apple bake, 186
  sundae, 196
Fruited cheese delight, 124
Fruited matzo kugel, 175

G
Garden pea soup, 114
Garlic bread, 175
Garlic vinaigrette, 183
Gazpacho, 115
Ginger
  –grilled Chicken, 130
  vinaigrette, 183
Goulash, pork, 136
Gravy, 182
Greek-style beans with mushrooms, 164
Greek-style fish, 159
Green beans
  and red cabbage, 114
  and sesame chicken, 131
  and tomatoes, Hungarian-style, 168
Green vegetable salad, 171
Grilled ham steak with pineapple, 139
Gypsy cheese salad, 122

H
Haddock, baked, 155
Hake, baked, 156
Halibut, poached with parmasan, 162

Ham
  and creamed cabbage, 148
  grilled, with pineapple, 139
  with rice and water chestnuts, 151
  and turkey casserole, 138
Haricot beans, and cheese potatoes, 167
Herb dressing, 184
Herbed vegetables, 168
Herring, soused, 188
Highland 'Fling', 192
Homemade bread, 174
Honey and coconut shake, 192
Honey-stewed prunes, 192
Hot mocha milk, 192
Hot mushroom turnover, 112

I
Irish stew, 144
Italian veal and peppers, 127

K
Kebabs
  chicken, 128
  lamb, 136
  rock fish, 159
Kedgeree and mushroom grill, 176
Kidney beans
  curried, 167
  're-fried', 167
  soup, 167
Kidneys, in red wine, 151
Kipper pate, 156
Knickerbocker glory, 196
Kugel, fruited matzo, 175

L
Lady fingers, 196
Lamb
  burgers, 138
  kebabs, 136
  lemon minted, 138
  liver creole, 143
  stew, 138
Layered sandwich, 174
Leeks
  and asparagus soup, 112
  cock-a-leekie, 111
  salad, 178
Lemon
  'butter' sauce, 184
  cod, 154
  juice with pancakes, 119
  –minted lamb, 137
  salad dressing, 182
  sauce, with skate, 156
Lemon sole, piquant, 158
Lemonade, 188
Lentil and mushroom pate, 165
Liver
  breadcrumbed, 146
  casseroled, 147
  casseroled, with noodles, 146
  chicken pilaf, 146
  chicken, sauteed in wine, 144
  chicken, with green noodles, 140
  chicken, with tarragon, 143
  lamb, creole, 143
  ox, with noodles, 146
  pate, 146
  sweet and sour, 147
  Venetian, 143
Lunch box fish and chese, 160

M
Macaroni
  –cheese salad, 122
  with cheese and peanut sauce, 176
Mackerel patties, 163
Marinated carrots, 168
Marinated rump steak, 150
Matzos
  brei, 118
  fruited kugel, 175
Meatball and vegetable stir-fry, 140
Mediterranean stew, 136
Meringue, apple, 195
Mexican beef patties, 142
Mince
  meatball and vegetable stir-fry, 140
  Mexican beef patties, 142
  savoury, with noodles, 139
Minestrone, 110
Mint sauce, 182
Minted carrots, 170
Minted passion cooler, 190
Mixed vegetable salad, 179
Mocha, 192
Mock kishka, 174
Mousse, salmon, 152
Mushroom (and mushroom dishes)
  and chicken, 132
  dip, 195
  and Greek-style beans, 164
  and kedgeree grill, 176
  and lentil pate, 165
  marinaded, 110
  omelette, 120
  sauce, with cauliflower, 171
  sauteed, with onions, 171
  soup, 115
  and split-pea stew, 165
  stuffed, 112
  stuffed eggs, 123
  stuffing with trout, 152
  turnovers, 112

N
Noodles
  and liver casserole, 144
  with savoury mince, 139

O
Oatmeal
  and apple breakfast, 176
  with spiced fruit ambrosia, 176
Omelette
  cheese, 120
  French, 120
  mushroom, 120
Onions and mushrooms, sauteed, 171
Orange
  broccoli, 170
  lamb rosemary, 139
  and pineapple 'cream', 188
  with pork, 142
  sauce with pancakes, 116
  spiced ambrosia, 187
Oregano vinaigrette, 183
Oriental beef, 150
Oven-baked burgers, 148

P
Pancakes
  Chinese-style, 117
  with jam, 196
  with lemon juice, 119
  with orange sauce, 116
Parsley soup, 175
Pate
  kipper, 156
  liver, 146
  mushroom and lentil, 165
Patties
  mackerel, 163
  Mexican beef, 142
Pea soup, 114
Peaches
  and cottage cheese mould, 126
  spiced, 195
Peanut
  and cheese sauce, with macaroni, 176
  sauce, shredded chicken in, 134
Pears
  baked spiced, 188
  frozen yogurt, 195
Peppers
  green, and Italian veal, 127
  red, with steak, 139
Pie, beef, 147
Pilaf, chicken liver, 146
Pineapple
  cheesecake, 190
  –coconut biscuits, 186
  and orange 'cream', 188
  and pumpkin, spiced, 187
  sorbet, 190
Piquant lemon sole, 158
Pitta bread
  baked 'cheesy' pittas, 122
  cheese salad sandwich, 119
Plum sauce, 184
Poached cod and French beans with tomatoes, 154
Poached halibut parmesan, 162
Pork
  and chicken meatballs, 142
  chili burgers, 142
  chops, barbecued, 143
  chops with orange slices, 142
  with fennel seeds, 142-3
  fillet, sweet and sour, 140
  goulash, 136
  and vegetable medley, 148
Potatoes
  with beans and cheese, 167
  cakes with tuna, 163
  with chicken capri, 134
  roast, 175
  salad, bacon-flavoured, 175
Prawns
  with crispy topping, 163
  sauteed with corn, 160
  thermidor, 155
Profiteroles, 194
Prunes, honey-stewed, 192
Pumpkin and pineapple, spiced, 187

Q
Quiche, broccoli, 120

R
Rabbit bourguignon, 130
Radish salad, 180
Red cabbage and green beans, 114

Red pepper steak, 138
Red salad, 172
Rice dishes
  cheese and vegetable risotto, 123
  chicken liver pilaf, 146
  rice salad with fish, 155
  with sausages in tomato sauce, 151
  with water chestnuts and ham, 151
Rice pudding, 190
Rich fruit pudding, 191
Risotto, cheese and vegetable, 123
Roast potatoes, 175
Rock fish kebabs, 159
Rosemary, orange lamb with, 139
Russian dressing, 184

S
Salads
  apple slaw, 180
  bacon-flavoured potato, 175
  bean, 179
  braised leek, 178
  broccoli, 179
  and cheese sandwich, 119
  chicken oriental, 135
  chickory and beetroot, 178-9
  Chinese, 180
  cole slaw vinaigrette, 178
  cucumber and tomato, 179
  curried chicken, 135
  curried cole slaw, 178
  green vegetable, 171
  gypsy cheese, 122
  macaroni cheese, 122
  mixed vegetable, 179
  radish, 180
  red, 172
  rice with fish, 155
  salmon, 162
  sardine, 156
  savoury butter beans, 166
Salad dressings
  creamy yogurt, 184
  Dijon-herb, 182
  herb, 184
  lemon, 183
  Russian, 184
  Thousand Island, 182
  vinaigrette, 183, 184
  Yogurt, 182
Salmon
  mousse, 152
  salad, 162
Sandwiches
  cheese and salad, 119
  grilled cheese, 122
  layered, 174
Sardine salad, 156
Sauces
  cheese and peanut, with macaroni, 176
  chocolate, 194
  gravy, 182
  lemon 'butter', 184
  mint, 183
  mushroom, with cauliflower, 171
  peanut, 134
  Spanish, 139
Sausages in tomato sauce with rice, 151

Sauteed dishes
  chick peas, Italian-style, 166
  curried veal and aubergine, 131
  chicken livers in wine, 144
  mushroom and onion, 171
  prawns and corn, 160
Savoury beans, 166
Savoury butter bean salad, 166
Savoury cabbage, 171
Savoury grilled tomatoes, 172
Savoury mince with noodles, 139
Savoury tripe, 150
Savoury vinaigrette, 183
Scallops, Far East style, 152
Seafood
  calamari with spaghetti, 155
  crab, Greek-style, 159
  crab meat mould, 160
  crab salad, curried, 160
  prawns thermidor, 155
  prawns and corn, sauteed, 160
  prawns with crispy topping, 163
  scallops, Far East style, 152
Sesame chicken with green beans, 131
Shredded chicken with peanut sauce, 134
Skate with lemon sauce, 156
Slow-cooked vegetable medley, 172
Sole,
  fillet Florentine, 159
  Italiano, 158
  lemon, 158
  veronique, 158
Sorbet, pineapple, 190
Souffle
  baked cheese, 116
  cheese, 116
Soup
  asparagus and leek, 112
  broccoli, 115
  cauliflower and courgette, 110
  cauliflower cream, 115
  cock-a-leekie, 111
  gazpacho, 115
  garden pea, 114
  minestrone, 110
  mushroom, 115
  parsley, 175
  split pea, 164
  tomato, 111
  tomato and marrow, 111
  Turkish chilled tomato, 194
  vegetable medley, 111
Soused herring, 158
Spaghetti
  and calamari, 155
  cheese with herbs, 124
Spanish sauce, with steak, 139
Spiced fruit ambrosia, 176
Spiced orange ambrosia, 187
Spiced peaches, 195
Spiced pineapple pumpkin, 187
Spicy plum sauce, 184
Spinach frittata, 126
Split pea
  and mushroom stew, 165
  soup, 164
Steak
  marinated, 150
  pizzaiola with Spanish sauce, 139

Stew
  Irish, 144
  lamb, 138
  Mediterranean, 136
  Split pea and mushroom, 165
  See also Casseroles
Stir-fried dishes
  chicken, 130
  frankfurter, 151
  meatballs and vegetables, 140
  sweet and sour chicken, 130
  tuna, 162
Strawberry
  –apple frost, 187
  cream, 186
Stuffed baked apple, 190
Stuffed French toast, 122
Swedish apple bake, 186
Sweet pancake with jam, 196
Sweet and sour dishes
  cabbage, 172
  chicken stir-fry, 131
  pork fillet, 140
Swiss cheese bake, 123

T
Tarragon
  chicken breasts with, 135
  chicken livers with, 143
  vinaigrette, 183
Thousand Island dressing, 182
Tomatoes
  and cucumber salad, 179
  and green beans, Hungarian-style, 168
  with herb cheese stuffing, 126
  and marrow soup, 111
  with onion and basil, 114
  savoury grilled, 172
  soup, 111
  Turkish chilled soup, 194
Tripe
  curried, 144
  savoury, 150
Tropical shake, 194
Trout with mushroom stuffing, 152
Tuna
  boats, 159
  lunch box and cheese, 162
  –potato cakes, 163
  stir-fry, 162
Turkey
  and cheese layer, 128
  oriental, 128
Turkish chilled tomato soup, 194

V
Veal
  Italian-style, with peppers, 127
  sauteed, curried, with aubergine, 131
  stew, 127
Vegetables (and vegetable dishes)
  cauliflower with mushroom sauce, 171
  Chinese cabbage and tomato medley, 171
  courgettes, Italian-style, 170
  courgette basil, 170
  curried vegetables, 170
  fennel and parmesan, 172
  green beans and tomatoes, Hungarian-style, 168
  green vegetable salad, 171
  herbed vegetables, 168
  marinaded carrots, 170
  minted carrots, 170
  orange broccoli, 170
  red salad, 172
  sauteed mushrooms and onion, 171
  savoury cabbage, 171
  savoury grilled tomatoes, 172
  slow-cooked vegetable medley, 172
  sweet and sour cabbage, 172
  vegetable and cheese platter, 118
  vegetable and cod bake, 154
Vegetable medley soup, 111
Vinaigrette
  basic, 183
  cider, 183
  dill, 183
  garlic, 183
  gingered, 183
  oregano, 183
  parmesan, 184
  savoury, 183
  tarragon, 183

W
Water chestnuts with ham and rice, 151
Welsh rarebit, 118
Wine, cooking with
  chicken livers sauteed in wine, 144
  chicken provencale, 132
  kidneys in red wine, 151
  rabbit bourguignon, 130

Y
Yogurt
  creamy salad dressing, 184
  dip, 182
  pear frozen, 195
  salad dressing, 182